A General Theory of Equilibrium Selection in Games

A General Theory of Equilibrium Selection in Games

John C. Harsanyi
and
Reinhard Selten

The MIT Press
Cambridge, Massachusetts
London, England

This book was set in Times New Roman by Asco Trade Typesetting Ltd. in Hong Kong, and printed and bound by Halliday Lithograph in the United States of America.

Library of Congress Cataloging-in-Publication Data

Harsanyi, John C.
 A general theory of equilibrium selection in games.

 Bibliography: p.
 Includes index.
 1. Equilibrium (Economics) 2. Cooperation. 3. Game theory. I. Selten, Reinhard. II. Title.
 HB145.H38 1988   339.5   87-35700
 ISBN 0-262-08173-3

Content

Foreword

The equilibrium concept of Nash is without doubt the single game-theoretic tool that is most often applied in economics; in recent years, especially, its use has increased dramatically. Together with this increased use has come a growing preoccupation with the philosophical and logical underpinnings of the concept. The current monumental work of John Harsanyi and Reinhard Selten, in the making for close to two decades, is a major contribution to this effort.

An equilibrium in a game is defined as an assignment to each player of a strategy that is optimal for him when the others use the strategies assigned to them. One of the oldest rationales for this concept, advanced already by von Neumann and Morgenstern (1944), is that any normative theory that advises players how to play games must pick an equilibrium in each game. A theory recommending anything other than an equilibrium would be self-defeating, in the sense that a player who believes that the others are following the theory will sometimes be motivated to deviate from it. Note that this holds only if the theory recommends a unique strategy for each player.

In general, a given game may have several equilibria. Yet uniqueness is crucial to the foregoing argument. Nash equilibrium makes sense only if each player knows which strategies the others are playing; if the equilibrium recommended by the theory is not unique, the players will not have this knowledge. Thus it is essential that for each game, the theory selects one unique equilibrium from the set of all Nash equilibria.

Of course the "theory" rationale makes sense only if all the players are advised by the same theory, and by no other theory, and they must be convinced that all will abide by the advice. This could happen if that theory alone were taught at the business (or law) schools that the players attended. An analogy is to industrial standardization, and to conventions such as driving on the right; indeed, such standards and conventions are illustrations of equilibrium selection.

In this book a coherent theory of equilibrium selection is constructed. The difficulties in constructing such a theory are formidable, as anybody reading this book will quickly realize. The major implication, like that of the first heavier-than-air flying machine, is that it can be done. The theory rationale for Nash equilibrium thus acquires a visible, demonstrated foundation.

The authors will probably be the first to acknowledge that their selection theory is not the only possible or reasonable one. Although the theory selects a unique equilibrium, as a theory it need not be unique. Every facet of the theory was carefully thought out; but as in any complex construction project, many decisions were made which, though far from arbitrary, could well have been made in some other way. During the fifteen or twenty years during which the theory was in the making, several of its aspects, both major and minor, were reconsidered and revised. No doubt, future streamlining and other improvements will be welcomed by the authors, and indeed, there is every chance that they themselves will participate in the process.

As a spin-off from demonstrating the feasibility of equilibrium selection, this book develops several new ideas that are important in their own right, quite independently of the selection problem. Prominent among these are the notions of risk dominance and the tracing procedure.

A consequence of the availability of a theory of equilibrium selection is the ability to implement what has been called the Nash program. A game is called cooperative if there is available a mechanism, such as a court, to enforce agreements. In a cooperative game any feasible outcome may be achieved if the players subscribe to the appropriate agreement. In the 1951 paper in which he defined equilibrium, Nash noted that by specifying and explicitly modeling the bargaining process by which agreements may be reached, one can view cooperative games as special instances of non-cooperative games. Nash suggested that the originally given cooperative game be analyzed by means of one of the noncooperative games associated with it in this way.

One difficulty with this program is that even when the bargaining process is fully specified and completely modeled, the resulting noncooperative game often has many equilibria that are very different from each other; in this case the Nash program is not very informative. By selecting a particular one of the many equilibria appearing in such models, the Harsanyi-Selten theory removes this difficulty.

The authors have not contented themselves with a purely theoretical construction. They realize that the proof of the pudding is in the eating of it, that a game-theoretic concept cannot be judged solely on the basis of abstract considerations of plausibility but where it leads in applications. Chapters 6 through 9 of the book are devoted to applications, with emphasis on bargaining and multilateral trade.

In summary, the publication of this book constitutes a major event in game theory; it is likely to have an important influence on the discipline itself as well as on its applications to economic and political theory. The authors are to be congratulated for bringing a long and arduous task to a successful conclusion.

Robert Aumann
Jerusalem, Israel

Acknowledgments

Without mentioning names, we want to thank those many game theorists who in the long process of the development of our theory helped us to clarify our ideas by their critical remarks. We are also grateful to four anonymous readers for the MIT Press. We are indebted to Franz Weissing and Michael Mitzkewitz who thoroughly read various preliminary versions of our book and eliminated some of our mistakes. We also want to thank those who gave technical assistance, especially Mary Ann Huisman, who prepared the drawings, and Mary Macgregor, who did most of the computations for chapter 9.

A General Theory of Equilibrium Selection in Games

1 The Need for a New Solution Concept

1.1 Our Solution Concept

The purpose of this book is to propose a new solution concept, primarily defined for noncooperative games but applicable also to cooperative games, because every cooperative game can be remodeled as a bargaining game having the structure of a noncooperative game. For any noncooperative game, including noncooperative bargaining games, our theory always selects *one* equilibrium point as the solution. By reducing cooperative games to noncooperative bargaining games, our approach unifies the theories of cooperative and noncooperative games into one general theory.

1.2 Cooperative and Noncooperative Games

In contrast, in classical game theory, cooperative and noncooperative games are treated quite differently, and the distinction between these two game classes plays a very fundamental role. Nash (1950a, 1951), who first introduced this distinction, defined cooperative games as games that permit *both* free communication and enforceable agreements among the players, in contrast to noncooperative games, which permit *neither* communication nor enforceable agreements.

A binary distinction based on two simultaneous criteria is logically unsatisfactory, however. We cannot define one category as a class of all objects possessing both properties A and B and the other category as a class of all objects possessing neither property. If we do so, then one must ask what about objects having property A but not B, and objects having property B but not A?

It is preferable therefore to use a one-criterion distinction—to define cooperative games simply as those permitting enforceable agreements and noncooperative games as those not permitting them. Certainly, how much communication is allowed among the players is important in many cases, but this turns out to be a less fundamental issue. To illustrate the problem, consider the Prisoner's Dilemma game shown in figure 1.1. (For an explanation of the term "Prisoner's Dilemma," see Luce and Raiffa 1957, pp. 94–95.) In each cell of the payoff table the number in the upper left-hand corner is player 1's payoff, and that in the lower right-hand corner is player 2's. The rows of the table represent player 1's strategies C^* and N^* and the columns represent player 2's strategies C^{**} and N^{**}.

Because this game is completely symmetric between the two players, both

Figure 1.1

players have positions of equal strength. Therefore it is natural to expect that they will agree on an outcome that yields them equal payoffs—by either choosing the strategy pair $C = (C^*, C^{**})$, which would yield the payoffs $(10, 10)$, or the strategy pair $N = (N^*, N^{**})$, which would yield the payoffs $(1, 1)$. If the game is played as a cooperative game (permitting enforceable agreements), then the players, assuming that they act rationally, will no doubt immediately agree to use the strategy pair C, since C will give them much higher payoffs than N would. Thus $C = (C^*, C^{**})$ may be called the *cooperative solution* of the game.

In contrast, if the game is played as a noncooperative game (i.e., if the players are unable to conclude enforceable agreements), then they cannot do any better than use the strategy pair $N = (N^*, N^{**})$, which may be called the *noncooperative solution*.

To establish this point, we will first show that if enforceable agreements are impracticable, then rational players cannot choose the strategy pair $C = (C^*, C^{**})$. Even if they did agree to use their C-strategies, they could not rationally expect each other to *keep* to this agreement, so any such agreement would be quite pointless. Suppose they were to make such an agreement and expect each other to keep it. Then player 1 would immediately have an incentive to violate this agreement by using strategy N^*, rather than C^*, because N^*, and not C^*, would be his best reply[1] to player 2's expected strategy C^{**}. Likewise player 2 would have an incentive to violate the agreement by using strategy N^{**}, rather than C^{**}, because N^{**}, and not C^{**}, would be his best reply to player 1's expected strategy C^*.

In a noncooperative game the strategy pair C cannot be chosen by rational players because it would be *self-destabilizing*: the fact that one player expects the other to abide by a C-strategy would give him a clear incentive to deviate from C. Our analysis also shows the mathematical reason why C has this undesirable property. The reason is that the two players' C-strategies are not best replies to each other. Rather, the best reply to C^{**} is N^*, and the best reply to C^* is N^{**}.

In contrast, the strategy pair $N = (N^*, N^{**})$ can be readily used by rational players in a noncooperative game because it is *self-stabilizing*: since N^* and N^{**} are mutually the best replies to each other, if the two players for any reason expect each other to use an N-strategy, then both of them will have a clear incentive to make this expectation come true by using N-strategies.

Clearly, in playing this game, the decisive question is whether the players can make enforceable agreements, and it makes little difference whether they are allowed to talk to each other. Even if they are free to talk and to negotiate an agreement, this fact will be of no real help if the agreement has little chance of being kept. An ability to negotiate agreements is useful only if the rules of the game make such agreements binding and enforceable. (In real life, agreements may be enforced externally by courts of law, government agencies, or pressure from public opinion; they may be enforced internally by the fact that the players are simply unwilling to violate agreements on moral grounds and know that this is the case.)

As Nash has already pointed out (1950a, 1951), similar considerations apply to all noncooperative games. Since in such games agreements are not enforceable, rational players will always choose a strategy combination that is *self-stabilizing* in the sense that the players will have some incentive to abide by a strategy combination (or at least will have no incentive not to do so) if they expect all *other* players to abide by it. Mathematically this means that they will always choose a strategy combination with the property that every player's strategy is a best reply to all other players' strategies. A strategy combination with this property is called an *equilibrium (point)*. Nash has also shown that every finite game[2] has at least one equilibrium point (in pure strategies or sometimes only in mixed strategies).

Nevertheless, the definitions of cooperative and noncooperative games are still in need of further clarification. As they stand, they may give the false impression that noncooperative games cannot be used for modeling game situations in which the players are able to make enforceable agreements (or to enter into other firm commitments,[3] e.g., irrevocable promises and threats). As we shall see in section 1.3, it is possible to incorporate self-commitment moves explicitly into the extensive form of a noncooperative game.

We propose therefore to rephrase our definitions as follows. A *non-*

cooperative game is a game modeled by making the assumption that the players are *unable* to make enforceable agreements (or other commitments), except insofar as the *extensive form of the game explicitly gives them an ability to do so*. In contrast, a *cooperative* game is a game modeled by making the assumption that the players are *able* to make enforceable agreements (and possibly other commitments) even if their ability to do so is not shown explicitly by the extensive form of the game.

1.3 Irrevocable Commitments within a Noncooperative Game

There are several ways of incorporating self-commitment moves into the extensive form of a game. For instance, we can define the payoffs in such a way that any violation of a commitment made by a player would carry heavy penalties, or we can add extra players to the game whose task is to punish violators. But the simplest method of doing it is this: At a suitable point of the game tree, we give the relevant player a choice between two moves, say, α and β, where α is interpreted as a commitment to do or not to do something at some later stage(s) of the game and β is interpreted as making no commitment. The commitment expressed by move α may be unconditional, or it may become operative only conditionally, subject to the occurrence of some future events. If the player chooses move β, then from that point the game will be governed by the remaining part of the original game tree, which we will call subtree T. But if he chooses move α, then from that point the game will be governed by a *modified* version of subtree T, to be called T'. T' will differ from T by having all branches *removed* that would correspond to moves violating the commitment that the player in question made when he chose move α (i.e., moves violating the commitment will simply not be available to this player).

It can of course happen that this removal of all commitment-violating moves will leave some of the players' information sets with one unique branch (one unique move), indicating that he no longer has a real choice at any of these information sets. Such information sets (and these unique branches) can always be omitted, since information sets permitting no real choice are irrelevant. This method can be easily generalized to cases where a player can choose not only between making and not making a specific commitment but rather among a number of alternative commitments.

For example, the extensive form of the game discussed in section 1.2 can be represented by the game tree in figure 1.2. The numbers 1 and 2 printed

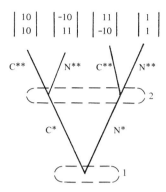

Figure 1.2

at the right of the two information-set symbols (the two ovals) indicate which player has a move at that particular information set.

Now we can represent the players' ability to make an enforceable agreement about using their C-strategies as follows: At the beginning of the game, we give player 1 a choice between moves α^* and β^*, where α^* means "I commit myself to using strategy C^*, provided that player 2 will commit himself to using strategy C^{**}," while move β^* means "I make no commitment." In case player 1 has actually chosen move α^*, we now give player 2 a choice between moves α^{**} and β^{**}, where α^{**} means "Yes, I do commit myself to using strategy C^{**} as player 1 has suggested," and move β^{**} means "I make no commitment."

Now, we can distinguish three cases:

1. If player 1 chooses α^* while player 2 chooses α^{**}, then both players will be committed to using their C-strategies. Consequently the remaining part of the game will now be reduced to the subtree T_1, shown in figure 1.3. But, since each of the two information sets in T_1 has only one branch arising from it, we can omit both of these information sets as well as the two branches (C^* and C^{**}), which amounts to replacing the entire subtree T_1 by the payoff vector $|{}^{10}_{10}|$ generated by it.

2. If player 1 chooses α^* while player 2 chooses β^{**}, then the two players will be under no commitment to restrict their freedom of action. Consequently the remaining part of the game will be governed by a subtree T_2 which is simply a copy of the original game tree.

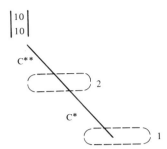

Figure 1.3

3. If player 1 chooses β^*, then once more the players will retain their freedom of action, and the remaining part of the game will be governed by a subtree T_3, which is again simply a copy of the original game tree.

Accordingly, the game tree of the enlarged game will be as shown in figure 1.4.

In the normal form of the enlarged game, we can characterize each player's strategies by three symbols. For example, the first symbol (α^* or β^* for player 1, and α^{**} or β^{**} for player 2) may be used to indicate the player's choice between commitment and no commitment, the second symbol (C^* or N^* for 1, and C^{**} or N^{**} for 2) may indicate the strategy that he would follow in subtree T_2, and the third symbol (C^* or N^*, or, alternatively, C^{**} or N^{**}) may indicate the strategy that he would follow in subtree T_3. Thus one possible strategy of player 1 would be $\alpha^* C^* N^*$. Obviously either player will have $2^3 = 8$ different pure strategies.

It is easy to verify that the enlarged game has only *one* perfect equilibrium point in pure strategies, $E_1 = (\alpha^* N^* N^*, \alpha^{**} N^{**} N^{**})$. In other words, if both players are able to commit themselves to C-strategies, it will be clearly in their interest to do so to obtain the payoffs $(10, 10)$. At the same time the definition of E_1 contains two N^* and two N^{**} symbols. These indicate that each player would use his N-strategy if his opponent refused to commit himself to use his C-strategy. (This part of either player's strategy plan will of course not be implemented since the opponent will make the required commitment.)

Intuitively one can identify E_1 with the cooperative solution (C^*, C^{**}) of the original game. Thus we can say that by incorporating the commitment moves α^* and α^{**} (as well as no-commitment moves β^* and β^{**}) into

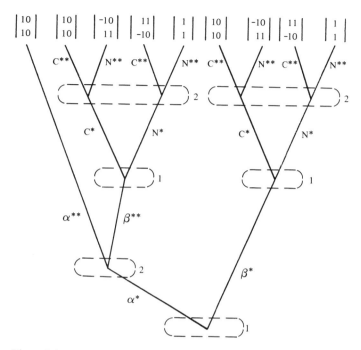

Figure 1.4

the extensive form of the game, we have essentially turned the cooperative solution (C^*, C^{**}) into an equilibrium point—so as to make it an outcome achievable by rational players even if the game (or, rather, the enlarged version of the game) is played as a formally noncooperative game. Indeed, since E_1 is the *only* perfect equilibrium point of the enlarged game, we have turned E_1 into the only outcome consistent with rational behavior by both players. (For a more detailed analysis of the enlarged game, see section 1.14. As we will try to show in sections 1.9 and 1.10, only *perfect* equilibrium points are compatible with rational behavior by all of the players in a noncooperative game.)

1.4 Limitations of the Classical Theory of Cooperative Games

The classical theory of *noncooperative* games is essentially a theory of one basic solution concept, that of equilibrium points. In contrast, the classical theory of *cooperative* games offers a rich variety of alternative solution concepts, namely the von Neumann-Morgenstern stable sets (1944), the Nash solution for two-person bargaining games (1950b, 1953), the Shapley value (1953), the core (Gillies 1959), the Aumann-Maschler bargaining sets (1964), among others.

Individually each of these solution concepts is of great theoretical interest. But as a group they fail to provide a clear, coherent theory of cooperative games. Indeed, most of the different solution concepts have very little logical connection and so cannot be interpreted as special cases of a general theory.

One may think that this fact is merely a conceptual limitation of classical game theory, which may be of some importance to the logician, methodologist, or philosopher but immaterial to the social scientist whose main interest lies in possible applications of game theory to economics, political science, and sociology. Yet, this conceptual limitation does in fact create major problems also in empirical applications.

First of all, although classical game theory offers a number of alternative solution concepts for cooperative games, it fails to provide a clear criterion as to *which* solution concept is to be employed in analyzing any real-life social situation. Nor does it give a clear answer to the obvious question of why so many different solution concepts are needed.

Many solution concepts generate some additional dimensions of indeterminacy. Even if the decision is made to analyze a given social situation in terms of some solution concept A, this will often fail to specify a well-defined outcome: it rather might tell us no more than that the outcome will be chosen from some (possibly very large) *set* S of "acceptable" outcomes; indeed, all it may tell us may be that the outcome will be a point lying in one of several alternative sets $S, S', S'', \ldots$, each equally consistent with the axioms of the chosen solution concept A.

An even more serious shortcoming of classical game theory is its failure to provide *any* usable solution concepts for some theoretically and empirically very important classes of cooperative (and of less than fully cooperative) games. These include:

1. Games *intermediate* between fully cooperative and fully noncooperative games. Examples are games where some types of agreements are enforceable while others are not; games where some groups of players are able to make enforceable agreements but others are not; and games where

enforceable agreements can be concluded at some stages of the game but not at other stages.

2. Cooperative games with a *sequential* structure. (There is some overlap between cases 1 and 2.) These are games involving two or more successive stages and permitting agreements to be built up gradually in several consecutive steps. Unlike classical cooperative games, in which any agreement made is final, such sequential games might allow renegotiation and modification of earlier agreements at later stages of the game under specified conditions.

3. Cooperative games with *incomplete information*. (Since games with incomplete information, both cooperative and noncooperative, raise some special problems; we will discuss them at some length in section 1.5.)

All these difficulties are due to the fact that the classical theory of cooperative games systematically neglects any analysis of the *bargaining process* among the players, which is probably the most important activity in any cooperative game. This is done by describing this bargaining as "preplay negotiations" and by assuming that it takes part *before* the "game" is actually played, and that it is therefore not part of the "game" at all. This approach of course amounts to relinquishing any serious attempt to understand how the outcome of the game depends on the specifics of the bargaining process among players.

1.5   Games with Incomplete Information

One of the most serious deficiencies of classical game theory is its inability to deal with games involving incomplete information. We say that a game is one with *complete information* if all players know the nature of the game, in the sense of knowing the extensive form of the game (the game tree) or the normal form of the game (the payoff matrix).

A game with complete information can be a game with either *perfect* or *imperfect information*. In a game with perfect information the players know both the nature of the game and all previous moves (made by other players or by chance) at every stage of the game; in a game with imperfect information the players know the nature of the game but have less than full information about the earlier moves during the game.

In contrast, in a game with *incomplete* information, the players have less than full information about (1) the strategy possibilities and/or (2) the payoff functions of the other players. Problem 2 may arise because the players may have limited information about:

1. the *physical consequences* to be produced by alternative strategy combinations,

2. the other players' *preference rankings* over these physical outcomes,

3. the other players' attitudes toward *risk taking*, or

4. some combination of these factors.

In addition the players may be ignorant about the amount of *information* that the other players have about any player's strategy possibilities and his payoff function.

Classical game theory cannot handle games with incomplete information at all (but does cover both games with *perfect* and with *imperfect* information as long as these have the nature of games with *complete* information). This obviously poses a very serious limitation since virtually all real-life game situations involve incomplete information. In particular, it very rarely happens that the participants of any real-life social situation have full information about each other's payoff functions. Uncertainty about the strategies available to the other players is also quite common.

We can, however, bring a game with incomplete information within the scope of game-theoretical analysis by using a probabilistic model to represent the incomplete information that the players have about various parameters of the game (Harsanyi 1967, 1968a, 1968b). In particular, the analysis of a game with incomplete information, G, can be reduced to analysis of a new game, G^*, involving suitably chosen random moves. We call G^* a *probabilistic model* for G. In this new game G^* the fact that (some or all of) the players have limited information about certain basic parameters of the game is mathematically represented by the assumption that these players have limited information about the outcomes of these *random moves*.

Formally, this probabilistic model game G^* will be a game with *complete* information. But it will be a game with *imperfect* information because of the players' having less than full information about the outcomes of the random moves occurring in the game. Thus our approach essentially amounts to reducing the analysis of a game with *incomplete* information, G, to the analysis of a game with *complete* (yet imperfect) information, G^*, which is fully accessible to the usual analytical tools of game theory.

By constructing suitable probabilistic models, we can produce games with any desired distribution of knowledge and ignorance among the players and can study how alternative informational assumptions will change the nature of the game. We can learn how a player can infer some pieces of information originally denied to him, by observing the moves of players who already possess this information, and also how a player can optimally convey information to other players or optimally withhold information in accordance with his own strategic interests. (We discuss the problem of optimally conveying information in chapter 9 where we analyze a two-person game with incomplete information on both sides. For the problem of optimally withholding information, see Aumann and Maschler's discussion, 1966, 1967, 1968, of infinitely repeated two-person zero-sum games under incomplete information, and also Stearns 1967; cf. Harsanyi 1977a.)

To be sure, the use of such probabilistic models provides only a partial solution for the problem of how to analyze games with incomplete information. For when a probabilistic-model game G^* is constructed for a game with incomplete information, G, there immediately arises the problem of what *solution concept* to use for this newly constructed game G^*.

If, in fact, the game G we start with is a *noncooperative* game with incomplete information, then this question has an easy answer. The probabilistic-model game G^* derived from G will also be a *noncooperative* game (though one with complete information), and G^* can be analyzed in terms of its equilibrium points; the concept of equilibrium points can be extended to games with incomplete information without difficulty (Harsanyi 1968a, pp. 320–329).

The situation is very different if the game G is a *cooperative* game with incomplete information. In this case the probabilistic-model game G^* derived from G will not admit of analysis in terms of *any* cooperative solution concept of conventional game theory. For example, the Nash solution for two-person bargaining games, which is an attractive solution concept for games with *complete* information, cannot be used for two-person bargaining games with *incomplete* information or for the probabilistic-model games derived from them. If we try to use the Nash solution for this purpose, we obtain completely nonsensical results (Harsanyi 1968a, pp. 329–334). Other classical cooperative solution concepts give equally unsatisfactory results when applied to incomplete information games. This lack of solution concepts applicable to games with incomplete information is another serious weakness of the classical theory of cooperative games.

1.6 Difficulties with the Concept of Equilibrium Points

Compared with the classical theory of cooperative games, the classical theory of noncooperative games presents a more satisfactory picture. It has more theoretical *unity* because it is based on one basic solution concept, that of equilibrium points. It is also a more complete theory because it tries to cover all aspects of a game and does not automatically exclude the players' bargaining moves from its analysis in the way the theory of cooperative games does. Furthermore the concept of equilibrium points— and therefore the classical theory of noncooperative games—can be easily extended to games with incomplete information.

Finally, the concept of equilibrium points is one of the very few game-theoretical solution concepts that has direct application to games, in *both* extensive and normal form. (This has many desirable consequences. One is that the classical theory of noncooperative games, unlike that of cooperative games, can easily handle games with sequential structure.)

Although the concept of equilibrium points has many strong points, it also has weaknesses, three of which are important to our discussion:

1. Almost every nontrivial game has many (sometimes infinitely many) different equilibrium points. Hence a theory that can only predict that the outcome of a noncooperative game is an equilibrium point—without specifying which equilibrium point it is—is an extremely weak and uninformative theory. This difficulty we call the *equilibrium selection problem*.

2. Any mixed-strategy equilibrium point is, or may appear to be, fundamentally unstable (see section 1.8), and therefore not a suitable solution of a game. This gives rise to what we call the *instability problem*: how are we to define a solution for a noncooperative game that has only mixed-strategy equilibrium points?

3. The third difficulty was pointed out by Reinhard Selten (1965, 1975): many equilibrium points require some or all of the players to use highly

irrational strategies (see sections 1.9 and 1.10). He proposed to call such equilibrium points *imperfect* equilibrium points, to distinguish them from *perfect* equilibrium points, which involve no irrational strategies. The problem posed by games that contain imperfect equilibrium points we call the *imperfectness problem*.

1.7   The Equilibrium Selection Problem

Among the three problems posed by the concept of equilibrium points, the equilibrium selection problem is of particular importance. To illustrate the nature of this problem, we consider a very simple two-person bargaining game, where two players have to agree on how to divide $100; the money is lost to them if they cannot agree. (We will assume that both players have linear utility functions for money.) This game can be represented by the following bargaining model: Each player has to name a real number, representing his payoff demand. The numbers named by players 1 and 2 will be called x_1 and x_2, respectively. If $x_1 + x_2 \leq 100$ (if the two players' payoff demands are mutually compatible), then both will obtain their payoff demands, with $u_1 = x_1$ and $u_2 = x_2$. In contrast, if $x_1 + x_2 > 100$ (if their payoff demands are incompatible), they will receive zero payoffs $u_1 = u_2 = 0$ (as this will be taken to mean that they could not reach an agreement).

If the players are free to divide the $100 in all mathematically possible ways, this game will have infinitely many equilibrium points in pure strategies because all possible pairs (x_1, x_2) satisfying $x_1 + x_2 = 100$, where $x_1 \geq 0$ and $x_2 \geq 0$, will be equilibrium points. But even if we restrict the players to payoff demands representing integer numbers of dollars, the game will still have 101 equilibrium points, from $(0, 100)$, $(1, 99), \ldots$, to $(100, 0)$. Clearly a theory telling us no more than that the outcome can be any one of these equilibrium points will not give us much useful information. We need a theory selecting one equilibrium point as the solution of the game. The purpose of our new solution concept is to provide a mathematical criterion that always selects one equilibrium point as the solution. In other words, with our one-point solution we attempt to overcome the equilibrium selection problem. (But, as we will try to show, our theory also overcomes the two other problems posed by the concept of equilibrium points—the instability problem and the imperfectness problem.)

1.8   The Instability Problem: A New Justification for Use of Mixed-Strategy Equilibrium Points

To illustrate the instability problem posed by games having only mixed-strategy equilibria, consider the game in figure 1.5. The only equilibrium in this game is in mixed strategies and has the form $E = (M, N)$, where $M = (\frac{1}{3}, \frac{2}{3})$ and $N = (\frac{4}{5}, \frac{1}{5})$ (i.e., player 1's equilibrium strategy M assigns the probabilities $\frac{1}{3}$ and $\frac{2}{3}$ to his two pure strategies A and B, respectively, while player 2's equilibrium strategy N assigns the probabilities $\frac{4}{5}$ and $\frac{1}{5}$ to his two pure strategies X and Y) To facilitate analysis of this game, we will add a new row, corresponding to M, and a new column, corresponding to N, to the payoff matrix (figure 1.6). As can be seen from this enlarged payoff matrix, if player 1 expects player 2 to use his equilibrium strategy N, then player 1 will have no real incentive to use his equilibrium strategy M. This is so because he will obtain the same payoff $u_1 = 36$, regardless of whether he uses his mixed equilibrium strategy M, either of his two pure strategies A and B, or any mixed strategy other than M. Likewise player 2 will have no real incentive to use his equilibrium strategy N, even if he expects player 1 to use the equilibrium strategy M. The reason is player 2 will obtain the same payoff $u_2 = 60$ regardless of whether he uses his equilibrium strategy N, either of his two pure strategies X and Y, or any mixed strategy other than N.

This is what we mean by saying that the equilibrium point $E = (M, N)$ is (seemingly) unstable: even if this does not provide an incentive for either player not to use his equilibrium strategy, it does not provide an incentive that would make it positively attractive for him to use his equilibrium strategy.

We now argue that the instability of such mixed-strategy equilibrium points is only apparent. Even if the players have as complete information about the payoff matrix of the game as they can possibly have, each player

	X	Y
A	45 / 30	0 / 90
B	30 / 75	60 / 45

Figure 1.5

will always have some irreducible minimum of *uncertainty* about the other player's actual payoffs. For example, even though the payoff matrix shows player 2's payoff associated with the strategy pair (A, X) to be $H_2(A, X) = 30$, player 1 will never be able to exclude the possibility that at this very moment this payoff may be in fact $30 - \varepsilon$ or $30 + \varepsilon$, where ε is a small positive number. This is so because every person's utility function is subject to at least some, very small, unpredictable random fluctuations because of changes in his mood or perhaps a sudden urge to use one of his pure strategies in preference to his other pure strategy.

This means that a realistic model of any given game will not have fixed payoffs but rather *randomly fluctuating* payoffs, even though these fluctuations may be very small. Mathematical analysis shows that such a game will have no mixed-strategy equilibrium points.[4] Rather, all its equilibrium points will be in pure strategies, in the sense that neither player will ever intentionally randomize between his two pure strategies. Instead, he will always find that one of his two pure strategies will yield him a higher expected payoff, and this is the pure strategy that he will actually use.

At the same time it can be shown that the random fluctuations in the two players' payoffs will interact in such a way that player 1 will find strategy A to be more profitable than strategy B almost exactly one-third of the time, and B more profitable than A almost exactly two-thirds of the time. As a result, though he may make no attempt to randomize, he will use his two pure strategies almost exactly with the probabilities prescribed by his equilibrium strategy $M = (\frac{1}{3}, \frac{2}{3})$. By the same token, though player 2 may make no attempt to randomize, he will use his two pure strategies X and Y almost exactly with the probabilities prescribed by his equilibrium strategy $N = (\frac{4}{5}, \frac{1}{5})$. (For detailed discussion and for mathematical proofs, see Harsanyi 1973a.)

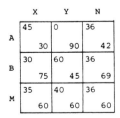

Figure 1.6

To conclude, when a given game is interpreted as a game with *fixed* payoffs, it will not provide incentives for the players at a mixed-strategy equilibrium point to use their pure strategies with the probabilities prescribed by their equilibrium strategies. But if the game is, more realistically, reinterpreted as a game with *randomly fluctuating* payoffs, then it will provide the required incentives, so that the instability problem associated with mixed-strategy equilibrium points will disappear.

1.9   The Imperfectness Problem

To illustrate the imperfectness problem, we consider a game in extensive form, because in the normal form the distinction between perfect and imperfect equilibrium points is often not clear. As an example, consider the extensive-form game shown in figure 1.7. In this game player 1 has the first move: he can choose between moves A and B. If he chooses B, the game will end immediately, with the payoffs $u_1 = 0$ and $u_2 = 2$. If he chooses A, player 2 will also have a move: he will be able to choose between moves X and Y. If he chooses X, the payoffs will be $u_1 = u_2 = 1$, whereas if he chooses Y, the payoffs will be $u_1 = u_2 = -1$. The normal form of this game is shown in figure 1.8.

Thus player 1 has two pure strategies: strategy A ("choose move A") and strategy B ("choose move B"). Player 2 also has two pure strategies: strategy X ("choose move X if player 1 has chosen A") and strategy Y ("choose move Y if player 1 has chosen A").

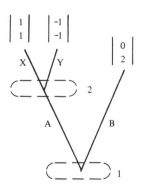

Figure 1.7

Obviously the game has two pure-strategy equilibrium points: the strategy pairs $E_1 = (A, X)$ and $E_2 = (B, Y)$. E_1 is a perfect equilibrium point, but E_2 is an imperfect equilibrium point, involving irrational strategies.

Strategy Y requires player 2 to choose move Y, which is surely irrational because it will yield him as well as player 1 the payoff $u_1 = u_2 = -1$, even though by choosing move X both he and player 1 could obtain the payoff $u_1 = u_2 = 1$. Strategy B is equally irrational: player 1 should know that if he chooses move A, then player 2 would surely choose move X, which would yield him the payoff $u_1 = 1$; therefore player 1 should not choose move B, which would yield him only $u_1 = 0$.[5]

How is it possible that an equilibrium point should involve such irrational strategies? In particular, how can an equilibrium point require a player to choose a move like Y when choosing this move is inconsistent with maximizing his own payoff?

The answer is that a move like Y will reduce the player's expected payoff only if this move occurs with a *positive probability*. Yet, if the two players act in accordance with equilibrium point $E_2 = (B, Y)$, then player 2 *will never come into a position of having to implement* this irrational move Y. In other words, move Y will occur with *zero probability* and therefore will not reduce player 2's expected payoff.

By definition, an equilibrium strategy must maximize the relevant player's expected payoff if the other players' strategies are kept constant. This means that no equilibrium strategy can prescribe an irrational (non-payoff-maximizing) move at any information set that will be reached with a *positive* probability if all players use their equilibrium strategies. But an equilibrium strategy may prescribe an irrational move for a player at any information set that will be reached with *zero* probability. Imperfect equilibrium points are precisely those equilibrium points that prescribe a move contrary to payoff maximization at some information set that will be reached with zero probability.

Figure 1.8

These considerations have the following implication. If the game contains enough random moves, then every information set will be reached with some positive probability, regardless of the strategies used by the players. A game with this property will contain only perfect equilibrium points. This fact can be used for a formal mathematical definition of perfect and imperfect equilibrium points (Selten 1975). Moreover, as we will see in chapter 2, it can also be used to eliminate all imperfect equilibrium points from the game. To ensure that the solution we obtain for each game G will be a perfect equilibrium point, we will apply our theory not to this game G but to a *uniformly perturbed* game in standard form with perfect recall, G', obtained from G.[6]

Intuitively this game G' will be obtained by assuming that whenever any player i wants to use a given pure strategy ϕ_i, he will make various "mistakes" with small but positive probabilities. In particular, if this strategy ϕ_i requires him to make a move ϕ_{ij} at his jth information set, he will have a small probability $\varepsilon > 0$ of making another move ($\phi'_{ij} \neq \phi_{ij}$) instead. For the sake of simplicity we will make a *uniformity assumption* to the effect that this mistake probability ε will be the *same* for all players i at all information sets and for all pairs of alternative moves ϕ_{ij} and ϕ'_{ij} available at any given information set. The resulting game G' will be called a *uniformly* perturbed game because of this uniformity assumption.[7]

1.10   Imperfect Equilibrium Points, Subjunctive Conditionals, and Self-commitment Moves

In modern logic the problem posed by imperfect equilibrium points can be restated as follows: The assumption that player 2 will use strategy Y is equivalent to the conditional statement S, "If player 1 were to make move A, then player 2 would make move Y." If this conditional statement is interpreted as a *Material Implication*, it will automatically become *vacuously true* whenever the stated condition (player 1's making move A) does not arise. But if this statement S is interpreted as a *Subjunctive Conditional* (as of course it is grammatically), it will be simply *false*. If player 1 does make move A, then player 2 (assuming that he is a rational individual who tries to maximize his payoff) would most certainly *not* make move Y.

The strategy pair $E_2 = (B, Y)$ is formally an equilibrium point. For this to be the case, all we need is that statement S should be true when it is interpreted as a Material Implication. (It is a common practice in mathematics to regard any conditional statement as being true as long as it is true when interpreted as a Material Implication.) Nevertheless, our game-theoretical intuition judges E_2 to be an *irrational* equilibrium point because this intuition would accept the truth of statement S only if it remained true even when interpreted as a Subjunctive Conditional, which is obviously not the case.

Our distinction between perfect and imperfect equilibrium points is closely related to the question of whether the players can make any firm *commitment* in a noncooperative game (see sections 1.2 and 1.3). The game we have been discussing contains no self-commitment moves. Accordingly, our analysis has been based on the assumption that player 2 cannot commit himself in advance to choose move X rather than Y at the time he reaches the information set where this choice has to be made. But it is easy to see that if he could make such commitment, then player 2 would have a clear interest to do so (in order to frighten player 1 into making move A rather than B). Yet the proper way of enabling player 2 to make such commitment is to give him a *self-commitment move* at the beginning of the game, instead of misconstruing a game not containing a self-commitment move as if it did.

To add the desired self-commitment move, we may proceed as follows: At the beginning of the game, we permit player 2 a choice between moves α and β, where α can be interpreted as saying, "I commit myself to choose move Y if player 1 chooses move A," whereas β can be interpreted as saying, "I make no commitment." If player 2 chooses β, then the future course of the game will be governed by subtree T_β, which is an exact copy of the original game tree. In contrast, if he chooses α, then the future course of the game will be governed by subtree T_α, which differs from the original game tree in having move X omitted (since it is excluded by player 2's self-commitment move α).

Once branch X has been omitted, we can remove the entire information set from which branch X used to arise (since player 2 will no longer have any real choice at this point), together with the one remaining single branch Y but not the other components of T_α. This reduced version of subtree T_α will be called subtree T_α^*. Subtrees T_α and T_α^* are shown in figures 1.9 and 1.10, and the game tree of the new enlarged game is shown in figure 1.11.

In the normal form of the new game, each player will have four different pure strategies. Those of player 1 will be AA, AB, BA, and BB, where the first letter always indicates the move player 1 would make in subtree T_α^*

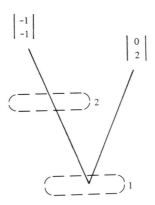

Figure 1.9

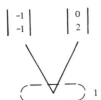

Figure 1.10

and the second letter the move he would make in subtree T_β. Player 2's pure strategies are αX, αY, βX, and βY.

It is easy to verify that the new game has only one perfect equilibrium point in pure strategies, namely $E_1^* = (BA, \alpha X)$. E_1^* has the following interpretation: At the beginning of the game player 2 will commit himself to make move Y, should player 1 make move A. This will deter player 1 from making move A. Instead, he will make move B, which will yield the payoffs $(0, 2)$ as desired by player 2. [If player 2 did not commit himself to move A, the players would use the strategy pair (B, Y) instead.] Intuitively, we can identify E_1^* with the strategy pair $E_2 = (B, Y)$ of the original game, except that in the original game this strategy pair was an imperfect equilibrium point whereas in the new enlarged game E_1^* is a perfect equilibrium point, and indeed the only perfect equilibrium point of the new game.

This is of course not at all surprising. Once player 2 is able to commit himself to use strategy Y, it becomes very rational for him to make this

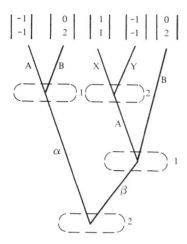

Figure 1.11

commitment, and then it becomes likewise rational for player 1 to use strategy *B*, as desired by player 2 (for a more detailed analysis of the extended game, see section 1.15).

1.11 Analysis of Cooperative Games by Means of Noncooperative Bargaining Models

The new solution theory we are proposing is formally a solution theory for noncooperative games, yet it grew out of our research on cooperative games.

When it became clear to us that the Nash solution in its original form could not be used as a solution concept for two-person bargaining games with incomplete information (Harsanyi 1968a, pp. 329–334), we decided to follow Nash's (1951, p. 285) suggestion that analysis of any cooperative game *G* should be based on a formal bargaining model *B(G)*, involving bargaining moves and countermoves by the various players and resulting in an agreement about the outcome of the game. Formally, this bargaining model *B(G)* would always be a noncooperative game in extensive form (or possibly in normal form), and the solution of the cooperative game *G* would be defined in terms of the equilibrium points of this noncooperative bargaining game *B(G)*.

At the same time we were fully aware of the fact that Nash's suggested approach could not work unless we could find a way of overcoming at least the equilibrium selection problem (and preferably also the *instability* and the *imperfectness* problems). Our first attempt to deal with the equilibrium selection problem was an ad hoc modification of the Nash solution (1950b), specifically designed to overcome the equilibrium selection problem in incomplete-information games we had been concerned with (Harsanyi and Selten 1972). But soon after this we came to the conclusion that thinking up solution concepts whenever a need for them arose was not really a satisfactory approach. Rather, a radically new theoretical departure was needed that would provide a *general* method of overcoming the equilibrium selection problem (as well as the instability and the imperfectness problems) for all possible noncooperative games.

Once these three problems are overcome—and our solution theory does overcome them—an analysis of cooperative games by means of non-cooperative bargaining models, as suggested by Nash, does provide a full remedy for the various problems posed by the classical theory of cooperative games. It yields a *uniform* approach to analyzing all classes of cooperative games. Even though different cooperative games may have to be analyzed in terms of very different bargaining models, the solution of each bargaining model (and therefore the solution of each cooperative game) can be defined in terms of the basic mathematical criteria specified by our solution theory. In other words, the problem of defining a solution for a cooperative game G can always be reduced to the problem of defining a solution for a *noncooperative* bargaining game $B(G)$.

Another advantage of this approach is that it shows *how* the solution (the theoretically predicted outcome) of any cooperative game G will depend on the nature of the postulated bargaining process among the players, as indicated by the bargaining model $B(G)$ used in analyzing this game G. For example, we can study how the outcome will depend on such factors as who can talk to whom, and who can talk to whom *first*; what the rules are for concluding agreements, for withdrawing from agreements already concluded, or for making tentative agreements irrevocable; how easily coalitions can be formed, enlarged, dissolved, combined, or recombined; and what threats can be made by whom against whom, and to what extent such threats are irrevocable.

In constructing bargaining models, we can take advantage of the great flexibility that bargaining games in extensive form provide—a flexibility not available to the classical theory of cooperative games which uses the more restrictive normal form (or the even more rigid characteristic-function form). Thus we can easily construct bargaining models that represent cooperative games wholly inaccessible to classical theory, such as partially cooperative games, cooperative games possessing a sequential structure, or cooperative games with incomplete information.

Additional flexibility is provided by adding specific self-commitment moves; so as to give each player the desired amount of self-commitment power in concluding enforceable agreements and in making irrevocable promises and/or threats.

1.12   The Modeling of Bargaining Moves

Most bargaining processes in the real world involve *successive* offers and counteroffers by the participants, without a clear upper limit on the permitted number of bargaining moves. This means that the strategies of the players have infinitely many degrees of freedom, which makes these bargaining processes infinite games.

Moreover two-person bargaining is usually a game with *perfect* information because each player knows all past moves at every stage. But three-or-more-person bargaining is often a game with *imperfect* information because one player may make a secret offer to another player. (Bargaining under *incomplete* information is of course always modeled as a game with *imperfect* information, namely as a game containing random moves whose outcomes are not fully known to all players; see section 1.5.)

One of Nash's important insights is that even though most real-life bargaining involves strategies with *infinitely* many degrees of freedom, it can be modeled by means of much simpler strategies that have only one (or very few) degrees of freedom. In other words, from a game-theoretical point of view, often only one parameter of the bargaining strategy of any player i is relevant, and this is the *lowest payoff x_i* that this player is willing to accept. Thus, at least in cases where the players cannot expect to learn any new information from each other during the bargaining process, we can assume without any real loss of generality that each player i will choose his payoff demand x_i at the beginning of the game independently of the other players, so that his bargaining strategy can be identified simply with this payoff demand x_i.[8]

In our opinion, even though most bargaining in the real world does involve successive offers and counteroffers, Nash's simultaneous-offers model of bargaining has significantly advanced our understanding of the bargaining process. It has clarified some important facts obscured by the successive-offers model, such as the basic *symmetry* between the two players in ordinary two-person bargaining situations, in contrast to the asymmetry characterizing *ultimatum games* where one player can make a unilateral take-it-or-leave-it offer to the other players. It has also helped us to understand the "blackmailer's fallacy" problem, which arises when a bargaining game proper is misinterpreted as an ultimatum game (Harsanyi 1977b, pp. 186–189).

Nevertheless, a simultaneous-offers model of bargaining *may* require more than one round of simultaneous offers. In cases where the bargaining is conducted with incomplete information, two or more rounds of simultaneous moves may be needed for the players to learn new information from each other. Moreover, even under the assumption of complete information, it may be necessary to use a two-stage model for analyzing two-person bargaining with variable threats (Nash 1953).

1.13   The Problem of Anticonflicts

In Nash's model of two-person bargaining with fixed threats (Nash 1950b) there are three possible outcomes:

1. The players' payoff demands x_1 and x_2 may be mutually incompatible, with $(x_1, x_2) \notin F$, where F is the feasible set. This case is interpreted as a conflict between the two players, in which they will obtain only their conflict payoffs c_1 and c_2.

2. These payoff demands x_1 and x_2 may be barely compatible, with $(x_1, x_2) \in \delta F$, where δF is the upper-right boundary of the feasible set F. This case obviously represents full agreement. Accordingly, the players will obtain their payoff demands x_1 and x_2.

3. The players' payoff demands x_1 and x_2 may be more than compatible (in the sense that even slightly larger payoff demands would have been compatible) because $(x_1, x_2) \in F^o$, where $F^o = F - \delta F$.

Nash regards case 3 as an agreement situation and assigns the players their payoff demands x_1 and x_2 in the same way as in case 2. But we will distinguish this case from case 2 by calling it *anticonflict*. Cases 1 and 2 correspond to conflict and to agreement, respectively, so Nash's definition of payoffs is appropriate. But questions may be raised about his treatment of the anticonflict case 3.

First of all, under the conditions of case 3 he permits the players to agree on an inefficient payoff vector (x_1, x_2). In many bargaining situations, however, such an outcome would be physically impossible, or at least prohibited by the rules of the game. Say the players are bargaining about how to divide a fixed sum of money, and the rules do not permit them to divide less than the available amount.

More fundamentally, the players cannot be said to have reached an agreement unless they have agreed on a *specific payoff vector* (and possibly also on a specific joint strategy for obtaining this payoff vector). Yet in the anticonflict case this condition fails. For example, let $f_2(x_1)$ be the highest payoff to player 2 compatible with player 1's receiving the payoff x_1, and let $f_1(x_2)$ be the highest payoff to player 1 compatible with player 2's receiving the payoff x_2. We submit that when player 1 makes the payoff demand x_1, he is implicitly proposing the payoff vector $\bar{x}_1 = (x_1, f_2(x_1))$ as the outcome for the game, and when player 2 makes the payoff demand x_2, he is implicitly proposing the payoff vector $\bar{x}_2 = (f_1(x_2), x_2)$ as the outcome. Now in case 2, $\bar{x}_1 = \bar{x}_2$, so we do have agreement between the players. But in case 3, $\bar{x}_1 \neq \bar{x}_2$, which means that there is no real agreement.

Unlike Nash, who treats an anticonflict like an agreement, we propose to treat it like a *conflict*, and we will assume that if the game ends with an anticonflict, the players will obtain only their conflict payoffs c_1 and c_2. Apart from being theoretically preferable, this approach also simplifies the computations in applying our solution theory to bargaining games.

We can illustrate our approach to anticonflicts by an analogy. Suppose two people meet in a narrow gateway. If they both insist on going through first, a conflict will result, and neither will get through. But if they can reach an agreement about who should go through first and who should go through second, they will both get through with very little delay. Suppose, however, that both insist that the other should go through first: this corresponds to an anticonflict, and it will create an impasse much the same way as a conflict proper would. Obviously under the proposed approach any bargaining game will have the nature of a *unanimity game*: agreement will be reached only if the two players (or all n players in the case of n-person bargaining) reach a unanimous agreement on the outcome. (For further discussion, see Harsanyi 1982a.)

In sum, we have considered the main difficulties of applying the classical theory of games to both cooperative and noncooperative games. We have indicated how our solution theory proposes to resolve these difficulties. Of the three main difficulties arising in *noncooperative* game theory, the instability problem can be overcome by the theory of games with randomly fluctuating (randomly disturbed) payoffs, the imperfectness problem by the uniformly (or nonuniformly) perturbed agent normal form (and, as we will see in chapter 2, by means of the standard form), and the equilibrium selection problem by suitable mathematical criteria for selecting an equilibrium point as the solution for a noncooperative game. Finally, the difficulties in the classical theory of *cooperative* games can be overcome by remodeling any cooperative game as a noncooperative bargaining game. We have discussed the modeling of bargaining processes and, in particular, the modeling of anticonflicts.

1.14 Appendix A

The normal form of the enlarged game discussed in section 1.3 is shown in figure 1.12. For readability we have omitted in the payoff matrix the * sym-

	αCC	αCN	αNC	αNN	βCC	βCN	βNC	βNN
αCC	10 / 10	10 / 10	10 / 10	10 / 10	10 / 10	10 / 10	-10 / 11	-10 / 11
αCN	10 / 10	10 / 10	10 / 10	10 / 10	10 / 10	10 / 10	-10 / 11	-10 / 11
αNC	10 / 10	10 / 10	10 / 10	10 / 10	11 / -10	11 / -10	1 / 1	1 / 1
αNN	10 / 10	10 / 10	10 / 10	10 / 10 ♦	11 / -10	11 / -10	1 / 1	1 / 1
βCC	10 / 10	-10 / 11	10 / 10	-10 / 11	10 / 10	-10 / 11	10 / 10	-10 / 11
βCN	11 / -10	1 / 1	11 / -10	1 / 1	11 / -10	1 / 1	11 / -10	1 / 1
βNC	10 / 10	-10 / 11	10 / 10	-10 / 11	10 / 10	-10 / 11	10 / 10	-10 / 11
βNN	11 / -10	1 / 1	11 / -10	1 / 1	11 / -10	1 / 1	11 / -10	1 / 1

Figure 1.12

bols after the letters characterizing player 1's strategies and also the **
symbols after the letters characterizing player 2's strategies—for instance,
player 1's strategy $\alpha^* N^* C^*$ will simply be written as $\alpha N C$.

In the payoff matrix, cells corresponding to equilibrium points are set
off by a heavy frame, and the cell corresponding to the unique perfect
equilibrium point is indicated by a diamond-shaped symbol.

As shown by the payoff matrix, apart from the perfect equilibrium point,
$E_1 = (\alpha^* N^* N^*, \alpha^{**} N^{**} N^{**})$, the enlarged game also has five imperfect
equilibrium points in pure strategies: $E_2 = (\alpha^* N^* C^*, \alpha^{**} C^{**} N^{**})$, $E_3 =$
$(\alpha^* N^* C^*, \alpha^{**} N^{**} N^{**})$, $E_4 = (\alpha^* N^* N^*, \alpha^{**} C^{**} N^{**})$, $E_5 = (\beta^* C^* N^*,$
$\beta^{**} N^{**} N^{**})$, and $E_6 = (\beta^* N^* N^*, \beta^{**} N^{**} N^{**})$. Three of these—$E_2$, E_3,
and E_4—agree with the perfect equilibrium E_1 in involving commitments
by both players to their C-strategies, but differ from E_1 on the unreached
subtrees T_2 and/or T_3.

In contrast, the two other imperfect equilibria, E_5 and E_6, involve
refusals by both players to commit themselves to their C-strategies and to
use instead their N-strategies. In fact E_6 can be intuitively identified with
$N = (N^*, N^{**})$, the unique equilibrium of the original game which we called
the noncooperative solution. E_5 is very similar to E_6 and differs from the
latter only on the unreached subtree T_2. By introducing commitment
moves into the game, we have made the noncooperative solution into an
imperfect equilibrium, and therefore into an outcome unavailable to rational players.

1.15   Appendix B

The normal form of the enlarged game discussed in section 1.9 is shown in
figure 1.13. As in figure 1.12, cells corresponding to equilibrium points are
set off by heavy frames, and the cell corresponding to the unique perfect
equilibrium point is indicated by a diamond-shaped symbol.

As shown by the payoff matrix, the enlarged game has only one perfect
equilibrium point, $E_1^* = (BA, \alpha X)$. But it has five imperfect equilibrium
points in pure strategies: $E_2^* = (AA, \beta X)$, $E_3^* = (AB, \beta Y)$, $E_4^* = (BA, \alpha Y)$,
$E_5^* = (BB, \alpha X)$, and $E_6^* = (BB, \alpha Y)$. Three of these imperfect equilibria—
E_4^*, E_5^*, and E_6^*—agree with the perfect equilibrium, E_1^*, in making player
2 commit himself to strategy Y, which then forces player 1 to use strategy
B, but they differ from E_1^* on the unreached subtree T_β.

	αX	αY	βX	βY
AA	-1 -1	-1 -1	1 1	-1 -1
AB	-1 -1	-1 -1	0 2	0 2
BA	0 ◆ 2	0 2	1 1	-1 -1
BB	0 2	0 2	0 2	0 2

Figure 1.13

In contrast, E_2^* and E_3^* make player 2 refrain from any commitment (on the mistaken expectation that he could not induce player 1 to use strategy B even if he did commit himself to strategy Y—this mistaken expectation is indicated by the letter A which is the first letter characterizing player 1's strategy). Nevertheless, E_3^* still makes the two players use the strategy pair (B, Y), even though, as we have argued, this will represent irrational behavior when player 2 is not committed to strategy Y in advance.

On the other hand, E_2^* makes the two players use the strategy pair (A, X) which is sensible enough once player 2 is not committed to strategy Y. Intuitively, E_2^* can be identified with the strategy pair $E_1 = (A, X)$ of the original game, except that in the original game E_1 was a perfect equilibrium (the only one of the game), whereas in the enlarged game E_2^* is an imperfect equilibrium because it is irrational for player 2 not to commit himself to strategy Y when he would be in a position to do so. This is so because, by making this commitment, he could obtain the payoff $u_2 = 2$, whereas, by not making this commitment, he reduces his payoff to $u_2 = 1$.

2 Games in Standard Form

2.1 Introduction

Our theory will be based on a game form that is intermediate between the extensive and the normal form. We call it the *standard form*. The standard form shows how the strategies are made up of choices at information sets without preserving more than the dependence of payoffs on choices. There are two reasons for using the standard form instead of the normal form. First, it is important to identify certain substructures called cells that correspond to subgames in the extensive form and are invisible in the normal form. Second, we want to select a perfect equilibrium point, and perfectness cannot be satisfactorily defined in the framework of the normal form.

We restrict our attention to games with perfect recall and substructures of such games. The reasons for this will be explained in section 2.2. In section 2.3 we introduce basic notations and definitions concerning the standard form. Section 2.4 explores the special properties of standard forms derived from extensive games with perfect recall. This leads us to a definition of perfect recall in the standard form. Important properties of standard forms with perfect recall are derived in section 2.5. Our solution concept is recursive in the sense that it is necessary to look at certain substructures of a game in order to solve it. A general definition of a substructure is given in section 2.6. Perturbed games and their substructures are of special importance for the theory. They belong to a class of substructures of the original game called *interior substructures*. Interior substructures of games with perfect recall have special properties that permit the decentralization of certain aspects of a player's strategy choice. These decentralization properties are discussed in section 2.7.

Uniformly perturbed games are introduced in section 2.8, and uniformly perfect equilibrium points in section 2.9. Then section 2.10 discusses the way in which our theory deals with the perfectness problem. The concepts of a solution function and a limit solution function are defined there. Solution functions select equilibrium points for perturbed games, and limit solution functions are obtained from solution functions by letting the perturbance parameter go to zero. In this way one selects a perfect equilibrium point for the unperturbed game. Formally, our solution concept is a limit solution function. The solution function on which it is based will be defined in chapter 5. In section 2.10 we are only concerned with the connection between solution functions and limit solution functions.

2.2   Reasons for the Exclusion of Imperfect Recall

Our solution theory will be in terms of the standard form, though it aims at the selection of a unique perfect equilibrium point for every extensive game with perfect recall. Perfect equilibrium points have been defined for such games only (Selten 1975).

An extensive game has perfect recall if every player at each of his information sets knows all his previous choices. We do not give a precise definition because we want to avoid the formalism of extensive games. Instead, we will later give a definition of perfect recall in the framework of the standard form. A precise definition of perfect recall in extensive games can be found elsewhere (Kuhn 1953; Selten 1975).

Clearly an absolutely rational player who is a single person should never forget what he has done before. Imperfect recall becomes important in games where some players are teams.

We take the view that games with teams as players are misspecified models. Each team member should be modeled as a separate player whose payoff is that of the team. A team is not really different from any other group of players who happen to have identical payoffs. We think of a player as an entity with completely integrated mental processes. This means that individual rationality alone is sufficient to enforce consistency of expectations within one player. Typically a team consists of several members whose expectations cannot be coordinated exclusively by individual rationality.

Consider the game of figure 2.1. In this game both players have the same payoffs. They face a typical team problem. Obviously both (A, A) and (B, C) realize the maximal payoff 2. Individual rationality alone does not provide a criterion on how to select between these two possibilities of receiving the maximal team payoff. The team members must either communicate to reach a common decision or apply some kind of game-theoretical reasoning

Figure 2.1
A two-person team problem

that permits them to select one of the two pure strategy equilibrium points (A, A) and (B, C). As we will show in chapter 5, our theory selects (A, A).

Of course in some games groups of persons can be modeled as a single player. If, for example, a group consists of a leader and several subordinates who must follow his orders, then only the leader is the real player. The orders to be given to his subordinates are choices he has to make.

Less trivial teams are groups of players with identical interests and special preplay communication opportunities. Here it must be admitted that preplay communication, and especially differential opportunities of preplay communication, pose modeling problems that are not automatically solved by our theory. We will come back to this point at the end of the book. The mere inclusion of formal communication moves into the game model proves to be insufficient.

Our theory aims mainly at extremely noncooperative games without communication. Such games are more basic than those with communication. To solve a game with communication, it is necessary to know what would happen if communication broke down. The breakdown of communication furnishes a threat point that may be of great importance. It is at least necessary to know whether a player should prefer the breakdown of communication.

In many cases it is not necessary to consider communication explicitly since, as in the example of figure 2.1, game-theoretic reasoning often is a good substitute for communication. Where communication is not really needed, it is reasonable to suppose that its presence or absence does not influence the solution of the game.

2.3 Games in Standard Form

The normal form of an extensive game describes the dependence of expected payoffs on pure strategies and abstracts from everything else. A pure strategy of a player is a function that assigns to everyone of his information sets a choice. The standard form does not only look at pure strategies and payoffs but also at the structure of pure strategies. It tells us of which choices a pure strategy is made up.

The standard form is derived from the extensive form by thinking of each information set of player i as administrated by a separate agent. Therefore the standard form does not only have a player set N but also an agent set M_i for every player $i \in N$. Every agent has a choice set that represents the choices at his information sets. A pure strategy of a player is conceptualized as a collection of choices for his agents. Otherwise, the standard form is not different from the normal form.

Notations and Definitions

We will use positive integers to represent the players. The player set N will be a nonempty finite set of positive integers. In many cases N will simply be the set $\{1, \ldots, n\}$ of the first n integers, but since we must look at substructures of games with fewer players, it is convenient to define player sets in a more general way.

We use pairs of positive integers ij to identify agents. The first of both integers represents the player to whom the agent belongs; the second represents the agent. Player i's agent set M_i is a nonempty finite set of pairs of integers of the form ij. The union of all M_i with $i \in N$ is denoted by M.

Each agent ij has a nonempty finite *choice set* Φ_{ij} of choices ϕ_{ij}. A pure strategy ϕ_i of player i may be thought of as a collection of choices for his agents:

$$\phi_i = (\phi_{ij})_{M_i}. \tag{2.3.1}$$

The lower index M_i indicates that ϕ_i contains one element ϕ_{ij} for every $ij \in M_i$. The same system of notation will be employed at other occasions too. Player i's *pure-strategy set* Φ_i is the set of all these collections:

$$\Phi_i = \underset{ij \in M_i}{\times} \Phi_{ij}. \tag{2.3.2}$$

A *pure-strategy combination* (or simply a *pure combination*) is a collection of pure strategies $\phi = (\phi_i)_N$, containing one strategy for each player $i \in N$. Alternatively, we may look at a pure-strategy combination as a collection of choices $\phi = (\phi_{ij})_M$, containing one choice $\phi_{ij} \in \Phi_{ij}$ for each agent $ij \in M$. We make no distinction between $(\phi_i)_N$ and $(\phi_{ij})_M$ if both prescribe the same choices to the agents in M. The *pure-strategy combination set* Φ is the set of all these collections ϕ:

$$\Phi = \underset{i \in N}{\times} \Phi_i = \underset{ij \in M}{\times} \Phi_{ij}. \tag{2.3.3}$$

Payoffs are defined only for players, not for agents. A *payoff function H on Φ* assigns a payoff vector

$$H(\phi) = (H_i(\phi))_N \tag{2.3.4}$$

to each $\phi \in \Phi$. As before, the lower index N indicates that $H(\phi)$ contains one component $H_i(\phi)$ for every $i \in N$. We look at Φ as a structure endowed with all the information on the sets N, M_i, and Φ_{ij}. We say that Φ is *admissible* if all these sets are finite and nonempty. We now can give a formal definition of a game in standard form.

STANDARD FORM   A *game in standard form* (or simply a *standard form*) $G = (\Phi, H)$ consists of an admissible set of pure-strategy combinations Φ, with the structure indicated by (2.3.3) together with a payoff function H on Φ.

Comment   A game in standard form differs from a normal-form game by the additional information on the structure of the pure-strategy sets Φ_i. It also differs from the agent normal form which has been introduced for the purpose of defining perfect equilibrium points (Selten 1975). In the agent normal form each agent becomes a separate player with the payoff of the player to whom he belongs in the original game. The agent normal form keeps the information on the agents' choices, but it neglects the information on the relationship between agents and players.

We feel that both players and agents must be identifiable for the purposes of our theory. One cannot define perfect equilibrium points without looking at agents (Selten 1975). For the purposes of perfectness it would be sufficient to work with the agent normal form. However, it is natural to look at players as centers of expectation formation. This will be important for the definition of risk dominance in chapter 5. We will make use of the idea that different agents of the same player should have the same expectations on other players. Therefore we need a game form with both agents and players.

A game in standard form combines the information of the normal form and the agent normal form. We may think of these two game forms as different aspects of the standard form.

NORMAL FORM   The *normal form* of a standard form $G = (\Phi, H)$ has the same structure as G except that the information on the internal structure of the pure strategy sets given by (2.3.2) is suppressed. Notationally, we need not make any distinction between a standard form and its normal form.

When we look at games in standard form where each player has only one agent, we need not distinguish between a player and his agent. The pure-strategy set of a player coincides with his agent's choice set. We refer to such games as games with *normal-form structure*.

AGENT NORMAL FORM   The agent normal form $G' = (\Phi, H')$ of a standard form $G = (\Phi, H)$ is a game with normal-form structure whose players are the agents of G with their choice sets Φ_{ij} as pure-strategy sets. The payoff $H'_{ij}(\phi)$ of $ij \in M_i$ is defined as $H_i(\phi)$. Sometimes it is convenient to think of the agents as renumbered by positive integers instead of pairs of positive integers when dealing with the agent normal form.

Use of the Word "Game"

Often a game in standard form can simply be called a *game* where this can be done without confusion. We will mainly be concerned with such games, although occasionally we will look at extensive forms to clarify conceptually important points.

The definitions that follow in the rest of this section refer to a fixed game in standard form $G = (\Phi, H)$.

MIXED STRATEGIES   A *mixed-strategy* q_i of player i is a probability distribution over player i's set of pure strategies. $q_i(\phi_i)$ denotes the probability assigned to ϕ_i. A mixed strategy q_i is called *completely mixed* if $q_i(\phi_i)$ is positive for every pure strategy $\phi_i \in \Phi_i$.

No distinction is made between a pure strategy ϕ_i and a mixed strategy that assigns probability 1 to ϕ_i and 0 to all other pure strategies. The set of all mixed strategies q_i of player i is denoted by Q_i.

A *combination* $q = (q_i)_N$ *of mixed strategies* (or simply a *mixed combination*) contains a mixed strategy q_i for every $i \in N$. The set of all combinations of this kind is denoted by Q. For $q = (q_i)_N$ and $\phi = (\phi_i)_N$, it is convenient to introduce the notation:

$$q(\phi) = \prod_{i \in N} q_i(\phi_i). \tag{2.3.5}$$

In other words, $q(\phi)$ is the product of all $q_i(\phi)$ with $i \in N$. The product $q(\phi)$ is called the *realization probability* of ϕ under q. The definition of the payoff function H is extended from Φ to Q in the usual way:

$$H(q) = \sum_{\phi \in \Phi} q(\phi)H(\phi). \tag{2.3.6}$$

Equations for H are to be understood as vector equations that hold for every component H_i of H.

i-INCOMPLETE COMBINATIONS   Combinations of the type $q_{-i} = (q_i)_{N\backslash\{i\}}$ that contain one mixed strategy for every player, with the exception of i, are called i-*incomplete*. The index $-i$ is used to designate i-incomplete combinations. $-i$ may be thought of as an abbreviation of $N\backslash\{i\}$.

Φ_{-i} denotes the set of all i-incomplete combinations of pure strategies, and the symbol Q_{-i} is used for the set of all i-incomplete mixed combinations. We use the notation $q_i q_{-i}$ to describe the $q \in Q$ that contains q_i and the components of q_{-i}. If, for all players with the exception of player i, the strategies in q_{-i} agree with those in q, we call q_{-i} *prescribed by* q. Similarly we say that each of the components of a combination q or an i-incomplete combination q_{-i} is prescribed by q or q_{-i}, respectively.

BEHAVIOR STRATEGIES   A *local strategy* b_{ij} of an agent ij is a probability distribution over his choice set Φ_{ij}. The probability assigned to $\phi_{ij} \in \Phi_{ij}$ by ij is denoted by $b_{ij}(\phi_{ij})$. No distinction is made between a choice ϕ_{ij} and the local strategy b_{ij} that selects ϕ_{ij} with probability 1. The set of all local strategies of ij is denoted by B_{ij}.

A *behavior strategy*

$$b_i = (b_{ij})_{M_i} \tag{2.3.7}$$

is a collection of local strategies b_{ij} containing one for each player i's agents. The set of all behavior strategies of player i is denoted by B_i. It is convenient to introduce the following notation:

$$b_i(\phi_i) = \prod_{ij \in M_i} b_{ij}(\phi_{ij}) \tag{2.3.8}$$

for $b_i = (b_{ij})_{M_i}$ and $\phi_i = (\phi_{ij})_{M_i}$. We call $b_i(\phi_i)$ the *realization probability* of ϕ_i under b_i.

Obviously the realization probabilities $b_i(\phi_i)$ for all $\phi_i \in \Phi_i$ are nonnegative and sum to 1. b_i can be regarded as a mixed strategy. If we know only the realization probabilities $b_i(\phi_i)$, we can easily reconstruct the local strategies b_{ij}. The probability $b_i(\phi_{ij})$ is the sum of all $b_i(\phi_i)$ for pure strategies ϕ_i that contain ϕ_{ij}. Therefore a behavior strategy is uniquely determined by its realization probabilities. This permits us to look at behavior strategies as special mixed strategies. We shall make no distinction between a behavior strategy b_i and the mixed strategy that assigns the realization probabilities $b_i(\phi_i)$ to the pure strategies. This has the consequence that B_i is identified with a subset of Q_i. If a player has at least two agents, then B_i

is a proper subset of Q_i. Not every mixed strategy permits a representation of the form (2.3.8).

A *behavior-strategy combination* $b = (b_i)_N$ (or simply a *behavioral combination*) contains a behavior strategy b_i for each player. The set of all such combinations is denoted by B. The definition of payoffs for mixed combinations automatically applies to behavioral combinations since they are special mixed combinations. A behavioral combination can also be regarded as a collection $b = (b_{ij})_M$ of local strategies for all agents.

PAYOFF EQUIVALENCE   Two mixed strategies r_i and s_i of player i are called *payoff equivalent* if we have

$$H(r_i\phi_{-i}) = H(s_i\phi_{-i}) \qquad\qquad\qquad\qquad (2.3.9)$$

for every $\phi_{-i} \in \Phi_{-i}$. Equation (2.3.9) implies that $H(r_iq_{-i})$ and $H(s_iq_{-i})$ are equal for all $q_{-i} \in Q_{-i}$. Note that (2.3.9) does not only concern player i's payoff but the whole payoff vector.

Comment   Our solution theory is restricted to games with perfect recall. Such games have special properties that will be examined in sections 2.4 and 2.5. Here we only want to explain why for some purposes one can restrict one's attention to behavior strategies. Kuhn's theorem expresses a very important property of games with perfect recall that deals with such strategies: for every mixed strategy $q_i \in Q_i$ a behavior strategy b_i can be found such that q_i and b_i are payoff equivalent (Kuhn 1953; Selten 1975).

Kuhn's theorem shows that in games with perfect recall a player does not lose anything of his range of strategic opportunities if he restricts his strategy selection to the set B_i of behavior strategies. However, because sometimes we have to look at substructures of games that are games with fewer players, we have to introduce the notion of a subcombination which specifies local strategies only for a subset of agents.

SUBCOMBINATIONS   Let $C \subseteq M$ be a nonempty subset of the set M of all agents. A collection $b_C = (b_{ij})_C$ of local strategies $b_{ij} \in B_{ij}$ containing one for each agent $ij \in C$ is called a *subcombination* for C. The set of all subcombinations for C is denoted by B_C.

Suppose that b_C and b_D are subcombinations for two nonintersecting subsets C and D of M. We use the notation $b_C b_D$ for the combination

$b_{C \cup D}$ that contains the components of b_C and b_D. A pure subcombination ϕ_C is a subcombination that contains a choice for every member of C. The set of all pure subcombinations for C is denoted by Φ_C.

Subcombinations for $M \setminus \{ij\}$ are called *ij-incomplete combinations*. The notation b_{-ij} is used for such subcombinations. Accordingly, B_{-ij} and Φ_{-ij} are the sets of mixed and pure *ij-incomplete combinations*, respectively. A subcombination for $M_i \setminus \{ij\}$ is called an *ij-incomplete behavior strategy*. We use the notation $b_{i \setminus ij}$ for *ij-incomplete behavior strategies*. $B_{i \setminus ij}$ and $\Phi_{i \setminus ij}$ are the sets of mixed and pure *ij-incomplete behavior strategies*, respectively. For $D \subseteq C$ we say that b_D is *prescribed* by b_C if b_D and b_C contain the same local strategies for the agents in D.

Comment   In our theory we will sometimes have to look at expectations that one player can form on the behavior of the other players. In a disequilibrium situation such expectations may take the form of *i-incomplete mixed combinations*, but this is not the most general case. A player may, for example, expect that with probability z all other players will behave according to ϕ_{-i} and with probability $1 - z$ all other players will behave according to ψ_{-i}, where ϕ_{-i} and ψ_{-i} are two *i-incomplete combinations* prescribed by two different solution theories between which the player cannot decide. To describe such expectations, we need the concept of *i-incomplete joint mixtures* that are probability distributions over the *i-incomplete pure combinations*.

JOINT MIXTURES   An *i-incomplete joint mixture* $q_{\cdot i}$ is a probability distribution over Φ_{-i}. The probability assigned to an *i-incomplete pure combination* by $q_{\cdot i}$ is denoted by $q_{\cdot i}(\phi_{-i})$. We use a dot before i as a lower index to distinguish *i-incomplete joint mixtures* from *i-incomplete combinations*. Wherever this can be done without risk of confusion, we shall drop the adjective "*i-incomplete*" and simply speak of joint mixtures. The set of all *i-incomplete joint mixtures* is denoted by $Q_{\cdot i}$.

REALIZATION PROBABILITIES   Let b_C be a mixed subcombination for $C \subseteq M$ We use the following notation:

$$b_C(\phi_C) = \prod_{ij \in C} b_{ij}(\phi_{ij}), \tag{2.3.10}$$

where ϕ_{ij} is prescribed by ϕ_C. We call $b_C(\phi_C)$ the *realization probability* of ϕ_C under b_C.

PLAYER SUBCOMBINATIONS   Let $D \subseteq N$ be a nonempty set of players. A *player subcombination* for D is a collection of mixed strategies containing one for each member of D. The set of all player subcombinations for D is denoted by Q_D. The realization probability of $\phi_D \in \Phi_D$ under q_D is defined as follows:

$$q_D(\phi_D) = \prod_{i \in D} q_i(\phi_i), \qquad (2.3.11)$$

where ϕ_i is prescribed by ϕ_D.

Obviously an i-incomplete mixed combination q_{-i} is a special player subcombination. The realization probabilities $q_{-i}(\phi_{-i})$ defined for q_{-i} by (2.3.11) form a probability distribution over Φ_{-i} or, in other words, a joint mixture. We make no distinction between q_{-i} and the i-incomplete joint mixture that assigns the realization probabilities under q_{-i} to the i-incomplete pure combinations. In this way, Q_{-i} is identified with a subset of $Q_{.i}$.

REALIZATION PROBABILITIES OF PURE SUBCOMBINATIONS   Let q_i be a mixed strategy of player i, and let ϕ_C be a pure subcombination for a subset $C \subseteq M_i$ of player i's agent set. The realization probability $q_i(\phi_C)$ of ϕ_C under q_i is defined as follows:

$$q_i(\phi_C) = \sum_{\phi_{M_i \setminus C} \in \Phi_{M_i \setminus C}} q_i(\phi_C \phi_{M_i \setminus C}). \qquad (2.3.12)$$

Obviously $q_i(\phi_C)$ is the probability that q_i selects a pure strategy ϕ_i that prescribes ϕ_C.

HYBRID COMBINATIONS   A *hybrid combination* $q_i q_{.i}$ for player i consists of a mixed strategy $q_i \in Q_i$ and a joint mixture $q_{.i} \in Q_{.i}$. The set of all hybrid combinations is the cartesian product $Q_i \times Q_{.i}$. The definition of the payoff function H is extended to hybrid combinations in the obvious way:

$$H(q_i q_{.i}) = \sum_{\phi_{-i} \in \Phi_{-i}} q_{.i}(\phi_{-i}) H(q_i \phi_{-i}). \qquad (2.3.13)$$

The payoff vector described by (2.3.13) can be interpreted as player i's expected value of the payoff vector if he uses q_i, and his expectations on the other players are described by $q_{.i}$.

We will also look at hybrid combinations of the form $b_C q_{.i}$, where $C \subseteq M_i$ is a subset of agents of player i. The cartesian product $B_C \times Q_{.i}$ is the set of all such combinations.

BEST REPLY $r_i \in Q_i$ is called a *best reply* to $q_{\cdot i} \in Q_{\cdot i}$ if we have

$$H_i(r_i q_{\cdot i}) = \max_{q_i \in Q_i} H_i(q_i q_{\cdot i}). \qquad (2.3.14)$$

An important fact on best replies deserves to be expressed as a lemma, but it need not be proved here for it is a well-known result of game theory:

LEMMA 2.3.1 (Lemma on best replies) r_i is a best reply to $q_{\cdot i}$ if and only if every $\phi_i \in \Phi_i$ with $r_i(\phi_i) > 0$ is a best reply to $q_{\cdot i}$.

Since *i*-incomplete mixed combinations are special *i*-incomplete joint mixtures, (2.3.14) also defines best replies to *i*-incomplete mixed combinations. We say that r_i is a best reply to $q \in Q$ if r_i is a best reply to the *i*-incomplete combination q_{-i} prescribed by q. A combination $r \in Q$ is called a *vector best reply* (or simply a best reply) to $q \in Q$ if every r_i in r is a best reply to q.

STRONG BEST REPLY r_i is called a *strong best reply* to $q_{\cdot i}$ if r_i is the only best reply to $q_{\cdot i}$. This means that player i receives a smaller payoff against $q_{\cdot i}$ if he uses any other strategy than r_i. In view of the lemma on best replies it is clear that a strong best reply must be a pure strategy.

LOCAL BEST REPLY   A *local best reply* r_{ij} of an agent $ij \in M$ to a hybrid combination $b_{i \setminus ij} q_{\cdot i}$ is a local strategy $r_{ij} \in B_{ij}$ with the following property:

$$H_i(r_{ij} b_{i \setminus ij} q_{\cdot i}) = \max_{b_{ij} \in B_{ij}} H_i(b_{ij} b_{i \setminus ij} q_{\cdot i}). \qquad (2.3.15)$$

A statement analogous to the lemma on best replies also holds for local best replies:

LEMMA 2.3.2 (Lemma on local best replies) r_{ij} is a local best reply to $b_{i \setminus ij} q_{\cdot i}$ if and only if every choice ϕ_{ij} with $r_{ij}(\phi_{ij}) > 0$ is a local best reply to $b_{i \setminus ij} q_{\cdot i}$.

The proof is analogous to that of the lemma on best replies and therefore need not be given here.

We say that r_{ij} is a local best reply to $b_i q_{\cdot i}$ if r_{ij} is a local best reply to $b_{i \setminus ij} q_{\cdot i}$, where $b_{i \setminus ij}$ is prescribed by b_i. A behavior strategy b_i is called a local best reply of player i to $q_{\cdot i}$ if every b_{ij} prescribed by b_i is a local best reply to $b_i q_{\cdot i}$. Since *ij*-incomplete combinations b_{-ij} can be interpreted as special hybrid mixtures, equation (2.3.15) also defines local best replies to *ij*-incomplete combinations. The combination $r \in B$ is a *local vector best reply* (or a local best reply) to $b \in B$ if every r_{ij} in r is a local best reply to the corresponding b_{-ij} prescribed by b.

STRONG LOCAL BEST REPLY r_{ij} is called a *strong local best reply* to $b_{i\setminus ij}q_{\cdot i}$ if r_{ij} is the only best reply to this hybrid combination. In view of the lemma on local best replies it is clear that a strong local best reply must be a choice.

Equilibrium Points

An *equilibrium point* in mixed strategies is a mixed combination $r \in Q$ that is a best reply to itself. Similarly, an *equilibrium point in behavior strategies* $b \in B$ and an *equilibrium point* $\phi \in \Phi$ *in pure strategies* are defined by the property of each being a best reply to itself. Obviously an equilibrium point in pure strategies is also an equilibrium point in behavior strategies, and an equilibrium point in behavior strategies is also an equilibrium point in mixed strategies.

Nash's theorem on the existence of equilibrium points for finite games guarantees that every game in standard form has at least one equilibrium point in mixed strategies (Nash 1951). Since we will restrict our attention to games with perfect recall where Kuhn's theorem holds, we will be able to reply on the existence of equilibrium points in behavior strategies. In the framework of our theory equilibrium points in behavior strategies will be the most important ones. Therefore, when we use the term "equilibrium point" without any qualifications we will always refer to an equilibrium point in behavior strategies.

LOCAL EQUILIBRIUM POINTS   A behavior-strategy combination $b \in B$ is a *local equilibrium point* if b is a local best reply to itself.

A local equilibrium point is not necessarily an equilibrium point in behavior strategies. However, our theory will be mainly concerned with standard forms where this is the case. The games to which our solution function is applied will have the property that a local best reply of a player is always a best reply.

STRONG EQUILIBRIUM POINTS   An equilibrium point r in mixed strategies is called *strong* if for every player i his strategy r_i in r is a strong best reply to r.

Note that this use of the term "strong equilibrium point" is different from that introduced by Aumann (1959). We feel that in view of the connection to strong inequalities, our use of the term is a very natural one. Moreover we do not need a name for Aumann's cooperative concept which does not appear in our strictly noncooperative theory.

A local equilibrium point $b \in B$ is called strong if for every agent $ij \in M$ the local strategy b_{ij} prescribed by b is a strong local best reply to b. Obviously strong equilibrium points and strong local equilibrium points must be pure-strategy combinations.

We say that an equilibrium point in mixed strategies r is *strong for player i* if this player's strategy r_i in r is a strong best reply to r, whereas the same condition is not necessarily satisfied for the other players. Similarily a local equilibrium point $b \in B$ is *strong for agent ij* if ij's local strategy b_{ij} in b is a strong local best reply to b.

2.4 Standard Forms with Perfect Recall

Games in standard form that can be derived from extensive games with perfect recall have important special properties. To find out what these special properties are, we have to investigate the distinguishing features of extensive games with perfect recall. We will do this in a somewhat informal way, for we do not want to burden the analysis with the formalism of the extensive game. Those who are familiar with the relevant definitions will have no difficulty in seeing that our conclusions are correct.

An extensive game has perfect recall if every player at each of his information sets knows all his previous choices. This has the consequence that the agents ij of player i and their choices ϕ_{ij} can be thought of as nodes of a tree whose structure is closely connected to the tree structure of the extensive game. To prepare the description of this "tree of player i," we first introduce a convenient way of speaking on the relevant details of the extensive form.

In this section we look at a fixed extensive game with perfect recall and the standard form $G = (\Phi, H)$ derived from it.

Precedence

Let ij and ik be two agents of player i. We say that ik *follows ij*, or equivalently that ij *precedes ik by* ϕ_{ij}, if at ik's information set player i knows that he has taken choice ϕ_{ij} at ij's information set. If in addition to this at ik's information set player i knows that ϕ_{ij} was the last choice he has made up to now, we say that ik *immediately follows ij* or equivalently that ij *immediately precedes ik by* ϕ_{ij}.

The definition of perfect recall has the consequence that ik follows ij if and only if there is at least one play that intersects first ij's information set and then ik's information set. An agent ij who is not preceded by any other agent of player i is called a *first agent*. If ik is not a first agent, then he immediately follows a uniquely determined agent ij by a uniquely determined choice ϕ_{ij}. We call this agent ij the *immediate predecessor* of ik, we speak of the choice ϕ_{ij} as the choice that immediately precedes ik, and we say that ik immediately follows ϕ_{ij}.

A choice ϕ_{ij} that is not immediately followed by any agent of player i is called *terminal*. If ϕ_{ij} is not terminal, one or several agents of player i may immediately follow ϕ_{ij}.

The Tree of a Player

We now look at a fixed player $i \in N$, and we construct a tree K_i *of player i*. This tree K_i has three kinds of *nodes*: (1) the origin o of the tree, (2) the *agents* $ij \in M_i$, and (3) the *choices* $\phi_{ij} \in \Phi_{ij}$ of the agents $ij \in M_i$. The *edges* of the tree are as follows: (1) For each first agent ij, there is an edge (o, ij) which connects the origin to this first agent. (2) For each agent $ij \in M_i$ and for each of his choices ϕ_{ij}, there is an edge (ij, ϕ_{ij}) that connects ij with ϕ_{ij}. (3) For each choice ϕ_{ij} and each ik, such that ik immediately follows ϕ_{ij}, the tree contains an edge (ϕ_{ij}, ik) (see figures 2.2 and 2.3). The terminal choices

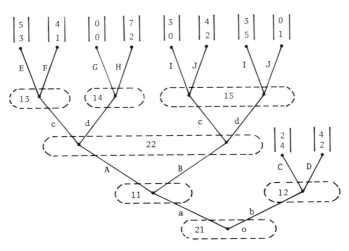

Figure 2.2
An extensive game with perfect recall. Information sets are represented by dotted lines, and payoffs as column vectors with the entries for player 1 above. The letter to the left of each edge denotes the choice to which it belongs.

are also called *end points* of the tree K_i. A path from the origin o to an end point of K_i is called a *quasi play*.

The extensive form does not specify the information of a player after the end of the game. Suppose that he receives only as much information as is implied by those information sets that are reached by the play. With this assumption a quasi play can be interpreted as a description of player i's information on the play after the end of the game.

Quasi-Play Combinations

Let C be the set of agents who are nodes on a fixed quasi play, and let ϕ_C be the subcombination for C that contains those choices of agents that are nodes on the quasi play. We call ϕ_C the *quasi-play combination* of the quasi play. The set of all subcombinations ϕ_C that are quasi-play combinations for some quasi play is denoted by Δ_i. Obviously there is a one-to-one correspondence between the quasi plays and the elements of Δ_i.

For every $\phi_i \in \Phi_i$, let $\delta(\phi_i)$ be the set of all quasi-play combinations $\phi_C \in \Delta_i$ such that the choices in ϕ_C are prescribed by ϕ_i. Since several agents ik may immediately follow an agent ij by the same choice ϕ_{ij}, the set $\delta(\phi_i)$ will generally contain more than one element.

Succession Probability

Let ik be an agent who immediately follows ij by the choice ϕ_{ij}. Let ξ_{ik} be the conditional probability that ik will be reached by a play of the game under the condition that ij has been reached and choice ϕ_{ij} has been taken.

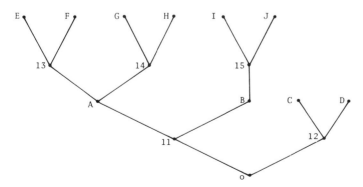

Figure 2.3
Player 1's tree K_1 for the game of figure 2.2

Obviously this probability depends on the strategies of the other players, but it does not depend on player i's strategy. To see this, suppose that a pure combination $\phi = \phi_i \phi_{-i}$ is being played. The condition that ij has been reached and choice ϕ_{ij} has been taken implies that ϕ_i prescribes the choices on the path from o to ϕ_{ij}. All strategies ϕ_i with this property will have the same effect on the other players' information, as long as no other agent of player i has been reached. We can conclude that ξ_{ik} is a function $\xi_{ik}(\phi_{-i})$ of the strategies of the other players. We call $\xi_{ik}(\phi_{-i})$ the *succession probability* of ik for ϕ_{-i}. A succession probability $\xi_{ij}(\phi_{-i})$ is also defined for first agents ij as the probability that ij is reached if ϕ_{-i} is played. It may of course happen that ij cannot be reached if ϕ_{-i} is played. In that case we define $\xi_{ij}(\phi_{-i})$ as zero.

Payoff Decompostion

Suppose that a pure combination $\phi = \phi_i \phi_{-i}$ is being played. The set C of all agents reached by a play and their choices prescribed by ϕ_i form a quasi-play combination $\phi_C \in \delta(\phi_i)$. The probability that a specific $\phi_C \in \delta(\phi_i)$ will be generated in this way by a play if ϕ is played is nothing else than the product of the succession probabilities of the agents in C. We denote this probability by $\xi(\phi_{-i})$.

Consider the conditional expectation of the payoff vector under the condition that $\phi_C \in \delta(\phi_i)$ has been generated by the play in the way described. This conditionally expected payoff depends only on ϕ_{-i}. The reasons are the same as those for the independence of the succession probabilities on ϕ_i. The product of the conditionally expected payoff vector with $\xi(\phi_{-i})$ is denoted by $h(\phi_C \phi_{-i})$. If ϕ_{-i} excludes the possibility that ϕ_C is generated, the value of h is defined as the zero vector. We call $h(\phi_C \phi_{-i})$ the contribution of ϕ_C to $H(\phi)$. It is clear that the following formula is true for every $\phi = \phi_i \phi_{-i} \in \Phi$:

$$H(\phi) = \sum_{\phi_C \in \delta(\phi_i)} h(\phi_C \phi_{-i}). \tag{2.4.1}$$

The payoff vector function h is defined on $\Delta_i \times \Phi_{-i}$. Equation (2.4.1) will be referred to as *player i's payoff decomposition* of $H(\phi)$.

Perfect Recall in the Standard Form

Consider a standard form $G = (\Phi, H)$ that may or may not have its origin in an extensive form. We say that player $i \in N$ has *perfect recall* if it is possible to construct a tree K_i with the following properties:

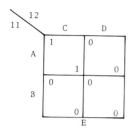
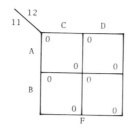

Figure 2.4
Example of a standard form with perfect recall. Player 1 has two agents 11 and 12. Agent 11 selects rows, agent 12 selects columns, and player 2 selects matrices. Payoffs of player 1 are shown in the upper left corner, and payoffs of player 2 in the lower right corner.

1. K_i has nodes at (a) the origin o, (b) the agents $ij \in M_i$, and (c) the choices $\phi_{ij} \in \Phi_{ij}$ of the agents $ij \in M_i$. The edges of K_i are (a) for every agent $ij \in M_i$ and every choice $\phi_{ij} \in \Phi_{ij}$ there is one edge (ij, ϕ_{ij}) that connects ij and ϕ_{ij}; (b) for every agent $ij \in M_{ij}$ there is either an edge (o, ij) that connects the origin o to ij or a choice ϕ_{ik} of another agent ik such that an edge (ϕ_{ik}, ij) connects ϕ_{ik} and ij.

2. K_i permits a payoff decomposition of the form (2.4.1)—that is, a payoff vector function h defined on $\Delta_i \times \Phi_{-i}$ can be found such that equation (2.4.1) holds.

In this definition it is understood that Δ_i and $\delta(\phi_i)$ have the same relationship to K_i as in the case of the tree of a player constructed from the extensive form. The definitions of "precedes," "follows," "first agent," "quasi play," and so forth, are transferred to the new context in the obvious way: a standard form $G = (\Phi, H)$ has perfect recall if in G every player $i \in N$ has perfect recall.

The tree K_i of player i need not be uniquely determined by the structure of the standard form. A very simple example is given by figure 2.4. Two ways of constructing the tree of player 1 are shown in figure 2.5. Note that even if K_i is uniquely determined, the payoff decomposition (2.4.1) need not be uniquely determined.

2.5 Properties of Standard Forms with Perfect Recall

In principle, it is always possible to check whether a given standard form has perfect recall. There are only finitely many possibilities to arrange

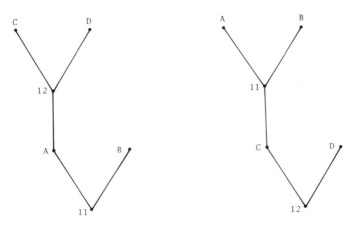

Figure 2.5
Two possibilities for the construction of player 1's tree K_1 in the example of figure 2.2

player i's agents and choices in a tree K_i with the properties required by condition 1 of the definition. To find out whether the payoff decomposition property holds, one has to look at (2.4.1) as a linear equation system for the vectors $h(\phi_C \phi_{-i})$. If a function h with (2.4.1) exists for a given K_i, one can find it by solving the system.

Luckily applications of our theory do not make it necessary to engage in such tedious computations. Models of substantial interest are usually given as normal forms or as extensive games with perfect recall. In such cases it is clear from the beginning that the standard forms under consideration have perfect recall.

The significance of the definition of perfect recall in the framework of the standard form lies in the fact that it enables us to develop our theory without formal reference to the extensive form. Thus one can avoid unnecessary complications without loss of precision.

Construction of Payoff-Equivalent Behavior Strategies

We now show how in a standard form with perfect recall a behavior strategy b_i can be constructed that is payoff equivalent to a given completely mixed strategy q_i. This amounts to a proof of a version of Kuhn's theorem in the framework of the standard form. The extension of the result to mixed strategies that are not completely mixed is easy, but we will not discuss this question here, since it has no significance for our theory.

Assume that $G = (\Phi, H)$ is a standard form with perfect recall and that q_i is a completely mixed strategy for player i. We can construct a tree K_i of player i with the properties required by the definition of perfect recall. Let K_i be a fixed tree of this kind, and let h be a payoff vector function that satisfies (2.4.1) with respect to this tree.

It is convenient to introduce the notation $\langle ij)$ for the set of all agents who precede ij in K_i. Let $\gamma_{\langle ij)}$ be the subcombination for $\langle ij)$ that contains the choices on the path from the origin o to ij. We call $\gamma_{\langle ij)}$ the *precombina-tion* of ij. In the case of a first agent ij, the set $\langle ij)$ is empty. In this case, $\gamma_{\langle ij)}$ is the *empty subcombination* containing no choice. For reasons of formal convenience we do not want to exclude the empty precombination.

The payoff decomposition property (2.4.1) has the consequence that agent ij's choice does not have any influence on the payoffs, unless ϕ_i prescribes the choices in the precombination to the agents in $\langle ij)$.

For every $\phi_{ij} \in \Phi_{ij}$ and every $ij \in M_i$, define

$$b_{ij}(\phi_{ij}) = \frac{q_i(\gamma_{\langle ij)}\phi_{ij})}{q_i(\gamma_{\langle ij)})}, \qquad (2.5.1)$$

where $\gamma_{\langle ij)}$ is the precombination of ij and where the denominator on the right-hand side is interpreted as 1 in the case of $\langle ij) = \varnothing$. In (2.5.1) we use the notation introduced by (2.3.10). Realization probabilities of the form $q_i(\phi_C)$ have been defined by (2.3.12).

Since q_i is completely mixed, the denominator in (2.5.1) is always positive. Moreover the sum of all $b_{ij}(\phi_{ij})$ with $\phi_{ij} \in \Phi_{ij}$ is clearly equal to 1. Consequently a local strategy b_{ij} is defined by (2.5.1). Let b_i be that behavior strategy of player i whose components are defined by (2.5.1). We will show that b_i is payoff equivalent to q_i. In view of (2.4.1) it is sufficient to prove

$$b_i(\gamma_D) = q_i(\gamma_D), \quad \text{for every } \gamma_D \in \Delta_i. \qquad (2.5.2)$$

Equation (2.5.2) is a consequence of (2.5.1). We obtain $b_i(\gamma_D)$ by the multiplication of all $b_{ij}(\gamma_{ij})$ along the quasi play corresponding to γ_D. In the product of the fractions taken from the right-hand side of (2.5.1), numerators cancel against denominators of the next term. The product is nothing else than the numerator of the last term. This is $q_i(\gamma_D)$. We have proved the following theorem:

THEOREM 2.5.1 (Kuhn's theorem)   Let $G = (\Phi, H)$ be a standard form with perfect recall, and let q_i be a completely mixed strategy of a player i in G. The behavior strategy b_i defined by (2.5.1) is payoff equivalent to q_i.

Further Properties of Standard Forms with Perfect Recall

Our theory makes use of two further properties of standard forms with
perfect recall. An important tool to be developed will be a payoff decomposition that focuses on the effects of a specific agent's choice. One may
think of this relation as a rearrangement of the payoff decomposition (2.4.1)
whose possibility is required by the definition of perfect recall in the
standard form. This agent payoff decomposition will involve the definition
of a local payoff for each agent. The second property to be investigated is
a recursive relationship between the local payoff of the agents of one player.

Agent Payoff Decomposition   Let $G = (\Phi, H)$ be a standard form with
perfect recall, let $i \in N$ be one of the players, and let ij be one of his agents.
According to the definition of perfect recall, we can construct a tree K_i of
player i. Let K_i be a fixed tree of this kind, and let h be a payoff vector
function defined on $\Delta_i \times \Phi_{-i}$ that satisfies (2.4.1) with respect to this tree.

It is convenient to introduce the notation $[ij\rangle$ for the set of agents that
consists of ij and all those agents of player i who follow ij in K_i. We call
$[ij\rangle$ agent ij's *forward set*. The rectangular bracket indicates that ij is
included in the set $[ij\rangle$. Agent ij is not included in the set $\langle ij)$ of agents who
precede him. A subcombination for $[ij\rangle$ will be called a *postcombination*
for agent ij.

For every postcombination $\phi_{[ij\rangle}$ we define a set of quasi-play combina-
tions $\delta(\phi_{[ij\rangle})$. The set $\delta(\phi_{[ij\rangle})$ is the set of all $\phi_C \in \Delta_i$ such that ϕ_C is prescribed
by $\gamma_{\langle ij)}\phi_{[ij\rangle}$. The quasi-play combinations in $\delta(\phi_{[ij\rangle})$ correspond to those
quasi plays in K_i that go through ij and after ij through choices in $\phi_{[ij\rangle}$
only. Define

$$H_{ij}(\phi_{[ij\rangle}\phi_{-i}) = \sum_{\phi_C \in \delta(\phi_{[ij\rangle})} h_i(\phi_C\phi_{-i}), \tag{2.5.3}$$

where h_i is the ith component of the payoff vector function h. We call H_{ij}
agent ij's *local payoff function*. Note that the definition of the local payoff
function is relative to a given graph K_i and a given payoff vector function
h. Local payoffs are not uniquely determined by the standard form.

One may think of H_{ij} as the part of player i's payoff that is influenced
by ij's choices. ij has no influence on payoffs obtained by quasi plays that
do not go through ij. Equation (2.5.3) is generalized to hybrid combinations
of the form $b_{[ij\rangle}q_{.i}$ by the following definition:

$$H_{ij}(b_{[ij\rangle}q_{.i}) = \sum_{\phi_{[ij\rangle} \in \Phi_{[ij\rangle}} \sum_{\phi_{-i} \in \Phi_{-i}} b_{[ij\rangle}(\phi_{[ij\rangle})q_{.i}(\phi_{-i})H_{ij}(\phi_{[ij\rangle}\phi_{-i}). \tag{2.5.4}$$

With the help of (2.4.1) it can be seen that player i's payoff $H_i(b_i q._i)$ can be split into two parts, one involving H_{ij} and the other not depending on local strategies of agents in ij's forward set; the second part is represented by a function h_{ij} defined on $B_{M_i \setminus [ij\rangle} \times Q._i$:

$$H_i(b_i q._i) = b_{\langle ij)}(\gamma_{\langle ij)}) H_{ij}(b_{[ij\rangle} q._i)$$

$$+ h_{ij}(b_{M_i \setminus [ij\rangle} q._i), \tag{2.5.5}$$

where the subcombinations $b_{\langle ij)}$, $b_{[ij\rangle}$, and $b_{M_i \setminus [ij\rangle}$ are those prescribed by b_i. We refer to (2.5.5) as the *agent payoff decomposition*. This relationship shows that the influence of ij's choice on player i's payoff works through his local payoff H_{ij}.

Recursive Local Payoff Relationship   We continue to work under the assumptions of the previous subsection. Let Θ_{ij} be the set of all terminal choices of agent ij. Agent ij's local payoff can be split into two parts: one obtained by his terminal choices $\phi_{ij} \in \Theta_{ij}$ and another due to his non-terminal choices $\phi_{ij} \in \Phi_{ij} \setminus \Theta_{ij}$. Define

$$h_{ij}(b_{ij} q._i) = \sum_{\phi_{ij} \in \Theta_{ij}} \sum_{\phi_{-i} \in \Phi_{-i}} b_{ij}(\phi_{ij}) q._i(\phi_{-i}) h_i(\gamma_{\langle ij)} \phi_{ij} \phi_{-i}), \tag{2.5.6}$$

where h_i stands for the ith component of h. Equation (2.5.6) describes that part of agent ij's local payoff that is due to his terminal choices. That part of his choices due to his nonterminal choices can be expressed with the help of the local payoffs of his immediate followers. We use the symbol $F(\phi_{ij})$ for the set of all agents of player i who immediately follow ij by ϕ_{ij}. With this notation we obtain the following relationship.

$$H_{ij}(b_{[ij\rangle} q._i) = h_{ij}(b_{ij} q._i)$$

$$+ \sum_{\phi_{ij} \in \Phi_{ij} \setminus \Theta_{ij}} \sum_{ik \in F(\phi_{ij})} b_{ij}(\phi_{ij}) H_{ik}(b_{[ik\rangle} q._i). \tag{2.5.7}$$

Equation (2.5.7) shows that agent ij's local payoff can be expressed as a function of his own local strategy b_{ij}, the i-incomplete mixture $q._i$ and the local payoffs of his immediate followers. We refer to (2.5.7) as the *recursive local payoff relationship*.

2.6   Substructures

In our theory it will often be necessary to look at substructures of standard forms with perfect recall. The solution concept is not applied directly to standard forms with perfect recall but to perturbed games derived from them. These perturbed games can be interpreted as special substructures. Moreover the solution concept is recursive in the sense that in many cases it is necessary to solve substructures of a perturbed game in order to find its solution. Substructures of standard forms are standard forms too, but the property of perfect recall is not necessarily inherited from the super-structure. The substructures appearing in our theory generally do not have perfect recall. Nevertheless, they have important special properties that in a sense are even stronger than those of games with perfect recall. It is necessary to investigate these properties.

We will give a general definition of a substructure that is sufficiently wide to cover a variety of quite different special cases that will be important for our theory. All substructures can be obtained by the application of two operations. The first one is fixing an agent at a local strategy; intuitively this has the interpretation that in the new game the agent must use this local strategy and thereby becomes a dummy who can be left out in the description of the new game. The new game does not contain this agent anymore. The second operation is narrowing the choice set of an agent; this means that in the new game his choice set consists of a finite number of his local strategies in the old game. This can be described as the restriction of his strategy choice to the convex hull of these local strategies.

In the most general case the transition from a standard form to a sub-structure will involve a set C of agents who are fixed at local strategies and a set D of agents whose choice sets are narrowed down. For convenience, we identify local strategies in the new game with local strategies in the old game. This can be done in a natural way. However, to avoid confusion, we must make sure that two different local strategies in the new game are also different in the old game. Therefore a linear independence restriction has to be imposed on a set of local strategies that is admissible as a new choice set.

The identification of local strategies of the substructure with local strate-gies of the original game avoids unnecessary notational complications. In this way we achieve the useful effect that a substructure of a substructure is also a substructure of the original game. The substructures important for our theory will be interior in the sense that the agents, including those who are fixed, are restricted to completely mixed local strategies of the old game. Interior substructures of standard forms with perfect recall have special features that will be called decentralization properties. The content and the significance of these decentralization properties will be discussed in section 2.7.

Fixing Agents

Let $G = (\Phi, H)$ be a game in standard form, and let $r_C = (r_{ij})_C$ be a sub-combination for a nonempty set C of agents with $C \neq M$. Let M' be the set $M \setminus C$, and let N' be the set of all players $i \in N$ with at least one agent in $M_i' = M_i \setminus C$. For every $i \in N'$ define

$$H_i'(\phi_{M'}) = H_i(\phi_M r_C). \tag{2.6.1}$$

Obviously $\Phi' = \Phi_{M'}$ together with $H' = (H_i)_{M'}$ forms a game $G' = (\Phi', H')$ with the player set N' and the agent set M'. This game G' is called the *game that results from G by fixing the agents in C at r_C*.

Narrowing Choice Sets

Let $G = (\Phi, H)$ be a game in standard form. Let D be a nonempty subset of the agent set M. For every $ij \in D$ let R_{ij} be a finite subset of ij's local strategy set B_{ij}. Define

$$R_D = \underset{ij \in D}{\times} R_{ij}, \tag{2.6.2}$$

$$\Phi' = \Phi_{M \setminus D} \times R_D. \tag{2.6.3}$$

We construct a game $G' = (\Phi', H')$ whose payoffs are defined as follows:

$$H'(\phi') = H(\phi'), \qquad \text{for every } \phi' \in \Phi'. \tag{2.6.4}$$

We say that $G' = (\Phi', H')$ *results from $G = (\Phi, H)$ by narrowing the choice sets in Φ_D to R_D*.

Not every game G' that can be obtained in this way will be considered to be a substructure of G. We thus impose a restriction on the new choice sets R_{ij} that enables us to identify local strategies in G' with local strategies in G without running into the difficulty that two different local strategies in G' must be identified with the same local strategy in G. Consider a local strategy b_{ij}' of an agent $ij \in D$ in G'. Suppose that in G agent ij uses each of his local strategies $r_{ij} \in R_{ij}$ with probability $b_{ij}'(r_{ij})$. If he does this, he will actually play a local strategy b_{ij} in G. Obviously the probabilities assigned to the choices $\phi_{ij} \in \Phi_{ij}$ by this local strategy are as follows:

$$b_{ij}(\phi_{ij}) = \sum_{r_{ij} \in R_{ij}} b_{ij}'(r_{ij}) r_{ij}(\phi_{ij}). \tag{2.6.5}$$

Let $|\Phi_{ij}|$ be the number of elements in Φ_{ij}. The local strategies $b_{ij} \in B_{ij}$ can be interpreted as $|\Phi_{ij}|$-dimensional vectors whose components are the probabilities $b_{ij}(\phi_{ij})$ arranged in some fixed order. We say that R_{ij} is a *set of independent local strategies* if the vectors corresponding to the elements of R_{ij} are linearly independent. Obviously the order in which the $b_{ij}(\phi_{ij})$ are arranged does not matter for this definition. If R_{ij} is a set of independent local strategies, then there can be at most one $b'_{ij} \in B'_{ij}$ for every $b_{ij} \in B_{ij}$ such that both local strategies are related as in (2.6.5). This becomes obvious if one looks at (2.6.5) as an equation system for the probabilities $b'_{ij}(\phi_{ij})$.

We want to use a system of notation that enables us to denote the right-hand side of (2.6.5) by $b'_{ij}(\phi_{ij})$. If this can be done, we need not use different symbols for a local strategy in G' and the corresponding local strategy in G. It is not quite sufficient to require that R_{ij} is a set of independent local strategies in order to achieve this goal. We must impose the following additional condition:

NOTATIONAL UNAMBIGUITY CONDITION   If $\phi_{ij} \in \Phi_{ij}$ belongs to R_{ij}, then $r_{ij}(\phi_{ij}) = 0$ holds for every $r_{ij} \neq \phi_{ij}$ in R_{ij}.

It is clear that this notational unambiguity condition excludes the possibility that different probabilities are assigned to ϕ_{ij} by b'_{ij} and the corresponding local strategy b_{ij} in (2.6.5).

We say that R_{ij} is an *admissible new choice set* if R_{ij} is a set of independent local strategies and if the notational unambiguity condition is satisfied for R_{ij}. If R_{ij} is an admissible new choice set, then we make no distinction between a local strategy b'_{ij} for G' and that local strategy b_{ij} for G that corresponds to it by (2.6.5).

We say the game $G' = (\Phi', H')$ that results from $G = (\Phi, H)$ by narrowing down the choice sets in Φ_D to R_D is *embedded* in G if all the R_{ij} in R_D are admissible new choice sets. If G' is embedded in G, then equation (2.6.4) can be immediately generalized to behavior-strategy combinations b' for G':

$$H'(b') = H(b'). \tag{2.6.6}$$

The identification of behavior-strategy combinations for G' with behavior-strategy combinations for G is a consequence of the identification of local strategies. In view of (2.6.3) the payoff function H' can be described as the restriction of H to B'.

Substructures of Standard Forms

We also say that $G' = (\Phi', H')$ is *embedded in* $G = (\Phi, H)$ if G' results from G by fixing agents at local strategies. In this case we face no problem of identification of local strategies since local strategies in G' are nevertheless local strategies in G.

Consider a sequence of games $G^1, \ldots, G^m$ such that for $k = 1, \ldots, m-1$, the game G^{k+1} results from G^k by either fixing agents or narrowing choice sets in such a way that G^{k+1} is embedded in G^k. A sequence of this kind will be called a *chain of substructures from* G^1 *to* G^m. A game $G' = (\Phi', H')$ will also be called *embedded* in G if there is a chain of substructures from G to G'. In a chain of substructures $G^1, \ldots, G^m$ the local strategies in G^{k+1} are local strategies in G^k. Therefore the local strategies in G^m are local strategies in G^1. This justifies the extended use of the word "embedded."

A game G' that is embedded in G will also be called a *substructure* of G. It is clear that every substructure G' of G can actually be obtained in two steps by first fixing those agents of G who do not belong to G' and then narrowing the choice sets of those agents who have different choice sets in G'. We can think of both operations being performed simultaneously since they do not interfere with each other. In this sense we speak of the game $G' = (\Phi', H')$ that *results from* $G = (\Phi, H)$ *by fixing the agents in* C *at* r_C *and by narrowing the choice sets in* Φ_D *to* R_D. This manner of speaking of course presupposes that C and D are nonintersecting and that the other conditions are satisfied that are required for both operations separately. If all choice sets in R_D are admissible, then a game G' that results from G in this way is embedded in G. All substructures of G can be obtained as games G' of this kind. We state the result in the form of a lemma:

LEMMA 2.6.1 (Lemma on substructures)   If $G' = (\Phi', H')$ is a substructure of a standard form $G = (\Phi, H)$, then for some $C, D, r_C,$ and R_C such that the R_{ij} in R_C are admissible new choice sets, the game $G' = (\Phi', H')$ results from $G = (\Phi, H)$ by fixing the agents in C at r_C and narrowing the choice sets in Φ_D to R_D.

Interior Substructures

Let $G = (\Phi, H)$ be a standard form, and let $G' = (\Phi', H')$ be a substructure of G. Assume that G' results from G by fixing the agents in C at r_C and by narrowing the choice sets in Φ_D to R_D. We say G' is an *interior substructure* of G if for every $ij \in C$ the local strategy r_{ij} in r_C is completely mixed and for every $ij \in D$ all choices r_{ij} in the new choice sets R_{ij} are completely mixed local strategies in G.

2.7 Decentralization Properties of Interior Substructures of Standard Forms with Perfect Recall

Interior substructures of standard forms with perfect recall have special features for which the interpretation suggests itself that they permit a player to delegate certain aspects of his strategy choice to his agents. We refer to these special features as decentralization properties. As we have seen, games with perfect recall have an important property of this kind which is expressed by Kuhn's theorem. Randomization need not be performed centrally by the player; one can rely on behavior strategies where randomization is decentralized. It is not quite obvious that Kuhn's theorem also holds for interior substructures of standard forms with perfect recall. We have to show that this is the case.

Another important decentralization property consists in the fact that a behavior strategy of a player is a best reply to a joint mixture for the other players if and only if it is a local best reply to this joint mixture. We call this the *local best-reply property*. It permits the player to delegate the task of checking the best-reply properties of a behavior strategy to his agents. It also has the consequence that local equilibrium points are equilibrium points. Generally, games with perfect recall do not have the local best-reply property, but their interior substructures do have this property.

The availability of a decentralized way of checking whether a given behavior strategy is a best reply to a joint mixture does not yet mean that a player can delegate the task of finding a best reply to his agents. Generally, an agent needs to know the local strategies of other agents of the same player in order to determine a local best reply of his own. This poses a co-ordination problem. As we shall see later, interior substructures of standard forms with perfect recall permit a decentralized iterative procedure that achieves coordination at a best reply for the player. We call this the *coordination property*.

Construction of Payoff-Equivalent Behavior Strategies

Let $G = (\Phi, H)$ be a standard form with perfect recall, and let $G' = (R, H')$ be an interior substructure of G that results from G by narrowing the choice sets in Φ to R. We will show that for every mixed strategy q'_i for G', we can find a payoff-equivalent behavior strategy b_i'. Obviously we do not have to look at a more general case since a subsequent fixing of agents at local strategies in G' will not destroy the possibility of constructing payoff-equivalent behavior strategies.

Let R_i be the set of pure strategies of player i in G'. Every $r_i \in R_i$ can be interpreted as a completely mixed strategy of player i. Suppose that in G player i uses each strategy $r_i \in R_i$ with its probability $q_i'(r_i)$. If he does this, he will actually play a mixed strategy where each $\phi_i \in \Phi_i$ is used with the following probability:

$$q_i'(\phi_i) = \sum_{r_i \in R_i} q_i'(r_i) r_i(\phi_i). \tag{2.7.1}$$

There is no risk of ambiguity in this notation since the strategies ϕ_i do not belong to R_i. Equation (2.7.1) permits us to interpret q_i' as a mixed strategy for G. Consider a specific agent ij of player i and one of his choices $s_{ij} \in R_{ij}$ in G'. Let S_i^j be the set of all pure strategies $r_i \in R_i$ in G' that contain s_{ij} as agent ij's component. Let K_i be a fixed tree of player i in G, and let $\gamma_{\langle ij \rangle}$ be agent ij's precombination in this tree. Define

$$b_{ij}'(s_{ij}) = \frac{\sum_{r_i \in S_i^j} q_i'(r_i) r_i(\gamma_{\langle ij \rangle})}{\sum_{r_i \in R_i} q_i'(r_i) r_i(\gamma_{\langle ij \rangle})}, \tag{2.7.2}$$

for every $s_{ij} \in R_{ij}$. Equation (2.7.2) defines a local strategy for ij in G'. As we shall see, (2.7.2) yields the same result as the construction (2.5.1) applied to q_i' as a mixed strategy for G. Obviously the denominator of (2.7.2) is nothing else than the realization probability $q_i'(\gamma_{\langle ij \rangle})$ of ij's precombination $\gamma_{\langle ij \rangle}$. The numerator can be interpreted as the probability that first the precombination is realized and then s_{ij} is played by q_i'. The probability of choosing $\phi_{ij} \in \Phi_{ij}$ by b_{ij}' is as follows:

$$b_{ij}'(\phi_{ij}) = \sum_{s_{ij} \in R_{ij}} b_{ij}'(s_{ij}) s_{ij}(\phi_{ij}). \tag{2.7.3}$$

This shows that the constructions (2.7.2) and (2.5.1) yield the same local strategy. For every agent ij of player i, let b_{ij}' be the local strategy obtained in this way. Moreover let b_i' be the behavior strategy that contains the b_{ij}' as components. Our version of Kuhn's theorem in section 2.5 shows that q_i' and b_i' are payoff equivalents. We state the result as a theorem:

THEOREM 2.7.1 (Theorem on substructures—Kuhn's theorem) Let $G' = (\Phi', H')$ be an interior substructure of a standard form $G = (\Phi, H)$ with perfect recall, and let q_i' be a mixed strategy of a player i in G'. Then the behavior strategy b_i' defined by (2.7.2) is payoff equivalent to q_i'.

LOCAL BEST-REPLY PROPERTY   A game $G = (\Phi, H)$ in standard form has the *local best-reply property* if the following is true for every player $i \in N$ and for every i-incomplete joint mixture $q_{.i} \in Q_{.i}$ in G: if $b_i \in B_i$ is a local best reply of player i to $q_{.i}$, then b_i is a best reply to $q_{.i}$.

THEOREM 2.7.2 (Theorem on local best replies)   Let $G' = (\Phi', H')$ be an interior substructure of a standard form $G = (\Phi, H)$ with perfect recall. Then G' has the local best-reply property.

Proof   As in the construction of payoff-equivalent behavior strategies, we can restrict our attention to the case that $G' = (\Phi', H')$ results from G by narrowing the choice sets in Φ to Φ'. Obviously a subsequent fixing of agents cannot destroy the local best-reply property.

For the purpose of this proof it is convenient to think of local strategies, behavior strategies, and i-incomplete joint mixtures in G' as special objects of this kind of G. Since G' is an interior substructure, every choice $\phi_{ij} \in \Phi_{ij}$ must be taken with positive probability. Let K_i be a fixed tree of player i in G. The realization probability of the precombination $\gamma_{\langle ij \rangle}$ will always be positive in G'. It follows by the agent payoff decomposition (2.5.5) that a local best reply of ij in G' must maximize ij's local payoff over the region B_{ij}' of local strategies of ij in G'.

Suppose that b_i' is a local best reply of player i in G' to $q_{.i}'$. Assume that b_i' is not a best reply of player i to $q_{.i}'$ in G'. Let r_i' be a best reply of player i in G' to $q_{.i}'$. There must be some agents ij for whom the following inequality holds:

$$H_{ij}(r_{\langle ij \rangle}'q_{.i}') \neq H_{ij}(b_{\langle ij \rangle}'q_{.i}'). \tag{2.7.4}$$

Otherwise, r_i' and b_i' would yield equal payoffs. This follows by the payoff decomposition (2.4.1) and by application of (2.5.3) to first agents. Among the agents for whom (2.7.4) holds, there must be at least one such that both local payoffs in (2.7.4) are equal for all agents who follow him. Let ij be an agent of this kind. Consider his local strategies b_{ij}' and r_{ij}' prescribed by b_i' and r_i', respectively. Since for all later agents the local payoffs on both sides of (2.7.4) are equal, it follows by the recursive local payoff relationship (2.5.7) that b_{ij}' is a local best reply both to $b_i'q_{.i}'$ and to $r_i'q_{.i}'$. This, together with (2.7.4), has the consequence that r_{ij}' cannot be a local best reply to $r_i'q_{.i}'$.

However, a behavior strategy cannot be a best reply unless it is a local best reply. This is a contradiction to the assumption that r_i' is a best reply. ∎

Remarks   Since a behavior strategy cannot be a best reply unless it is a local best reply, the local best-reply property has the consequence that $b_i' \in B_i'$ is a best reply to q_{-i}' if and only if b_i' is a local best reply to q_{-i}'.

To prepare the statement of the coordination property, it is necessary to introduce some additional definitions and notations that will refer to a game $G = (\Phi, H)$ in standard form.

CENTROID   Let $\Psi_{ij} \subseteq \Phi_{ij}$ be a nonempty set of choices of agent ij. The *centroid* $c(\Psi_{ij})$ of Ψ_{ij} is the following local strategy b_{ij} of ij:

$$b_{ij}(\phi_{ij}) = \begin{cases} \dfrac{1}{|\Psi_{ij}|}, & \text{for } \phi_{ij} \in \Psi_{ij}, \\ 0, & \text{for } \phi_{ij} \notin \Psi_{ij}, \end{cases} \qquad (2.7.5)$$

where $|\Psi_{ij}|$ is the number of elements in Ψ_{ij}. The centroid of ij's choice set Φ_{ij} is denoted by c_{ij}. We call c_{ij} the centroid of agent ij. The centroid c_i of player i is that one of his behavior strategies that prescribes the centroid $c_{ij} = c(\Phi_{ij})$ to every agent $ij \in M_i$.

LOCAL BEST-REPLY SET   For every hybrid combination of the form $b_{i \setminus ij} q_{-i}$ we define a *local best-reply set* $A_{ij}(b_{i \setminus ij} q_{-i})$. The set $A_{ij}(b_{i \setminus ij} q_{-i})$ is the set of all choices $\phi_{ij} \in \Phi_{ij}$ that are local best replies to $b_{i \setminus ij} q_{-i}$. In this way local best-reply correspondences A_{ij} from $B_{i \setminus ij} \times Q_{-i}$ to Φ_{ij} are defined for every $ij \in M$.

CENTRAL LOCAL BEST REPLY   The centroid $c[A_{ij}(b_{i \setminus ij} q_{-i})]$ of the local best-reply set $A_{ij}(b_{i \setminus ij} q_{-i})$ is denoted by $a_{ij}(b_{i \setminus ij} q_{-i})$. This local strategy of agent ij is called ij's *central local best reply* to $b_{i \setminus ij} q_{-i}$.

Comment on the Coordination Problem   Suppose that $b_{i \setminus ij} q_{-i}$ describes the expectations of agent ij. Then, from his point of view, only the choices in $A_{ij}(b_{i \setminus ij} q_{-i})$ are reasonable ones, and all of them are equally good. Under these circumstances it is very natural to assume that he will use all these choices with equal probabilities. This is the idea behind the definition of the central local best reply.

Assume that q_{-i} represents player i's expectations on the other players before he has decided on his own strategy. Suppose that the local best-reply property holds for the game $G = (\Phi, H)$ under consideration. However, this alone does not permit the player to delegate the task of choosing a best reply to his agents. Since the local best-reply set $A_{ij}(b_{i\setminus ij}q._i)$ depends on $b_{i\setminus ij}$ the agents of player i have to form expectations on the other agents of the same player in order to be able to determine local best replies. Moreover the local best-reply property does not guarantee a global best reply unless all agents form correct expectations on each other.

Actually for interior substructures of standard forms with perfect recall the agents' problem of forming coordinated expectations is less severe than it might seem at first glance. The recursive local payoff relationship permits a recursive determination of local best replies for the agents of player i. One starts with the agents not followed by others and continues with the immediately preceding ones, until a local best reply for player i is obtained.

However, this way of coordinating the expectations of player i's agents on each other is not completely satisfactory. It is based on the tree of player i which fails to be uniquely determined. For the purpose of our theory it is necessary to select a unique best reply of player i. Moreover it seems to be desirable to avoid explicit use of the tree of player i if one wants to obtain a theory that is as simple as possible.

Our iterative procedure arrives at a uniquely determined local best reply of player i without explicit reference to his tree. Actually the construction is not essentially different from the procedure based on the tree which has been outlined earlier. This will become apparent in the proof of its effectiveness for interior substructures of standard forms with perfect recall.

The iterative procedure can be thought of as a decentralized interaction process involving the player and his agents. First the player sends to his agents a message containing an initial hybrid combination $b_i^o q._i$. Then the agents determine central local best replies to $b_i^o q._i$ and inform the player. He puts these central best replies together and thereby forms a new hybrid combination $b_i^1 q._i$. The agents again determine central local best replies, and so on. For interior substructures of standard forms with perfect recall the procedure converges after a finite number of steps. Moreover the end result does not depend on the initial strategy b_i^o.

It is justified to speak of a decentralized procedure since the player performs a passive role as a clearinghouse for messages.

Central Local Best Reply of a Player

Let $G = (\Phi, H)$ be a game in standard form, and let $q._i$ an i-incomplete joint mixture for G. Moreover let b_i^o be a behavior strategy for player i. We construct a sequence $b_i^o, b_i^1, \ldots$, of behavior strategies for player i. The local strategies b_{ij}^k prescribed by b_i^k are defined as follows:

$$b_{ij}^k = a_{ij}(b_{i \setminus ij}^{k-1} q_{.i}) \tag{2.7.6}$$

for every $ij \in M_i$ and for $k = 1, 2, \ldots$, where $b_{i \setminus ij}^{k-1}$ is the ij-incomplete behavior strategy prescribed by b_i^{k-1}. We call the sequence $b_i^o, b_i^1, \ldots$, the *reply sequence for* $q_{.i}$ *starting from* b_i^o.

Suppose that all reply sequences for $q_{.i}$ regardless of the initial strategy b_i^o converge to the same behavior strategy b_i. If this is the case, the common limit b_i of all reply sequences for $q_{.i}$ is called *player i's central local best reply to* $q_{.i}$. Player i's central local best reply to $q_{.i}$ is denoted by $a_i(q_{.i})$.

COORDINATION PROPERTY   A game $G = (\Phi, H)$ in standard form has the *coordination property* if for every $i \in N$ and for every i-incomplete joint mixture $q_{.i} \in Q_{.i}$ all reply sequences $b_i^o, b_i^1, \ldots$, defined by (2.7.6) converge to the same limit b_i after a finite number of steps.

THEOREM 2.7.3 (Theorem on coordination)   Let $G' = (\Phi', H')$ be an interior substructure of a standard form $G = (\Phi, H)$ with perfect recall. Then $G' = (\Phi', H')$ has the coordination property.

Proof   As far as the assertion to be proved is concerned, there is no essential difference between a substructure where the agents in C are fixed at r_C and another one where the choice sets of these agents are narrowed down to sets $\{r_{ij}\}$ containing the local strategy in r_C as the only element. Therefore we assume that $G' = (\Phi', H')$ results from $G = (\Phi, H)$ by narrowing the choice sets in Φ to Φ'.

Let K_i be a fixed tree of player i in G. Let M_i^1 be the set of all agents who in K_i are not followed by other agents of player i. For $k = 1, 2, \ldots$, let M_i^{k+1} be the set of all agents of player i such that all the agents who follow an agent of this kind are in $M_i^1 \cup \cdots \cup M_i^k$. It is clear that there can be only finitely many nonempty sets M_i^k. The number $|M_i|$ of agents of player i is an upper bound for the number of nonempty sets M_i^k.

Since G' is an interior substructure, a local best reply in G' can be described a local strategy that maximizes local payoffs in G'. This follows by the agent payoff decomposition (2.5.5).

The recursive local payoff relationship (2.5.7) has the consequence that in G' the central local best replies of agents in M_i^1 to hybrid combinations of the form $b_i' q_{.i}'$ depend only on $q_{.i}'$. Similarly, the central local best replies of agents in M_i^{k+1} depend only on $q'_{\cdot i}$ and the local strategies b'_{ij} of agents ij in $M_i^1 \cup \ldots \cup M_i^k$. This has the consequence that in the reply sequence $b_i'^{o}, b_i'^{1}, \ldots$, the local strategies of agents in M_i^1 do not change after $b_i'^{1}$, and those of agents in M_i^k do not change after $b_i'^{k}$. The sequence converges after at most $|M_i|$ steps.

The final result does not depend on the initial strategy b'_o. This is clear for the agents in M_i^1 and immediately follows by induction for the agents in every one of the sets M_i^k. ∎

Remark   The proof has shown that the number $|M_i|$ of agents of player i is an upper bound for the number of steps needed until convergence of the reply sequence is reached.

2.8   Uniformly Perturbed Games

Our solution theory is not directly applied to games in standard form. As we have explained in the introduction of this chapter, we first determine solutions of uniformly perturbed games and then find the limit solution by letting the perturbance go to zero.

Uniformly perturbed games of a standard form, or ε-perturbations as we will call them by a shorter name, differ from the original game only by the fact that every choice must be taken with at least probability ε. Formally, an ε-perturbation will be defined as an interior substructure whose new choice sets consist of "extreme" local strategies from which one selects a choice with maximal admissible probability.

ε-Perturbations

Consider a standard form $G = (\Phi, H)$ and a positive number ε that is sufficiently small in the sense that the following condition is satisfied:

$$\varepsilon < \frac{1}{|\Phi_{ij}|}, \quad \text{for every } ij \in M_i, \tag{2.8.1}$$

where $|\Phi_{ij}|$ is the number of choices of agent ij. For every $\varepsilon > 0$ with (2.8.1) we shall define the ε-perturbation $G_\varepsilon = (\Phi_\varepsilon, H_\varepsilon)$ of G. This game will be an interior substructure of G obtained by narrowing the choice sets in Φ to Φ_ε. To define the new choice sets $\Phi_{\varepsilon ij}$, we introduce the notion of an ε-extreme local strategy.

The *ε-extreme* local strategy $\phi_{\varepsilon ij}$ for an agent ij in G *corresponding to his* choice $\phi_{ij} \in \Phi_{ij}$ is defined as follows:

$$\phi_{\varepsilon ij}(\psi_{ij}) = \begin{cases} 1 - (|\Phi_{ij}| - 1)\varepsilon, & \text{for } \psi_{ij} = \phi_{ij}, \\ \varepsilon, & \text{for } \psi_{ij} \neq \phi_{ij}. \end{cases} \qquad (2.8.2)$$

For every $ij \in M$, the set of all ε-extreme local strategies of ij is agent ij's new choice set $\Phi_{\varepsilon ij}$ in $G_\varepsilon = (\Phi_\varepsilon, H_\varepsilon)$. To show that G_ε is a substructure of G, we have to prove that the $\Phi_{\varepsilon ij}$ are admissible new choice sets. The notational unambiguity condition is trivially satisfied since no ϕ_{ij} belongs to $\Phi_{\varepsilon ij}$. In view of inequality (2.8.1), together with (2.8.2), it is clear that none of the ε-extreme local strategies can be obtained as a linear combination of the others. $\Phi_{\varepsilon ij}$ is a set of independent local strategies. Consequently $\Phi_{\varepsilon ij}$ is an admissible new choice set.

Since all ε-extreme local strategies are completely mixed, the ε-perturbations of G are interior substructures of G. Our notational conventions for the standard form are also used for ε-perturbations, with the only difference that the lower index ε is added everywhere in front of other lower indexes if there are any. Where several different standard forms and their ε-perturbations appear, upper indexes are used to make the necessary distinctions.

A behavior-strategy combination b_ε for G_ε is also a behavior-strategy combination for G. In view of the definition of G_ε as the game that results from G by narrowing the choice sets in Φ to Φ_ε, we have

$$H_\varepsilon(b_\varepsilon) = H(b_\varepsilon). \qquad (2.8.3)$$

In many cases we can shorten formulas by using H instead of H_ε.

Interpretation

The interpretation of uniformly perturbed games is based on the following idea. Agent ij cannot avoid to select any of his choices by mistake. The probability of selecting any given choice ϕ_{ij} by mistake is ε. There will be a probability $|\Phi_{ij}|\varepsilon$ of making a mistake. The probability of making no mistake is $1 - |\Phi_{ij}|\varepsilon$. Whenever a mistake is made all choices are equally likely, including the one that should have been chosen intentionally. The probabilities $b_{\varepsilon ij}(\phi_{\varepsilon ij})$ describe the agent's intentions, whereas the probabilities $b_{\varepsilon ij}(\phi_{ij})$ describe his actual behavior. We now look at the connection between the probabilities of corresponding choices in G and G_ε assigned by a local strategy in G_ε.

Probabilities of Choices in G

Define

$$\eta_{ij} = 1 - |\Phi_{ij}|\varepsilon \tag{2.8.4}$$

for every $ij \in M$. According to the interpretation given earlier, this is agent ij's probability of making no mistake. The following relationship is a consequence of (2.8.2):

$$b_{\varepsilon ij}(\phi_{ij}) = \varepsilon + \eta_{ij}b_{\varepsilon ij}(\phi_{\varepsilon ij}), \tag{2.8.5}$$

where $\phi_{\varepsilon ij}$ corresponds to ϕ_{ij}. The choice ϕ_{ij} is selected with probability ε by mistake and with probability $\eta_{ij}b_{\varepsilon ij}(\phi_{\varepsilon ij})$ intentionally. η_{ij} can be interpreted as *realization probability of ij's intentions*.

Payoffs in Pure-Strategy Combinations for G

For some purposes it will be important to express the payoffs for a combination $\psi_{\varepsilon} \in \Phi_{\varepsilon}$ in terms of payoffs for combinations $\phi \in \Phi$. To obtain a simpler formula, we introduce the following notation:

$$\eta_C = \prod_{ij \in C} \eta_{ij} \tag{2.8.6}$$

for every $C \subseteq M$ with $\eta_C = 1$ for $C = \varnothing$. If we look at ψ_{ε} as a behavior-strategy combination for G, we see that η_C can be interpreted as the probability that the agents in C make no mistake. The payoff vector for ϕ_{ε} is easily obtained if, in addition to this, one takes into account that $\varepsilon^{|M|-|C|}$ is the probability for the agents in $M \setminus C$ of jointly selecting a specific ϕ_{-C} by mistake:

$$H(\psi_{\varepsilon}) = \sum_{C \subseteq M} \sum_{\phi_{-C} \in \Phi_{-C}} \varepsilon^{|M|-|C|}\eta_C H(\psi_C\phi_{-C}), \tag{2.8.7}$$

where ψ_C corresponds to the subcombination $\psi_{\varepsilon C}$ for C prescribed by ψ_{ε}.

Absence of Perfect Recall

Consider a standard form $G = (\Phi, H)$ with perfect recall and an ε-perturbation $G_{\varepsilon} = (\Phi_{\varepsilon}, H_{\varepsilon})$ of G. It is interesting to point out that generally G_{ε} does not have perfect recall. The reasons are as follows: Let $\psi_{\varepsilon} \in \Phi_{\varepsilon}$ and $\psi \in \Phi$ be pure-strategy combinations in G_{ε} and G that correspond to each other, and let ψ_i be player i's strategy in ψ. Let K_i be a tree of player i in G. One might think that with this tree the definition of perfect recall is also satisfied for G_ε. However, with the help of the payoff decomposition (2.4.1) and the relationship (2.8.7), it can be seen immediately that this is not the case. Equation (2.8.7) shows that $H(\psi_\varepsilon)$ does not only depend on the quasi-play combinations in $\delta(\psi_i)$ but on all quasi-play combinations in Δ_i, and therefore on all choices prescribed by ψ_i.

Generally, it will also not be possible to find another tree, say $K_{\varepsilon i}$, such that the requirements of the definition of perfect recall are satisfied in G_ε. With the exceptions of special cases, $H(\psi_\varepsilon)$ will depend on all choices ψ_{ij} in ψ_i. Therefore all these choices would have to appear in each quasi-play combination in $\delta(\psi_{\varepsilon i})$. This is impossible unless the tree $K_{\varepsilon i}$ has only one quasi play, which would mean that $H(\psi_\varepsilon)$ does not depend on $\psi_{\varepsilon i}$.

The absence of perfect recall in ε-perturbations is in complete agreement with the interpretation of perfect recall in the extensive form. Let ij be an agent who is preceded by an agent ik. In the ε-perturbation agent ij does not know which of his choices $\phi_{\varepsilon ik}$ agent ik has selected. Agent ij knows ϕ_{ik} but not $\phi_{\varepsilon ik}$; in other words, he does not know whether ϕ_{ik} has been selected intentionally or by mistake.

2.9   Uniform Perfectness

Perfect equilibrium points can be losely described as equilibrium points that can be approximated with any degree of precision by equilibrium points of perturbed games. In our theory we are interested only in uniformly perfect equilibrium points that can be approximated by equilibrium points of ε-perturbations of the game under consideration. We will not give a formal definition of perfectness, only a general one of uniform perfectness.

Limit Equilibrium Points

Let $G = (\Phi, H)$ be a standard form with perfect recall. Consider a monotonically decreasing sequence $\varepsilon_1, \varepsilon_2, \ldots$, of positive numbers converging to zero where ε_i is sufficiently small to satisfy condition (2.8.1) which has been imposed on perturbance parameters in the previous section. Let G^i be the ε_i-perturbation of G. A sequence $G^1, G^2, \ldots$, of ε-perturbations of G, which arises from a sequence $\varepsilon_1, \varepsilon_2, \ldots$, of this kind, is called a *test sequence* for G.

A behavior strategy combination r for G is called a *limit equilibrium point* of the test sequence $G^1, G^2, \ldots$, if for $k = 1, 2, \ldots$, an equilibrium point r^k in behavior strategies of G^k can be found such that for $k \to \infty$ the sequence of the r^k converges to r. In this definition the r^k are interpreted as behavior strategies for G. Convergence is to be understood in this way. A behavior-strategy combination r for G is called a limit equilibrium point of G if it is a limit equilibrium point of at least one test sequence for G.

The fact that a limit equilibrium point of G is an equilibrium point of G needs to be pointed out formally because it is not an immediate consequence of the definition. The proof will be omitted here since essentially the same result has been obtained elsewhere (Selten 1975, lemma 3). The argument used there can be easily transferred to the framework of the standard form.

LEMMA 2.9.1 (Lemma on limit equilibrium points)   A limit equilibrium point of a standard form $G = (\Phi, H)$ with perfect recall is an equilibrium point of G.

Uniformly Perfect Equilibrium Points

A behavior-strategy combination r for a standard form $G = (\Phi, H)$ with perfect recall is a *uniformly perfect equilibrium point* of G if it is a limit equilibrium point of G.

A theorem on the existence of uniformly perfect equilibrium points will be stated without proof since the result can be obtained in essentially the same way as a similar result which has been proved elsewhere (Selten 1975, theorem 5). In addition to the argument given there, one has to make use of the fact that Kuhn's theorem holds for interior substructures of games with perfect recall, and therefore especially for ε-perturbations of games with perfect recall. This implies the existence of equilibrium points in behavior strategies for ε-perturbations of games with perfect recall.

THEOREM 2.9.1 (Theorem on uniformly perfect equilibrium points)   Let $G = (\Phi, H)$ be a standard form with perfect recall. Then G has at least one uniformly perfect equilibrium point.

2.10   Solution Functions and Limit Solution Functions

The equilibrium selection theory proposed in this book specifies a solution function that selects a unique equilibrium point for every interior substructure of a standard form with perfect recall. In particular, a solution is determined for every ε-perturbation of a standard form with perfect recall. A limit solution for the unperturbed game is obtained by letting the perturbance parameter go to zero. The limit solution is a uniformly perfect equilibrium point. This is the way in which our theory deals with the imperfectness problem.

Solution Function

A *solution function* L for a class $\mathscr{G}$ of games in standard form is a function that assigns an equilibrium point $r = L(G)$ of G to every standard form $G \in \mathscr{G}$.

The class of all standard forms with perfect recall is denoted by $\mathscr{R}$. We call $\mathscr{R}$ the *perfect recall class*. If $\mathscr{G}$ is a class of games, then $\mathscr{I}(\mathscr{G})$ denotes the class of all interior substructures of games in $\mathscr{G}$. We call $\mathscr{I}(\mathscr{G})$ the *interior substructure class* of $\mathscr{G}$. The solution concept in this book is based on a solution function for the interior substructure class $\mathscr{I}(\mathscr{R})$ of the perfect recall class $\mathscr{R}$.

For the purpose of studying desirable properties of solution functions, it will often be useful to look at solution functions defined on more limited classes of games.

Limit Solution Functions

Let $\mathscr{G}$ be a class of games with perfect recall or, in other words, a subclass of $\mathscr{R}$. Let L be a solution function for the interior substructure class $\mathscr{I}(\mathscr{G})$ of $\mathscr{G}$. Let G be a game in $\mathscr{G}$. For the case that the limit exists, define

$$\underset{\rightarrow}{L}(G) = \lim_{\varepsilon \to 0} L(G_\varepsilon), \tag{2.10.1}$$

where G_ε is the ε-perturbation of G. Obviously $\mathscr{I}(\mathscr{G})$ contains all ε-perturbations G_ε of G. We call $\underset{\rightarrow}{L}(G)$ the *limit solution of* G *with respect to* L. Suppose that the limit solution $\underset{\rightarrow}{L}(G)$ exists for all games $G \in \mathscr{G}$. Then a solution function $\underset{\rightarrow}{L}$ on $\mathscr{G}$ is defined by (2.10.1). We call this solution function $\underset{\rightarrow}{L}$ the *limit solution function of* L.

The Existence Problem

The answer to the question whether a limit solution function $\underset{\rightarrow}{L}$ for given solution function L on $\mathscr{I}(\mathscr{G})$ exists depends on the mathematical structure of L. Although we deal with finite games only, the mathematical structure of the solution function for $\mathscr{I}(\mathscr{R})$ specified by the equilibrium selection theory proposed in this book is not a very easy one. The solution function involves piecewise algebraic functions and limits of such functions. The limit solution adds an additional step of taking a limit. In an unpublished paper the authors have achieved a result on iterated limits of piecewise algebraic functions that suggests that no difficulties should arise with respect to the existence of the limit solution. (Harsanyi and Selten 1977). In this book we will not attempt to give a detailed and rigorous existence proof which is bound to be lengthy and very technical.

Uniform Perfectness of the Limit Solution

Suppose that $\mathcal{G}$ is a class of standard forms with perfect recall and that L is a solution function for $\mathscr{I}(\mathcal{G})$. If the limit solution $\underset{\rightarrow}{L}(G)$ of a game $G \in \mathcal{G}$ with respect to L exists, then $\underset{\rightarrow}{L}(G)$ is a uniformly perfect equilibrium point of G. This is an immediate consequence of (2.10.1) and the definition of uniform perfectness.

3 Consequences of Desirable Properties

3.1 Introduction

The nature of the problem of equilibrium point selection in noncooperative games does not seem to permit a satisfactory solution concept that can be characterized by a set of simple axioms. Nevertheless, it is useful to look at desirable properties and to explore their consequences.

Even if full-scale axiomatization cannot be achieved, important conclusions can be drawn from axiomatic considerations of limited scope. The simplest class of games where the equilibrium point selection problem occurs is that of all 2×2 games with two strong pure-strategy equilibrium points. Risk dominance which is a central notion of our theory can be fully axiomatized for this admittedly very restricted class of games. It is also important to see that certain properties that may seem to be desirable at first glance cannot be achieved. As we shall see, it is impossible to define a continuous solution function.

A reasonable solution concept should neither be influenced by positive linear payoff transformations nor by renamings of players, agents, and choices. The notion of an isomorphism combines both kinds of operations. We look at invariance with respect to isomorphisms as an indispensable requirement.

One might wish to require that an increase of payoffs at a strong equilibrium point always enhances its chance to become the solution. However, examples of games with more than two players show that this kind of payoff monotonicity is not very convincing as a general requirement.

Structural features like subgames of extensive games cannot be neglected by a reasonable solution concept. In order to transfer this idea to the framework of the standard form, we will introduce special substructures called cells. This gives rise to powerful requirements called *cell consistency* and *truncation consistency*. These requirements reduce the task of finding a solution for general games to the simpler one of finding a solution for games without cells.

An impossibility result to be derived in this chapter concerns a way of subdividing one information set into two which we call "sequential agent splitting." An agent who has to choose between three choices α, β, and γ is subdivided into two agents: one who first chooses between "α or β" and γ, and another who then, if necessary, decides between α and β. Unfortunately, it is not possible to require that this kind of agent splitting not change the limit solution of the game without violating other axioms like cell consistency and truncation consistency which we judge to be intuitively more compelling.

Further desirable requirements concern the elimination of superfluous strategic possibilities. An agent may have two choices α and β such that β is a local best reply wherever α has this property, but not vice versa. In this case α is called inferior to β. One might want to require that the removal of an inferior choice does not change the solution of the game. Unfortunately, we have to be satisfied with a much weaker partial invariance property with respect to inferior choices.

A similar requirement concerns classes of choices that are distinguished only by name. Such duplicate classes should be replaceable by their centroids. An anologous requirement is considered for classes of semiduplicates which are indistinguishable in a weaker sense. Here too we have to be satisfied with partial invariance properties. It may matter in which order various superfluous strategic possibilities are eliminated.

Standard forms without cells, inferior choices, duplicate classes, and semiduplicate classes are called irreducible. The three partial invariance properties mentioned earlier, together with cell consistency, truncation consistency, and invariance with respect to isomorphisms, uniquely determine the extension of a solution function for irreducible games to general games. If these six requirements are satisfied, the task of finding the solution of a general game can be transformed to the task of solving certain irreducible games. This can be done by a procedure of decomposition and reduction described by the flowchart of figure 3.29.

It will often be convenient to look at examples of games with normal form structure. Many important phenomena arise already there and can be more easily discussed in the simpler framework of such games where we need not distinguish between a player and his only agent. For two-person games of this kind we will employ the conventional bimatrix representation.

3.2   Continuity

Consider the class of all 2×1 games shown in figure 3.1. For $t \neq 0$ the game has only one equilibrium point, namely A for $t > 0$ and B for $t < 0$.

For $t = 0$ every mixed strategy of player 1 is an equilibrium strategy. Clearly no solution concept can assign a unique equilibrium point to every game in the class in a continuous way. Not only player 1's strategy but

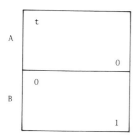

Figure 3.1
A class of 2 × 1 games. Player 1's payoff is given above, and player 2's payoff below

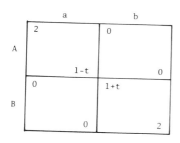

Figure 3.2
A class of 2 × 2 games

also player 2's payoff must behave discontinuously as a function of t at $t = 0$.

If a payoff parameter is varied continuously, some equilibrium points may suddenly disappear and others that have not been there before may suddenly appear. To show how this problem may arise in a less trivial way, we add a further example. Consider the class of games given by figure 3.2. Here for $t < -1$ the strategy combination Aa is the only equilibrium point of game. For $-1 \leq t \leq +1$ both Aa and Bb are equilibrium points. Moreover for $-1 \leq t \leq +1$ the game has a third equilibrium point in mixed strategies where player 1 uses A with probability $2/(3 - t)$ and player 2 uses a with probability $(1 + t)/(3 + t)$. For $-1 < t < +1$ the game has no further equilibrium point. For $t = -1$ and $t = +1$ there are infinitely many equilibrium points, but this does not matter as far as our argument is concerned. Any function that assigns a unique equilibrium point to every game in the class must behave discontinuously with respect to t at some point in the interval $-1 \leq t \leq +1$.

It is now clear that a certain amount of discontinuity cannot be avoided in a theory of equilibrium point selection. Continuity considerations seem to be of little relevance for the problem.

3.3 Positive Linear Payoff Transformations

The payoffs of the players are von Neumann-Morgenstern utilities. Interpersonal comparisons may be possible, but they are not relevant for the noncooperative solution theory where each player is assumed to be motivated by his own payoff exclusively.

Interpersonal utility comparisons are important for ethical theory, but they have no room in a solution concept that is exclusively based on the assumption of individualistic rationality. Since von Neumann-Morgenstern utilities are determined only up to positive linear transformations and since interpersonal comparisons are considered irrelevant, a game remains essentially unchanged if each player's payoff is subjected to a different positive linear transformation. This leads to the following definition of equivalence between games:

EQUIVALENCE   To games in standard form $G = (\Phi, H)$ and $G' = (\Phi, H')$ with the same set Φ of pure strategy combinations are *equivalent* if constants $\alpha_i > 0$ and β_i can be found for every i in the player set N, such that

$$H_i'(\phi) = \alpha_i H_i(\phi) + \beta_i \tag{3.3.1}$$

holds for every $\phi \in \Phi$ and every $i \in N$.

INVARIANCE WITH RESPECT TO POSITIVE LINEAR PAYOFF TRANSFORMATIONS A solution function L for a class $\mathscr{G}$ of games in standard form is called *invariant with respect to positive linear payoff transformations*, if for two equivalent games G and G' in $\mathscr{G}$ we always have $L(G) = L(G')$.

Invariance with respect to positive linear payoff transformations is a very important requirement. In our judgment it is more than a desirable property; it is indispensable.

3.4 Symmetry

A rational theory of equilibrium selection must determine a solution that is independent of strategically irrelevant features of the game. Names and numbers used to distinguish players, agents, and choices should not matter. Games that do not differ in other ways must be considered as isomorphic and should not be treated differently.

Invariance with respect to renaming of players, agents, and choices may be considered a symmetry property because it implies that the solution must reflect the symmetries of the game.

Renamings

A renaming of players, agents, and choices in a standard form $G = (\Phi, H)$ may be thought of as a system of mappings that relates G to another game $G' = (\Phi', H')$. The old names of players, agents, and choices in G are replaced by new names in G'. We shall use the notation indicated in figure 3.3.

Three kinds of mappings are involved: a mapping σ from the player set N of G onto the player set N' of G', for each player i a mapping ρ_i from his agent set M_i onto $\sigma(i)$'s agent set $M'_{\sigma(i)}$, and finally for every agent ij a mapping f_{ij} that maps his choice set Φ_{ij} onto agent $\sigma(i)\rho_i(j)$'s choice set in G'. All these mappings are one to one.

Actually it is sufficient to describe the system $f = (f_{ij})_M$ of mappings from choice sets onto choice sets in order to specify a renaming. If one knows which choice in G is mapped on which choice in G', one also knows which player is mapped on which player and which agent is mapped on which agent. Therefore it is natural to think of the system f as endowed with all the information on the mappings σ and ρ_i for $i \in N$. These auxiliary mappings need not be mentioned explicitly if we describe how G' results from G by a renaming.

We may look at f as a mapping from Φ to Φ'. This suggests the notation $f(\phi)$ for that combination $\phi' \in \Phi'$ whose components are related to those

	old name	new name
player	i	$\sigma(i)$
agent	ij	$\sigma(i)\rho_i(j)$
choice	ϕ_{ij}	$f_{ij}(\phi_{ij})$

Figure 3.3
The system of notation used for renaming

of ϕ as follows:

$$\phi'_{kl} = f_{ij}(\phi_{ij}), \quad \text{with } k = \sigma(i) \text{ and } l = \rho_i(j) \quad \text{for every } ij \in M. \tag{3.4.1}$$

It is convenient to adopt a notion of isomorphism that permits us to say that equivalent games are isomorphic. Therefore our definition of an isomorphism will involve a combination of a renaming with a system of positive linear payoff transformations.

Isomorphism

An *isomorphism* from $G = (\Phi, H)$ to $G' = (\Phi', H')$ is a system $f = f(\phi_{ij})_M$ of one-to-one mappings f_{ij} of ij's choice set M_{ij} in G onto $\sigma(i)\rho_i(j)$'s choice set $M'_{\sigma(i)\phi_i(j)}$ in G' such that the following conditions are satisfied:

1. The mapping σ is a one-to-one mapping of the player set N of G onto the player set N' of G'.

2. For every $i \in N$ the mapping ρ_i is a one-to-one mapping from player i's agent set M_i in G onto player $\sigma(i)$'s agent set $M'_{\sigma(i)}$ in G'.

3. The payoff functions H and H' are related as

$$H'_{\sigma(i)}(f(\phi)) = \alpha_i H_i(\phi) + \beta_i, \quad \text{for every } i \in N \text{ and every } \phi \in \Phi \atop \text{with constants } \alpha_i > 0 \text{ and } \beta_i. \tag{3.4.2}$$

An isomorphism is called a *renaming* if in condition 3 we have $\alpha_i = 1$ and $\beta_i = 0$ for every $i \in N$. Two games G and G' are called *isomorphic* if at least one isomorphism from G to G' exists.

Simplifications for Games with Normal-Form Structure

In a game $G = (\Phi, H)$ with normal-form structure where each player i has just one agent, it is convenient not to distinguish between a player and his only agent. For such games an *isomorphism* for $G = (\Phi, H)$ to $G' = (\Phi', H')$ can be described as a system of mappings $f = (f_i)_N$ where f_i maps i's pure-strategy set Φ_i in G onto $\sigma(i)$'s pure-strategy set $\Phi_{\sigma(i)}$ in G'. The notation $\phi' = f(\phi)$ is used in the sense that the components of ϕ' and ϕ are connected by $\phi'_{\sigma(i)} = f_i(\phi_i)$ for every $i \in N$. Conditions 1 and 3 must of course hold as in the more general case.

Extension of the Mapping f

Consider an isomorphism $f = (f_{ij})_M$ from a standard form $G = (\Phi, H)$ to a standard form $G' = (\Phi', H')$. Let b_{ij} be a local strategy of agent ij in G. We write

$$b'_{km} = f_{ij}(b_{ij}) \tag{3.4.3}$$

if we have

$$b'_{km}(f_{ij}(\phi_{ij})) = b_{ij}(\phi_{ij}), \quad \text{with } k = \sigma(i) \text{ and } m = \rho_i(j) \text{ for every } \phi_{ij} \in \Phi_{ij}. \tag{3.4.4}$$

In this way f_{ij} is extended from Φ_{ij} to B_{ij}. We write $b' = f(b)$ if the local strategies in the behavior strategy combination b' are related to those of b as in (3.4.4). Obviously (3.4.2) and (3.4.4) imply

$$H_{\sigma(i)}(f(b)) = \alpha_i H_i(b) + \beta_i, \quad \text{for every } b \in B \text{ and every } i \in N. \tag{3.4.5}$$

Clearly an isomorphism f that is considered a mapping defined on B preserves best-reply relationships and carries equilibrium points into equilibrium points.

Invariance with Respect to Isomorphisms

A solution function L for a class of standard form games $\mathcal{G}$ is invariant with respect to isomorphisms if for every isomorphism f from a game $G \in \mathcal{G}$ to a game $G' \in \mathcal{G}$ (which may or may not be different from G) we have

$$L(G') = L(G). \tag{3.4.6}$$

Interpretation Equation (3.4.6) is the formal expression of what is meant by saying that isomorphic games should not be treated differently. Invariance with respect to isomorphisms includes invariance with respect to positive linear utility transformations to which it adds an invariance with respect to renaming. A formal description of this latter invariance need not be given here. In our judgment invariance with respect to isomorphisms is an indispensable requirement for any rational theory of equilibrium point selection that is based on strategic considerations exclusively. With the help of the notion of an isomorphism we can give a precise meaning to the idea that the solution should correctly reflect the symmetries of a game.

SYMMETRIES   A symmetry of a game $G = (\Phi, H)$ is an isomorphism from G to itself.

Symmetry-Invariant Equilibrium Points

An equilibrium point r of $G = (\Phi, H)$ is called *symmetry invariant* if for every symmetry f of G we have $r = f(r)$.

THEOREM 3.4.1 (Theorem on symmetry invariance)   Let $G = (\Phi, H)$ be an interior substructure of a game in standard form with perfect recall. Then G has a symmetry-invariant equilibrium point in behavior strategies.

Proof   Nash has shown that every finite game in normal form has a symmetry-invariant equilibrium point (Nash 1951). From this result we can conclude that G has a local equilibrium point in behavior strategies. The local best-reply property of interior substructures of standard forms with perfect recall (see section 2.7) has the consequence that a local equilibrium point of G is an equilibrium point.

A solution function L that is invariant with respect to isomorphisms must assign a symmetry-invariant equilibrium point to every game in the class where it is defined. An example of a game with a symmetry is given in figure 3.4. The game is a two-person game with normal-form structure. It has three equilibrium points, two in pure strategies, namely Aa and Bb and a mixed one $r = (r_1, r_2)$ with $r_1(A) = \frac{2}{3}$ and $r_2(a) = \frac{1}{3}$. The symmetry f carries Aa to Bb, and vice versa. The mixed equilibrium point r is the only one that is symmetry invariant. Any solution function L that is invariant with respect to isomorphism cannot assign anything but $L(G) = r$ to this game. The payoff vector of r is $H(r) = (\frac{2}{3}, 1\frac{1}{3})$. Note that both players receive more at each of the two pure-strategy equilibrium points. Nevertheless, invariance with respect to isomorphism forces us to adopt r as the solution. ■

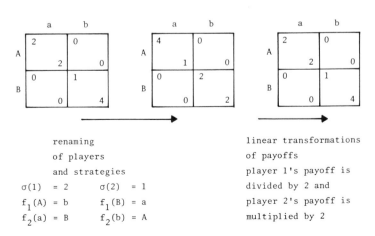

Figure 3.4
An example of a symmetry

3.5 Best-Reply Structure

In the preceding section we argued that invariance with respect to positive linear payoff transformations has to be supplemented by invariance with respect to renamings of players, agents, and strategies. In this way we obtained the stronger notion of invariance with respect to isomorphisms.

As we have seen, isomorphisms preserve best-reply relationships. One may take the view that these relationships contain the essence of a non-cooperative game because no other information is needed to determine the set of all equilibrium points. This suggests the idea that two games should be treated in the same way if they do not differ with respect to their best reply relationships. Unfortunately, invariance requirements of this kind turn out to be too strong if they are imposed on the solution function. As we shall see in a later section, one would have to accept counterintuitive consequences.

Our solution concept is composed of a number of different parts that interact in a process of equilibrium point selection. An important concept embedded in the definition of the solution as a building block is risk dominance. Risk dominance will be explained in later sections. In the limited context of 2×2 games it will be possible to axiomatize it. One of the axioms will be an invariance requirement based on best-reply considerations. As far as risk dominance in 2×2 games is concerned, the requirement is a very natural one, even if it is doubtful whether it should be extended to a wider context.

It is necessary to introduce the notion of a best-reply structure to obtain a formal description of the best-reply relationships. However, we will do this for games with normal-form structure only because we do not want to pursue the subject of invariance requirements based on best-reply relationships beyond a very limited scope.

In the rest of this section all definitions will refer to a game $G = (\Phi, H)$ with normal-form structure. No distinction is made between a player i and his only agent.

BEST-REPLY STRUCTURE   The set of all pure best replies of player i to $q_{.i}$ is denoted by $A_i(q_{.i})$. The correspondence A_i which assigns the set $A_i(q_{.i})$ to $q_{.i} \in Q_{.i}$ is called *player i's best-reply correspondence*. $A = (A_i)_N$ is the *system of best-reply correspondences*.

The *best-reply structure* $B = (\Phi, A)$ of $G = (\Phi, H)$ consists of the set of pure-strategy combinations $\Phi = \bigtimes_{i \in N} \Phi_i$ and the system $A = (A_i)_N$ of best-reply correspondences. It is clear that an isomorphism f from G to G' carries the best-reply structure of G to that of G'.

Stability Sets

The set of all $q_{\cdot i} \in Q_{\cdot i}$ such that a given pure strategy ϕ_i is a best reply to $q_{\cdot i}$ is denoted by $S(\phi_i)$. The set $S(\phi_i)$ is called the *stability set* of ϕ_i. Obviously $S(\phi_i)$ is the set of all $q_{\cdot i}$ with $\phi_i \in A_i(q_{\cdot i})$. One may regard S as a correspondence from the union of all Φ_i to the union of all $Q_{\cdot i}$. In a sense the correspondence S is the inverse of the system A of best-reply correspondences. The pair (Φ, S) could also serve as a formal description of the best-reply structure.

Graphic Representation for 2 × 2 Games

The best-reply structure of 2 × 2 games can be visualized with the help of a simple graph. Consider the class of 2 × 2 games described by figure 3.5. These games have strong equilibrium points in the upper left- and lower right-hand corners. It is convenient to introduce the notation u_i and v_i for the losses faced by player i if he deviates from the equilibrium points $U = U_1 U_2$ and $V = V_1 V_2$, respectively, while the other player plays his equilibrium strategy.

A mixed strategy q_i in a 2 × 2 game is fully described by both probabilities. We will use the notation

$$p_i = q_i(V_i). \tag{3.5.1}$$

Player 1's strategy U_1 is a best reply for

	U_2	V_2
U_1	a_{11} b_{11}	a_{12} b_{12}
V_1	a_{21} b_{21}	a_{22} b_{22}

$$u_1 = a_{11} - a_{21} > 0$$
$$u_2 = b_{11} - b_{12} > 0$$
$$v_1 = a_{22} - a_{12} > 0$$
$$v_2 = b_{22} - b_{21} > 0$$

Figure 3.5
2 × 2 games with strong equilibrium points in upper left and lower right corners

$$a_{11}p_2 + a_{12}(1 - p_2) \geq a_{21}p_2 + a_{22}(1 - p_2), \tag{3.5.2}$$

and V_1 is his best reply for

$$a_{11}p_2 + a_{12}(1 - p_2) \leq a_{21}p_2 + a_{22}(1 - p_2). \tag{3.5.3}$$

This yields

$$U_1 \in A_1(q_2), \quad \text{for } 0 \leq p_2 \leq \frac{u_1}{u_1 + v_1}, \tag{3.5.4}$$

$$V_1 \in A_1(q_2), \quad \text{for } \frac{u_1}{u_1 + v_1} \leq p_2 \leq 1. \tag{3.5.5}$$

Similarily, we obtain

$$U_2 \in A_2(q_1), \quad \text{for } 0 \leq p_1 \leq \frac{u_2}{u_2 + v_2}, \tag{3.5.6}$$

$$V_2 \in A_2(q_1), \quad \text{for } \frac{u_2}{u_2 + v_2} \leq p_1 \leq 1. \tag{3.5.7}$$

We can draw a diagram that represents all mixed-strategy combinations as points (p_1, p_2) in a rectangular coordinate system. This is done in figure 3.6 for a special case ($u_1 = 2$, $u_2 = 6$, $v_1 = 8$, $v_2 = 4$). The diagram will be called the *stability diagram* of the game. The regions where the four pure strategy combinations are best replies are indicated in figure 3.6. We call these regions the stability regions of the respective pure-strategy combinations.

The stability regions are closed rectangles, all with one corner in common representing the mixed equilibrium point with $p_1 = u_2/(u_2 + v_2)$ and $p_2 = u_1/(u_1 + v_1)$. The equilibrium points U and V belong to their stability region, but the "cross combinations" $U_1 V_2$ and $V_1 U_2$ belong to the stability region of the opposite cross combination.

Interestingly the best-reply structure of a game in the class of figure 3.5 does not depend on anything but the ratios u_1/v_1 and u_2/v_2 of the players' deviation losses at both strong equilibrium points. Absolute payoff levels do not matter. Only ratios of payoff differences are important.

Payoff Transformations That Preserve the Best-Reply Structure

Let $G = (\Phi, H)$ be a game with normal-form structure, and let ψ_{-j} be a fixed j-incomplete pure-strategy combination for G. We construct a new game $G' = (\Phi, H')$ with the same set Φ of pure-strategy combinations. For

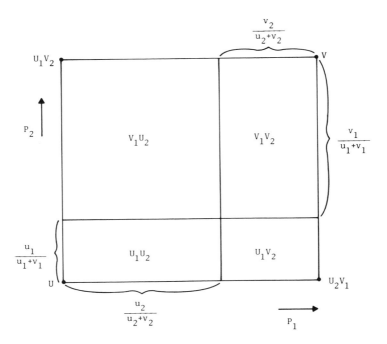

Figure 3.6
Stability diagram of the game of figure 3.5

$i \neq j$ define

$$H_i'(\phi) = H_i(\phi), \quad \text{for every } \phi \in \Phi. \tag{3.5.8}$$

Let λ be a constant. Player j's payoff is defined as follows:

$$H_j'(\phi_j \psi_{-j}) = H_j(\phi_j \psi_{-j}) + \lambda, \tag{3.5.9}$$

$$H_j'(\phi_j \phi_{-j}) = H_j(\phi_j \phi_{-j}), \quad \text{for } \phi_{-j} \neq \psi_{-j}. \tag{3.5.10}$$

We say that G' results from G by adding λ to player j's payoff at ψ_{-j}.

It is clear that the same amount $\lambda q_{.j}(\psi_{-j})$ is added to every payoff of the form $H_j(q_j q_{.j})$ in the transition from H_j to H_j'. Therefore we obtain the following result: adding λ to player j's payoff at ψ_{-j} does not change the best-reply structure. Consider the game of figure 3.5. We receive the game of figure 3.7 if we make the following changes one after the other:

1. Add $-a_{21}$ to player 1's payoffs at U_2.

2. Add $-b_{12}$ to player 2's payoffs at U_1.

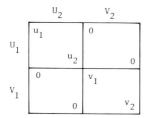

Figure 3.7
Games received by best-reply structure preserving transformations from those of figure 3.5

	c		d		e	
a	1		0		0	
		2		$1-t$		0
b	0		0		1	
		0		$1+t$		$\frac{4}{3} + \frac{2}{3}t$

$0 < t < 1$

c is best reply for $0 \le q_1(b) \le \frac{1}{2}$

d is best reply for $\frac{1}{2} \le q_1(b) \le \frac{3}{4}$

e is best reply for $\frac{3}{4} \le q_1(b) \le 1$

Figure 3.8
A class of 2 × 3 games with the same best-reply structure

3. Add $-a_{12}$ to player 1's payoffs at V_2.

4. Add $-b_{21}$ to player 2's payoffs at V_1.

This confirms once more what we already know from the investigation of the best-reply structure of the games of figure 3.5: every game in this class has the same best-reply structure as the corresponding game of figure 3.7.

It may be worthwhile to point out that not every payoff transformation that preserves the best-reply structure can be obtained by a combination of positive linear payoff transformations with the repeated application of the operation of adding a constant to player j's payoffs at ψ_{-j}. In this respect 2 × 2 games are exceptional. Already in 2 × 3 games other best-reply structure preserving payoff transformations are possible.

An example is the class of games in figure 3.8. A positive linear transformation or adding a constant at player 2's payoffs at a or b cannot change the quotient

$$\frac{H_2(bd) - H_2(bc)}{H_2(be) - H_2(bd)} = 3\frac{1+t}{1-t} \qquad (3.5.11)$$

which clearly depends on t. Therefore a combination of such transformations cannot yield the same result as a transition from one t to another.

Invariance with Respect to Payoff Transformations That Preserves the Best-Reply Structure

A solution function L for a class $\mathscr{G}$ of games with normal-form structure is called *invariant with respect to payoff transformations that preserve the best-reply structure* (or simply *best-reply invariant*) if for any two games $G = (\Phi, H)$ and $G' = (\Phi, H')$ in $\mathscr{G}$ with the same best-reply structure we have $L(G) = L(G')$.

Comment   As we have said before, we do not insist on best-reply invariance as a desirable property of a solution function. But it is an intuitively attractive requirement that should not be violated without a good reason. We want to keep as much of it as possible.

3.6   Payoff Dominance

Consider the game of figure 3.9. The equilibrium point $U = U_1 U_2$ yields higher payoffs for both players than the other pure-strategy equilibrium point $V = V_1 V_2$. The mixed equilibrium point with probabilities of 0.4 and 0.8 for U_1 and U_2, respectively, yields even worse payoffs, namely 7.2 for player 1 and 4 for player 2. Clearly, among the three equilibrium points of

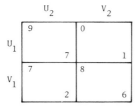

Figure 3.9
Example of a 2×2 game with payoff dominance

the game, $U_1 U_2$ is the most attractive one for both players. This suggests that they should not have any trouble coordinating their expectations at the commonly preferred equilibrium point $U_1 U_2$. The solution of the game should be $U_1 U_2$. The idea that equilibrium points with greater payoffs for all players should be given preference in problems of equilibrium point selection leads to the following definition.

PAYOFF DOMINANCE   Let r and s be two equilibrium points of $G = (\Phi, H)$ with $\Phi = \bigtimes_{i \in N} \Phi_i$. We say that r *payoff-dominates* s if we have

$$H_i(r) > H_i(s), \quad \text{for every } i \in N, \tag{3.6.1}$$

In (3.6.1) we require strict inequality since we want to restrict considerations of payoff dominance to cases where the interest of all players unambiguously points in the same direction.

The idea of payoff dominance must be handled with care. We cannot require that $L(G)$ should never be payoff dominated by any other equilibrium point. As we have seen in section 3.4, invariances with respect to isomorphisms forces us to accept the mixed equilibrium point as the solution of the game in figure 3.4 even if it is payoff dominated by both pure-strategy equilibrium points.

The example of figure 3.4 shows that we should not pay attention to payoff-dominance relationships where the dominating equilibrium point fails to be symmetry invariant. This leads to the following definitions:

PAYOFF EFFICIENCY   A symmetry-invariant equilibrium point r of a game $G = (\Phi, H)$ is called *payoff efficient* if G has no other symmetry-invariant equilibrium point s that payoff-dominates r.

A solution function L for a class of games $\mathscr{G}$ is *payoff efficient* if $L(G)$ is payoff efficient for every $G \in \mathscr{G}$. Unfortunately, payoff efficiency is a very

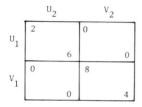

Figure 3.10
Game with the best-reply structure of the game in figure 3.9

strong requirement that cannot be easily satisfied by a solution concept such as ours. There are reasons why it should not be satisfied in general. One of these reasons will be discussed in the section on cells. Another reason is connected to the fact that a situation similar to that in figure 3.4 may arise with symmetry invariance. Two equilibrium points that payoff-dominate a third one, but not each other, may be equally strong in the sense that the theory does not yield a sufficient reason to select one rather than the other. In such situations it may be unavoidable to select an equilibrium point that fails to be payoff efficient. Despite these difficulties payoff dominance is an important criterion of equilibrium point selection that cannot be ignored.

Payoff-dominance relationships can easily be reversed by repeated additions of constants to a player j's payoff at some ψ_{-j}. Any strong equilibrium point ψ can be made the only payoff efficient one by performing the operations of adding a sufficiently great constant λ_j to the payoffs of every player j at his j-incomplete ψ_{-j} derived from ψ. This shows that best-reply invariance and payoff efficiency are in conflict.

In the construction of our solution concept, we have rejected full best-reply invariance in favor of keeping the possibility of giving some room to considerations of payoff dominance without going as far as imposing the requirement of payoff efficiency.

3.7   The Intuitive Notion of Risk Dominance

Consider the game of figure 3.11. There is no payoff-dominance relationship between both pure-strategy equilibrium points $U = (U_1, U_2)$ and $V = (V_1, V_2)$. Player 1 has higher payoffs at U, and player 2 has higher payoffs at V.

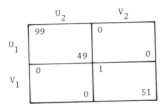

Figure 3.11
An extreme example of risk dominance

Suppose that the players are in a state of mind where they think that either U or V must be the solution of the game. What is the risk of deciding one way or the other? If player 1 expects that player 2 will choose U_2 with a probability of more than 0.01, it is better for him to choose U_1. Only if player 2 chooses V_2 with a probability of at least 0.99, player 1's strategy V_1 will be the more profitable one. In this sense U_1 is much less risky than V_1.

Now let us look at the situation of player 2. His strategy V_2 is the better one if he expects player 1 to select V_1 with a probability of more than 0.49, and U_2 is preferable if he expects U_1 with a probability greater than 0.51. In terms of those numbers V_2 seems to be slightly less risky than U_2.

It is obvious that player 1's reason to select U_1 rather than V_1 is much stronger than player 2's reason to select V_2 rather than U_2. The players must take this into account when they try to form subjective probabilities on the other player's behavior. Presumably player 1 will select U_1 with high probability, and since player 2 knows this, he is likely to think that it is better for him to choose U_2 rather than V_2. It is plausible to assume that in the end both players will come to the conclusion that both will play the equilibrium point U.

The same line of reasoning can be followed for less extreme situations. Consider a game of the form of figure 3.7 with $u_1 > v_1$ and $v_2 > u_2$. Player 1's risk situation is connected to the ratio u_1/v_1, and player 2's risk situation to the ratio v_2/u_2. Player 1 is more strongly attracted to U than player 2 to V if u_1/v_1 is greater than v_2/u_2. This is the case if and only if we have $u_1 u_2 > v_1 v_2$.

These considerations suggest the following notion of risk dominance for the games under consideration: U risk-dominates V for $u_1 u_2 > v_1 v_2$, and V risk-dominates U for $v_1 v_2 > u_1 u_2$. The heuristic arguments that lead to this conclusion are fully in terms of the best-reply structure. We have compared probabilities of the form $u_i/(u_i + u_i)$ and $v_i/(u_i + v_i)$. The probabilities that must be compared are the same in the more general situation of figure 3.5. These probabilities depend only on the best-reply structure.

Since similar products appear in Nash's cooperative bargaining theory, we call $u_1 u_2$ and $v_1 v_2$ the Nash-products of U and V, respectively. Interestingly the areas of the stability regions of U and V (see figure 3.6) are proportional to the Nash-products of U and V. This is a further argument for a notion of risk dominance based on the comparison of Nash-products.

Risk dominance and payoff dominance may point in different directions.

An example is the game of figure 3.9 where U payoff-dominates V but V has the greater Nash-product (the Nash-products are the same as in figure 3.10). The notion of risk dominance between strong equilibrium points which has been obtained heuristically can be characterized by a set of simple axioms. This will be done in a later section.

3.8 Payoff Monotonicity

In this section we will discuss the requirement of payoff monotonicity which we mentioned at the beginning of the chapter. Since we will argue that this property is less reasonable than it might seem, we will restrict our attention to games with normal form structure, in which the phenomenon that we want to exhibit already occurs.

Consider a game $G = (\Phi, H)$ with normal form structure, and let ψ be a pure-strategy equilibrium point of G. We construct a new game $G' = (\Phi, H')$ with the same set Φ of pure-strategy combinations. Let λ_i with $i \in N$ be non-negative constants at least one of which is positive. Define

$$H'(\phi) = H(\phi), \quad \text{for } \phi \neq \psi, \tag{3.8.1}$$

$$H_i'(\psi) = H_i(\psi) + \lambda_i, \quad \text{for every } i \in N. \tag{3.8.2}$$

If G and G' are related in this way, we say that G' *results from G by strengthening ψ*. The only difference between G and G' consists in the fact that some players receive more at ψ.

PAYOFF MONOTONICITY   A solution function L for a class of games with normal form structure is called payoff monotonous if the following is true: if the solution $L(G)$ of a game $G \in \mathcal{G}$ is a pure-strategy equilibrium point and if G' results from G by strengthening $L(G)$, then we have $L(G') = L(G)$.

Interpretation   The requirement of payoff monotonicity is a very appealing one. Why should an equilibrium point become less attractive if some of its payoffs are increased? Nevertheless, an objection can be raised that makes it doubtful whether one should insist on payoff monotonicity as a general property.

To explain the nature of the counterargument, we look at the example of the three-person games of figures 3.12 and 3.13. The game of figure 3.13 results from that of figure 3.12 by strengthening $U = U_1 U_2 U_3$. In the

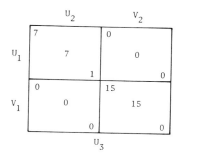
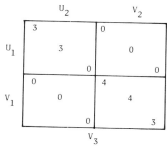

Figure 3.12
A three-person game. Player 3 chooses between the left and the right matrix

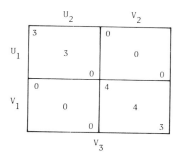

Figure 3.13
A game that results from that of figure 3.12 by strengthening U

second game player 3 receives 1 unit more at U than in the first one. Otherwise, both games agree in all payoffs.

It is reasonable to start a crude analysis of the risk situation in both games with the assumption that player 3 is more likely to choose U_3 in the second game. But does this strengthen U more than $V = V_1 V_2 V_3$?

Suppose that players 1 and 2 expect each other to behave in the same way in both games. Then an increase of their subjective probability for U_3 will increase their incentive to use their strategies V_1 and V_2. The numbers are chosen in such a way that it is not unreasonable to expect that the change from the first game to the second enhances the stability of V more than that of U.

The solution concept that we will propose here actually assigns the solution U to the first game and the solution V to the second. It does not have the payoff monotonicity property. Although we reject payoff monotonicity as a general property, we think that it is a very reasonable requirement for 2 × 2 games. There we cannot find any reason to suppose that one of two strong equilibrium points can be made more attractive by strengthening the other. The nature of the example seems to indicate that at least three players are needed to produce an example where payoff monotonicity fails to be convincing.

3.9 Axiomatic Characterization of Risk Dominance between Strong Equilibrium Points in 2 × 2 Games

Let $\mathcal{K}$ be the class of all 2 × 2 games with two strong equilibrium points. We will axiomatize a *risk-dominance relationship* that is defined between the two strong equilibrium points of any game in $\mathcal{K}$. The notation $U \succ V$ is used to indicate that U risk-dominates V. We also permit that neither U risk-dominates V nor V risk-dominates U, and we write $U|V$ if this is the case. For any game $G \in \mathcal{K}$ with strong equilibrium points U and V, one of the following statements must hold:

1. $U \succ V$ (U risk-dominates V in G).

2. $V \succ U$ (V risk-dominates U in G).

3. $U|V$ (there is no risk dominance between U and V in G).

This is part of the definition of the concept of a risk-dominance relationship and not yet a requirement to be imposed on it. It will always be understood that U and V are the strong equilibrium points of a game $G = (\Phi, H) \in \mathcal{K}$. The axioms are stated as follows:

AXIOM 1 (Invariance with respect to isomorphisms)   Let f be an isomorphism from G to G'. Then we have $f(U) \succ f(V)$ in G' if and only if we have $U \succ V$ in G.

AXIOM 2 (Best-reply invariance)   Let $G' = (\Phi, H')$ be a game that has the same best-reply structure as $G = (\Phi, H)$. Then $U \succ V$ holds in G' if and only if it holds in G.

AXIOM 3 (Payoff monotonicity)   Let $G' = (\Phi, H')$ be a game that results from $G = (\Phi, H)$ by strengthening U. If $U \succ V$ or $U|V$ holds in G, then $U \succ V$ holds in G'.

Interpretation   It is clear that we must require invariance with respect to isomorphisms. The reasons are the same as those discussed in section 3.4.

As we have seen in section 3.7, the intuitive arguments that we have used to compare risks attached to different equilibrium points run in terms of the best-reply structure. Imposing axiom 2 means that we look for a concept of this kind without specifying a precise way in which risk comparisons should be made.

Payoff monotonicity has been discussed in section 3.8. As far as 2×2 games are concerned, it seems to be a very desirable property even if for more complicated games the situation is less clear.

THEOREM 3.9.1   There is one and only one risk-dominance relationship for $\mathcal{K}$ that satisfies axioms 1, 2, and 3. As in figure 3.5 let u_i and v_i, with $i = 1$, 2, be the deviation losses of player i at the strong equilibrium points U and V of a game $G \in \mathcal{K}$. Then we have

$$U \succ V, \qquad \text{for } u_1 u_2 > v_1 v_2, \tag{3.9.1}$$

$$V \succ U, \qquad \text{for } v_1 v_2 > u_1 u_2, \tag{3.9.2}$$

$$U \mid V, \qquad \text{for } u_1 u_2 = v_1 v_2. \tag{3.9.3}$$

Proof   Up to renamings of the strategies every game $G \in \mathcal{K}$ is in the class of games of figure 3.5. Any such game has the same best-reply structure as the corresponding game of figure 3.7 (see section 3.5). Multiplication of player 1's payoff by $1/v_1$ and player 2's payoff by $1/u_2$ transforms a game of figure 3.7 into a game of figure 3.14.

For $u = v$ the game of figure 3.14 has a symmetry that carries U to V (renaming of strategies and exchanging the players). Therefore, in view of axiom 1, for $u = v$ we must have $U \mid V$.

A game of figure 3.14 with $u > v$ results from a game with $u = v$ from strengthening U. Therefore, in view of axiom 3, we must have $U \succ V$ for every game of figure 3.14 with $u > v$ and similarly $V \succ U$ for every game

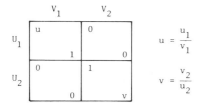

Figure 3.14
Games equivalent to those of figure 3.7

of figure 3.14 with $v > u$. Since the best-reply structure of a game of figure 3.5 is the same as that of the corresponding game of figure 3.14, we must have $U \succ V$ for $u > v$ there too. We have $u > v$ if and only if $u_1 u_2 > v_1 v_2$. Analogously, we have $V \succ U$ if and only if $v_1 v_2 > u_1 u_2$. This proves the theorem. ∎

Comment   The theorem gives a firm basis to our intuitive considerations on risk dominance between strong equilibrium points in 2×2 games. The only notion of risk dominance that agrees with the axioms can be described as a comparison of Nash-products of deviation losses. It is interesting that our result supports Nash's bargaining theory under fixed threats without relying on anything similar to the axiom of irrelevant alternatives that plays a crucial role in his axiomization.

Referring to the risk-dominance relationship characterized by theorem 3.9.1, we can define a solution function, which we will call the *pure risk-dominance solution function* because it completely ignores the aspect of payoff dominance.

The Pure Risk-Dominance Solution

The pure risk-dominance solution function $\bar{L}$ on $\mathcal{K}$ is defined as follows: Let U and V be the strong equilibrium points of $G = (\Phi, H)$, and let u_i and v_i for $i = 1, 2$, be the deviation losses at U and V (as in figure 3.5). Let $r = (r_1, r_2)$ with

$$r_1(U_1) = \frac{v_2}{u_2 + v_2}, \quad r_2(U_2) = \frac{v_1}{u_1 + v_1} \tag{3.9.4}$$

be the third equilibrium point of G. Then we have

$$\bar{L}(G) = \begin{cases} U, & \text{for } u_1 u_2 > v_1 v_2, \\ V, & \text{for } v_1 v_2 > u_1 u_2, \\ r, & \text{for } u_1 u_2 = v_1 v_2. \end{cases} \tag{3.9.5}$$

Conflict between Risk Dominance and Payoff Dominance

We have already pointed out in section 3.7 that a risk-dominance relationship in one direction is compatible with a payoff-dominance relationship in the other direction. It may be useful to look at the extreme example of figure 3.15. Here U payoff-dominates V but V strongly risk-dominates U. It is reasonable to expect that most players would prefer to play V_i rather

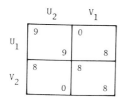

Figure 3.15
Example of payoff dominance and risk dominance in opposite directions

than U if the game is played for a considerable amount of money (say \$1,000 per unit) without preplay communication. On the other hand, with preplay communication they may come to the conclusion that they can trust each other to choose $U = (U_1, U_2)$. An agreement to do so is self-stabilizing and does not need any commitment power.

If each player knows the other to be fully rational, then there should not be any need for them to enter preplay communication before the game starts since the outcome can be easily predicted. Even under conditions that do not permit preplay communication, they should trust each other to play U.

The pure risk-dominance solution involves a certain lack of rationality. Nevertheless, under certain circumstance distrust may be justified. Suppose, for example, that in the game under consideration preplay communication has taken place and for some mysterious reason the players could not agree on U. Then after the breakdown of communication it is certainly justified to ignore payoff dominance and to rely only on risk dominance.

For a long time the authors took the view that everything beyond pure risk dominance should be captured by formal models of preplay communication that describe how trust is developed rationally under the threat of conflict. In a theory of this type the pure risk-dominance solution would serve as a threat point of preplay bargaining. Preplay bargaining itself would be described as a game where an equilibrium point has to be selected, hopefully without conflict between risk and payoff dominance. Otherwise, one would meet with the difficulty of bargaining on bargaining before the start of the bargaining game. Despite the difficulties involved in this approach, it may still be worth trying.

Our impression now is that a theory that considers both payoff and risk dominance is more in agreement with the usual image of what constitutes rational behavior. Moreover it avoids some of the difficulties of the approach outlined earlier even if models of preplay communication may still be necessary for some purposes.

The Proposed Solution Function for 2 × 2 Games with Two Strong Equilibrium Points

The solution function L for $\mathcal{K}$ that results from the application of our general concept to this class gives absolute priority to payoff dominance. It can be described as follows: Let U and V be the strong equilibrium points of $G = (\Phi, H)$. Then we have

$$L(G) = \begin{cases} U, & \text{if } H_i(U) > H_i(V), \text{ for } i = 1, 2, \\ V, & \text{if } H_i(U) < H_i(V), \text{ for } i = 1, 2, \\ \bar{L}(G), & \text{else,} \end{cases} \tag{3.9.6}$$

where $\bar{L}(G)$ is the pure risk dominance solution function introduced in this section. We call this solution L the *proposed solution function* for $\mathcal{K}$.

One may ask how the solution function L should be extended to the class of all 2×2 games. Obviously games that have only one equilibrium point raise no difficulties. Some degenerate cases with an infinity of equilibrium points like the example of figure 3.16 cannot be fully discussed before the introduction of further basic concepts. An important definition, namely that of a cell, will be introduced in the next section in order to prepare the discussion of further desirable properties. The notion of a cell permits us to decompose some games into smaller games. The game of figure 3.16 turns out to be decomposable in this sense. We will come back to this example in section 3.11.

3.10   Cells

It is natural to require that a solution function for extensive games is subgame consistent in the sense that the behavior prescribed on a subgame is nothing else than the solution of the subgame. After all, once the subgame has been reached all other parts of the game are strategically irrelevant.

It is not immediately clear how subgame consistency can be achieved in the framework of the standard form. The definition of a subgame depends on the tree structure of the extensive form. The standard form abstracts from the information on the sequential order in which choices are made.

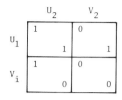

Figure 3.16
A degenerate 2 × 2 game

A further complication is added by the fact that we do not apply our solution function directly to the standard form of an extensive game, but to its ε-perturbations. We must do this in a way that achieves subgame consistency of the limit solution for the original game.

The essential features of a subgame are not lost in the transition from the extensive form to the ε-perturbed form. To capture these essential features, we will define special substructures of the standard form as cells. As we shall see, a subgame always corresponds to a cell of an ε-perturbation, but it is also possible that an ε-perturbation has a cell that does not arise from a subgame of the underlying extensive form.

It may seem to be somewhat confusing that a subgame of an extensive game generally does not correspond to a cell of its unperturbed standard form. In the unperturbed standard form a subgame corresponds to a slightly different kind of substructure which we will call a *semicell*. A semicell is very similar to a cell, but its distinguishing properties are less stringent.

Since subgames are related to problems of perfectness, it is not too surprising that the substructures generated by subgames in ε-perturbed standard forms have better properties than those generated in the unperturbed standard form. Before we go on to define semicells and cells, we will discuss this problem with the help of a specific example. In this way it will be easier to understand the intuitive ideas underlying our definitions.

The Notion of a Subgame

Since we want to avoid the formalism of extensive games, we cannot give a precise definition of a subgame. However, the following description will be sufficient for our purposes: Consider a node x of the tree of an extensive game Γ. Let K_x be the subtree containing x and all nodes after x. The subtree K_x is the tree of a subgame Γ_x if the following condition is satisfied:

every information set with nodes in K_x does not contain any nodes outside K_x. The rules of Γ_x are those specified by Γ after x has been reached.

The Example of Figure 3.17

Let Γ be the game of figure 3.17. This game has a subgame Γ_w at w. The information sets of agents 12 and 22 do not contain any nodes outside the subtree K_w at w. The standard form of Γ is shown in figure 3.18. It is represented as an array of four bimatrices. The subgame Γ_w is reached if agent 11 chooses r and agent 21 chooses l. Therefore the strategic situation of the subgame Γ_w is that of the 2×2 game represented by the bimatrix in the lower left corner of figure 3.18. We refer to this bimatrix as the *bimatrix of the subgame* Γ_w.

The bimatrix of the subgame Γ_w can be obtained as a substructure of the standard form by fixing agent 11 at r and agent 21 at l. What are the special

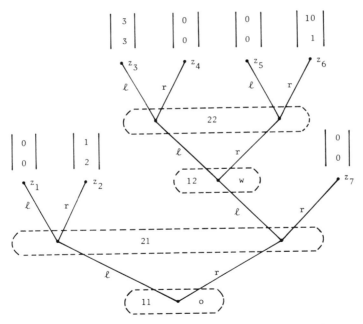

Figure 3.17
An extensive game with a subgame Γ_w at w. The names of the agents of both players are given within the dotted lines representing their information sets. Player 1's payoff is above, and player 2's payoff below. Choices are indicated by the letters l and r, standing for left and right.

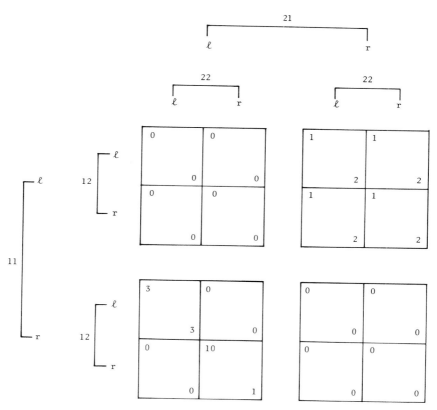

Figure 3.18
The standard form of the extensive game of figure 3.17. The choices controlled by agent *ij* are indicated by connecting lines marked by *ij*. Agent 11 selects a row of bimatrices, 21 selects a column of bimatrices, 12 selects a row within the bimatrix, and 22 selects a column within the bimatrix. Player 1's payoffs are shown above, and player 2's payoffs below.

features that distinguish this substructure from other substructures obtainable in a similar way? To answer this question, we look more closely at the payoff functions H_1 and H_2 of both players in the standard form of figure 3.18. Let x_{ij} be agent ij's probability of choosing l, and let y_{ij} be agent ij's probability of choosing r. A behavior strategy combination can be represented by a vector

$$x = (x_{11}, x_{12}, x_{21}, x_{22}). \tag{3.10.1}$$

Accordingly, we write $H_i(x)$ for i's expected payoff if the behavior strategy combination corresponding to x is played. The payoffs are as follows:

$$H_1(x) = x_{11}y_{21} + y_{11}x_{21}[3x_{12}x_{22} + 10y_{12}y_{22}], \tag{3.10.2}$$

$$H_2(x) = 2x_{11}y_{21} + y_{11}x_{21}[3x_{12}x_{22} + y_{12}y_{22}]. \tag{3.10.3}$$

The expression in the rectangular brackets has an obvious interpretation. Let $H_{w1}(x_{12}x_{22})$ and $H_{w2}(x_{12}x_{22})$ be player 1's and player 2's payoffs in the 2×2 game represented by the bimatrix of Γ_w. We have

$$H_{w1}(x_{12}x_{22}) = 3x_{12}x_{22} + 10y_{12}y_{22}, \tag{3.10.4}$$

$$H_{w2}(x_{12}x_{22}) = 3x_{12}x_{22} + y_{12}y_{22}. \tag{3.10.5}$$

Obviously agents 12 and 22 need not be concerned with anything but H_{w1} and H_{w2}. The local strategies of agent 11 and 21 do not really matter for them. This is because H_1 is always a non-negative linear transformation of H_{x1} and H_2 is always a non-negative linear transformation of H_{x2}. The coefficients of these transformations are determined by the local strategies of agents 11 and 21, but these coefficients do not have any essential influence on the strategic situation of agents 12 and 22. It does not matter what 12 and 22 do if we have $y_{11}x_{21} = 0$, but for $y_{11}x_{21} > 0$, it always matters in the same way. As far as the subgame agents 12 and 22 are concerned, a transition from one pair of completely mixed local strategies for the outside agents 11 and 21 to another amounts to a positive linear payoff transformation and therefore is analogous to the transition to an equivalent game.

The fact that H_1 and H_2 are non-negative linear transformations of expressions involving the local strategies of 12 and 22 with coefficients determined by the local strategies of 11 and 21 can be checked in the standard form without reference to the underlying extensive form. It can be seen immediately that a subgame will always lead to an analogous situation in the standard form. Total payoffs can be written as subgame payoffs multiplied by the probability of reaching the subgame supplemented by an additional term that reflects the payoffs at endpoints outside the subgame.

If we want to obtain a substructure that corresponds to the subgame, it does not really matter where we fix the agents outside the subgame as long as we avoid local strategies that produce zero probability of reaching the subgame. It will be convenient to define semicells and cells in such a way that all outside agents kj are fixed at the centroids c_{ij} of their choice sets Φ_{ij}. (For the definition of the centroid, see section 2.7.)

It is useful to look at the situation in uniformly perturbed games before we begin to state formal definitions. Consider an ε-perturbation of the standard form shown in figure 3.18. Obviously there H_1 and H_2 will always be positive linear transformations of H_{w1} and H_{w2}, since no choice can be taken with a probability less than ε. It is clear that a subgame will always lead to an analogous situation in the ε-perturbation of the standard form.

The definition of a semicell will involve non-negative linear payoff transformations, and the definition of a cell will involve positive linear transformations. In this way we solve the task of recognizing subgames like substructures in the standard form. However, semicells of standard forms and cells of ε-perturbed standard forms do not always correspond to subgames in an underlying extensive game. An example for this will be given later.

Semicells and Cells

Let $G = (\Phi, H)$ be a game in standard form with

$$\Phi = \underset{i \in N}{\times} \Phi_i = \underset{ij \in M}{\times} \Phi_{ij}. \tag{3.10.6}$$

Let C be a nonempty proper subset of M. Let $G^C = (\Phi^C, H^C)$ be the game that results from G by fixing the agents $ij \in M \setminus C$ at the centroids c_{ij} of their choice sets Φ_{ij}. We will use the symbol $-C$ as an abbreviation for $M \setminus C$.

The game G^C is a semicell if for every $\psi_{-C} \in \Phi_{-C}$ and for every i with $M_i \cap C \neq \varnothing$ a number $\alpha_i(\psi_{-C}) \geq 0$ and a number $\beta_i(\psi_{-C})$ can be found such that

$$H_i(\psi_{-C}\phi_C) = \alpha_i(\psi_{-C})H_i^C(\phi_C) + \beta_i(\psi_{-C}). \tag{3.10.7}$$

G^C is a cell if for every $\psi_{-C} \in \Phi_{-C}$ and for every i with $M_i \cap C \neq \varnothing$ a number $\alpha_i(\psi_{-C}) > 0$ and a number $\beta_i(\psi_{-C})$ can be found such that (3.10.7) holds.

We say that C *forms a semicell* or a *cell* if G^C is a semicell or cell, respectively. Then G^C is called the semicell or cell *formed* by C.

Remark   An immediate consequence of (3.10.7) is that numbers $\alpha_i(b_{-C})$ and $\beta_i(b_{-C})$ can be found for every subcombination $b_{-C} \in B_{-C}$ such that (3.10.7) holds with b_{-C} in place of ψ_{-C}, with $\alpha_i(b_{-C}) \geq 0$ in the case of a semicell and with $\alpha_i(b_{-C}) > 0$ in the case of a cell. Obviously

$$\alpha_i(b_{-C}) = \sum_{\phi_{-C} \in \Phi_{-C}} b_{-C}(\phi_{-C}) \alpha_i(\phi_{-C}) \tag{3.10.8}$$

and

$$\beta_i(b_{-C}) = \sum_{\phi_{-C} \in \Phi_{-C}} b_{-C}(\phi_{-C}) \beta_i(\phi_{-C}) \tag{3.10.9}$$

satisfy these requirements.

Interpretation   A semicell or a cell may have fewer players than the original game because $M_i \cap C$ may be empty for some players. If a semicell or a cell arises from a subgame of an underlying extensive form, then (3.10.7) can be satisfied for these outside players, too. Moreover, if $\alpha_i(\psi_{-C})$ is the probability of reaching the subgame by ψ_{-C}, then the multiplicative constant in (3.10.7) does not depend on i.

Although, as the preceding explanation shows, subgamelike substructures may be defined in a more restrictive way, our definitions are based on the idea that any subset C of agents that is strategically independent should be treated in the same way.

The standard form does not permit us to reconstruct subgames of the extensive form. This is shown by the example of figure 3.19. The upper game has a subgame, the lower has none, and both have the same standard form. Should these games be treated differently? We disregard the fact that in the lower game player 2's information set does not tell him whether x or y has been reached. His decision is important for him only if x has been reached. The next example throws further light on the cell definition.

Example of a Cell Not Arising from a Subgame

Suppose that the two players 1 and 2 who have linear utilities for money are involved in a bimatrix game whose entries are in unknown currencies. Before they make their choice, a third player secretly selects between two alternative possibilities:

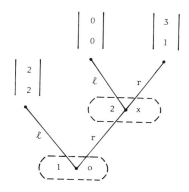

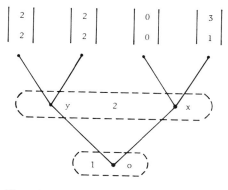

Figure 3.19
Two extensive games with the same standard form. The upper one has a subgame at x; the lower one has no subgame. For the conventions of graphic representation, see figure 3.17.

1. Player 1 receives U.S. dollars, and player 2 receives Israeli shekels.

2. Player 1 receives French francs, and player 2 receives German marks.

It is reasonable to cover the strategic situation of players 1 and 2 in this game by the definition of a cell. For every fixed strategy choice of player 3 their situation is the same. Therefore they do not even have to think about player 3's strategy choice. They only interact with each other and as far as they are concerned the game is a two-person game.

Remark If G is the standard form of an extensive game Γ and C is the set of all agents in a subgame of Γ, then C forms a semicell in G. Moreover C forms a cell in every ε-perturbation G_ε of G. This is clear from the discussion preceding the definition of semicells and cells.

It is worthwhile to show that a semicell of a standard form always corresponds to a cell of its ε-perturbation, regardless of whether it arises from a subgame of an underlying extensive form or not. This is a consequence of the following lemma:

LEMMA 3.10.1 (Lemma on semicells) Let $G = (\Phi, H)$ be a standard form, and let C be a subset of agents in G that forms a semicell of G. Then C forms a cell of every interior substructure $G' = (\Phi', H')$ of G such that the agent set M' of G' contains C.

Proof With the help of (3.10.8) and (3.10.9) we can determine numbers $\alpha_i(\phi'_{M'\backslash C})$ and $\beta_i(\phi'_{M'\backslash C})$ that satisfy the requirements for a semicell in G'. Assume that at least one—the $\alpha_i(\phi_{-C})$—is positive. Then all $\alpha_i(\phi'_{M\backslash C})$ are positive, since the choices in G' are completely mixed local strategies in G. In this case C forms a cell in G'. Assume, on the contrary, that $\alpha_i(\phi_{-C}) = 0$ holds for every $\phi_{-C} \in \Phi_{-C}$. Then by (3.10.7) we have

$$H_i(\psi_{-C}\phi_C) = \beta_i(\psi_{-C}) \qquad (3.10.10)$$

for players with agents in C. Moreover we also have

$$H_i^C(\phi_C) = \beta_i(\psi_{-C}) \qquad (3.10.11)$$

by the definition of the semicell payoff function. Define $\hat{\alpha}_i(\phi_{-C}) = 1$ and $\hat{\beta}_i(\phi_{-C}) = 0$ for every $\phi_{-C} \in \Phi_{-C}$. With these coefficients instead of $\alpha_i(\phi_{-C})$ and $\beta_i(\phi_{-C})$, respectively, (3.10.7) holds too, and the conditions required by the definition of a cell are satisfied. C forms a cell already in G, and as we have seen earlier, in G' too. ∎

Comment   The solution function of our theory is not directly applied to standard forms but to their ε-perturbations. The fact that semicells of a standard form correspond to cells of its ε-perturbations permits us to concentrate attention on cells. Some further results on cells will be derived in the following:

LEMMA 3.10.2 (Lemma on cells)   Let C and C' with $C \cap C' \neq \varnothing$ be two proper subsets of M, both of which form cells of $G = (\Phi, H)$ with

$$\Phi = \underset{i \in N}{\times} \Phi_i = \underset{ij \in M}{\times} \Phi_{ij}. \tag{3.10.12}$$

Then $D = C \cap C'$ forms a cell of G as well.

Proof   Any change of the subcombination b_{-D} for $M \backslash D$ can be achieved by two successive changes such that first only the local strategies of agents in $M \backslash C$ are changed and then those of the agents in $C \backslash D$. Both changes are connected with the positive linear payoff transformations for the players i, with $M_i \cap D \neq \varnothing$ in the first case because C forms a cell and in the second case because C' forms a cell. Two successive positive linear transformations performed one after another are equivalent to one positive linear transformation. In this way we receive the positive linear transformations whose existence are required by the definition of a cell as applied to G. ∎

Counterexample

One may think that the union of two subsets C and C' forms a cell if C and C' form a cell. The example of figure 3.20 shows that this is not necessarily true. The game of figure 3.20 is a game with normal-form structure. We need not distinguish between a player and his only agent. Both $\{1\}$ and $\{2\}$

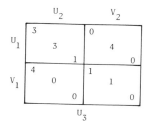 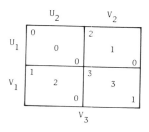

Figure 3.20
A counterexample: 1 and 2 form cells but 1, 2 does not form a cell. Players 1, 2, and 3 choose rows, columns, and matrices, respectively.

form cells because, for fixed strategies of the other players, the difference between the payoffs for U_i and V_i is always 1 for $i = 1, 2$. Nevertheless, $\{1, 2\}$ does not form a cell and not even a semicell because a shift from U_3 to V_3 reverses the payoff differences between $U_1 U_2$ and $V_1 V_2$. No non-negative linear payoff transformation can produce this result.

Elementary Cells

Let $G = (\Phi, H)$ be a standard form, and let C be a nonempty proper subset of its agent set M such that C forms a cell G^C of G. The cell G^C is called *elementary* if no proper subset of C forms a cell of G. It follows by the lemma on cells that subsets that form elementary cells do not intersect.

Comment

The fact that elementary cells do not intersect is important. It enables us to define a solution function based on the idea that a game with cells should be solved by first solving the elementary cells and then solving the game that results by fixing the agents of the elementary cells at the local strategies prescribed by the solution of these cells.

3.11   Cell Consistency and Truncation Consistency

In this section we look at two desirable properties of solution functions. Roughly speaking, cell consistency requires that the solution of the whole game agrees with that of its cells as far as the cell agents are concerned. Truncation concerns the "truncated" game that results if the agents in a cell are fixed at the solution of the cell. The requirement postulates that the solution of the truncated game should agree with the solution of the whole game as far as its agents are concerned.

Completeness

A class $\mathscr{G}$ of games in standard form is called *complete* if a substructure G' of a game $G \in \mathscr{G}$ always belongs to $\mathscr{G}$. Obviously $\mathscr{G}$ is complete if $\mathscr{G}$ is the interior substructure class $\mathscr{I}(\mathscr{G}')$ of another class $\mathscr{G}'$ of standard forms. In our theory we only consider solution functions for complete subclasses of the class $\mathscr{I}(\mathscr{R})$ of all interior substructures of standard forms with perfect recall.

Truncations

Let L be a solution function for a complete class $\mathscr{G} \subseteq \mathscr{I}(\mathscr{R})$. Let $G \in \mathscr{G}$ be a game with a cell G^C. The *truncation of G with respect to G^C and L* is the Game $\bar{G}$ that results from G by fixing the agents G^C at their local strategies in the solution $L(G^C)$ of G^C.

Remark The completeness of $\mathscr{G}$ is important because it guarantees that both G^C and the truncation $\bar{G}$ of G with respect to G^C and L are in $\mathscr{G}$ if G^C is a cell of G. Both G^C and $\bar{G}$ result from G by fixing some of the agents but not all of them.

Cell Consistency

A solution function L for a complete class $\mathscr{G} \subseteq \mathscr{I}(\mathscr{R})$ is called *cell consistent* if for a cell G^C of a game $G \in \mathscr{G}$ the solution $L(G^C)$ and $L(G)$ of G^C and G always prescribe the same local strategies to all agents in G^C.

Truncation Consistency

A solution function L for a complete class $\mathscr{G} \subseteq \mathscr{I}(\mathscr{R})$ is called *truncation consistent*, if for a truncation $\bar{G}$ of a game $G \in \mathscr{G}$ with respect to a cell G^C and L the solutions $L(\bar{G})$ and $L(G)$ of $\bar{G}$ and G always prescribe the same local strategies for all agents of $\bar{G}$.

Interpretation As far as their strategic situation is concerned, the agents in a cell do not depend on outside agents. This was discussed in the last section. Obviously cell consistency is a very natural requirement.

  If cell consistency is accepted, then truncation consistency becomes an almost unavoidable additional requirement. If it is rational to expect the cell agents to play their local strategies of the cell solution, it should be possible to replace the analysis of the whole game by the analysis of the cell and the truncated game. As we shall see, cell consistency and truncation consistency have the consequence that it is sufficient to know the solutions of games without cells in order to compute the solution for all games in the complete class $\mathscr{G} \subseteq \mathscr{I}(\mathscr{R})$ where the solution function is defined.

Decomposibility

A game G is called *decomposable* if it has at least one cell. Games without cells are called *indecomposable*. We say that G is fully decomposable if every agent belongs to an elementary cell. Decomposable games that are not fully decomposable are called *partially decomposable.*

Main Truncation

Let L be a solution function for a complete class $\mathscr{G} \subseteq \mathscr{I}(\mathscr{R})$. For every partially decomposable game $G \in \mathscr{G}$ we construct a game $\hat{G}$ that is called the *main truncation of G with respect to L.* Let $G^1, \ldots, G^k$ be the elementary cells of G. The game $\hat{G}$ results from G by fixing the agents of the elementary cells at their local strategies in the solutions $L(G^1), \ldots, L(G^k)$ of the elementary cells.

Composition

Let L be a solution function for a complete class $\mathscr{G} \subseteq \mathscr{I}(\mathscr{R})$, and let $G \in \mathscr{G}$ be a fully decomposable game. Let r be that behavior-strategy combination for G that contains for every agent ij his local strategy prescribed by the solution $L(G^j)$ of the elementary cell to which he belongs. This behavior-strategy combination r is called the *composition of the elementary cell solutions.* Now consider a partially decomposable game $G \in \mathscr{G}$. Let r be that behavior-strategy combination for G that (1) for every agent in an elementary cell G^j of G contains his local strategy in $L(G^j)$ and (2) for every agent in the main truncation $\hat{G}$ of G with respect to L contains his local strategy in $L(\hat{G})$. This behavior-strategy combination r is the *composition of the main truncation and elementary cell solutions.*

LEMMA 3.11.1 (Composition lemma) Let L be a solution function for a complete class $\mathscr{G} \subseteq \mathscr{I}(\mathscr{R})$. Then for every fully decomposable $G \in \mathscr{G}$ the composition of the main truncation and elementary cell solutions is an equilibrium point of G.

Proof L assigns equilibrium points in behavior strategies to game $G \in \mathscr{G}$. Since these games are interior substructures of standard forms with perfect recall, they have the local best-reply property (see theorem 2.7.2, the theorem on local best replies). The local best replies of the cell agents do not depend on local strategies of outside agents. The construction of the main truncation embodies the expectation that cell agents use their local strategies in the cell solution. Therefore in both cases (full and partial decomposibility) the composition is a local equilibrium of G and consequently an equilibrium point of G. ∎

Extension   Let $\mathcal{G}_o$ be the subclass of all indecomposable games in a class $\mathcal{G} \subseteq \mathcal{I}(\mathcal{R})$, and let L_o be a solution function for $\mathcal{G}_o$. On the basis of L_o we will construct a solution function L for $\mathcal{G}$ that will be called the *extension of L_o to $\mathcal{G}$*. The extension L is recursively defined by the following properties:

1. For $G \in \mathcal{G}_o$ we have $L(G) = L_o(G)$.

2. If $G \in \mathcal{G}$ is fully decomposable, then $L(G)$ is the composition of the elementary cell solutions.

3. If $G \in \mathcal{G}$ is partially decomposable, then $L(G)$ is the composition of the main truncation and the cell solutions.

LEMMA 3.11.2 (Extension lemma)   Let L_o be a solution function for the subclass $\mathcal{G}_o$ of all indecomposable games in a class $\mathcal{G} \subseteq \mathcal{I}(\mathcal{R})$. There is one and only one solution function L for $\mathcal{G}$ with the properties 1, 2, and 3.

Proof   It is clear that a unique behavior-strategy combination $L(G)$ is defined by properties 1, 2, and 3 for every $G \in \mathcal{G}$. Property 3 may have to be applied several times, first to the game itself, then to its main truncation, and so on. But finally a main truncation will arise that is either indecomposable or fully decomposable. An easy induction argument based on the composition lemma 3.11.1 shows that $L(G)$ is an equilibrium point in behavior strategies of G. ■

THEOREM 3.11.1 (Extension theorem)   Let L_o be a solution function for the subclass $\mathcal{G}_o$ of all indecomposable games in a class $\mathcal{G} \subseteq \mathcal{I}(\mathcal{R}_o)$; let L_o be invariant with respect to positive linear payoff transformations. There is one and only one cell consistent and truncation consistent solution function for $\mathcal{G}$ that agrees with L_o on $\mathcal{G}_o$, namely the extension L of $\mathcal{G}_o$ to $\mathcal{G}$.

To prove this theorem, we need the following decomposition lemma:

LEMMA 3.11.3 (Decomposition lemma)   Let L be a solution function for a complete class $\mathcal{G} \subseteq \mathcal{I}(\mathcal{R})$. Let G^C be a cell of a game $G \in \mathcal{G}$, and let $\bar{G}$ be the truncation of G with respect to G^C and L. Then every agent subset D with $C \cap D = \varnothing$ that forms a cell in G forms a cell in $\bar{G}$ too. Moreover the cells formed by D in G and $\bar{G}$ are equivalent games.

Proof   In the same way as in the proof of the lemma 3.10.1 on semicells in the last section one can use (3.10.8) and (3.10.9) to find the linear transformations that show that D forms a cell in $\bar{G}$ and that the cells formed by D in G and $\bar{G}$ are equivalent. ■

Proof of the Extension Theorem 3.11.1   We first show that a cell consistent and truncation consistent solution function L that agrees with L_o on $\mathscr{G}_o$ must be the extention of L_o to $\mathscr{G}$.

Suppose that the agent subsets $C_1, \ldots, C_k$ form the elementary cells $G^1, \ldots, G^k$ of the standard form $G \in \mathscr{G}$. Let $\tilde{G}$ be the truncation with respect to one of the elementary cells, say G^1, and to L. The decomposition lemma 3.11.3 permits us to conclude that $C_2, \ldots, C_k$ form cells $\tilde{G}^2, \ldots, \tilde{G}^k$. Moreover $\tilde{G}^j$ and G^j are equivalent for $j = 2, \ldots, k$. Since L_o is invariant with respect to positive linear transformations, we have $L(G^j) = L(\tilde{G}^j)$ for $j = 2, \ldots, k$. It is now clear that we can obtain properties 2 and 3 of the extension by repeated application of cell consistency and truncation consistency. It does not matter in which order the elementary cells are removed one after the other.

It remains to show that the extension of L of L_o has the properties of cell consistency and truncation consistency. This will be done by induction on the number m of agents in G.

Both properties trivially hold for games in $\mathscr{G}$ with only one agent. Assume that they hold for games with at most $m - 1$ agents. Consider a decomposable game $G \in \mathscr{G}$ with m agents. Let C be a subset of agents that forms a cell G^C of G. Let $\bar{G}$ be the truncation of G with respect to G^C and L.

The elementary cells of G^C are also elementary cells of G. Suppose that G^C is fully decomposable or indecomposable. In this case the agreement of $L(G)$ with $L(G^C)$ and $L(\bar{G})$ is an immediate consequence of properties 2 and 3.

Now suppose that G^C is partially decomposable. Then G is partially decomposable as well. Let $\hat{G}$ be the main truncation of G, and let G^D be the main truncation of G^C, where D stands for the set of agents in G^D. Obviously, the agents in D are also agents of $\hat{G}$.

It follows by properties 2 and 3 that $L(G)$ agrees with $L(G^C)$ and $L(\hat{G})$ as far as the agents in the elementary cells of G are concerned. Therefore G^D is a cell of $\hat{G}$. Since C has less than m agents, truncation consistency can be applied to G^C. Therefore $L(G^C)$ agrees with $L(G^D)$ for the agents in D. Consequently the truncation of $\hat{G}$ with respect to G^D is $\bar{G}$. Since $\hat{G}$ has fewer than m agents, we can rely on cell consistency and truncation consistency to conclude that $L(\hat{G})$ is the composition of $L(\bar{G})$ and $L(G^D)$. Since, by definition, $L(G)$ agrees with $L(\hat{G})$ for the agents in $\hat{G}$, it follows that $L(G)$ is the composition of $L(G^C)$ and $L(\bar{G})$. ∎

Comment   The extension theorem 3.11.1 shows that cell consistency and truncation consistency are powerful properties that reduce the task of defining a solution concept to the task of defining a solution concept for indecomposable games.

Cell consistency and truncation consistency require that all considerations that may influence the selection of equilibrium points are applied strictly locally—only to those indecomposable games that appear in the process of computing the solution with the help of all three properties on the basis of a solution concept for indecomposable games. These indecomposable games shall be called the *bricks* of the original game.

Local and Global Payoff Efficiency

Payoff efficiency is an example of a selection criterion that cannot be applied to the game as a whole but only locally to its bricks. Figure 3.21 shows an extensive game Γ that may serve as an example. The game has two subgames Γ_l after agent 11's choice l and Γ_r after agent 11's choice r. Let G_ε be an ε-perturbed standard form of Γ, and let G_ε^l be the cells G_ε that correspond to Γ_l and Γ_r, respectively. For every agent let l_ε and r_ε be his ε-extreme local-strategy corresponding to l and r, respectively. Note that player 1 does not belong to G_ε^l and G_ε^r. Each of both cells has only one payoff-efficient equilibrium point. In both cases the payoff-efficient equi-

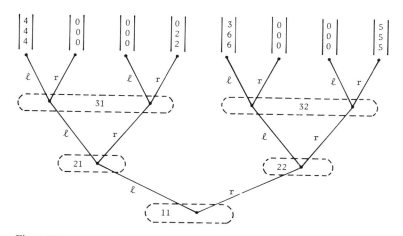

Figure 3.21
Example of a conflict between local and global payoff efficiency. For the conventions of graphic representation, see figure 3.17.

librium point prescribes l_ε to both agents. This shows that local payoff efficiency—the application of the principle to bricks of the game rather than to the whole game—together with cell consistency and truncation consistency result in the selection of that equilibrium point of G_ε that prescribes l_ε to each of the agents. However, this equilibrium point is not globally payoff efficient in G_ε. The equilibrium point that prescribes r_ε to all agents yields better payoffs for all players.

It is in the interest of all players to play r_ε everywhere rather than l_ε everywhere. Unfortunately, this is true only in the beginning of the game. In the subgame Γ_r the interests of player 1 do not count any more. Agents 22 and 32 must be expected to choose l_ε rather than r_ε.

The Degenerate 2 × 2 Game of Figure 3.16

The game of figure 3.16 has only one payoff-efficient equilibrium point, namely $U = (U_1, U_2)$. Nevertheless, our theory does not select this equilibrium point as the limit solution. This is a consequence of cell consistency together with invariance with respect to isomorphisms. Obviously $\{1\}$ and $\{2\}$ form cells in all ε-perturbations of this game. These cells are one-person games with only one agent who gets the same payoff for both of his choices. In view of invariance with respect to isomorphisms the solution assigns probability 0.5 to each of both choices. Cell consistency leads to the result that the limit solution of the game of figure 3.16 is that equilibrium point where both players choose each of their pure strategies with probability $\frac{1}{2}$. Although this equilibrium point fails to be payoff efficient, the result is not unreasonable. Each player is interested in his own payoff only. He does not care for the other player's payoff and has no reason to prefer one of his pure strategies over the other for any fixed expectation on the other player's behavior.

Decomposition Properties of the Limit Solution

One may ask the question whether cell consistency and truncation consistency induce similar properties on the limit solution. After all, the most important reason for the introduction of the cell notion was the idea that the limit solution should be *subgame consistent* in the sense that as far as the agents of a subgame are concerned, the solution of the subgame agrees with the solution of the whole game. Of course, if we speak of the limit solution of an extensive game, we really mean the limit solution of its standard form. The preceding definition of subgame consistency should be understood in this way. We use the symbol $\underrightarrow{L}(\Gamma)$ for the limit solution of an extensive game.

Cell consistency of a solution function L implies subgame consistency of the limit solution function $\underrightarrow{L}$ of L. This follows by the lemma 3.10.1 on semicells. One might expect that an analogous result can be obtained with respect to truncation consistency. However, this is not the case. To show this, we must first define the *truncation* $\bar{\Gamma}$ of an extensive game Γ with respect to a subgame Γ' of Γ and $\underrightarrow{L}$. One obtains this extensive game $\bar{\Gamma}$ if in Γ the subgame Γ' is replaced by its solution payoff $H'(\underrightarrow{L}(\Gamma'))$. This means that the starting point of Γ' becomes an end point with payoffs according to $H'(\underrightarrow{L}(\Gamma'))$ and that nothing is changed outside the subgame Γ'.

We say that $\underrightarrow{L}$ is *subgame truncation consistent* if the following condition is satisfied: let $\bar{\Gamma}$ be an extensive form and Γ' be a subgame of Γ such that $\underrightarrow{L}$ is defined for Γ, Γ' and the truncation $\bar{\Gamma}$ of Γ with respect to Γ' and $\underrightarrow{L}$; then $\underrightarrow{L}(\Gamma)$ and $\underrightarrow{L}(\bar{\Gamma})$ prescribe the same local strategies to the agents in $\bar{\Gamma}$.

Before we go on to show why a limit solution function cannot be expected to have the property of subgame truncation consistency, we want to clarify a small point concerning the standard form of an extensive game. Our definition of the standard form does not permit players without agents. However, such players are possible in extensive games. In the transition to the standard form we simply remove such players and their payoffs. This has the consequence that the standard form of a subgame or a truncation with respect to a subgame may have fewer players than the standard form of the whole game. This must be kept in mind in the interpretation of the properties of subgame consistency and subgame truncation consistency.

Consider the extensive game Γ of figure 3.22. This game has a subgame Γ_x at node x. Since Γ_x has only one equilibrium point, namely player 2's choice of r, this equilibrium point is the limit solution $\underrightarrow{L}(\Gamma_x)$ of the subgame. Figure 3.23 shows the truncation $\bar{\Gamma}$ of Γ with respect to Γ_x and $\underrightarrow{L}$. The standard form of $\bar{\Gamma}$ has a symmetry that maps one choice to the other. The same is true for all its ε-perturbations. If L satisfies the requirement of invariance with respect to isomorphisms, then $\underrightarrow{L}(\bar{\Gamma})$ must assign equal probabilities to l and r in figure 3.23.

Every ε-perturbation of the standard form of the game Γ of figure 3.22 has only one equilibrium point that prescribes the ε-extreme choices r_ε corresponding to r to both agents. Therefore the limit solution $\underrightarrow{L}(\Gamma)$ assigns r to both agents. We have obtained the following result:

Result   Let L be a solution function for the interior substructure class $\mathscr{I}(\mathscr{G})$ of a class of standard forms $\mathscr{G}$, such that $\mathscr{G}$ contains the standard forms of the extensive games of figure 3.22 and 3.23. If L is invariant with respect to isomorphisms, then the limit solution $\underrightarrow{L}$ of L is not subgame truncation consistent.

Comment   Since invariance with respect to isomorphism is an indispensible requirement, we cannot expect subgame truncation consistency of the limit solution function. The nature of the example shows why we need not be disturbed by this lack of subgame truncation consistency. In the only equilibrium point of the ε-perturbed standard form of figure 3.22, player 1 receives a payoff of $2 + \varepsilon - \varepsilon^2$. A deviation to his ε-extreme strategy l_ε corresponding to l would yield only $2 + \varepsilon^2$. The loss of $\varepsilon(1 - 2\varepsilon)$ approaches the limit 0 for $\varepsilon \to 0$. The fact that the choice of r_ε by both agents is a strong

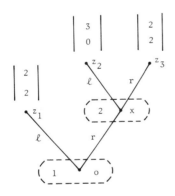

Figure 3.22
An extensive two-person game

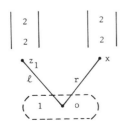

Figure 3.23
"Truncation" of the game of figure 3.22

equilibrium point is lost in the transition to the limit. One can say that important information on the game structure may be suppressed if the truncation with respect to a subgame and $\underrightarrow{L}$ is formed. Truncations formed in ε-perturbations with respect to the corresponding cells preserve this information. Clearly this is an advantage rather than a disadvantage.

The result just obtained remains correct if invariance with respect to isomorphisms is required of $\underrightarrow{L}$ rather than L. This shows that any solution concept addressed directly to unperturbed standard forms is bound to run into difficulties. Our roundabout approach via the ε-perturbations may seem to be cumbersome, but it recommends itself by more than one reason.

3.12   Sequential Agent Splitting

Figure 3.24 shows what sequential agent splitting means in the extensive form. An agent hk of a player h who has to choose between α, β, and γ is

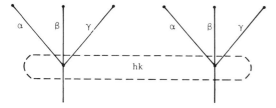

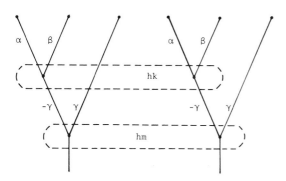

Figure 3.24
An example of sequential agent splitting in the extensive form

split into two agents hm and hk such that hm has to select either γ or $-\gamma$ and then in case of $-\gamma$ agent hk has to choose between α and β. The symbol $-\gamma$ is used as an abbreviation for "α or β." One has to imagine the graphic representation of an extensive form where the upper part of figure 3.24 is taken out and is replaced by the lower part of figure 3.24. Of course we have to assume that originally there was no agent hm in the game.

At least at first glance it is hard to imagine why sequential agent splitting should in any way change the strategic situation. Nevertheless, as we shall see, one cannot avoid the conclusion that sequential agent splitting does have a considerable influence on risk comparisons between equilibrium points in some games. To connect sequential agent splitting to our theory of equilibrium selection, we have to introduce a formal definition in the framework of the standard form.

Sequential Agent Splitting in the Standard Form

Let $G' = (\Phi, H)$ with

$$\Phi = \underset{i \in N}{\times} \Phi_i = \underset{ij \in M}{\times} \Phi_{ij} \tag{3.12.1}$$

be a game in standard form. Let $hk \in M_h$ be one of the agents of a player $h \in N$, and let $\gamma \in \Phi_{hk}$ be one of agent hk's choices. Moreover let m be a positive integer with $hm \notin M_h$. We construct a standard form $G' = (\Phi', H')$ with

$$\Phi' = \underset{i \in N}{\times} \Phi'_i = \underset{ij \in M'}{\times} \Phi'_{ij}, \tag{3.12.2}$$

$$M' = M \cup \{hm\}, \tag{3.12.3}$$

$$\Phi'_{ij} = \Phi_{ij}, \quad \text{for } ij \in M \setminus \{hk\}, \tag{3.12.4}$$

$$\Phi'_{hk} = \Phi_{hk} \setminus \{\gamma\}, \tag{3.12.5}$$

$$\Phi'_{hm} = \{\gamma, -\gamma\}. \tag{3.12.6}$$

[In (3.12.6) agent hm's alternative of not choosing γ is symbolized by $-\gamma$]. We say that the behavior-strategy combination $b' = (b'_{ij})_{M'}$ corresponds to $b = (b_{ij})_M$, and we write $b' \to b$ if we have

$$b'_{ij} = b_{ij}, \quad \text{for } ij \in M \setminus \{hk\}, \tag{3.12.7}$$

$$b'_{hm}(\gamma) = b_{hk}(\gamma), \tag{3.12.8}$$

$$b'_{hm}(-\gamma)b'_{hk}(\phi_{hk}) = b_{hk}(\phi_{hk}), \quad \text{for } \phi_{hk} \in \Phi'_{hk}. \tag{3.12.9}$$

The payoffs of G' are defined as

$$H'(\phi') = H(\phi), \quad \text{with } \phi' \to \phi. \tag{3.12.10}$$

The game $G' = (\Phi, H')$ is called the game that *results from* $G = (\Phi, H)$ *by splitting off an agent hm for hk's choice* γ.

Remark The following equation is an immediate consequence of (3.12.7) to (3.12.10):

$$H'(b') = H(b), \quad \text{for } b' \to b. \tag{3.12.11}$$

Interpretation Even if the formal definition may seem to be somewhat complicated, it can easily be seen that is the correct translation of the idea of sequential agent splitting into the language of the standard form.

The operations of ε-perturbation and sequential agent splitting are not interchangeable, however. It matters what is done first. If in the example of figure 3.24 we first form an ε-perturbation and then split off agent km, then the task of the new agents hm and hk can be described as the choice between the ε-extreme local strategies α_ε, β_ε, and γ_ε corresponding to α, β, and γ. One may think of the new agents as decision makers who do not make their own mistakes but simply administrate the mistakes of the old agent hk. Each of the choices α, β, and γ will be taken with minimum probability ε.

The picture is different if agent hm is split off first and then the ε-perturbation is formed. If the intentional choices are $-\gamma$ and α, then β will be chosen with probability $\varepsilon(1 - \varepsilon)$ and γ with probability ε; the situation is analogous if the intentional choices are $-\gamma$ and β. These probabilities are almost the same as in the reversed case considered earlier. However, if agent hm intends to choose γ, then the probabilities of α and β depend on the intentions of agent hk; if he intends to choose β, then α is chosen with probability ε^2 and β with probability $\varepsilon(1 - \varepsilon)$. The situation is analogous if he intends to choose α.

Obviously one has to expect that for specific values of ε, sequential agent splitting before and after ε-perturbation leads to essentially different solutions. This suggests that one should not be concerned about the solutions of ε-perturbations as such but only about limit solutions. At least at first glance it seems to be reasonable to require that for unperturbed standard forms with perfect recall, sequential agent splitting does not produce an essential change of the limit solution.

Invariance with Respect to Sequential Agent Splitting

Let $\mathscr{G}$ be a class of games with perfect recall, and let L be a solution function for the interior substructure class $\mathscr{I}(\mathscr{G})$ of $\mathscr{G}$. We say that L is *invariant with respect to sequential agent splitting* if the following condition is always satisfied: let G and G' be two games in $\mathscr{G}$ such that G' results from G by splitting off an agent hm for a choice γ of an agent hk; if $\underrightarrow{L}(G)$ and $\underrightarrow{L}(G')$ exist, then we have $\underrightarrow{L}(G') \to \underrightarrow{L}(G)$.

Interpretation The requirement postulates that the limit solution of G' corresponds to the limit solution of G, provided that both limit solutions exist. In the case that $\underrightarrow{L}(G)$ prescribes γ with probability 1, agent hk's behavior in the limit solution of G' is not restricted by the requirement because it does not matter what he does if agent hm selects γ.

We next prove an impossibility theorem that forces us to reject the requirement of invariance with respect to sequential agent splitting. The proof makes use of the 3×3 game shown in figure 3.25. Therefore we need the technical presupposition that this game has a limit solution. In a reasonable solution theory nonexistence of a limit solution should not be a problem for games as simple as that of figure 3.25.

THEOREM 3.12.1 (Impossibility theorem)   Let $\mathscr{G}$ be a class of standard form games that contains all two-person games with at most two agents for each player and at most three choices for each agent. Let L be a solution function for the interior substructure class $\mathscr{I}(\mathscr{G})$ of $\mathscr{G}$ that satisfies the requirement of cell consistency and truncation consistency and that for 2×2 games with two strong equilibrium points either agrees with the proposed solution function or with the pure risk-dominance solution function (see section 3.9).

	α	β	γ
α	7 5	0 2	0 2
β	0 0	2 9	0 0
γ	0 0	0 2	8 4

Figure 3.25
A special 3×3 game

Moreover let L be such that the limit solution $\underset{\rightarrow}{L}$ of L exists for the game of figure 3.25. Then L does not satisfy the requirement of invariance with respect to sequential agent splitting.

Proof The two different ways of sequential agent splitting in the game of figure 3.25 in fact lead to a contradiction. Figure 3.26 summarizes the argument of the proof. At the top of figure 3.26 we find the game G of figure 3.25. Two arrows point to two standard forms G^1 and G^2 with two agents for each player. Both games are obtainable from G by repeated sequential agent splitting.

G has only the two agents 11 and 21. The game G^1 results from G by first splitting of an agent 12 for agent 11's choice β and then splitting off an agent 22 for agent 21's choice β. In G^1 the agents 11 and 21 form a semicell $\hat{G}^1$. The choice between α and γ does not matter unless the other agents 12 and 22 both choose $-\beta$. In every ε-perturbation G^1_ε of G^1 this semicell $\hat{G}^1$ corresponds to a cell $\hat{G}^1_\varepsilon$.

For sufficiently small ε the solution $L(\hat{G}^1_\varepsilon)$ of the cell is (γ, γ). This follows by a comparison of the Nash-products for (α, α) and (γ, γ) which for small ε are near to 21 and 32, respectively. Let $\bar{G}^1_2$ be the truncation of G^1_ε with respect to G^1_ε and L. For $\varepsilon \rightarrow 0$ the payoffs of $\bar{G}^1_\varepsilon$ approach those of the game G^3 shown below G^1 in figure 3.26. In this sense we may say that G^3 is the "limit truncation" of G^1 with respect to $\hat{G}^1_\varepsilon$ and L. A comparison of Nash-products in G^3 shows that for sufficiently small ε we must have $L(\bar{G}^1_\varepsilon) = (\beta, \beta)$.

Cell consistency and truncation consistency of L lead to the conclusion that $L(G^1_\varepsilon)$ prescribes the choices β, γ, β, γ to the agents 11, 12, 21, 22 in that order. Obviously the same is true for the limit solution $\underset{\rightarrow}{L}(G^1)$. Invariance with respect to sequential agent splitting requires that the limit solution of G^1 corresponds to that of G. Therefore we must have $\underset{\rightarrow}{L}(G) = (\beta, \beta)$.

A similar argument is indicated by the right-hand side of figure 3.26. The game G^2 results from G by splitting off agents for the choice α. The cell formed by 12 and 22 in the ε-perturbation G^1_ε of G^1 has the solution (β, β). The "limit truncation" G^5 shows that we must have $\underset{\rightarrow}{L}(G) = (\alpha, \alpha)$. ∎

Remark Could the result be avoided by a more restrictive definition of a cell that would narrow down the applicability of the cell and truncation consistency requirement? A more restrictive definition of a cell would have to cover those substructures that correspond to subgames in the ε-perturbed standard form. Therefore note that G^1 and G^2 can be inter-

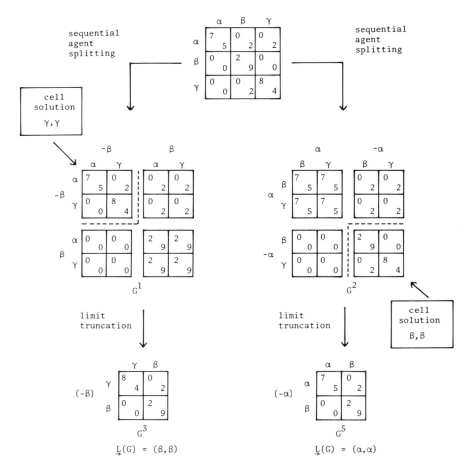

Figure 3.26
Proof of the impossibility theorem. Player 1's payoffs are shown above, and player 2's payoffs below. Agents 11 and 21 choose between α and γ in G^1 and between β and γ in G^2. Agents 12 and 22 choose between β and $-\beta$ in G^1 and between α and $-\alpha$ in G^2.

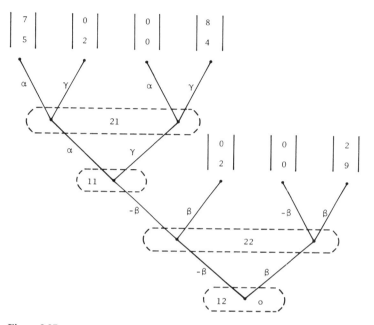

Figure 3.27
The extensive game Γ^1 whose standard form agrees with G^1 in figure 3.26

preted as the standard forms of two extensive forms Γ^1 and Γ^2 both of which have subgames corresponding to the respective semicells formed by agents 11 and 12. These extensive forms are shown in figures 3.27 and 3.28. Consequently the impossibility result cannot be avoided by a more restrictive definition of cells.

Interpretation We draw the conclusion that it is by no means irrelevant whether a choice α, β, or γ has a sequential structure. Games where a simultaneous choice has to be made can be different from others where the decision is split into two steps involving choices between "α or β" and γ in the first step and between α and β in the second step. If we do not want to give up the idea of a solution function altogether, we must abolish one of the properties that lead to the impossibility result. Among those properties invariance with respect to sequential agent splitting seems to be the least compelling one. But it does not appear to be an unreasonable idea that risk comparisons among three alternatives may be changed by the imposition of a sequential structure.

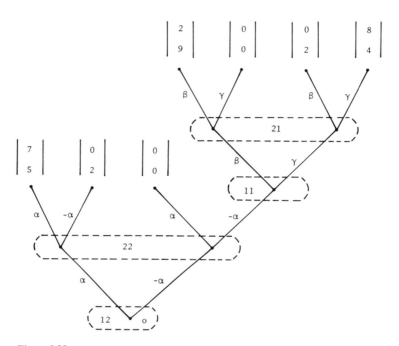

Figure 3.28
The extensive game Γ^2 whose standard form agrees with G^2 in figure 3.26

After all, consider the fact that after a decision between "α or β" and γ has been made in favor of "α or β," alternative γ has become irrelevant, and the risk comparisons may look quite different from those that would arise in a simultaneous choice situation. Different sequential orders may require different ways of looking at the situation. Even if it is not easy to understand why this should be so, it is reasonable to suppose that the basic reason for the impossibility result must be searched in this direction.

The proof of the impossibility result makes use of the fact that both ways of sequential agent splitting in figure 3.26 reduce the risk-dominance comparisons to comparisons in 2×2 games that result from G by removing α, β, or γ from the pure strategy sets of both players. The three comparisons that can be made in this way result in an intransitive pattern: (α, α) dominates (β, β) and (β, β) dominates (γ, γ), but (γ, γ) dominates (α, α). Moreover each way of sequential agent splitting removes one of the three comparisons, namely that between (α, α) and (β, β) in the case of G^1 and that between (γ, γ) and (α, α) in the case of G^2. Thus we can see already here that the impossibility result is connected to intransitivities of risk dominance. We shall return to the phenomenon in chapter 5 (section 5.4) after introducing our general definition of risk dominance.

3.13 Decomposition and Reduction

As we have shown in section 3.11, cell consistency and truncation consistency reduce the task of finding solutions for decomposable games to the simpler one of finding solutions for indecomposable games. An indecomposable game may be further simplified by the elimination of superfluous strategic possibilities. We will look at the elimination of inferior choices, duplicate classes, and semiduplicate classes. These concepts have already been mentioned in the introduction of the chapter. The partial invariance properties with respect to the elimination of such superfluous strategic possibilities were also mentioned there, as well as the difficulties confronting stronger requirements of a similar nature.

Our solution concepts permit the simultaneous elimination of all inferior choices in indecomposable games, the simultaneous elimination of all duplicate classes in indecomposable games without inferior choices, and the simultaneous elimination of all semiduplicate classes in indecomposable games without inferior choices and duplicate classes. The solution is not changed by these operations. This is expressed by the three partial invariance properties.

In section 3.11 we defined extensions of solution functions for indecomposable games to decomposable games. In a similar fashion we will define extensions of solution functions for irreducible games to general games. Irreducible games are indecomposable games without inferior choices, duplicate classes, and semiduplicate classes.

Unfortunately we cannot subdivide the extension of a solution function for irreducible games to general games into two steps, one from irreducible games to decomposable games and another from decomposable games to general games. This is because the application of one of the three elimination operations to an indecomposable game may produce a decomposable game.

If we speak of reduction as opposed to decomposition, we mean the application of the three elimination operations. Decomposition into a cell and the truncation with respect to this cell substitutes the analysis of two games for the analysis of one game. Reduction simply reduces the size of the game to be analyzed. The procedure of decomposition and reduction described by the flowchart of figure 3.29 shows how both types of operations interact in the determination of the solution of a general game.

Stability Sets

Let $G = (\Phi, H)$, with

$$\Phi = \underset{i \in N}{\times} \Phi_i = \underset{ij \in M}{\times} \Phi_{ij}, \tag{3.13.1}$$

be a game in standard form, and let $\phi_{ij} \in \Phi_{ij}$ be a choice of an agent $ij \in M$. The set of all hybrid combinations $b_{i \setminus ij} q_{.i}$ such that ψ_{ij} is a local best reply to $b_{i \setminus ij} q_{.i}$ is denoted by $S_{ij}(b_{i \setminus ij} q_{.i})$. This set is called the *stability set* of ψ_{ij}. The stability set of ψ_{ij} may be described as the set of all hybrid combinations $b_{i \setminus ij} q_{.i}$ such that ψ_{ij} is in the local best reply set $A_{ij}(b_{i \setminus ij} q_{.i})$ (see section 2.7).

Elimination of Inferior Choices

As before, let $G = (\Phi, H)$ be a game in standard form with (3.13.1), and let $ij \in M$ be an agent in G. A choice $\phi_{ij} \in \Phi_{ij}$ is called *inferior to a choice* $\psi_{ij} \in \Phi_{ij}$ if we have

$$S_{ij}(\phi_{ij}) \subset S_{ij}(\psi_{ij}). \tag{3.13.2}$$

A choice $\phi_{ij} \in \Phi_{ij}$ is called *inferior* if it is inferior to at least one other choice $\psi_{ij} \in \Phi_{ij}$. Choices that are not inferior to any other choice are called *noninferior*. For every $ij \in M$, let Ψ_{ij} be the set of all noninferior choices of agent ij. Obviously Ψ_{ij} cannot be empty. Define

$$\Psi = \underset{i \in N}{\times} \Psi_i = \underset{ij \in M}{\times} \Psi_{ij}. \tag{3.13.3}$$

The game $G' = (\Psi, H')$ that results from $G = (\Phi, H)$ by narrowing the choice sets in Φ to Ψ (see section 2.6) is called the game that *results from G by elimination of inferior choices*.

Comment Consider a choice ϕ_{ij} that is *weakly dominated* by a choice ψ_{ij} in the sense that for every $\phi_{-ij} \in \Phi_{-ij}$ player i's payoff $H_i(\phi_{ij}\phi_{-ij})$ is not greater than $H_i(\psi_{ij}\phi_{-ij})$ and smaller than $H_i(\psi_{ij}\phi_{-ij})$ for at least one $\phi_{-ij} \in \Phi_{-ij}$. A weakly dominated choice is always inferior, but an inferior choice need not be weakly dominated.

We feel that in the framework of our theory the notion of an inferior choice is more relevant than that of a weakly dominated choice. A Bayesian player will always play a best reply to his expectations on the other players, that is, to a joint mixture $q_{.i}$. The games to which our solution function is applied are interior substructures of standard forms with perfect recall. Such games have the local best-reply property (see section 2.7). This has the consequence that a behavior strategy b_i which is a best reply to $q_{.i}$ assigns positive probabilities only to such choices that are local best replies to $b_i q_{.i}$. Therefore a choice is superfluous if it is less suitable as a local best reply than another one. This idea is expressed by condition (3.13.2) in the definition of an inferior choice.

Duplicates and Semiduplicates

Two choices ϕ_{ij} and ψ_{ij} of an agent ij in a standard from $G = (\Phi, H)$ are called *duplicates* if the condition

$$H(\phi_{ij}\phi_{-ij}) = H(\psi_{ij}\phi_{-ij}) \tag{3.13.4}$$

is satisfied for every $\phi_{-ij} \in \Phi_{-ij}$. They are called *semiduplicates* if instead of (3.13.4) the weaker condition

$$H_i(\phi_{ij}\phi_{-ij}) = H_i(\psi_{ij}\phi_{-ij}) \tag{3.13.5}$$

is satisfied for every $\phi_{-ij} \in \Phi_{-ij}$. Obviously both the duplicate and semi-duplicate relations are equivalence relations. Equivalence classes with respect to relations that contain more than one element are called *duplicate classes* and *semiduplicate classes*, respectively.

Remarks (Equation 3.13.4) continues to hold if ϕ_{-ij} is replaced by an arbitrary hybrid combination $b_{i \setminus ij} q_{.i}$. The same is true for (3.13.5) if ϕ_{ij} and ψ_{ij} are semiduplicates.

Elimination of Duplicate Classes and Semiduplicate Classes

Let R_{ij} be that subset of agent ij's local-strategy set B_{ij} that contains all choices without duplicates and the centroids $c(\Lambda_{ij})$ of all duplicate classes Λ_{ij} in Φ_{ij}. It is clear that R_{ij} is an admissible new choice set of agent ij (see section 2.6).
Define

$$R = \underset{i \in N}{\times} R_i = \underset{ij \in N}{\times} R_{ij}. \tag{3.13.6}$$

The game $G' = (R, H')$ that results from $G = (\Phi, H)$ by narrowing the choice sets in Φ to R is called the game that *results from G by elimination of duplicate classes*. The game that *results from G by elimination of semiduplicate classes* is defined analogously. Instead of the duplicate classes, the semiduplicate classes are removed from Φ_{ij} and replaced by their centroids.

Comment   Unlike the definition of inferior choices which is based on local best-reply properties, the definition of duplicates and semiduplicates is in terms of payoffs. Two choices, ϕ_{ij} and ψ_{ij}, with the same stability set need not be semiduplicate because payoffs may differ where both choices fail to be local best replies. One may ask why we approach the conceptual problems behind inferior choices, on the one hand, and duplicates and semiduplicates, on the other, differently. We feel that this is justified in view of important differences between the elimination of inferior choices and the elimination of duplicate and semiduplicate classes. The arguments in favor of the removal of inferior choices are considerations of comparative strategic suitability. The elimination operations for duplicate and semiduplicate classes do not really remove strategic alternatives but simply stipulate that choices that are in some sense indistinguishable are used with equal probabilities. Structural indistinguishability is similar to symmetry. Payoff relationships underly the definition of isomorphisms. This suggests payoff-oriented notions of duplicates and semiduplicates.

Partial Invariance Properties

At least at first glance it seems reasonable to require that the solution of a game not be changed by the elimination of inferior choices, duplicate classes, or semiduplicate classes. Unfortunately, such requirements cannot be imposed in full generality.

The order in which the three operations of elimination are applied successively does sometimes influence the final result. After the elimination of inferior choices, some semiduplicates may become duplicates; after the elimination of semiduplicate classes, choices may be inferior that were not inferior before. A choice that is inferior in a decomposable game may be a duplicate or a semiduplicate in a truncation of this game.

To avoid conflicts with cell consistency and truncation consistency, we adopt the view that properties related to the three operations should be strictly local; that is, they should not apply directly to a decomposable game but rather to the indecomposable games that arise in the computation of its solution. This means that cell decomposition is given priority over the three elimination operations.

Of the three elimination operations, elimination of inferior choices is clearly the most important one. We shall require that elimination of inferior choices does not change the solution of any indecomposable games. Among the remaining two operations it seems reasonable to give precedence to the elimination of duplicate classes since duplicates are more closely related to each other than semiduplicates. These considerations lead us to the following partial invariance requirements:

1. *Partial invariance with respect to inferior choices.* A solution function L for a complete class $\mathcal{G} \subseteq \mathcal{I}(\mathcal{R})$ is called *partially invariant with respect to inferior choices* if $L(G) = L(G')$ holds for every indecomposable game $G \in \mathcal{G}$ and the game G' that results from G by elimination of inferior choices.

2. *Partial invariance with respect to duplicates.* A solution function L for a complete class $\mathcal{G} \subseteq \mathcal{I}(\mathcal{R})$ is called *partially invariant with respect to duplicates* if $L(G) = L(G')$ holds for every indecomposable game $G \in \mathcal{G}$ without inferior choices and for the game G' that results from G by elimination of duplicate classes.

3. *Partial invariance with respect to semiduplicates.* A solution function L for a complete class $\mathcal{G} \subseteq \mathcal{I}(\mathcal{R})$ is called *partially invariant with respect to semiduplicates* if $L(G) = L(G')$ holds for every indecomposable game $G \in \mathcal{G}$ without inferior choices and with duplicate classes and for the game G' that results from G by elimination of semiduplicate classes.

Irreducible Games

A game G in standard form is called *irreducible* if it is indecomposable and has no inferior choices, duplicate classes, or semiduplicate classes. Other games are called *reducible*.

Extension

Let $\mathcal{G}'$ be the subclass of all irreducible games in a complete class $\mathcal{G} \subseteq \mathcal{I}(\mathcal{R})$. Moreover let L' be a solution function for $\mathcal{G}'$. On the basis of L' we will construct a solution function L for $\mathcal{G}$ that will be called the *extension of L' to $\mathcal{G}$*. The extension is defined recursively by the following properties:

1. For $G \in \mathcal{G}'$ we have $L(G) = L'(G)$.

2. If $G \in \mathcal{G}$ is fully decomposable, then $L(G)$ is the composition of the elementary cell solutions.

3. If $G \in \mathcal{G}$ is partially decomposable, then $L(G)$ is the composition of the main truncation and the elementary cell solutions.

4. If $G \in \mathcal{G}$ is an indecomposable game with inferior choices, then we have $L(G) = L(G')$, where G' is the game that results from G by elimination of inferior choices.

5. If $G \in \mathcal{G}$ is an indecomposable game without inferior choices and with duplicate classes, then we have $L(G) = L(G')$, where G' is the game that results from G by elimination of duplicate classes.

6. If $G \in \mathcal{G}$ is an indecomposable game without inferior choices and without duplicate classes but with semiduplicate classes, then we have $L(G) = L(G')$, where G' is the game that results from G by elimination of semiduplicate classes.

It has to be shown that these properties determine a unique solution function. This is done by the following lemma:

LEMMA 3.13.1 (Extension lemma) Let $\mathcal{G}'$ be the subclass of all irreducible games in a complete class $\mathcal{G} \subseteq \mathcal{I}(\mathcal{R})$. Moreover let L' be a solution function for $\mathcal{G}'$. Then there is one and only one solution function L for $\mathcal{G}$ with properties 1 through 6.

Proof We have to show (1) that $L(G)$ is uniquely determined by all six properties and (2) that L is a solution function (i.e., a function that assigns an equilibrium point to every $G \in \mathcal{G}$). Both assertions are proved by induction on the total number Z of choices of all agents in G. The assertions are trivially true for $Z = 1$. Suppose that they hold for total numbers of choices up to $Z - 1$. Let G be a game whose total number of choices is Z. Exactly one of the six properties is applicable to G. If G is irreducible, then $L(G)$ is a uniquely determined equilibrium point. If G is decomposable, the compositions in properties 2 and 3 are uniquely determined equilibrium points (see the composition lemma 3.11.1). If one of the properties 4, 5, and 6 applies, it can be seen immediately that $L(G)$ is a uniquely determined equilibrium point of G. All properties relate the solution of G to solutions of games with a smaller total number of choices. ■

Comment The extension defined earlier will be used as a part of our solution concept. It permits us to define a solution function for the class $\mathcal{I}(\mathcal{R})$ of all interior substructures of standard forms with perfect recall, starting from a solution function for the subclass of irreducible games in $\mathcal{I}(\mathcal{R})$. In this way we want to secure cell consistency, truncation consistency, and the three partial invariance properties as well as invariance with respect to isomorphisms. We have to show that we really reach this aim. This will be done by an "extension theorem." The proof will not immediately follow the theorem. It will be based on several results to be derived first.

THEOREM 3.13.1 (Extension theorem)   Let $\mathscr{G}'$ be the subclass of all irreducible games in a complete class $\mathscr{G} \subseteq \mathscr{I}(\mathscr{R})$. Let L' be a solution function for $\mathscr{G}'$ that is invariant with respect to isomorphisms. Then the extension L of L' to $\mathscr{G}$ is cell consistent, truncation consistent, partially invariant with respect to inferior choices, duplicates, and semiduplicates and invariant with respect to isomorphisms. Moreover there is no other solution function for $\mathscr{G}$ that agrees with L' on $\mathscr{G}'$ and satisfies these six requirements.

LEMMA 3.13.2 (Lemma on partial invariance properties)   Under the assumptions of the extension theorem 3.13.1 the extension L is partially invariant with respect to inferior choices, duplicates, and semiduplicates.

Proof   The assertion is an immediate consequence of properties 4, 5, and 6, in the definition of the extension. ∎

LEMMA 3.13.3 (Lemma on consistency properties)   Under the assumptions of the extension theorem 3.13.1 the extension L is cell consistent and truncation consistent.

Proof   To prove the lemma, it is sufficient to show by induction on the number m of agents that no violation of cell consistency and truncation consistency can occur for decomposable games. The same argument as in the second part of the proof of the extension theorem 3.11.1 can be used here. We need not repeat this argument. ∎

LEMMA 3.13.4 (Lemma on invariance with respect to isomorphisms)   Under the assumptions of the extension theorem 3.13.1 the extension L is invariant with respect to isomorphisms.

Proof   Let G and G' be two isomorphic games in $\mathscr{G}$, and let f be an isomorphism from G to G'. We have to show $L(G') = f(L(G))$ is trivially true in the case $Z = 1$, where both games have only one agent with only one choice. Assume that the assertion holds for total numbers of choices up to $Z - 1$ where both games have only one agent with only one choice. Assume that the assertion hold for total numbers of choices up to $Z - 1$, and let G and G' be games with Z choices. We distinguish three cases:

1. G and G' are irreducible.

2. G and G' are indecomposable and reducible.

3. G and G' are decomposable.

Since an isomorphism carries inferior choices, duplicate classes, semi-duplicate classes, and cells to inferior choices, duplicate classes, semiduplicate classes, and cells, respectively, the three cases are mutually exclusive and exhaustive.

Nothing needs to be proved in case 1. Consider case 2. One of the properties 4, 5, and 6 in the definition of the extension is applicable. Let $\hat{G}$ and $\hat{G}'$ be the games that result from G and G', respectively, by the application of the relevant elimination operation. Obviously an isomorphism $\hat{f}$ from $\hat{G}$ to $\hat{G}'$ is induced by f. Since $\hat{G}$ and $\hat{G}'$ have fewer than Z choices, we have $L(\hat{G}') = \hat{f}(L(\hat{G}))$. It follows that $L(G') = f(L(G))$ holds.

Now consider case 3. The isomorphism f carries an elementary cell of G to an elementary cell of G'. An elementary cell will always have fewer than Z choices. Therefore f carries the solution of an elementary cell of G to the solution of its counterpart in G'. It follows that the main truncation of G (if it exists) is carried to the main truncation of G'. Since the main truncation has fewer than Z choices, the solution of the main truncation is carried to the solution of the main truncation of G'. It follows that we have $L(G') = f(L(G))$. ∎

Proof of the Extension Theorem 3.13.1   The results obtained up to now show that the extension L satisfies the six requirements. It remains to show that there is no other solution function $\bar{L}$ for $\mathscr{G}$ that agrees with L' on $\mathscr{G}'$ and satisfies the six requirements. Let Z be the smallest number such that a game $G \in \mathscr{G}$ with a total number of Z choices and with $\bar{L}(G) \neq L(G)$ can be found. Let G be a game of this kind. Obviously G must be reducible since L and $\bar{L}$ agree with L' for reducible games.

Suppose that G is indecomposable. The three partial invariance properties applied to $\bar{L}$ together with the properties 4, 5, and 6 of L lead to the conclusion that we must have $\bar{L}(G) = L(G)$ because the relevant elimination operation yields a game with less than Z choices. This shows that G cannot be indecomposable.

Now assume that G is decomposable. In the same way as in the proof of the extension theorem in section 3.10, it can be seen that properties 2 and 3 of L can be obtained as a consequence of cell consistency, truncation consistency, and invariance with respect to positive linear payoff transformations. The result of applying properties 2 or 3 is achieved if truncations are formed for one elementary cell after the other. The order of doing this does not matter (see the first part of the proof of the extension theorem 3.11.1). This shows that properties 2 and 3 also hold for $\bar{L}$. Since the elementary cells and the main truncation of G (if it exists) have fewer than Z choices, we must have $\bar{L}(G) = L(G)$. This shows that G cannot be decomposable either. Consequently L is the only solution function for $\mathscr{G}$ that agrees with L' and $\mathscr{G}'$ and satisfies the six requirements. ■

Comment   The extension theorem 3.13.1 shows that the way in which we reduce the task of solving games to the task of solving irreducible games is not an arbitrary one. If we want to obtain the properties mentioned in the theorem, we have essentially no alternative approach.

However, the partial invariance properties with respect to inferior choices, duplicates, and semiduplicates are very weak. Our definition severely restricts the applicability of the three elimination operations to special classes of games. The elimination also always removes all inferior choices, duplicate classes, or semiduplicate classes at the same time. Nothing is said about what happens if only some inferior choices, duplicate classes, or semi-duplicate classes are removed. It is doubtful whether significantly stronger forms of the partial invariance properties can be satisfied together with cell consistency and truncation consistency by any solution function for the class of all interior substructures of standard forms with perfect recall.

The Procedure of Decomposition and Reduction

As before, let L' be a solution function for the subclass $\mathscr{G}'$ of irreducible games in a complete class $\mathscr{G} \subseteq \mathscr{I}(\mathscr{R})$ such that L' is invariant with respect to isomorphisms, and let L be the extension of L' to $\mathscr{G}$. On the basis of the knowledge of L' we can compute $L(G)$ for every $G \in \mathscr{G}$. In principle, the recursive definition of the extension enables us to do this, so it is not really necessary to say more about the computation of L on the basis of L'. Yet additional insight may be gained, it is not without interest by a more detailed procedure, where the task of finding the solution is broken down into a succession of elementary steps. Also the application of the solution concept becomes easier by a more detailed description of what should be done in which order to which games. These questions will be answered by the *procedure of decomposition and reduction* described by the flowchart of

figure 3.29. In the following discussion we will give further explanations
and show why under the assumptions made earlier the procedure succeeds
in computing the solution $L(G)$ of the game G under consideration.

Dynamic Notation

A dynamic notational convention is used in the flowchart. At any step of
the procedure there will be a list of games $G^1, \ldots, G^m$. The length of this
list and the meaning of the symbol G^k varies during the procedure.

Solution Agreement

At any point during the procedure every game G^k on the list will have the
property that its solution $L(G^k)$ agrees with the solution $L(G)$ of the game
G to be solved, as far as the agents in G^k are concerned. We shall refer to
this property of G^k as *solution agreement*. Wherever a new game is introduced, one of the six requirements satisfied by L in view of the extention
theorem will guarantee solution agreement for the newly introduced game.

Course of the Procedure

The procedure starts at rectangle 1 where the game G to be solved becomes
the game G^1. Then the procedure moves to rhomboid 2. Rhomboids contain questions whose answers determine the next step. Rectangles contain
operations to be performed including the change of names.

If G^1 is decomposable, the procedure moves from rhomboid 2 to rectangle 3. Whenever rectangle 3 is reached, the indexes of $G^1, \ldots, G^m$ are
moved up by 1. Thereby these games receive the new names $G^2, \ldots, G^{m+1}$.
An arbitrarily selected elementary cell of G^2 (formerly G^1) becomes the new
game G^1. Cell consistency guarantees solution agreement for the new game
G^1.

Rhomboid 4 can be reached from rectangle 3 or directly from rhomboid
2. In both cases G^1 is indecomposable at rhomboid 4. Elimination of
inferior choices at rectangle 5 creates a new game G^1 whose solution
agreement is guaranteed by partial invariance with respect to inferior
choices.

If at rhomboid 4 the game G^1 has no inferior choices, then rhomboid 6
is reached. Solution agreement for the new game G^1 created at rectangle 7
follows by partial invariance with respect to duplicates.

If rhomboid 8 is reached, then G' has neither inferior choices nor dupli-

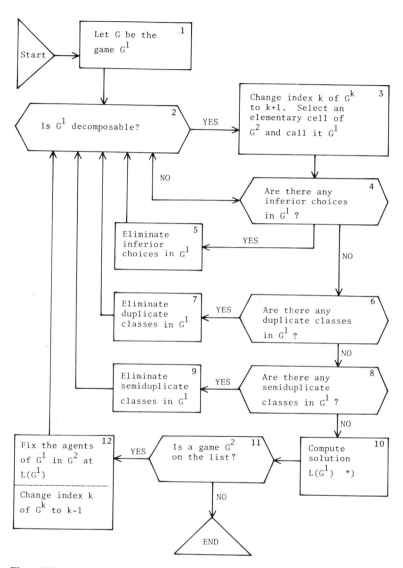

Figure 3.29
Flowchart for the procedure of decomposition and reduction. [*By solution agreement $L(G^1)$ agrees with $L(G)$ for the agents in G^1.]

cate classes. Solution agreement of the new game G^1 created at rectangle 9 follows by partial invariance with respect to semiduplicates.

The procedure always turns back to rhomboid 2 after rectangles 5, 7, and 9. Therefore at rectangle 10 the game G^1 will be irreducible. The computation of $L(G^1) = L'(G^1)$ determines the components of $L(G)$ for the agents in G^1.

If at rhomboid 11 the game G^1 is not the only one on the list, the procedure must have passed rectangle 3 at least once in the past. Consider the last time when this has happened. At that time G^1 was an elementary cell, say G' of the game now called G^2. In view of cell consistency and solution agreement we have $L(G^1) = L(G')$. This shows that at rectangle 12 the truncation of G^2 with respect to G' and L is formed by fixing the agents on G^1 at $L(G^1)$. Temporarily, this truncation will be called G^2 in rectangle 12, but then the indexes are moved down by 1 and the truncation becomes the new game G^1 to be considered at rhomboid 2. Solution agreement for this game follows by truncation consistency.

Note that as long as there are several games $G^2, \ldots, G^m$ on the list, G^k is derived by reduction at rectangles 5, 7, and 9 and/or by truncation at rectangle 12 from an elementary cell of G^{k+1} ($k = 1, \ldots, m - 1$). In the same way the game G^m is derived from G. This is still true if at rhomboid 11 we have $m = 1$. Consequently the local solution strategies have been computed for all agents as soon as at rhomboid 11 there is no game G^2 on the list.

Comment Compared with the recursive definition of the extension by all six properties, the procedure of decomposition and reduction is nearer to an algorithm. To write a computer program on the basis of the flowchart of figure 3.29, one would have to supply subprograms for the rhomboids and rectangles. As an example consider rhomboid 2. For every nonempty proper subset G of agents we would have to check whether a linear equation system derived from (3.10.7) can be solved with positive $\alpha_i(\psi_{-c})$.

The computational procedure may seem unwieldy because of the number of agents and choices involved. However, this impression is misleading. In economics and other social sciences game models often have a special structure that permits many complications to be excluded beforehand. It may, for example, be clear from the structure of the model that the answer to the question in rhomboid 2 is always "no."

Our theory will be based on a solution function for the class $\mathscr{I}(\mathscr{R})$ of all interior substructures of standard forms with perfect recall. It will be the extension of a solution function for the subclass of all irreducible games in $\mathscr{I}(\mathscr{R})$. In this way we obtain a solution function with the six properties mentioned in the extention theorem 3.13.1. Moreover the extension theorem axiomatizes the way in which we connect solutions of reducible games to solutions of irreducible games.

4 The Tracing Procedure

4.1 A Bayesian Approach

The mathematical basis of our solution concept is the tracing procedure, which is a mathematical procedure for defining rational outcomes for non-cooperative games by use of a Bayesian conceptual framework. Bayesian decision theory has been eminently successful in analyzing one-person decision problems involving uncertainty. The purpose of the tracing procedure is to extend the Bayesian approach to the n-person decision problems posed by n-person noncooperative games. Such games pose decision problems involving uncertainty because they require each player to choose his strategy without knowing the strategies the other players will choose. We will first define the tracing procedure for situations where the players use *mixed strategies*. But in section 4.15 we will extend our definition to situations where they use *behavior strategies*.

4.2 Strategies

We will consider an n-person noncooperative game G, in which any player i ($i = 1, \ldots, n$) has K_i *pure strategies*. For strategies and strategy combinations we will use the same notations as in chapter 2, except that for convenience we will now number player i's pure strategies as $\phi_i^1, \ldots, \phi_i^k, \ldots,$ $\phi_i^{K_i}$. But we will also go on using the symbol ϕ_i as a generic notation for any pure strategy of player i. The number of elements in any finite set S will be denoted as $|S|$.

Since $|\Phi_i| = K_i$, for $i = 1, \ldots, n$, the number of complete pure-strategy combinations ϕ in the game will be

$$|\Phi| = K = \prod_{i \in N} K_i, \tag{4.2.1}$$

where N is the set of all n players. On the other hand, the number of *i-incomplete* combinations ϕ_{-i} will be

$$|\Phi_{-i}| = K_{-i} = \frac{K}{K_i}, \quad \text{for } i = 1, \ldots, n. \tag{4.2.2}$$

A *mixed strategy* q_i of any player can be regarded as a probability vector $q_i = (q_{i1}, \ldots, q_{iK_i})$, where q_{ik} ($k = 1, \ldots, K_i$) is the probability that this mixed strategy assigns to the pure strategy ϕ_i^k. We must of course have

$$q_{ik} \geq 0, \quad \text{for } k = 1, \ldots, K_i, \tag{4.2.3}$$

$$\sum_{k=1}^{K_i} q_{ik} = 1. \tag{4.2.4}$$

Thus the *set* $Q_i = \{q_i\}$ of player i's mixed strategies will be a closed simplex of $(K_i - 1)$ dimensions.

If a given mixed strategy q_i concentrates all probability on one pure strategy ϕ_i^k, then it will be called an *improper* mixed strategy and will be identified with this pure strategy; thus we will write $q_i = \phi_i^k$. But, if q_i assigns positive probabilities to all of i's pure strategies, it will be called *completely* mixed. A mixed strategy will be called *proper* if it is not improper, and it will be called *incompletely* mixed if it is not completely mixed.

In general, the set $Z(q_i)$ of all pure strategies that a given mixed strategy q_i uses with positive probabilities will be called the *carrier* of q_i.

Suppose that the probability vectors $q_i^o, q_i^1, \ldots, q_i^M$ satisfy an equation of the form

$$q_i^o = \sum_{m=1}^{M} \lambda_m q_i^m, \quad \text{with } \lambda_1, \ldots, \lambda_M \geq 0 \text{ and } \sum_{m=1}^{M} \lambda_m = 1. \tag{4.2.5}$$

Then we will say that the mixed strategy q_i^o is a *probability mixture* (or a convex combination) of the mixed strategies $q_i^1, \ldots, q_i^M$.

The *set* $Q = \{q\} = Q_1 \times \cdots \times Q_n$ of all *complete* mixed-strategy combinations q will be a closed polyhedron of $(\bar{K} - n)$ dimensions, where

$$\bar{K} = \sum_{i \in N} K_i. \tag{4.2.6}$$

Q will be called the *strategy space* of the game.

In contrast, the set $Q_{-i} = \{q_{-i}\} = Q_1 \times \cdots \times Q_{i-1} \times Q_{i+1} \times \cdots \times Q_n$ of all *i-incomplete* strategy combinations q_{-i} will be a closed polyhedron of $\bar{K}_{-i} - (n - 1) = \bar{K}_{-i} - n + 1$ dimensions, where

$$\bar{K}_{-i} = \sum_{\substack{j \neq i \\ j \in N}} K_j = \bar{K} - K_i, \quad \text{for } i = 1, \ldots, n. \tag{4.2.7}$$

As was stated in section 2.3, joint mixtures over *i*-incomplete pure strategy combinations ϕ_{-i}—that is, probability distributions over the set $\Phi_{-i} = \{\phi_{-i}\}$—will be denoted by symbols having a subscript $._i$. (But the subscript $-i$ will always indicate an *i*-incomplete mixed-strategy combination.) Now suppose the $(n-1)$ players other than player i use the i-incomplete mixed-strategy combination $q_{-i} = (q_1, \ldots, q_{i-1}, q_{i+1}, \ldots, q_n)$. According to the probability multiplication law the implication is then that any i-incomplete pure-strategy combination $\phi_{-i} = (\phi_1, \ldots, \phi_{i-1}, \phi_{i+1}, \ldots, \phi_n)$ will be realized with a probability

$$r_{\cdot i}(\phi_{-i}) = \prod_{\substack{j \neq i \\ j \in N}} q_j(\phi_j). \tag{4.2.8}$$

Here $q_j(\phi_j)$ denotes the probability that player j's mixed strategy q_j assigns to the pure strategy ϕ_j. [Thus, if $\phi_j = \phi_j^k$, then $q_j(\phi_j) = q_{jk}$.] This probability distribution $r_{\cdot i}$ will be called the joint mixture *generated* by q_{-i}. For simplicity of notation, we will also use brackets to denote this joint mixture: $r_{\cdot i} = [q_{-i}]$ and $r_{\cdot i}(\phi_{-i}) = [q_{-i}](\phi_{-i})$.[1]

4.3 Payoff Vectors

Any payoff $H_i(\phi)$ that a given player i would derive from any one of the K possible complete pure-strategy combinations ϕ in the game will be called a *pure* payoff. For each player i, the K-vector $v_i(G)$ listing the K possible pure payoffs $H_i(\phi)$, $\phi \in \Phi$, that he can obtain in game G will be called his *personal vector*. Finally, the nK-vector $v(G)$ listing the components of all n personal vectors will be called the *defining vector* of game G.

We will say that a given game G is *free of payoff ties* if each of its n personal vectors $v_i(G)$ consists of K *different* numbers—that is, if, for each $i \in N$, $\phi \neq \phi'$ implies that $H_i(\phi) \neq H_i(\phi')$.

If we know all of player i's pure payoffs $H_i(\phi)$, we can always compute his (expected) payoff $H_i(q)$ for any mixed-strategy combination $q = (q_1, \ldots, q_n)$ by using the probability multiplication law. In particular we can write

$$H_i(q) = \sum_{\phi \in \Phi} \prod_{i \in N} q_i(\phi_i) H_i(\phi_1, \ldots, \phi_n). \tag{4.3.1}$$

4.4 The Phrase "Almost All"

Suppose that $X = \{x\}$ is a finite-dimensional set. We will say that a given mathematical statement is true for *almost all* elements x of this set X if the set $\bar{X}(S)$ of all those elements x for which this statement S is *not* true can be covered by a closed subset X^* of X, having measure zero in X.

We need, however, a somewhat more complicated definition for the phrase "almost all games" because the set of all possible games has infinitely many dimensions. We propose the following definition.

The size of any game G can be characterized by the vector $\sigma = (n; K_1, \ldots, K_n)$, specifying the number of players and the number of pure strategies available to each player. We will call σ the *size vector* of game G. For any possible size vector σ, the set $\mathscr{G} = \mathscr{G}(\sigma) = \mathscr{G}(n; K_1, \ldots, K_n)$ of all games G possessing this vector σ as their size vector will be called the *size class* corresponding to σ.

Every game G in this size class $\mathscr{G}(\sigma)$ will have a defining vector $v(G)$ that lists exactly nK payoffs. If we identify each game G with its defining vector $v(G)$, then we can identify the size class $\mathscr{G}(\sigma)$ itself with the set of all possible real vectors of size nK, that is, with an nK-dimensional Euclidean space.

On the basis of these identifications, we can define the phrase "almost all games" as follows. A given mathematical statement S will be said to be true for *almost all games* if, for every possible size class $\mathscr{G}$, the set $\overline{\mathscr{G}}(S)$ of all games G in $\mathscr{G}$ for which this statement S is *not* true can be covered by a closed subset $\mathscr{G}^*$ of $\mathscr{G}$, having measure zero in $\mathscr{G}$.

4.5   Best Replies and Equilibrium Points

Best replies, vector best replies, and equilibrium points were defined in section 2.3. We now state some further properties of these concepts.

Obviously a given strategy q_i^* of player i is a best reply to an i-incomplete strategy combination q_{-i} if and only if

$$H_i(q_i^* q_{-i}) \geq H_i(q_i q_{-i}), \quad \text{for all } q_i \text{ in } Q_i. \tag{4.5.1}$$

On the other hand, q_i^* is a *strong* best reply to q_{-i} if and only if, for any strategy q_i *different* from q_i^*, condition (4.5.1) is satisfied with a *strong* inequality sign $>$. For the reader's convenience, we restate the following lemma, already stated in section 2.3:

LEMMA 4.5.1   A mixed strategy q_i^* is a best reply to a given i-incomplete strategy combination q_{-i} if and only if all pure strategies ϕ_i in the carrier $Z(q_i^*)$ of q_i^* are themselves best replies to q_{-i}.

By this lemma, once we know all pure-strategy best replies to q_{-i}, we can easily obtain all best replies to q_{-i}: the latter will be simply all possible *probability mixtures* of these pure-strategy best replies.

For any given (pure or mixed) strategy q_i^*, the set $P(q_i^*)$ of all i-incomplete strategy combinations q_{-i} *to which* this strategy q_i^* is a best reply is called the *stability set* of q_i^*. According to lemma 4.5.1 our main interest will be in the stability sets $P(\phi_i^k)$ of the various *pure* strategies ϕ_i^k of each player i. These will be called *pure* stability sets. For shorter notation, we will write

$$P(\phi_i^k) = P_i^k, \quad \text{for } i = 1, \ldots, n, \quad k = 1, \ldots, K_i. \tag{4.5.2}$$

From (4.5.1) we see that any stability set is always defined by *weak* inequalities. Consequently we can state:

LEMMA 4.5.2   The stability set $P(q_i^*)$ of any strategy q_i^* of player i is always a *closed* subset (possibly empty) of the set Q_{-i} of all i-incomplete strategy combinations.

Lemma 4.5.1 implies the following lemma:

LEMMA 4.5.3   The stability set $P(q_i^*)$ of any mixed strategy q_i^* is simply the *intersection* of the stability sets P_i^k, $P_i^{k'}, \ldots$ of the pure strategies $\phi_i^k \, \phi_i^{k'}, \ldots,$ belonging to the *carrier* $Z(q_i^*)$ of q_i^*.

Clearly every possible i-incomplete strategy combination q_{-i} will always have at least one best reply. Recalling lemma 4.5.1 this implies:

LEMMA 4.5.4   The pure stability sets $P_i^1, \ldots, P_i^{K_i}$ always cover the entire polyhedron $Q_{-i} = \{q_{-i}\}$.

In any game G free of payoff ties, the intersection of two different pure stability sets P_i^k and $P_i^{k'}$, $k \neq k'$, is either empty or is a hypersurface (hyperboloid) $\mathcal{H}^{kk'}$ defined by the equation

$$H_i(\phi_i^k q_{-i}) = H_i(\phi_i^{k'} q_{-i}), \quad \text{for all } q_{-i} \text{ in } Q_{-i}. \tag{4.5.3}$$

$\mathcal{H}^{kk'}$ will be a hyperboloid because, by (4.3.1), the last equation is multilinear in the probabilities q_{jk} for $j = 1, \ldots, i - 1, i + 1, \ldots, n$ and for $k = 1, \ldots, K_j$. [In contrast, in a game with payoff ties, some sets P_i^k and $P_i^{k'}$, $k \neq k'$, may coincide because (4.5.3) may become an identity.] Consequently:

LEMMA 4.5.5   For *almost all* games G (i.e., for those without payoff ties) the following statement is true: for almost all incomplete strategy combinations q_{-i} (for those not lying on the boundary of two pure stability sets P_i^k and $P_i^{k'}$), the set of all best replies q_i^* to q_{-i} will consist of a *unique pure* strategy $q_i^* = \phi_i$.

In view of condition (4.5.1) and lemma 4.5.1, equilibrium points can be characterized by the following property. Any complete strategy combination q will be an *equilibrium point* if and only if every component strategy q_i of q satisfies the two requirements:

$$H_i(\phi_i^k q_{-i}) = H_i(\phi_i^{k'} q_{-i}), \tag{4.5.4}$$

if both ϕ_i^k and $\phi_i^{k'}$ are in the carrier $Z(q_i)$ of q_i, and

$$H_i(\phi_i^k q_{-i}) \geq H_i(\phi_i^{k'} q_{-i}), \tag{4.5.5}$$

if ϕ_i^k belongs to $Z(q_i)$ while $\phi_i^{k'}$ does not.

Another implication of lemma 4.5.1 is that any *strong* equilibrium point must be in *pure* strategies. (Yet not all pure-strategy equilibrium points are strong, even though *almost all* games do have the property that *all* of their pure-strategy equilibrium points, if they have any, are strong.)

We will now state three more, easily verifiable, lemmas:

LEMMA 4.5.6 Suppose that both strategies q_i^* and q_i^{**} are best replies to a given i-incomplete strategy combination q_{-i}. Then any probability mixture q_i^o of q_i^* and of q_i^{**} will be likewise a best reply to q_{-i}.

LEMMA 4.5.7 Suppose that the two i-incomplete strategy combinations q_{-i}^* and q_{-i}^{**} agree in $(n-2)$ components but differ in player j's strategy, so that $q_k^* = q_k^{**}$ for all $k \neq i$ and $\neq j$ but $q_j^* \neq q_j^{**}$. Moreover suppose that strategy q_i is a best reply to both q_{-i}^* and q_{-i}^{**}. Then q_i will be a best reply also to any i-incomplete strategy combination q_{-i}^o that can be obtained from q_{-i}^* (or from q_{-i}^{**}) by replacing player j's strategy q_j^* (or q_j^{**}) with a strategy q_j^o that is a probability mixture of q_j^* and of q_j^{**}.

The last two lemmas imply:

LEMMA 4.5.8 Suppose that:

1. The three strategy combinations q^*, q^{**}, and q^o agree in all components except in the strategy of player i.

2. The first two strategy combinations q^* and q^{**} are equilibrium points.

3. Strategy q_i^o is a probability mixture of strategies q_i^* and q_i^{**}.

Then the third strategy combination, q^o, will be likewise an equilibrium point.

4.6   Vector Best Replies

Using the concept of vector best replies, we define a *stability set P*(q*) of a complete strategy combination q** as the set of all complete strategy combinations *q to which q** is a vector best reply. We can now state the following simple lemmas:

LEMMA 4.6.1   A given complete strategy combination q will be an equilibrium point if and only if q is a vector best reply to itself.

LEMMA 4.6.2   A given complete strategy combination q will be an equilibrium point if and only if it lies within its own stability set $P^*(q)$.

LEMMA 4.6.3   The stability set $P^*(q)$ of an equilibrium point q will be a *full-dimensional* subset of the game's strategy space $Q = \{q\}$ if and only if q is a *strong* equilibrium point.

DEFINITION OF THE TRACING PROCEDURE

4.7   The Prior Probability Distributions (Prior Strategies)

By the tracing procedure we are trying to model a process of *convergent expectations*, to be called the *outcome-selection process*, by which rational players will come to adopt, and to *expect* each other to adopt, one particular equilibrium point $q^* = (q_1^*, \ldots, q_n^*)$ as the outcome for a given non-cooperative game G. At the beginning of this outcome-selection process, the players will as yet lack any specific theory predicting the strategies to be used by the other players. Accordingly, each player j will express his expectations about the strategy choice of any other player $i \neq j$ in the form of a *subjective probability distribution* $p_i = (p_{i1}, \ldots, p_{iK_i})$ over player i's pure strategies, where p_{ik} $(k = 1, \ldots, K_i)$ is the subjective probability that player j assigns to the hypothesis that player i will actually use his kth pure strategy ϕ_i^k. These subjective distributions p_i will be called *prior probability distributions*, or simply *priors*.

An important assumption of our model is that *all* other players $j \neq i$ will associate the *same* prior probability distribution p_i with any given player i. This assumption is based on the fact that, as we will see later, our theory always uniquely specifies the prior distribution p_i to be assigned to the strategies of each player i in any given case, and our model will assume that all the $(n-1)$ fellow players of player i will always use this particular prior distribution p_i prescribed by our theory.

The specific prior distributions our theory uses will be described in chapter 5. As we shall see, in some cases it uses *uniform* prior distributions, assigning *equal* prior probabilities to all eligible strategies of a given player. In other cases it uses *nonuniform* priors, assigning *higher* prior probabilities to those pure strategies that would be best replies to the other players' expected strategies in *wider* ranges of possible situations that may arise in the game.

Mathematically every prior distribution p_i is a probability distribution over player i's pure-strategy set $\Phi_i = \{\phi_i\}$ and therefore has the nature of a *mixed strategy* by player i. Of course its game-theoretical interpretation is quite different from that of an ordinary mixed strategy q_i. First of all, the probabilities q_{ik} associated with a mixed strategy q_i are *objective* probabilities freely chosen by player i *himself*, whereas the probabilities p_{ik} associated with a prior probability distribution p_i are *subjective* probabilities expressing the *other* players' expectations about player i's likely behavior.

Moreover, if another player, say, player j, expects player i to use a (proper) mixed strategy q_i, then this amounts to making the assumption that i will intentionally randomize between two or more different pure strategies. In contrast, if player j assigns a prior probability distribution p_i to i's pure strategies, then he is making no such assumption. Even if j were fully convinced that i would always use a pure strategy and would never randomize between different pure strategies, it might still make very good sense for him to assign subjective probabilities p_{ik} to i's different pure strategies ϕ_i^k—as long as j were uncertain about *which* particular pure strategy player i would in fact use.

The n-tuple of all n prior probability distributions will be written as $p = (p_1, \ldots, p_n)$, whereas the $(n-1)$-tuple obtained from p by omitting the ith component p_i will be written as $p_{-i} = (p_1, \ldots, p_{i-1}, p_{i+1}, \ldots, p_n)$. We will call p a *(complete) prior vector* and p_{-i} an *i-incomplete prior vector*.

In our model an *i-incomplete prior vector* p_{-i} will be used to summarize player i's expectations about the other $(n-1)$ players' strategies. On the other hand, a complete prior vector p will be used to summarize all n players' *mutual* expectations about each other's behavior.

Because each prior p_i has the mathematical form of a mixed strategy by the relevant player i, we will sometimes call p_i player i's *prior strategy*, and the vectors p and p_{-i} *prior strategy combinations*.

4.8   The Prediction Problem

Now suppose we know the n players' mutual expectations as expressed by the prior vector p. How can we then predict the strategy combination $q = (q_1, \ldots, q_n)$ these players will actually use in the game? For convenience we will call this problem simply the *prediction problem*. The purpose of the tracing procedure is to offer a solution to this very problem.

Note that, at least at an informal level, this problem as well as its close relatives continually arise in applied game-theoretical analysis and in economic and other social-science research. For example, a game theorist may argue that in a given game G, the players will use the strategies $q_1, \ldots, q_n$ corresponding to a specific equilibrium point q because a "sufficiently large" subset of these players will expect with a "sufficiently high" probability that q will be the outcome of the game, and this fact will be known to all players, giving them a strong incentive to use their q-strategies. Or an economist may argue that the price of a given commodity X will be (say) \$5 because a "sufficiently large" percentage of the producers will expect with a "sufficiently high" probability that the price of X will be \$5, and so on.

The tracing procedure can be regarded as a formally precise restatement of informal arguments of this kind.

4.9   The "Naive" Bayesian Approach

On a formal level the simplest answer to the prediction problem would be this. In our model, given the complete prior vector p entertained by the players, and expectations of each player i about the other players' strategies will be expressed by the i-incomplete prior vector p_{-i} derived from p. Accordingly, one may argue that each player i will simply choose a strategy q_i^o that is his best reply to this prior vector p_{-i}; that is, he will choose a strategy $q_i = q_i^o$ maximizing his expected payoff

$$H_i^o = H_i(q_i p_{-i}). \tag{4.9.1}$$

By the same token one may propose to define the *outcome* of the game as the strategy combination $q^o = (q_1^o, \ldots, q_n^o)$, consisting of these best reply strategies q_i^o for the various players. In other words, the outcome would be defined as a *vector best reply q^o to the complete prior vector p*. This simpleminded outcome-selection theory we will call the *naive Bayesian approach*.

Unfortunately this simple theory will not work because this best reply strategy combination q^o will generally not be an equilibrium point of the game, and therefore it cannot be the outcome chosen by a rational outcome-selection theory.

The difficulty with the naive Bayesian approach can also be stated as follows: The players' initial information about each other's behavior is expressed by the complete prior vector $p = (p_1, \ldots, p_n)$. We will say that p expresses the players' *first-order* information about each other's likely behavior. In contrast, any information the players may have about each other's *reactions* to this first-order information will be called *second-order* information. Thus, if the naive Bayesian approach were right in concluding that the players' reaction to p would be to adopt the best-reply strategy combination $q^o = (q_1^o, \ldots, q_n^o)$, then this would be second-order information.

Now in cases where q^o is not an equilibrium point, the basic objection to the naive Bayesian approach is this. If q^o is not an equilibrium point, then there must be at least one player i whose q^o-strategy q_i^o is not a best reply to the strategy combination $q_{-i}^o = (q_1^o, \ldots, q_{i-1}^o, q_{i+1}^o, \ldots, q_n^o)$ supposedly used by the other players. Yet the naive Bayesian approach still predicts that player i will use this strategy q_i^o.

This prediction is consistent with the *first-order* information that the naive Bayesian approach attributes to him because, by definition, q_i^o is a best reply to p_{-i}. But the prediction is inconsistent with the *second-order* information he is supposed to have (to the effect that the other players will use the strategy combination q_{-i}^o) because, by assumption, q_i^o is not a best reply to q_{-i}^o.

Yet, even though the naive Bayesian approach as such would not be a satisfactory outcome-selection theory, it can be used as a starting point for a more satisfactory theory. In fact, the tracing procedure always starts with the strategy combination q^o, representing a vector best reply to the prior vector p which is assumed to express the players' first-order information. Whereas the naive Bayesian approach would make the players act as if they completely disregarded all their second-order information, the tracing procedure does gradually feed back this second-order information more and more into the system, until in the end all the discrepancy between first- and second-order information completely disappears.

At the beginning of the tracing procedure, just as under the naive Bayesian approach, the players' *expectations* (first-order information) about each other's behavior are given by the prior vector p, whereas their tentative *strategy plans* (second-order information) are given by the best-reply strategy combination q^0. As the tracing procedure progresses, both p and q^0 are subjected to systematic and continuous transformations until both of them finally converge to a specific equilibrium point $q^* = (q_1^*, \ldots, q_n^*)$ of the game. Thus at the end of the tracing procedure both the players' actual strategy plans and expectations about each other's strategy plans will correspond to the same equilibrium point q^*, representing the predicted outcome of the game.

4.10 The Linear Tracing Procedure

The tracing procedure has two versions which we will distinguish by the adjectives "linear" and "logarithmic." In this section we will describe the linear tracing procedure. The logarithmic version of the procedure will be described later.

The linear procedure is based on a one-parameter family of auxiliary games Γ^t with $0 \leq t \leq 1$. In any game Γ^t, every player i $(i = 1, \ldots, n)$ will have the same strategy set $Q_i = \{q_i\}$ as he would have in the original game G we are analyzing. But his payoff function H_i^t in game Γ^t will be

$$H_i^t(q_i q_{-i}) = t H_i(q_i q_{-i}) + (1 - t) H_i(q_i p_{-i}), \tag{4.10.1}$$

where H_i is his payoff function in the original game G. Clearly we have

$$H_i^1(q_i q_{-i}) = H_i(q_i q_{-i}) \tag{4.10.2}$$

so that $\Gamma^1 = G$. On the other hand,

$$H_i^0(q_i q_{-i}) = H_i(q_i p_{-i}). \tag{4.10.3}$$

Thus Γ^0 is a game of a rather special structure in which the payoff H_i^0 of each player i will depend only on his *own* strategy q_i and will be independent of the *other* players' strategy combination q_{-i}. [This can be seen from the fact that the right-hand side of (4.10.3) does not contain q_{-i}. It does of course contain the incomplete prior vector p_{-i}. But the latter is actually a basic parameter of game Γ^0, independent of the strategies $q_1, \ldots, q_n$ actually used by the players in Γ^0.]

Consequently game Γ^0 naturally decomposes into n mutually independent and separate maximization problems, one for each player. Because of this rather unusual property, Γ^0 will be called a *separable game*.

Note that Γ^0 is conceptually closely related to what we have described as the naive Bayesian approach: as a comparison of (4.9.1) and (4.10.3) will show, game Γ^0 requires each player i to maximize the *same* payoff function $H_i^o = H_i^0 = H_i(q_i p_{-i})$ as he would have to maximize under the latter approach.

Note also that by (4.10.1), the payoff function H_i^t of any player i in any auxiliary game Γ^t will be simply a convex combination of his payoff function $H_i = H_i^1$ in the original game $G = \Gamma^1$ and of his payoff function $H_i^o = H_i^0$ in the separable game Γ^0.

In discussing various auxiliary games Γ^t and in comparing them with the original game G, we will often make use of the following convenient terminology. Instead of saying that (say) q_i^* is a best reply to q_{-i} in game Γ^t (or in game G), we will say simply that q_i^* is a Γ^t best reply (or a G best reply) to q_{-i}. Likewise, instead of saying that q is an equilibrium point in game Γ^t (or in game G), we will say that q is a Γ^t equilibrium point (or is a G equilibrium point, etc.).

Using lemma 4.5.5 and the separability of game Γ^0, we can now state:

LEMMA 4.10.1   For *almost all* games G, the following statement is true: for *almost all* choices of the prior vector p, the resulting separable game $\Gamma^0 = \Gamma^0(G, p)$ will have exactly *one* equilibrium point q^o, and the latter will be a *strong* Γ^0 equilibrium point in *pure* strategies.

This lemma can also be stated in the following slightly different form:

LEMMA 4.10.2   For any given choice of p, *almost all* games G will give rise to a separable game $\Gamma^0 = \Gamma^0(G, p)$ having only *one* equilibrium point q^o, which is a *strong* equilibrium point in *pure* strategies.

Obviously this Γ^0 equilibrium point q^o is identical to the best-reply strategy combination q^o we have discussed in connection with the naive Bayesian approach (in section 4.9).

By the definition of equilibrium points, every Γ^t equilibrium point $q = (q_1, \ldots, q_n)$ will have the property that each component q_i of q will be a Γ^t best reply to the $(n-1)$-tuple q_{-i} formed by the other $(n-1)$ components. Alternatively, in terms of the concept of G best replies, any Γ^t equilibrium point can be characterized as follows:

LEMMA 4.10.3   If a strategy combination $q = (q_1, \ldots, q_n)$ is a Γ^t equilibrium point, then each component q_i of q will be a G best reply to the probability distribution

$$p(i, t, q) = t[q_{-i}] + (1 - t)[p_{-i}]. \tag{4.10.4}$$

Here $[q_{-i}]$ and $[p_{-i}]$ are the probability distributions generated by q_{-i} and p_{-i}, respectively, over the set Φ_{-i} of all possible i-incomplete pure-strategy combinations ϕ_{-i}. On the other hand, $t[q_{-i}] + (1 - t)[p_{-i}]$ denotes the probability distribution generated by the assumption that probability distribution $[q_{-i}]$ will apply with probability t, whereas probability distribution $[p_{-i}]$ will apply with probability $(1 - t)$.

Equivalently, $t[q_{-i}] + (1 - t)[p_{-i}]$ is that particular probability distribution that assigns to each i-incomplete pure-strategy combination ϕ_{-i} the probability

$$t[q_{-i}](\phi_{-i}) + (1 - t)[p_{-i}](\phi_{-i}). \tag{4.10.5}$$

The preceding lemma follows from equation (4.10.1). By this equation, in game Γ^t, if player i uses strategy q_i while the other players use strategy combination q_{-i}, then his payoff will be $H_i^t = tH_i(q_i q_{-i}) + (1 - t)H_i(q_i p_{-i})$. This is of course the same payoff expectation that player i would have in game G itself if he used strategy q_i, whereas the other players with probability t used strategy combination q_{-i} and with probability $(1 - t)$ used the strategy combination corresponding to the prior vector p_{-i}.

For any auxiliary game Γ^t, the set of all equilibrium points in Γ^t will be called E^t. By Nash's (1951) existence theorem for equilibrium points, all of these sets E^t will be nonempty. Let $X = X(G, p)$ be the graph of the correspondence $t \to E^t$ for $0 \le t \le 1$. X will be typically a collection of pieces of one-dimensional algebraic curves, though in degenerate cases it may also contain isolated points and/or subsets of more than one dimension.

Each point x of X will have the mathematical form $x = (t, q)$, where q is an equilibrium point of game Γ^t. We will refer to t as the *t-coordinate* and to q as the *strategy part* of this point x. Since $t \in I$, where $I = [0, 1]$ is the closed unit interval, whereas $q \in Q$, where Q is a copy of the strategy space of game G (because by construction every game Γ^t will have the same strategy space Q as G itself has), our graph X will always be a subset of the closed cylindrical set $Y = I \times Q$.[2]

Suppose that graph X contains a path L connecting a point $x^0 = (0, q^o)$, corresponding to an equilibrium point q^o of the separable game Γ^0, with a point $x^1 = (1, q^*)$, corresponding to an equilibrium point q^* of the original game $\Gamma^1 = G$. Then L will be called a *feasible path*, whereas x^0 and x^1 will be called the *starting point* and the *end point* of this path L, respectively. Moreover the strategy part q^* of this end point x^1 will be called the *outcome* selected by path L. This strategy combination q^* can be rationally selected as outcome of the game because it will always be an equilibrium point of the original game G.

We can now define the *linear tracing procedure*: it consists in selecting an outcome q^* for any noncooperative game G by tracing (i.e., by following) a feasible path L from its starting point $x^0 = (0, q^o)$ to its end point $x^1 = (1, q^*)$.

For any given pair (G, p), we will call the linear tracing procedure *feasible* if the graph $X = X(G, p)$ contains *at least* one feasible path L, and we will call it *well defined* if X contains *exactly* one feasible path L. In the latter case this unique feasible path L will be called a *distinguished path*. Since this distinguished path L will depend on both G and p, we will write $L = L(G, p)$.

For any given pair (G, p) for which the linear tracing procedure is well defined, this procedure will always select a unique equilibrium point

$$q^* = (q_1^*, \ldots, q_n^*) = T(G, p) \tag{4.10.6}$$

of game G as outcome. It is important to note that operator T of the linear tracing procedure is a *two-argument* operator: in other words, the outcome q^* it selects for game G will depend (and in most cases very crucially depend) not only on the nature of game G but also on the prior-distribution vector p the players are assumed to use.

As we shall see:

1. For *any* possible pair (G, p), the linear tracing procedure is always feasible but is not always well defined.

2. For any specific vector p of prior probability distributions, *almost all* games G will give rise to a well-defined linear tracing procedure.

Thus the linear tracing procedure will select a unique solution q^* in "almost all" cases, but not in "all" cases. Yet we want a method that always works. Therefore in section 4.13 we will describe the logarithmic tracing procedure which is always well defined. (Moreover, as we shall see, it is a true generalization of the linear tracing procedure in the sense that in all cases where also the linear tracing procedure is well defined, it always selects the same equilibrium point q^* as the linear procedure would select for outcome.)

4.11 Three Numerical Examples for the Linear Tracing Procedure

Consider the two-person non-zero-sum game G, defined by figure 4.1. For convenience, player 1's pure strategies have been denoted by a and b, whereas those of player 2 by c and d. (Thus $\phi_1^1 = a$, $\phi_1^2 = b$, $\phi_2^1 = c$ and $\phi_2^2 = d$.)

The game has two equilibrium points in pure strategies: $E_1 = (a, c)$ and $E_2 = (b, d)$. It also has one equilibrium point in mixed strategies: $E_3 = (q_1^*, q_2^*)$, where $q_1^* = (q_{11}^*, q_{12}^*) = (\frac{4}{5}, \frac{1}{5})$ while $q_2^* \doteq (q_{21}^*, q_{22}^*) = (\frac{1}{3}, \frac{2}{3})$.

The strategy space of the game can be represented by the square $ABCD$ of figure 4.2 (or of figure 4.3). Any point X of this square will represent a mixed-strategy pair $q = (q_1, q_2) = ((q_{11}, q_{12}), (q_{21}, q_{22}))$. In particular, the vertical distances XV and UX will represent the probabilities q_{11} and $q_{12} = 1 - q_{11}$, respectively, whereas the horizontal distances XZ and YX will represent the probabilities q_{21} and $q_{22} = 1 - q_{21}$ (see figure 4.2). Accordingly the two pure-strategy equilibrium points E_1 and E_2 will be represented by the corner points A and C, since $E_1 = (a, c) = ((1, 0), (1, 0))$ while $E_2 = (b, d) = ((0, 1), (0, 1))$. On the other hand, the mixed-

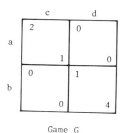

Game G

Figure 4.1

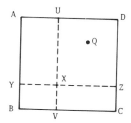

Figure 4.2

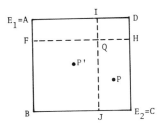

Figure 4.3

strategy equilibrium point E_3 will be represented by point Q (see figure 4.3).

Note that the *stability sets* of the equilibrium points $E_1 = A$ and $E_2 = C$ will be the closed rectangles $AFQI$ and $QJCH$. This can be verified as follows: For the equilibrium point $E_1 = (a, c)$ to be a vector best reply to any given strategy pair $q = (q_1, q_2) = ((q_{11}, q_{12}), (q_{21}, q_{22}))$, it is both necessary and sufficient that a should be a best reply to q_2 and that c should be a best reply to q_1 so that

$$H_1(a, q_2) = 2q_{21} \geq H_1(b, q_2) = q_{22} \tag{4.11.1}$$

while

$$H_2(q_1, c) = q_{11} \geq H_2(q_1, d) = 4q_{12}.$$

But $q_{11} + q_{12} = q_{21} + q_{22} = 1$. Therefore (4.11.1) is equivalent to the requirements that

$$q_{11} \geq \tfrac{4}{5} \quad \text{and} \quad q_{21} \geq \tfrac{1}{3}. \tag{4.11.2}$$

Yet the points q satisfying these requirements are exactly the points of the closed rectangle $AFQI$. This is so because, by construction, point Q has the coordinates $q_{11}^* = \tfrac{4}{5}$ and $q_{21}^* = \tfrac{1}{3}$. The statement concerning the rectangle $QJCH$ can be verified in a similar way.

By the same reasoning the stability set of the pure-strategy pair $B = (b, c)$ will be the closed rectangle $IQHD$, whereas that of the pure-strategy pair $D = (a, d)$ will be $FBJQ$. It will be noted that in accordance with lemma 4.6.2, the two equilibrium points $E_1 = A$ and $E_2 = C$ lie *within* their own stability sets, whereas the two non-equilibrium-point strategy pairs $B = (b, c)$ and $D = (a, d)$ lie *outside* their own stability sets.

Finally, the stability set of the mixed-strategy equilibrium point $E_3 =$

$Q = (q_1^*, q_2^*)$ is a one-point set consisting of only $E_3 = Q$ itself. This follows from lemma 4.5.1: if a given point $q = (q_1, q_2)$ lies within the stability set of E_3, then q_2 must have the properties that *both* a and b are best replies to q_2, which means that q must lie on the line FG. At the same time q_1 must have the property that *both* c and d are best replies to q_1, which means that q must lie on the line HI. Consequently q must lie on the intersection of FH and of IJ, so that we must have $q = E_3 = Q$.

First Example Suppose the players' initial expectations correspond to a prior vector $p = (p_1, p_2)$ lying in the relative interior of the stability set of either pure-strategy equilibrium point (both of which are strong equilibrium points with full-dimensional, i.e., two-dimensional, stability sets). For instance, suppose that $p_1 = (p_{11}, p_{12}) = (\frac{1}{3}, \frac{2}{3})$ whereas $p_2 = (p_{21}, p_{22}) = (\frac{1}{6}, \frac{5}{6})$. This prior vector p is represented by point P on figure 4.3 and therefore lies in the relative interior of the rectangle $QJCH$, the stability set of equilibrium point $E_2 = C$.

In cases like this the naive Bayesian approach would work quite well: the vector best reply to this prior vector is the strategy pair $q^o = (q_1^o, q_2^o) = (b, d) = E_2 = C$, which is of course an equilibrium point of the game. Thus we could follow the naive Bayesian approach and define the outcome as this equilibrium point E_2. This is what we will do. As we shall see, also the linear tracing procedure selects E_2 as the outcome for this choice of the prior vector p.

It may be noted that in small games, such as our example (and even in somewhat larger games with a simple structure), the linear tracing procedure can be implemented with very little computation because all one has to do is to find the distinguished path $L = L(G, p)$ generated by the postulated prior vector p. But we have felt it may be helpful to the reader if, for the three tracing problems to be discussed, we provide a rather detailed analysis, not only of the distinguished path L itself but rather of the entire graph $X = X(G, p)$ used in the linear tracing procedure.

To implement the linear tracing procedure, we will first construct the separable auxiliary game Γ^0 generated by our prior vector p. By (4.10.3) the pure payoffs of this game Γ^0 will be as follows:

$$H_1^0(a, c) = H_1^0(a, d) = H_1(a, p_2) = \frac{2}{6} = \frac{1}{3}. \tag{4.11.3}$$

$$H_1^0(b, c) = H_1^0(b, d) = H_1(b, p_2) = \frac{5}{6}. \tag{4.11.4}$$

$$H_2^0(a, c) = H_2^0(b, c) = H_2(p_1, c) = \frac{1}{3}. \tag{4.11.5}$$

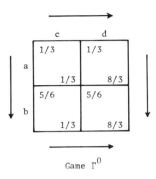

Game Γ^0

Figure 4.4

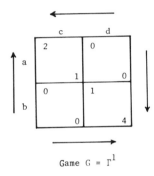

Game $G = \Gamma^1$

Figure 4.5

$$H_2^0(a,d) = H_2^0(b,d) = H_2(p_1,d) = \tfrac{8}{3}. \qquad\qquad (4.11.6)$$

The payoff matrix of Γ^0 is summarized in figure 4.4. For convenience, figure 4.5 reproduces the payoff matrix of the original game $G = \Gamma^1$.

The four arrows next to each matrix indicate the *best replies* to the various pure strategies. Thus the left-hand and the right-hand arrows show what strategies are player 1's best replies to strategies c and d, respectively (e.g., in figure 4.4 the left-hand arrow points down to show that player 1's best reply to strategy c is strategy b because $\tfrac{5}{6} > \tfrac{1}{3}$). On the other hand, the upper and the lower arrows show what strategies are player 2's best replies to strategies a and b. (The rather exceptional case, not arising in figures 4.4 and 4.5, where *both* pure strategies of a given player are best replies will be indicated by double-headed arrows, like $\updownarrow$ and $\leftrightarrow$.)

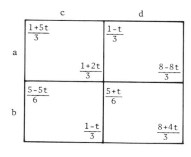

Game Γ^t

Figure 4.6

For any given 2 × 2 game the directions of the four arrows also indicate the locations of its pure-strategy equilibrium points. Since the two strategies associated with an equilibrium point must be mutually best replies to each other, a given field of a game matrix will correspond to an equilibrium point if and only if this field has both a vertical and a horizontal arrow pointing to it (like →↓, etc.).

By this criterion, game Γ^0 has only one pure-strategy equilibrium point, the strategy pair $(b, d) = C$. (Moreover it cannot have any mixed-strategy equilibrium point because strategy b strongly dominates strategy a, whereas strategy d strongly dominates strategy c.) In contrast, game $G = \Gamma^1$ has the two pure-strategy equilibrium points $(a, c) = A = E_1$ and $(b, d) = C = E_2$. As we have seen, it also has one mixed-strategy equilibrium point $E_3 = Q$.

In view of (4.10.1) we can obtain the payoff matrix of a generic auxiliary game Γ^t, with $0 \leq t \leq 1$, by taking a convex combination of the payoff matrices of games G and Γ^0, assigning weight t to G, and assigning weight $(1 - t)$ to Γ^0. This will yield the payoff matrix for game Γ^t shown in figure 4.6.

A comparison of figures 4.4 and 4.5 will show that as t moves from $t = 0$ to $t = 1$, the left-hand and the upper arrows must somewhere reverse their directions. Simple computation indicates that the left-hand arrow is reversed at the t-value $t = \frac{1}{5}$ since the equation

$$\frac{1 + 5t}{3} = \frac{5 - 5t}{6}$$

(4.11.7)

has this t-value as solution. (At this reversal point the left-hand arrow will of course become double-headed, like $\updownarrow$.) In contrast, the upper arrow is reversed at $t = 7/10$ since the equation

$$\frac{1 + 2t}{3} = \frac{8 - 8t}{3} \tag{4.11.8}$$

has this t-value as solution. This means that the various auxiliary games Γ^t for $0 \le t \le 1$ will have the following arrow patterns:

Region 1:

$0 \le t < \frac{1}{5}$.   Arrow pattern .

Region 2:

$t = \frac{1}{5}$.   Arrow pattern .

Region 3:

$\frac{1}{5} < t < \frac{7}{10}$.   Arrow pattern .

Region 4:

$t = \frac{7}{10}$.   Arrow pattern .

Region 5:

$\frac{7}{10} < t \le 1$.   Arrow pattern .

These arrow patterns show that auxiliary games Γ^t with $0 \le t < 7/10$ have only the one pure-strategy equilibrium point, $(b, d) = C$. (As in all these games strategy d strongly dominates strategy c, so these games have no mixed-strategy equilibrium point.)

On the other hand, all auxiliary games Γ^t with $7/10 \le t \le 1$ have two pure-strategy equilibrium points: $(a, c) = A$ and $(b, d) = C$. With the exception of game $\Gamma^{7/10}$ corresponding to $t = 7/10$, these games also have exactly one mixed-strategy equilibrium point $q(t) = (q_1(t), q_2(t))$, where

$$q_1(t) = \left(\frac{5t + 7}{15t}, \frac{10t - 7}{15t} \right), \tag{4.11.9}$$

$$q_2(t) = \left(\frac{t+1}{6t}, \frac{5t-1}{6t}\right).$$
                                                                                                    (4.11.10)

Note that if we set $t = 1$, then we obtain $q_1(1) = (\frac{4}{5}, \frac{1}{5})$ and $q_2(1) = (\frac{1}{3}, \frac{2}{3})$, so that $q(1) = E_3 = Q$.

Finally, game $\Gamma^{7/10}$ has the same three equilibrium points as the games Γ^t of region 5 do: $(a, c) = A$, $(b, d) = C$, and $q(t)$. But it also has infinitely many additional equilibrium points. This is so because now the two component strategies of $q(t) = q(7/10)$ take the form:

$$q_1(\tfrac{7}{10}) = (1, 0) = a,$$
                                                                                                    (4.11.11)

$$q_2(\tfrac{7}{10}) = (\tfrac{17}{42}, \tfrac{25}{42}).$$
                                                                                                    (4.11.12)

Yet by lemma 4.5.8, if both (a, c) and $(q_1(7/10), q_2(7/10)) = (a, q_2(7/10))$ are equilibrium points of game $\Gamma^{7/10}$, then so must be all strategy pairs

$$\bar{q}(\mu) = (a, \bar{q}_2(\mu)),$$
                                                                                                    (4.11.13)

where

$$\bar{q}_2(\mu) = (\mu, 1 - \mu) \quad \text{with } \tfrac{17}{42} \leq \mu \leq 1.$$
                                                                                                    (4.11.14)

If we represent the strategy space of this game $\Gamma^{7/10}$ by the square $ABCD$ of figure 4.7, then its equilibrium points will be represented by the one point $C = (b, d)$ and by the infinitely many points of the closed interval AR.

The first end point A of this interval will of course represent the pure-strategy equilibrium point (a, c), whereas the second end point R will represent the half-mixed equilibrium point $q(7/10) = \bar{q}(17/42) = (a, (17/42, 25/42))$. Consequently graph X of the linear tracing procedure will be as shown in figure 4.8.

As the figure shows, graph X has two unconnected branches, $CC'C''$ and

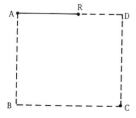

Figure 4.7

$A''A'RQ$. Branch $CC'C''$ corresponds to the same strategy pair $(b, d) = C$ in all auxiliary games Γ'. In our terminology all points $x = (t, (b, d))$ of $CC'C''$ have the same strategy part $(b, d) = C$. A branch with this property is called a *constant* branch. By the same token segment $A''A'$ of the second branch is a constant segment since, in the region $7/10 \leq t \leq 1$ where it is located, all its points correspond to the same strategy pair $(a, c) = A$. On the other hand, segment RQ of the second branch is a variable segment, because its points $x = (t, (q_1(t), q_2(t)))$ have a strategy part $q(t) = (q_1(t), q_2(t))$ which is a nonconstant function of t. Finally, segment $A'R$ is called a *jump* segment because the strategy part $\bar{q}(\mu)$ of its points varies from A to R' [or, more precisely, player 2's strategy varies from $c = (1, 0)$ to $q_2(7/10) = (17/42, 25/42)$, while player 1's strategy stays constant at a], even though the t-coordinate keeps the same value $t = 7/10$ along the entire segment $A'R$. [Thus, if we imagine t to represent time, we would have to say that player 2 "jumps"—at infinite speed—from strategy c to strategy $q_2(7/10)$.]

In nondegenerate cases *constant* branches and constant segments correspond to *strong* equilibrium points in *pure* strategies (as they do in our example). *Variable* segments correspond to equilibrium points in *mixed* strategies. Finally, *jump* segments correspond to situations where one player uses variable probability mixtures of two pure strategies while the other player or players use constant pure strategies.

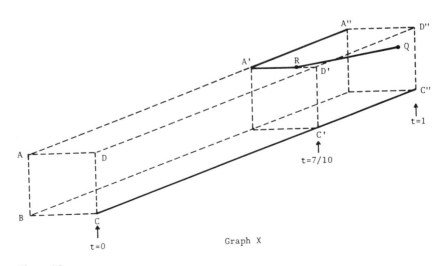

Graph X

Figure 4.8

Of the two branches, $A''A'RQ$ is restricted to the region $7/10 \le t \le 1$, whereas $CC'C''$ extends to the entire range $0 \le t \le 1$. Consequently $CC'C''$ is the only feasible path, and it yields equilibrium point $(b, d) = C = E_2$ as the outcome.

Second Example   Now we will assume that the players' initial expectations correspond to a prior vector $p = (p_1, p_2)$ lying *outside* the stability sets $AFQI$ and $QJCH$ of the two pure-strategy equilibrium points $E_1 = A$ and $E_2 = C$. For example, suppose that $p_1 = (\frac{1}{2}, \frac{1}{2})$ and $p_2 = (\frac{2}{3}, \frac{1}{3})$. This prior vector corresponds to point P' of figure 4.3.

This prior vector will yield the following separable auxiliary game Γ^0 (see figure 4.9). For convenience, figure 4.10 again reproduces the payoff matrix of the original game $G = \Gamma^1$.

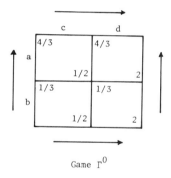

Game Γ^0

Figure 4.9

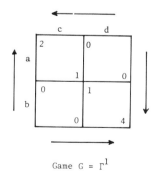

Game $G = \Gamma^1$

Figure 4.10

Γ^0 has only the one equilibrium point $(a, d) = D$. This is not an equilibrium point for the original game $G = \Gamma^1$. This means that at least one player will have to change his strategy during the tracing procedure. In fact, the decisive question is *which* player will be the one to shift. For example, if it is player 1 who shifts from strategy a to b, then from that point on the players will be using the strategy pair $(b, d) = C$, and the latter will be the actual outcome because no further strategy change will occur during the tracing procedure. In contrast, if it is player 2 who shifts from strategy d to strategy c, then from that point on the players will be using the strategy pair $(a, c) = A$, and this will be the actual outcome.

If we compare figures 4.9 and 4.10, then it becomes clear that the upper and the right-hand arrows must be reversed somewhere as t moves from $t = 0$ to $t = 1$. The nature of the outcome will depend on which arrow is reversed *first*. If the upper arrow is reversed first, then after this reversal we will have a game with an arrow pattern $\uparrow \overset{\leftarrow}{\to} \uparrow$, which means a game with $(a, c) = A$ as equilibrium point, indicating a shift by player 2 from strategy d to strategy c. In contrast, if the right-hand arrow is reversed first, then we will obtain a game with an arrow pattern $\uparrow \overset{\to}{\to} \downarrow$, which means a game with $(b, d) = C$ as equilibrium point, indicating a shift by player 1 from strategy a to strategy b. In either case the new equilibrium point arising after the first arrow reversal will emerge as the actual outcome. Thus in the first case the outcome will be $(a, c) = A = E_1$, whereas in the second case it will be $(b, d) = C = E_2$. (As we will see in the third example, in the degenerate case where the two arrows are reversed *simultaneously* at the same t-value, the linear tracing procedure will permit either player to shift his strategy, so that the players will be free to move to either E_1 or E_2—or even to the mixed-strategy equilibrium point E_3. In this case the linear tracing procedure will not be well defined.)

To find the t-values at which the two arrows are reversed, we have computed the payoff matrix of a generic auxiliary game Γ^t for $0 \leq t \leq 1$, by taking the appropriate convex combination of the payoff matrices for games G and Γ^0 in accordance with (4.10.1) (see figure 4.11).

Using this payoff matrix, we can conclude that the upper arrow will be reversed at $t = \frac{3}{5}$ because this t-value is the solution of the equation

$$\frac{1 + t}{2} = 2 - 2t. \tag{4.11.15}$$

On the other hand, the right-hand arrow will be reversed at $t = \frac{1}{2}$ since this t-value is the solution of the equation

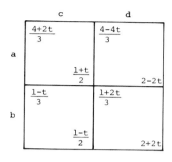

Game Γ^t

Figure 4.11

$$\frac{4-4t}{3} = \frac{1+2t}{3}.$$

(4.11.16)

This means that the right-hand arrow will be reversed *first*. As a result player 1 will shift his strategy from a to b, whereas player 2 will keep his strategy constant at d, and the solution will be $(b, d) = C = E_2$. A different choice of the prior vector p would of course have yielded the opposite result.)

A more detailed analysis is as follows. We obtain the following arrow patterns in the various auxiliary games Γ^t:

Region 1:

$0 \leq t < \frac{1}{2}$.   Arrow pattern ⌐⌐ .

Region 2:

$t = \frac{1}{2}$.   Arrow pattern ⌐⌐ .

Region 3:

$\frac{1}{2} < t < \frac{3}{5}$.   Arrow pattern ⌐⌐ .

Region 4:

$t = \frac{3}{5}$.   Arrow pattern ⌐⌐ .

Region 5:

$\frac{3}{5} < t \le 1$.   Arrow pattern ⌐→⌐ .

Thus all auxiliary games Γ^t with $0 \le t < \frac{1}{2}$ will have only the one pure-strategy equilibrium point $(a, d) = D$. In contrast, game $\Gamma^{1/2}$ will have the two pure-strategy equilibrium points $(a, d) = D$ and $(b, d) = C$. This, however, implies, in view of lemma 4.5.8, that all half-mixed strategy pairs of the form (q_1, d) will be likewise equilibrium points, with q_1 ranging over all possible mixed strategies of player 1 (see figure 4.12 where all points of the line DC are equilibrium points).

On the other hand, all games Γ^t with $\frac{1}{2} < t < \frac{3}{5}$ will have only the one pure-strategy equilibrium point $(b, d) = C$. Finally, all games Γ^t with $\frac{3}{5} < t \le 1$ will have the two pure-strategy equilibrium points $(b, d) = C$ and $(a, c) = A$. They will also have a mixed-strategy equilibrium point $q(t) = (q_1(t), q_2(t))$, where

$$q_1(t) = \left(\frac{5t + 3}{10t}, \frac{5t - 3}{10t}\right),\qquad\qquad (4.11.17)$$

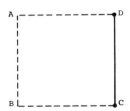

Figure 4.12

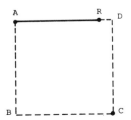

Figure 4.13

$$q_2(t) = \left(\frac{2t-1}{3t}, \frac{t+1}{3t}\right).$$

(4.11.18)

Note that for game $G = \Gamma^1$, we obtain $q(t) = q(1) = ((\frac{4}{5}, \frac{1}{5}), (\frac{1}{3}, \frac{2}{3})) = E_3 = Q$.

Among these games, game $\Gamma^{3/5}$ represents a rather special situation. In this game, equilibrium point $q(t) = q(\frac{3}{5})$ has the form:

$$q_1(\tfrac{3}{5}) = (1, 0) = a,$$

(4.11.19)

$$q_2(\tfrac{3}{5}) = (\tfrac{1}{9}, \tfrac{8}{9}).$$

(4.11.20)

In view of lemma 4.5.8, this implies that all half-mixed strategy pairs $\bar{q}(\mu) = (a, \bar{q}_2(\mu))$ will also be equilibrium points, where $\bar{q}_2(\mu) = (\mu, 1 - \mu)$, with $1/9 \leq \mu \leq 1$. Figure 4.13 shows the location of all equilibrium points in game $\Gamma^{3/5}$: they correspond to the points of the closed interval AR and to point C. Figure 4.14 shows the entire graph X of the linear tracing procedure.

Like the graph of figure 4.8, the new graph X also has two unconnected branches, $DD'C'C'''$ and $A'''A''RQ$. $DD'C'C'''$ consists of three segments. Segment DD' is a *constant* segment, on which the players always use the strategy pair $(a, d) = D$. $D'C'$ is a *jump* segment, on which player 1 shifts from strategy a to strategy b while player 2 keeps his strategy constant at d, and the t-coordinate stays constant at $t = \frac{1}{2}$. Finally, $C'C'''$ is again

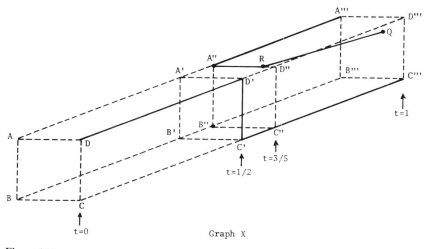

Graph X

Figure 4.14

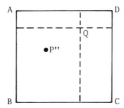

Figure 4.15

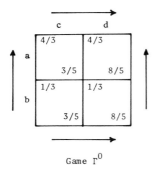

Game Γ^0

Figure 4.16

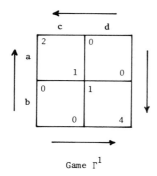

Game Γ^1

Figure 4.17

a constant segment, on which the players always use the strategy pair $(b, d) = C$.

Branch $A'''A''RQ$ also consists of three segments. $A'''A''$ is a constant segment, corresponding to $(a, c) = A$. $A''R$ is a jump segment, on which player 2 moves from strategy $(1, 0) = c$ to strategy $(1/9, 8/9)$ while player 1 keeps his strategy constant at a, and the t-coordinate stays constant at $t = 7/10$. Finally, RQ is a *variable* segment, on which the players use the mixed strategies $q_1(t)$ and $q_2(t)$, which are nonconstant functions of t.

Since branch $A'''A''RQ$ is restricted to the region $7/10 \le t \le 1$, the only feasible path is branch $DD'C'C'''$. At the end point C''' of this path, the players use the equilibrium point $(b, d) = C = E_2$. Therefore this equilibrium point $C = E_2$ is the outcome selected by the linear tracing procedure.

Third Example Now we will assume that the players' initial expectations are expressed by the prior vector $p = (p_1, p_2)$ with $p_1 = (\frac{3}{5}, \frac{2}{5})$ and $p_2 = (\frac{2}{3}, \frac{1}{3})$. If the strategy space of the game is represented by the square $ABCD$ of figure 4.15, then the new prior vector p will correspond to point P''. The payoff matrix of the separable auxiliary game Γ^0 generated by p is given in figure 4.16. Finally, for convenience, the payoff matrix of game $G = \Gamma^1$ itself is reproduced in figure 4.17.

A comparison of figures 4.16 and 4.17 will show that as we move from $t = 0$ to $t = 1$ during the tracing procedure, the upper and the right-hand arrows must somewhere reverse their directions. To find the t-values where these reversals occur, we have computed the payoff matrix of a generic auxiliary game Γ^t for $0 \le t \le 1$ (see figure 4.18).

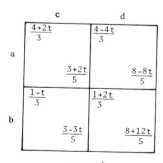

Game Γ^t

Figure 4.18

Clearly the upper arrow will be reversed at $t = \frac{1}{2}$ since this t-value is the solution of the equation

$$\frac{3 + 2t}{5} = \frac{8 - 8t}{5}. \tag{4.11.21}$$

But now the right-hand arrow will also be reversed at the same t-value $t = \frac{1}{2}$ since this t-value is the solution also of the equation

$$\frac{4 - 4t}{3} = \frac{1 + 2t}{3}. \tag{4.11.22}$$

As has already been stated, when two arrows are reversed simultaneously at the *same* t-value, then the linear tracing procedure will tend to be ill defined, and this is what will actually turn out to be the case in this example.

For the various auxiliary games Γ^t, $0 \leq t \leq 1$, the arrow patterns will be as follows:

Region 1:

$0 \leq t < \frac{1}{2}$. Arrow pattern

Region 2:

$t = \frac{1}{2}$. Arrow pattern

Region 3:

$\frac{1}{2} < t \leq 1$. Arrow pattern

Clearly all auxiliary games Γ^t with $0 \leq t < \frac{1}{2}$ will have only the one equilibrium point $(a, d) = D$. In contrast, game $\Gamma^{1/2}$ will have the three pure-strategy equilibrium points $(a, c) = A$, $(a, d) = D$, and $(b, d) = C$. In view of lemma 4.5.8, however, this implies that all half mixed strategy pairs of the form (a, q_2) will also be equilibrium points, with q_2 ranging over all of player 2's mixed strategies, and that all half-mixed strategy pairs of the form (q_1, d) will also be equilibrium points, now with q_1 ranging over all of player 1's mixed strategies. The equilibrium points of game $\Gamma^{1/2}$ are shown on figure 4.19.

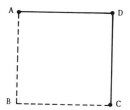

Figure 4.19

Finally, all auxiliary games Γ^t with $\frac{1}{2} < t \leq 1$, will have the two pure-strategy equilibrium points $(a, c) = A$ and $(b, d) = C$. They will also have the one mixed-strategy equilibrium point $q(t) = (q_1(t), q_2(t))$, with

$$q_1(t) = \left(\frac{3t + 1}{5t}, \frac{2t - 1}{5t}\right),$$

(4.11.23)

$$q_2(t) = \left(\frac{2t - 1}{3t}, \frac{t + 1}{3t}\right).$$

(4.11.24)

Note that $q(\frac{1}{2}) = ((1, 0), (0, 1)) = (a, d) = D$, whereas $q(1) = ((\frac{4}{5}, \frac{1}{5}), (\frac{1}{3}, \frac{2}{3})) = E_3 = Q$. Graph X of the linear tracing procedure now will be as shown in figure 4.20.

In this case the entire graph X is connected. In the region $0 \leq t < \frac{1}{2}$ it has only one branch, consisting of the one constant segment DD' on which the players use the strategy pair $(a, d) = D$. But at the t-value $t = \frac{1}{2}$, the graph divides into three different branches. One of these, $D'A'A''$, consists of two segments. One is the jump segment $D'A'$, on which player 2 moves from strategy d to strategy c while player 1 keeps his strategy constant at a, and the t-coordinate stays constant at $t = \frac{1}{2}$. The other is the constant segment $A'A''$, on which the players use the strategy pair $(a, c) = A$. Another branch, $D'C'C''$, also consists of two segments: (1) the *jump* segment $D'C'$, on which now player 1 moves from strategy a to strategy b while player 2 keeps his strategy constant at d, and the t-coordinate stays constant at $t = \frac{1}{2}$, and (2) the constant segment $C'C''$, on which the players use the strategy pair $(b, d) = C$. Finally, the third branch, $D'Q$, is a variable branch, on which the two players' strategies $q_1(t)$ and $q_2(t)$ are nonconstant functions of t.

Accordingly our graph now contains *three* different feasible paths. The first, $DD'A'A''$, leads to equilibrium point $(a, b) = A = E_1$ as the outcome.

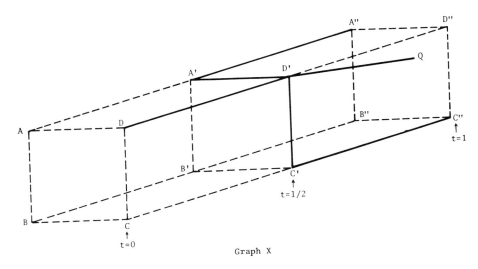

Graph X

Figure 4.20

The second, $DD'C'C''$, leads to equilibrium point $(b,d) = C = E_2$ as the outcome. Finally, the third path, $DD'Q$, leads to the mixed-strategy equilibrium point $Q = E_3$ as the outcome. Obviously in this case the linear tracing procedure is not well defined.

4.12   Decision and Game-Theoretic Interpretation: The Outcome-Selection Process

As has already been stated, the tracing procedure is meant to model the *outcome-selection process*, envisaged as a process of analysis, computation, expectation formation, and strategy choice, by which a group of n rational players will come to adopt, and to expect each other to adopt, one equilibrium point as the outcome of the game they are going to play. In discussing the outcome-selection process, we will have primarily in mind the nondegenerate case, where the linear tracing procedure is well defined and uniquely specifies one particular distinguished path $L = L(G, p)$. But our analysis can be easily extended also to the degenerate case where selection of a unique distinguished path requires use of the logarithmic tracing procedure (see section 4.13).

For each player i, the outcome-selection process will produce gradual changes both in his own tentative *strategy plans* and in his *expectations* about the other players' likely strategies. At any given moment both his plans and his expectations will be determined by a specific point $x^t = (t, q)$ of the distinguished path L, to be called his *position point* at that moment. As the outcome-selection process progresses, this position point x^t will continuously move along this path L, from its starting point $x^0 = (0, q^o)$ to its end point $x^1 = (1, q*)$.

At any given moment, when player i's position point is x^t, his tentative strategy plan will be to use the strategy q_i prescribed by the strategy part $q = (q_1, \ldots, q_i, \ldots, q_n)$ of this point x^t. He will of course know that any other player j who has reached the same position point x^t will likewise entertain the tentative strategy plan of using his own q-strategy q_j.[3] But player i will also know that as long as the t-value associated with this position point x^t is *less* than unity, the strategy part q of x^t may not in fact correctly indicate the final outcome of the game. (Indeed, as long as $t < 1$, the strategy part q of x^t need not be even an equilibrium point of game G, even though, by construction, it will always be an equilibrium point of the auxiliary game Γ^t.) Consequently player i will know that even if q_j is the strategy preferred by player j at the moment, there is absolutely no assurance that q_j will actually be player j's final strategy (outcome strategy) in the game.

In particular, we will assume that player i will assign only probability t to the hypothesis that the other $(n - 1)$ players' behavior will in fact correspond to the strategy combination $q_{-i} = (q_1, \ldots, q_{i-1}, q_{i+1}, \ldots, q_n)$ predicted by the strategy part q of this position point x^t, and that he will reserve the remaining probability $(1 - t)$ to his original hypothesis that the other players' behavior will correspond to the prior vector p_{-i}. This means that his actual *expectations* about the other players' likely behavior will correspond to the probability distribution $\rho(i, t, q) = t[q_{-i}] + (1 - t)[p_{-i}]$ defined by equations (4.10.4) and (4.10.5).

This assumption in turn can be used to justify the assumption that player i's tentative *strategy plan* at that moment will be to use strategy q_i. This is so because, by lemma 4.10.3, this strategy q_i will be his *best reply* to the probability distribution $\rho(i, t, q)$, which, as we have argued, will represent his *expectations* about the other players' likely behavior.

Thus, at each moment of the outcome-selection process, the t-value associated with his position point x^t will measure the *degree of confidence* that each player i will have in the tentative prediction provided by this position point x^t, to the effect that the other players will use the strategy combination q_{-i} prescribed by the strategy part q of x^t. As this

t-value associated with x^t gradually increases[4] from $t = 0$ to $t = 1$ during the outcome-selection process, the players will gradually move from a state of complete predictive uncertainty to a state of complete predictive certainty.

At the beginning of this outcome-selection process, the complete uncertainty in which each player will find himself about the other players' likely behavior will express itself in an exclusive reliance on the prior vector p_{-i} in forming his expectations, in that he will entertain a probability distribution $\rho(i, 0, q^o)$, assigning unity probability weight to p_{-i} and zero probability weight to the strategy combination q^o_{-i} associated with his position point $x^0 = (0, q^o)$. In contrast, at the end of the outcome-selection process, he will be in a state of complete predictive certainty because he will feel able to predict with full assurance that the other players will use their outcome strategies, since now he will entertain a probability distribution $\rho(1, q^*)$, assigning unity probability weight to the strategy combination q^*_{-i} prescribed by the outcome q^* of the game.

In terms of our distinction between first- and second-order information, under our model at any position point $x^t = (t, q)$ the *first-order* information to which each player i will react will consist of the probability distribution $\rho(i, t, q) = t[q_{-i}] + (1 - t)[p_{-i}]$. In contrast, his *second-order* information will consist of knowing that the other players' tentative reaction to their own first-order information will be the strategy combination q_{-i}. Formally, we can define his second-order information as the probability distribution $[q_{-i}]$ generated by this strategy combination q_{-i}.

Of course, if we disregard the very special case where q_{-i} and p_{-i} happen to coincide, then at any position point x^t associated with a t-value *smaller* than unity, we have

$$\rho(i, t, q) = t[q_{-i}] + (1 - t)[p_{-i}] \neq [q_{-i}], \tag{4.12.1}$$

which means that as long as $t < 1$, there will be a definite discrepancy between each player's first- and second-order information. As we have seen, our model explains this discrepancy by the fact that as long as $t < 1$, the strategy combination q_{-i} predicted by the position point $x^t = (t, q)$ will represent only some very *tentative* strategy choices by the other players, which in general will not correspond to their final strategy choices at all. This is why the probability distribution $\rho(i, t, q)$ used by player i will assign only the less-than-unity probability weight t to this strategy combination q_{-i} when he tries to predict his fellow players' final strategies.

As the outcome-selection process moves to its end point, the parameter t will approach unity, and so this discrepancy between the players' first- and second-order information will become smaller and smaller, and in the end, when t does become unity, this discrepancy will entirely disappear, with the players' expectations—as well as both their first- and second-order information—coming to be completely focused on the same equilibrium point q^* representing the outcome of the game.

4.13 The Logarithmic Tracing Procedure

The purpose of the logarithmic tracing procedure is to approximate the *piecewise* algebraic graph X of the linear tracing procedure by a *fully* algebraic graph $\overline{X}$, possessing some desirable mathematical properties not possessed by X itself.

We will again define a one-parameter family of auxiliary games $\overline{\Gamma}^t$ for $0 \leq t \leq 1$, but this time these games will also depend on a very small positive constant η, which for the time being will be assumed to be given. In any game $\overline{\Gamma}^t$, every player i $(i = 1, \ldots, n)$ will have the same strategy set $Q_i = \{q_i\}$ as he would have in the original game G (and as he would have also in the auxiliary games Γ^t used in the linear tracing procedure). But his payoff function $\overline{H}_i^t$ in game $\overline{\Gamma}^t$ will be

$$\overline{H}_i^t(q_i q_{-i}) = t H_i(q_i q_{-i}) + (1 - t) H_i(q_i p_{-i})$$

$$+ \eta(1 - t)\alpha_i \sum_{k=1}^{K_i} \log q_{ik}, \qquad (4.13.1)$$

where α_i is a positive constant to be defined later and where η is a very small positive number.

The payoff functions $\overline{H}_i^t$ differ from the payoff functions H_i^t used in the linear tracing procedure in containing also a logarithmic term. This is why the procedure based on these payoff functions is called the logarithmic tracing procedure, in distinction from the linear tracing procedure, whose payoff functions H_i^t are linear in the probabilities $q_{i1}, \ldots, q_{iK_i}$ for each player i.

This logarithmic term of course vanishes when $t = 1$. But when $t < 1$, then its effect is to give each player i an incentive to shift his strategy q_i closer to his *centroid strategy* $c_i = (1/K_i, \ldots, 1/K_i)$, which assigns the same probability $q_{ik} = 1/K_i$ to each of his pure strategies ϕ_i^k. (The logarithmic term has this effect since the quantity $\Sigma_k \log q_{ik}$ will be maximized at the point $q_i = c_i$.)

Since the logarithmic term is multiplied by η, which is a very small positive number, this effect of the logarithmic term will usually be very small and will go to zero when η itself is sent to zero. But the effect of the logarithmic term will be quite important when, without this term, two or more different pure strategies of player i would be best replies to the strategy combination q_{-i} used by the other players: in such cases the logarithmic term will give him a clear incentive to use all of these best reply strategies with the same probabilities. More generally, the logarithmic term will ensure that each player i will always have a unique best reply to any given strategy combination of the other players (as shown later in lemma 4.13.1).

We will now define the positive constant α_i of (4.13.1). As the first two terms of the equation are quantities measured in player i's *payoff units* (utility units), α_i must be defined in such a way as to be likewise a quantity expressed in these payoff units. In particular, suppose the $(n-1)$ players other than player i use the strategy combination q_{-i}. Then the quantity

$$\Delta H_i(q_{-i}) = \max_{q_i \in Q_i} H_i(q_i q_{-i}) - \min_{q_i' \in Q_i} H_i(q_i' q_{-i}) \tag{4.13.2}$$

will be the *largest payoff difference* that player i's own strategy choice can yield, since it is the difference between what his *best-reply* strategy and what his *worst-reply* strategy to q_{-i} would give him. We now set

$$\alpha_i^* = \max_{q_{-i} \in Q_{-i}} \Delta H_i(q_{-i}), \quad \text{with } \alpha_i = \alpha_i^* \text{ if } \alpha_i^* > 0. \tag{4.13.3}$$

Thus, whenever that definition yields a positive quantity, we define α_i as the *largest possible payoff difference* to player i, associated with any strategy combination q_{-i} of the other players. Now, by (4.13.2), α_i^* cannot be negative, and it can be zero only in two cases:

1. If player i has only *one* strategy ϕ_i^1.

2. If he has more than one strategy, but if all his strategies would always yield him the *same payoff* when the other players' strategy combination q_{-i} is given.[5]

In both cases 1 and 2 we can arbitrarily choose any positive number as our coefficient α_i because all positive α_i's will yield the same solution. This is so because any positive α_i will give player i a clear incentive always to use his centroid best reply c_i, regardless of the strategies used by the other players. (In case 1, of course, $c_i = \phi_i^1$.)

Inspection of (4.12.1) will show that $\bar{H}_i^1 = H_i$, so that $\bar{\Gamma}^1 = G$. On the other hand,

$$\bar{H}_i^0(q_i q_{-i}) = H_i(q_i p_{-i}) + \eta \alpha_i \sum_{k=1}^{K_i} \log q_{ik}. \tag{4.13.4}$$

Thus the auxiliary game $\bar{\Gamma}^0$, like the auxiliary game Γ^0 used in the linear tracing procedure, is a *separable game*, in which the payoff $\bar{H}_i^0$ of each player i will depend only on his own strategy q_i and be independent of the strategy combination q_{-i} used by the other $(n-1)$ players.

LEMMA 4.13.1   In any auxiliary game $\bar{\Gamma}^t$ with $0 \le t < 1$, to any possible strategy combination q_{-i} of the other players each player i will always have a *unique* best reply q_i, which will always be a *completely mixed* strategy.

Proof Uniqueness of the best reply q_i follows from the fact that, in any such game $\bar{\Gamma}^t$, player i's payoff function $\bar{H}_i^t$ will be a *strictly convex* function in the probabilities $q_{i1}, \ldots, q_{iK_i}$. On the other hand, q_i must be completely mixed because, if any probability q_{ik} took a zero value, then $\bar{H}_i^t$ would take an infinite negative value since $\log 0 = -\infty$; however if all probabilities q_{ik} are positive, then $\bar{H}_i^t$ will always be finite. ∎

Lemma 4.13.1 and the separability of game $\bar{\Gamma}^0$ imply:

LEMMA 4.13.2   The auxiliary game $\bar{\Gamma}^0$ will always have exactly *one* equilibrium point $q^o = (q_1^o, \ldots, q_n^o)$, and this will be in *completely mixed* strategies for all players.

LEMMA 4.13.3   In an auxiliary game $\bar{\Gamma}^t$ with $0 < t < 1$, any strategy combination $q = (q_1, \ldots, q_n)$ will be an equilibrium point if and only if all of its components q_i (for $i = 1, \ldots, n$) satisfy the conditions

$$\sum_{k=1}^{K_i} q_{ik} - 1 = 0, \tag{4.13.5}$$

$$t[H_i(\phi_i^k q_{-i}) - H_i(\phi_i^1 q_{-i})]$$

$$+ (1-t)[H_i(\phi_i^k p_{-i}) - H_i(\phi_i^1 p_{-i})] + \frac{\eta(1-t)\alpha_i(q_{i1} - q_{ik})}{(q_{i1} q_{ik})} = 0, \tag{4.13.6}$$

$$\text{for } k = 2, \ldots, K_i.$$

Equation (4.13.6) can also be written in the form:

$$tq_{i1}q_{ik}[H_i(\phi_i^k q_{-i}) - H_i(\phi_i^1 q_{-i})]$$
$$+ (1 - t)q_{i1}q_{ik}[H_i(\phi_i^k p_{-i}) - H_i(\phi_i^1 p_{-i})] \qquad (4.13.7)$$
$$+ \eta(1 - t)\alpha_i(q_{i1} - q_{ik}) = 0, \quad \text{for } k = 2, \ldots, K_i.$$

Proof Equation (4.13.5) is a restatement of (4.2.4). The $(K_i - 1)$ equations of form (4.13.6) are the first-order conditions for maximizing the payoff function $\bar{H}_i^t$ defined by (4.13.1) if q_{-i} and p_{-i} are kept constant. Since $\bar{H}_i^t$ is a strictly concave function in the probabilities $q_{i1}, \ldots, q_{iK_i}$, these first-order conditions are not only necessary conditions for maximization but rather are also sufficient conditions. Finally, the admissibility of writing (4.13.6) in the form (4.13.7) follows from the fact that, by lemma 4.13.1, both q_{i1} and q_{ik} $(k = 2, \ldots, K_i)$ will always be positive quantities. ∎

LEMMA 4.13.4 Any equilibrium point q of game $\bar{\Gamma}^1 = G$ will satisfy conditions (4.13.5) and (4.13.7). But, in general, not every strategy combination satisfying these conditions will be an equilibrium point.

Proof The first sentence of the lemma follows from (4.5.4). The second sentence follows from the fact that any pure-strategy combination will satisfy (4.13.7) whether or not it is an equilibrium point.

The set of all equilibrium points in any given game $\bar{\Gamma}^t$ will be called $\bar{E}^t$. By using Brouwer's fixed-point theorem, it is easy to show that all of these sets $\bar{E}^t$ will be nonempty. Let $\bar{X}$ be the graph of the correspondence $t \to \bar{E}^t$ for $0 \le t \le 1$.

On the other hand, let X^* be the set of all vectors $x = (t, q)$ satisfying all n equations of form (4.13.5) and all $(\bar{K} - n)$ equations of form (4.13.7), that is, all together $n + (\bar{K} - n) = \bar{K}$ different algebraic equations. Obviously each vector x will contain all together $(\bar{K} + 1)$ variables: the one variable t and the $\bar{K}$ variables of form q_{ik} that define the n components $q_1, \ldots, q_n$ of the strategy combination q. This means that we have all together $\bar{K}$ algebraic equations to characterize our $(\bar{K} + 1)$ different variables. Consequently X^* will be typically an algebraic variety of one dimension; that is, it will be an *algebraic curve*, even though in degenerate cases it may contain isolated points and/or subsets of more than one dimension.

Finally, let $X^o = X^* \cap Y$, where Y is the cylindrical set defined in section 4.10. Thus X^o is the set of all points $x = (t, q)$ in X^* that satisfy the

$\bar{K}$ inequalities of form (4.2.3) as well as the one additional inequality $0 \le t \le 1$. ∎

LEMMA 4.13.5 $\bar{X} \subseteq X^o$. In particular, in the region $0 \le t < 1$, $\bar{X}$, and X^o will exactly coincide, but in the region $t = 1$, X^o may include some points not belonging to $\bar{X}$.

The lemma follows from lemmas 4.13.3 and 4.13.4. By lemma 4.13.5, our new graph $\bar{X}$, unlike graph X used in the linear tracing procedure, will be a *fully* algebraic curve instead of merely being a *piecewise* algebraic curve.[6] Let δQ be the *boundary* of the strategy space Q. Thus δQ is the set of all strategy combinations q having at least one component q_i that is a pure strategy or is an incompletely mixed strategy. We set $\hat{Y} = \delta Q \times I^o$, where $I^o = (0, 1)$ is the open unit interval. Let Y^0 and Y^1 be the sets of all points $x = (t, q)$ in Y whose t-coordinate is $t = 0$ or $t = 1$, respectively. Clearly the boundary δY of set Y will consist of the three disjoint sets Y^0, $\hat{Y}$, and Y^1.

LEMMA 4.13.6   Let q^o denote the unique equilibrium point of game Γ^0 (see lemma 4.13.2). Then graph $\bar{X}$ will always have a one-dimensional branch $\bar{L}$ starting at the point $x^0 = (0, q^o)$, and locally unique within some finite neighborhood of this point. If we continue this branch $\bar{L}$ analytically long enough, then it will eventually intersect the boundary δY of set Y once more within set Y^1 at some point $x^1 = (1, \bar{q})$.

Proof   We will define $\bar{K}$ functions f_{ik} in the one variable t and in the $\bar{K}$ variables q_{ik} as follows. For $i = 1, \ldots, n$ and for $k = 1$, we define $f_{ik} = f_{i1}$ as the left-hand side of equation (4.13.5). For $i = 1, \ldots, n$ and for $k = 2, \ldots, K_i$, we define f_{ik} as the left-hand side of the relevant equation of form (4.13.7). Finally, we define the Jacobian

$$J = J(t, q) = \frac{\partial(\ldots, f_{ik}, \ldots)_{i=1,\ldots,n; k=1,\ldots,K_i}}{\partial(\ldots, q_{ik}, \ldots)_{i=1,\ldots,n; k=1,\ldots,K_i}}. \tag{4.13.8}$$

It is easy to verify that at the point $x^0 = (0, q^o)$, this Jacobian can never vanish. Consequently, by the implicit function theorem, graph $\bar{X}$ will always have a branch $\bar{L}$ starting at x^0 and locally unique in some finite neighborhood of x^0. On the other hand, since $\bar{L}$ will be an algebraic curve, if $\bar{L}$ is analytically continued long enough, it will leave set Y and therefore it will once more intersect the boundary δY of Y (see Harsanyi, 1973b pp. 241–242, lemmas 2 and 3). However, this second intersection point $x = (t, q)$ cannot coincide with the first intersection point x^0 because then

$\bar{L}$ would not be locally unique around x^0. Nor can x be another point $x \neq x^0$ of set Y^0 because, by lemma 4.13.2, game $\bar{\Gamma}^0$ can have only one equilibrium point. Finally, x cannot be a point of set $\hat{Y}$ because, by lemma 4.13.1, no game $\bar{\Gamma}^t$ with $0 < t < 1$ can have an equilibrium point lying on the boundary δQ of the strategy space Q. Consequently the second intersection point x must lie in set Y^1 and therefore must have the form $x = x^1 = (1, \bar{q})$. ∎

LEMMA 4.13.7   The strategy part $\bar{q} = (\bar{q}_1, \ldots, \bar{q}_n)$ of the intersection point x^1, mentioned in the last lemma, must be an equilibrium point of game $\bar{\Gamma}^1 = G$.

Proof   Let $\tilde{L} = \bar{L} - \{x^1\}$. Since $\tilde{L} \subseteq X^*$, all points $x = (t, q)$ of $\tilde{L}$ must satisfy (4.13.7). Moreover $\eta > 0$, and, by lemma 4.13.1, for each $x \in \tilde{L}$ we must have $q_{i1} > 0$ and $q_{ik} > 0$ for $k = 2, \ldots, K_i$. Therefore the expression

$$\Delta = t[H_i(\phi_i^k q_{-i}) - H(\phi_i^1 q_{-i})]$$
$$+ (1 - t)[H_i(\phi_i^k p_{-i}) - H_i(\phi_i^1 p_{-i})] \tag{4.13.9}$$

must have the same sign as the expression $(q_{ik} - q_{i1})$ does. Consequently we can write

$$\Delta(q_{ik} - q_{i1}) \geq 0. \tag{4.13.10}$$

On the other hand, point $x^1 = (1, \bar{q})$ is a limit point of $\tilde{L}$, and therefore its strategy part $\bar{q}$ must satisfy (4.13.7) and (4.13.10) if we set $t = 1$. This means that

$$\bar{q}_{i1} \bar{q}_{ik}[H_i(\phi_i^k \bar{q}_{-i}) - H_i(\phi_i^1 \bar{q}_{-i})] = 0 \tag{4.13.11}$$

and

$$(\bar{q}_{ik} - \bar{q}_{i1})[H_i(\phi_i^k \bar{q}_{-i}) - H_i(\phi_i^1 \bar{q}_{-i})] \geq 0. \tag{4.13.12}$$

Without loss of generality we can assume that player i's pure strategies are numbered in such a way that

$$\bar{q}_{i1} \geq \bar{q}_{ik}, \quad \text{for } k = 2, \ldots, K_i. \tag{4.13.13}$$

According to (4.13.5), this implies that

$$\bar{q}_{i1} > 0. \tag{4.13.14}$$

But, by (4.13.11), we must have

$$H_i(\phi_i^k \bar{q}_{-i}) = H_i(\phi_i^1 \bar{q}_{-i}), \quad \text{whenever } \bar{q}_{ik} > 0, \qquad (4.13.15)$$

and by (4.13.12), (4.13.13), and (4.13.14), we must have

$$H_i(\phi_i^k \bar{q}_{-i}) \le H_i(\phi_i^1 \bar{q}_{-i}), \quad \text{whenever } \bar{q}_{ik} = 0. \qquad (4.13.16)$$

Yet (4.13.15) and (4.13.16) imply (4.5.4) and (4.5.5). Consequently the strategy part $\bar{q}$ of point $x^1 = (1, \bar{q})$ will be in fact an equilibrium point of game G, as desired.

The curve $\bar{L}$ defined by lemma 4.13.6 will of course depend on game G, on the prior-distribution vector p, and on the parameter η. The same will be true for the equilibrium point $\bar{q}$ defined by the end point x^1 of $\bar{L}$. Therefore we will write $\bar{L} = \bar{L}(G, p, \eta)$ and $\bar{q} = \bar{q}(G, p, \eta)$. Moreover we define

$$q^* = \bar{T}(G, p) = \lim_{\eta \to 0} \bar{q}(G, p, \eta). \quad \blacksquare \qquad (4.13.17)$$

LEMMA 4.13.8   The limit indicated by (4.13.17) will always exist. Moreover the limit point q^* will always be an equilibrium point of game G.

Proof   Existence of the limit follows from the fact that $\bar{q}$, being a limit point of the algebraic curve $\tilde{L}$, must be an algebraic, or at least a piecewise algebraic, function of η. On the other hand, since each point $\bar{q}(G, p, \eta)$ for $\eta > 0$ is an equilibrium point of game G, q^* is a limit point of the set $E^1 = \bar{E}^1$ of all equilibrium points of G. Since E^1 is a closed set, q^* itself must also be an equilibrium point of G. $\quad \blacksquare$

We are now in a position to give our *first* definition for the logarithmic tracing procedure and for the solution q^* specified by this procedure. (Shortly we will also propose a second definition which, however, will always yield the same solution q^*.) For any game G, and for any vector p of prior probability distributions, the *logarithmic tracing procedure* consists in constructing the curve $\bar{L} = \bar{L}(G, p, \eta)$ for various alternative small positive values of the parameter η, following this curve $\bar{L}$ from its starting point $x^0 = (0, q^0)$ to its end point $x^1 = (1, \bar{q})$ in order to find the equilibrium points $\bar{q} = \bar{q}(G, p, \eta)$ corresponding to these η-values, and finally defining the solution q^* of the game by means of the limit operation specified by (4.12.17).

The second definition of the logarithmic tracing procedure will be based on the *limit curve* L^* which we obtain from the curves $\bar{L} = \bar{L}(G, p, \eta)$ if we let η go to zero.

More specifically, for any point $x = (t, q)$ of a given curve $\bar{L} = \bar{L}(G, p, \eta)$, let $\lambda(x^0, x)$ denote the *distance* of x from the starting point $x^0 = (0, q^0)$ as measured along this curve $\bar{L}$. We define

$$\kappa(x^0, x) = \frac{\lambda(x^0, x)}{\lambda(x^0, x^1)}, \tag{4.13.18}$$

where $x^1 = (1, \bar{q})$ is the end point of $\bar{L}$. The variable $\kappa = \kappa(x^0, x)$ can be used to parametrize any given curve $\bar{L}(G, p, \eta)$ by means of one equation of the form

$$t = \gamma_o(\kappa, \eta) \tag{4.13.19}$$

and by means of $\bar{K}$ equations of the form

$$q_{ik} = \gamma_{ik}(\kappa, \eta), \quad \text{for } i = 1, \ldots, n; \text{ for } k = 1, \ldots, K_i. \tag{4.13.20}$$

In vector notation these $\bar{K}$ equations can be summarized in the form of one equation

$$q = \gamma(\kappa, \eta). \tag{4.13.21}$$

We now define the limit curve $L^* = L^*(G, p)$ by the scalar equation

$$t = \bar{\gamma}_o(\kappa) = \lim_{\eta \to 0} \gamma_o(\kappa, \eta) \tag{4.13.22}$$

and by the vector equation

$$q = \bar{\gamma}(\kappa) = \lim_{\eta \to 0} \gamma(\kappa, \eta). \tag{4.13.23}$$

Since each curve $\bar{L}(G, p, \eta)$ is defined by a system of algebraic equations in the variables t and q_{ik} ($i = 1, \ldots, n; k = 1, \ldots, K_i$), the limits indicated by (4.13.22) and by (4.13.23) will always exist.

Now we can state our *second* definition for the logarithmic tracing procedure and for the outcome q^* specified by this procedure. Under this definition the logarithmic tracing procedure consists in following the limit curve $L^* = L^*(G, p)$ from its starting point $x^0 = (0, q^0)$, corresponding to the κ-value $\kappa = 0$, to its end point $x^1 = (1, q^*)$, corresponding to the κ-value $\kappa = 1$. The outcome specified by the logarithmic tracing procedure then is simply the strategy part q^* of this end point $x^1 = (1, q^*)$ of the limit curve L^*.

LEMMA 4.13.9   The outcomes specified by the first and by the second definitions of the logarithmic tracing procedure are identical.

Proof For any finite η, the strategy part of the end point x^1 of the curve $\bar{L}(G, p, \eta)$ has been denoted as $\bar{q} = \bar{q}(G, p, \eta)$. Since this end point x^1 corresponds to the κ-value $\kappa = 1$, we can write

$$\bar{q}(G, p, \eta) = \gamma(1, \eta). \tag{4.13.24}$$

Consequently

$$\lim_{\eta \to 0} \bar{q}(G, p, \eta) = \lim_{\eta \to 0} \gamma(1, \eta). \tag{4.13.25}$$

In view of (4.13.17) and (4.13.22), this in turn implies that

$$\bar{T}(G, p) = \bar{\gamma}(1). \tag{4.13.26}$$

Yet the left-hand side of this equation is the outcome as specified by the first definition, whereas the right-hand side is the strategy part of the end point $x^1 = (1, q^*)$ of the limit curve $L^*(G, p)$ and therefore is the outcome as specified by the second definition. This proves the lemma. ∎

THEOREM 4.13.1   The outcome $q^* = \bar{T}(G, p)$ specified by the logarithmic tracing procedure always exists and is always unique, so that the logarithmic tracing procedure is always feasible and is always well defined.

The theorem follows from lemmas 4.13.6 to 4.13.9.

LEMMA 4.13.10   The limit curve $L^*(G, p)$ is always a subset of graph $X(G, p)$ used in the linear tracing procedure.

Proof For any given κ-value $\kappa = \hat{\kappa}$ with $0 \leq \hat{\kappa} \leq 1$, we have to show that the strategy combination $\hat{q} = \bar{\gamma}(\hat{\kappa})$ will be an equilibrium point of the auxiliary game $\Gamma^{\hat{t}}$, where $\hat{t} = \bar{\gamma}_o(\hat{\kappa})$. For $\hat{\kappa} = 1$, this follows from lemma 4.13.9. Thus we can restrict ourselves to the case where $0 \leq \hat{\kappa} < 1$. For any positive η, the variables $t = \gamma_o(\hat{\kappa}, \eta)$ and $q_{ik} = \gamma_{ik}(\hat{\kappa}, \eta)$ will satisfy equation (4.13.7) because the vector (t, q) will be a point of curve $\bar{L}(G, p, \eta)$. In view of (4.10.1) this equation can also be written in the form

$$q_{i1} q_{ik} [H_i^t(\phi_i^k, q_{-i}) - H_i^t(\phi_i^1, q_{-i})] + \eta(1 - t)(q_{i1} - q_{ik}) = 0. \tag{4.13.27}$$

Moreover, since $\hat{\kappa} < 1$, we have $t < 1$ and $1 - t > 0$. Also $\eta > 0$. Furthermore, by lemma 4.13.1, $q_{i1} > 0$ and $q_{ik} > 0$. Consequently the expression in square brackets in (4.13.27) must have the same sign as the expression $(q_{ik} - q_{i1})$. Therefore we can write

$$(q_{ik} - q_{i1})[H_i^t(\phi_i^k q_{-i}) - H_i^t(\phi_i^1 q_{-i})] \geq 0. \tag{4.13.28}$$

Since the vector $(\hat{t}, \hat{q})$ is the limit of such points (t, q) when η goes to zero, the variables $\hat{t}$, $\hat{q}_{i1}$, and $\hat{q}_{ik}$ must also satisfy (4.13.27) and (4.13.28) if we set $\eta = 0$. Moreover we can assume without loss of generality that player 1's pure strategies are numbered in such a way that

$$q_{i1} \geq q_{ik}, \quad \text{for } k = 2, \ldots, K_i \qquad (4.13.29)$$

so that

$$q_{i1} > 0. \qquad (4.13.30)$$

But then, by (4.13.27) and (4.13.30), we must have

$$H_i^t(\phi_i^k q_{-i}) = H_i^t(\phi_i^1 q_{-i}), \quad \text{whenever } q_{ik} > 0, \qquad (4.13.31)$$

$$H_i^t(\phi_i^k q_{-i}) \leq H_i^t(\phi_i^1 q_{-i}), \quad \text{whenever } q_{ik} = 0. \qquad (4.13.32)$$

Yet conditions (4.13.31) and (4.13.32) imply conditions (4.5.4) and (4.5.5) as applied to game Γ^i. Consequently the strategy combination $\hat{q}$ will be in fact an equilibrium point of game Γ^i, as desired. ∎

THEOREM 4.13.2   For any possible choice of G and p, the linear tracing procedure is always feasible.

Proof   We have to show that every graph $X = X(G, p)$ always contains a feasible path. Yet this follows from lemma 4.13.10, which implies that the limit curve $L^*(G, p)$ itself is such a feasible path. ∎

THEOREM 4.13.3   For some choices of G and p, the linear tracing procedure is not well defined.

Proof   To establish the theorem, it is sufficient to adduce one numerical example where the linear tracing procedure is ill defined. Such an example is the *third example* discussed in section 4.12. ∎

LEMMA 4.13.11   Whenever the linear tracing procedure is well defined, the distinguished path $L(G, p)$ of the linear tracing procedure and the limit curve $L^*(G, p)$ of the logarithmic tracing procedure will coincide.

Proof   When the linear tracing procedure is well defined, then graph X will contain only one feasible path L, which is called the distinguished path. Yet, by lemma 4.13.10, the limit curve L^* is always a feasible path contained by X. Therefore we must have $L = L^*$. ∎

THEOREM 4.13.4   Whenever the linear tracing procedure is well defined, the solutions $q^* = T(G, p)$ specified by the linear and by the logarithmic tracing procedures will coincide.

The theorem directly follows from lemma 4.13.11. Finally, the following theorem will be stated without a proof:

THEOREM 4.13.5   For any given complete prior vector p, *almost all* games G will give rise to a well-defined linear tracing procedure. (A proof, based on Sard's, 1942, theorem, can be found in Harsanyi, 1975, pp. 83–92.)

4.14   The Tracing Map for a Simple Class of Games

For a given game G, the set of all prior vectors p for which the tracing procedure yields a particular equilibrium point q as the outcome, so that $T(G, p) = q$, is called the *source set* of this equilibrium point q. A map showing a partitioning of the game's strategy space $Q = \{q\} = \{p\}$ into the various source sets existing in the game is called the *tracing map* of the game. In this section we will describe the tracing map of a simple class of two-person non-zero-sum games. (This class will contain the game discussed in section 4.12.) The games G to be considered will have a payoff matrix of the form shown in figure 4.21.

All games of this class have three equilibrium points. Two of these, $(a, c) = E_1$ and $(b, d) = E_2$, are in pure strategies. The third, $(q_1^*, q_2^*) = E_3$, is in mixed strategies, with

$$q_1^* = \left(\frac{\delta}{\beta + \delta}, \frac{\beta}{\beta + \delta} \right),$$

$$q_2^* = \left(\frac{\gamma}{\alpha + \gamma}, \frac{\alpha}{\alpha + \gamma} \right).$$

Figure 4.22 shows the strategy space of a typical game in this class (that of game G discussed in section 4.12). The three equilibrium points of the game are $A = E_1$, $C = E_2$, and $Q = E_3$. FQ is an extension of line QD (not shown on the diagram). QH is an extension of line BQ.

Simple computation gives the following results. Any point p lying above the broken line FQH will yield $A = E_1$ as the solution by the linear tracing procedure, whereas any point p lying below that line will yield $C = E_2$ as the outcome. On the other hand, all points p lying on the line FQH will

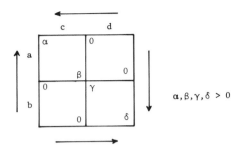

Figure 4.21

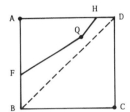

Figure 4.22

give rise to an ill-defined linear tracing procedure, with feasible paths leading to all three equilibrium points of the game as possible outcomes. Thus, for points p lying on this boundary line FQH, only the logarithmic tracing procedure will provide unique results.

These results are as follows:

Case 1:
Q, and therefore the entire border line FQH, lies above the diagonal BD (as is the case in figure 4.22). This will happen if $\alpha\beta < \gamma\delta$. In this case all points p on the border line FQH will yield $C = E_2$ as the outcome.

Case 2:
Q, as well as FQH, lies below the diagonal BD. This will happen if $\alpha\beta > \gamma\delta$. In this case all points p on FQH will yield $A = E_1$ as the outcome.

Case 3:
Q lies on the diagonal BD (so that the boundary line FQH will coincide with BD). This will happen if $\alpha\beta = \gamma\delta$. In this case all points p on the boundary line $FQH = BD$ will yield $Q = E_3$ as the outcome.

Note that for any game G in this class and for any possible choice of the prior vector p, we will obtain the same outcome whether we apply the tracing procedure to G or to the *uniformly perturbed* version G_ε of G; then we let the mistake-probability parameter ε go to zero.

Yet there is one interesting difference with respect to prior vectors p lying on the boundary line FQH, at least when the game comes under case 1 or 2. As we have seen, if we apply the linear tracing procedure to such vectors p on the boundary line, then we will obtain an indeterminate result, and only the logarithmic tracing procedure will yield a unique outcome. But if we apply the linear tracing procedure to a uniformly perturbed game G_ε, then also these boundary vectors may yield a unique outcome, even without use of the logarithmic tracing procedure. This is true only in cases 1 and 2. In case 3, these boundary vectors will give rise to an ill-defined linear tracing procedure, even if we use the uniformly perturbed game G_ε, and only the logarithmic procedure will yield a unique outcome.

This fact has the following mathematical interpretation. In cases 1 and 2, if we apply the linear tracing procedure to the uniformly perturbed game G_ε rather than to the original unperturbed game G, this is mathematically equivalent to slightly displacing the prior vector p toward the centroid of square $ABCD$, that is, toward the strategy pair $c = (c_1, c_2)$, where $c_1 = (\frac{1}{2}, \frac{1}{2})$ and also $c_2 = (\frac{1}{2}, \frac{1}{2})$. As a result p will be removed from the boundary FQH, where the linear tracing procedure is indeterminate to a region where it is well defined. Using the logarithmic tracing procedure instead of the linear tracing procedure will have a similar effect.

On the other hand, in case 3 this mechanism will not work because in this case the boundary line FQH will coincide with the diagonal BD. Now, if we displace a given point p of this diagonal toward the centroid c, this will not remove this point from this diagonal and will not move it to a region where the linear tracing procedure is well defined.

The tracing map described in this section illustrates the important fact that even in very simple games G, the outcome $q^* = T(G, p)$ selected by the tracing procedure will very strongly depend on the prior vector p used as a starting point. This of course means that to obtain a satisfactory solution theory, the tracing procedure must be supplemented by a satisfactory theory of how to choose prior probability distributions, and that the theory of prior distributions is at least as important a part of our outcome theory as is the theory of the tracing procedure itself.

4.15   The Tracing Procedure in Behavior Strategies

We now have to extend our definition of the tracing procedure—of both its linear and logarithmic versions—to the case where the players use behavior strategies. This is so because our theory of equilibrium selection will be based on the assumption that the players use behavior strategies, rather than mixed strategies, in accordance with our definition of the *standard form* in chapter 2.

To define the *linear* tracing procedure in behavior strategies, all we have to do is to replace all references to mixed strategies by references to behavior strategies in equation (4.10.1). This yields the equation

$$H_i^t(b_i b_{-i}) = tH_i(b_i b_{-i}) + (1 - t)H_i(b_i p_{-i}) \tag{4.15.1}$$

as our new definition of player i's payoff $(i = 1, \ldots, n)$ in any auxiliary game $\Gamma^t(0 \le t \le 1)$.

On the other hand, to define the *logarithmic* tracing procedure in behavior strategies, it would be natural to use the following equation:

$$\hat{H}_i^t(b_i b_{-i}) = tH_i(b_i b_{-1}) + (1 - t)H_i(b_i p_{-i})$$

$$+ \eta(1 - t)\alpha_i \sum_{ij \in M_i} \sum_{k=1}^{K_{ij}} \log b_{ijk}, \tag{4.15.2}$$

where again η is a very small positive constant and α_i the quantity defined by (4.13.2) and (4.13.3). M_i denotes the set of all agents ij of player i. K_{ij} is the number of local pure strategies available to any agent ij. Let $\hat{\Gamma}^t(0 \le t \le 1)$ be the auxiliary game in which the function $\hat{H}_i^t$ defined by (4.15.2) is player i's payoff function, $i = (1, \ldots, n)$.

This definition of the payoff functions $\hat{H}_i^t$, however, would give rise to the following problem. Whereas for $t < 1$ the payoff function $\bar{H}_i^t$ defined by (4.13.1) is always a *strictly concave* function of the probabilities q_{ik} characterizing player i's mixed strategy q_i, the payoff function $\hat{H}_i^t$ defined by (4.15.2) is in general not a concave function of the probabilities b_{ijk} characterizing player i's behavior strategy b_i. (This is so because the first two terms on the right-hand side of (4.13.1) are *linear* functions of the probabilities q_{ik}, whereas the corresponding terms in (4.15.2) are in general multilinear, rather than linear, functions of the probabilities b_{ijk}.) Consequently we cannot any longer argue that the separable game $\hat{\Gamma}^0$ corresponding to $t = 0$ must have a *unique* equilibrium point because of the strict concavity of the payoff functions $\hat{H}_i^t$. Yet we would need this uniqueness property in order to provide the logarithmic tracing procedure in behavior strategies with a well-defined starting point.

To overcome this difficulty, we will proceed as follows: Let $\hat{b}_i$ denote player i's unique central local best reply to the i-incomplete prior vector p_{-i}. (On the uniqueness of central local best replies, see chapter 2, section 2.7). Accordingly, $\hat{b}_{i \backslash ij}$ will denote the local-strategy combination that $\hat{b}_i$ assigns to player i's agents other than agent ij. We will give up the assumption that in each auxiliary game $\hat{\Gamma}^t$ every agent of player i will try to maximize the *same* payoff function $\hat{H}_i^t$. Instead, we will assume that in general each agent ij will try to maximize a somewhat *different* payoff function $\hat{H}_{ij}^t$, defined as

$$\hat{H}_{ij}^t(b_{ij}b_{-ij}) = tH_i(b_{ij}b_{-ij}) + (1-t)\tau H_i(b_{ij}b_{i \backslash ij}p_{-i})$$

$$+ (1-t)(1-\tau)H_i(b_{ij}\hat{b}_{i \backslash ij}p_{-i}) + \eta(1-t)\alpha \sum_{k=1}^{K_{ij}} \log b_{ijk}, \qquad (4.15.3)$$

where

$$\tau = t\frac{\eta+1}{\eta+t}. \qquad (4.15.4)$$

Clearly the right-hand side of (4.15.3) differs from that of (4.15.2) in two ways. One is that the last term omits the logarithms of the probabilities $b_{ij'k}$ associated with the local strategies $b_{ij'}$ of player i's *other* agents $ij' \neq ij$. The other difference is that the second term on the right-hand side of (4.15.2) is now replaced by two terms. But the first difference is mathematically irrelevant because, in maximizing the payoff function $\hat{H}_{ij}^t$, agent ij would in any case have to treat the logarithms of the probabilities $b_{ij'k}$ characterizing the strategies $b_{ij'}$ of the *other* agents $ij' \neq ij$ as *constants* without any effect on his maximization problem. On the other hand, the second difference would become a mere difference in notation if, in the third term on the right-hand side of (4.15.3), the strategy combination $\hat{b}_{i \backslash ij}$ were replaced by $b_{i \backslash ij}$.

Although, owing to the second difference, maximization of $\hat{H}_{ij}^t$ by agent ij is *non*equivalent to maximization of $\hat{H}_i^t$ by him, the two maximization problems will be *very nearly* equivalent. To show this, let $\hat{\Gamma}_1^t$ denote the auxiliary game $\hat{\Gamma}^t$ defined in terms of the payoff functions $\hat{H}_i^t$, and let $\hat{\Gamma}_2^t$ denote the auxiliary game $\hat{\Gamma}^t$ defined in terms of the payoff functions $\hat{H}_{ij}^t$. Now it is easy to verify that if η is small enough, then at any equilibrium point $b = (b_1, \ldots, b_n)$ of an auxiliary game $\hat{\Gamma}_1^t$ corresponding to a small enough t value, each player i will use a strategy b_i very close to his central local best reply $\hat{b}_i$ to p_{-i}. Consequently for small enough η and t values, the fact that in one term of equation (4.15.3) the strategy combination $\hat{b}_{i\backslash ij}$ occurs rather than the strategy combination $b_{i\backslash ij}$ can only make a minor difference. Moreover the parameter τ in equation (4.15.3) has been defined in such a way that as the parameter t moves from $t = 0$ to slightly larger t values, τ will *very fast* move from $\tau = 0$ to a τ value very close to 1, giving a near-zero weight to the term containing $\hat{b}_{i\backslash ij}$ by the time when $\hat{b}_i$ might significantly differ from player i's equilibrium strategy b_i in the various auxiliary games $\hat{\Gamma}_2^t$ corresponding to larger t values.

Note that both payoff functions $\hat{H}_i^t$ and $\hat{H}_{ij}^t$ are strictly concave functions of the probabilities b_{ijk} characterizing the local mixed strategy b_{ij} of agent ij, but that neither is a concave function of the probabilities b_{ijk} characterizing the entire behavior strategy b_i of player i.

Yet there is an important difference between the logarithmic tracing procedures defined in terms of the payoff functions $\hat{H}_i^t$ and $\hat{H}_{ij}^t$. It lies in the fact that whereas the auxiliary game $\hat{\Gamma}_1^0$, defined in terms of the payoff functions $\hat{H}_i^0$, is *separable* only with respect to the individual *players* i, the auxiliary game $\hat{\Gamma}_2^0$, defined in terms of the payoff functions $\hat{H}_{ij}^0$ is *separable* also with respect to the individual *agents* ij. That is to say, game $\hat{\Gamma}_2^0$ decomposes into as many mutually independent one-person maximization problems as the number of all agents in the game. This separability, together with the fact that each payoff function $\hat{H}_{ij}^0$ is a strictly convex function of the local mixed strategy b_{ij} of the relevant agent ij, ensures that for any positive value of η, game $\hat{\Gamma}_2^0$ will always have *one* and *only* one equilibrium point, providing a well-defined unique starting point for the logarithmic tracing procedure—or, more exactly, for that version of the latter that uses the payoff functions $\hat{H}_{ij}^t$.

Note that the close relationship between the payoff functions $\hat{H}_i^t$ and $\hat{H}_{ij}^t$ for small values of η, as already discussed, ensures that as η goes to zero, the graphs defined by both versions of the logarithmic tracing procedure in behavior strategies will converge to some subset of the graph of the linear tracing procedure. This fact in turn can be used to show that theorems 4.13.1 to 4.13.5 of section 4.13 are just as true for the linear and the logarithmic procedures in *behavior* strategies as they are for their counterparts in *mixed* strategies, provided that we define the logarithmic tracing procedure in behavior strategies in terms of the payoff functions $\hat{H}_{ij}^t$.

COMPUTATIONALLY USEFUL FACTS ABOUT THE TRACING PROCEDURE

4.16 Classification of the Line Segments of Linear Tracing Graphs

Suppose that a one-dimensional subset S of graph $X = X(G, p)$, used in the linear tracing procedure, can be parametrized in such a way that all its defining equations are analytic. Then S will be called a *line segment* of graph X. As was mentioned in section 3.11, in nondegenerate cases this graph X will contain only three types of line segments:

1. *Constant segments.* These are line segments whose points have the form (t, q), where q is a constant strategy combination while t ranges over a closed subinterval $I^* = [t^*, t^{**}]$ of the closed unit interval $I = [0, 1]$.

A very important special case is constant segments using a constant pure-strategy combination $q = \phi$. In nondegenerate cases this pure-strategy combination ϕ will always be a strong equilibrium point for all games Γ^t with a t-value belonging to the interior I^o of the relevant interval I^*.

2. *Jump segments.* These are line segments whose points have the form $(t^*, (q_i \phi_{-i}))$, where t^* is a constant t-value, ϕ_{-i} is a constant i-incomplete pure-strategy combination, whereas q_i ranges over some or all probability mixtures of two specific pure strategies ϕ_i and ϕ_i'.

3. *Variable segments.* These are line segments whose points have the form $(t, q(t))$, where t ranges over a closed subinterval of I while $q(t)$ is a nonconstant function of t. [Typically at least two component strategies $q_i(t)$ of q will be mixed strategies varying with t. The other component strategies, if any, *may* stay constant. Such constant components will be usually pure strategies.]

Unlike other branches of a graph X, a distinguished (or even a feasible) path L has a well-defined direction, from its starting point $x^0 = (0, q^o)$ to its end point $x^1 = (1, q^*)$. Accordingly, among variable segments V belonging to a distinguished (or feasible) path L, we can distinguish *forward-moving* and *backward-moving* ones, depending on whether the parameter t increases or decreases along V as we trace L from x^0 to x^1. (An example for a backward-moving variable segment will be given in section 4.18.) Presumably constant segments belonging to such paths L can also be both forward moving and backward moving, though in our computing experience we have so far encountered only forward-moving ones.

4.17 Some Useful Lemmas

We will now state a few definitions and lemmas. It will always be assumed
that we are considering the linear tracing procedure generated by a given
game G and by a given prior vector p.

Suppose the linear tracing graph X contains a path L connecting a point
$x^0 = (0, q^o)$ with a point $x^{t^*} = (t^*, q^*)$, $0 < t^* \leq 1$. Then L will be called a
subfeasible path. (Obviously a feasible path is a subfeasible path with
$t^* = 1$.)

A feasible or subfeasible path L will be called *unbranching* if every point
$x = (t, q)$ of L, with the possible exception of its end point x^{t^*}, has a
neighborhood $N(x)$ containing no point x' belonging to graph X yet not
belonging to L itself.

LEMMA 4.17.1   Any unbranching feasible path L will be a distinguished
path.

Proof   The lemma follows from the definition of a distinguished path. ∎

For convenience, we will often say that "q_i is a best reply to q_{-i} at $t = t^*$,"
or that "q is an equilibrium point at $t = t^*$," instead of saying that "q_i is a
best reply to q_{-i} in game Γ^{t^*}," and so on.

LEMMA 4.17.2   The set $I^*(\phi_i q_{-i})$ of all t-values at which a given pure
strategy ϕ_i is a best reply to a given strategy combination q_{-i} will be either
empty or a one-point set or a closed interval of finite length.

Proof   By (4.10.1), each payoff function H_i^t is linear in the parameter t. On
the other hand, best replies are defined by weak payoff inequalities. These
two facts imply the lemma. ∎

LEMMA 4.17.3   For any given strategy combination q_{-i}, the two sets
$I^*(\phi_i q_{-i})$ and $I^*(\phi_i' q_{-i})$ with $\phi_i \neq \phi_i'$ will be either identical or disjoint or
possessing only *one* point in common.

The lemma follows from the same facts as the preceding lemma.

A subinterval I^* of the closed unit interval I will be called *relatively open*
if it can be obtained as the intersection of I with an open set.

LEMMA 4.17.4   The set $\hat{I}(q)$ of all t-values at which a given strategy combination q is an equilibrium point will be a closed subinterval (possibly
empty) of I, whereas the set $\check{I}(q)$ of all t-values at which q is a strong

equilibrium point will be a relatively open subinterval (possibly empty) of I. Moreover, if $\breve{I}(q)$ is nonempty, then it will cover the entire interior of $\breve{I}(q)$.

Proof To be at least a weak equilibrium point, q must satisfy a set of weak payoff inequalities. To be a strong equilibrium point, it must satisfy some strong payoff inequalities. These facts, together with the linearity of the payoff functions H_i^t in t, imply the lemma. ∎

LEMMA 4.17.5 Suppose that, at $t = t^*$, ϕ_i is a strong best reply (or is not a best reply) to a given i-incomplete strategy combination $\hat{q}_{-i}$. Then at this t-value $t = t^*$, ϕ_i will be a strong best reply (or will not be a best reply) to any i-incomplete strategy combination q_{-i} within some neighborhood $N(\hat{q}_{-i})$ of $\hat{q}_{-i}$.

Proof The payoff function $H_i^{t^*}(\phi_i q_{-i})$ is *continuous* in q_{-i}. Moreover, for ϕ_i to be a *strong* best reply (or *not* to be a best reply), it must satisfy some *strong* inequalities. These facts imply the lemma. ∎

LEMMA 4.17.6 Suppose that, at $t = t^*$, the strategy combination ϕ is a *strong* equilibrium point. Then, at this t-value, ϕ will be the *only* equilibrium point within some neighborhood $N(\phi)$ of ϕ.

Proof The lemma follows from the previous lemma. ∎

LEMMA 4.17.7 Suppose that ϕ is a *strong* equilibrium point at $t = 0$ and an equilibrium point, whether strong or weak, at $t = 1$. Then $\phi = T(G, p)$ will be the outcome selected by the linear tracing procedure.

Proof For each player i, at $t = 0$, ϕ_i is a *strong* best reply to ϕ_{-i}, and at $t = 1$, it is at least a *weak* best reply to ϕ_{-i}. Therefore, by (4.10.1), ϕ_i will be a *strong* best reply to ϕ_{-i} at *all* t with $0 \le t < 1$. Thus graph X will contain a *constant segment* C, using ϕ at all t-values. Hence C will be a feasible path. Moreover, by lemma 4.17.6, C will be unbranching, and by lemma 4.17.1, it will be a distinguished path. This establishes the lemma. ∎

LEMMA 4.17.8 Suppose that L is an unbranching subfeasible path whose end point is $\hat{x} = (\hat{t}, \phi)$ and whose last line segment is a *constant segment* C, with points of the form (t, ϕ) for some range $\breve{t} \le t \le \hat{t}$. Moreover suppose at the t-value $t = \hat{t}$:

1. Player i has exactly *two* pure-strategy best replies ϕ_i and ϕ_i' to the other players' strategy combination ϕ_{-i}.

2. Every other player $j \ne i$ has only the *one* best reply ϕ_j to ϕ_{-j}.

Then C will be joined by a *jump segment* J connecting $\hat{x} = (\hat{t}, \phi)$ with some point $\tilde{x} = (\hat{t}, \tilde{q})$, where $\tilde{q} = (\tilde{q}_i \phi_{-i})$, with $\tilde{q}_i$ being a probability mixture of ϕ_i and of ϕ_i'.

Proof Let $q_i(\mu)$ be a mixed strategy assigning probability μ to ϕ_i' and assigning probability $(1 - \mu)$ to ϕ_i. By lemma 4.17.4, if μ is small enough, then $q(\mu) = (q_i(\mu)\phi_{-i})$ will be an equilibrium point at $t = \hat{t}$. This establishes the lemma. ∎

LEMMA 4.17.9   Under the assumptions of lemma 4.17.8, suppose also that:

3. Every player $j \neq i$ has only the one best reply ϕ_j, not only to ϕ_{-j} itself but also to the j-incomplete strategy combination ϕ_{-j}' obtained from ϕ_{-j} if player i's strategy ϕ_i is replaced by ϕ_i'.

Then the jump segment J mentioned in lemma 4.17.8 will extend all the way to the point $\bar{x} = (\hat{t}, \phi')$, where $\phi' = (\phi_i' \phi_{-i})$. Moreover the extended path $L' = L \cup J$ will be, like L itself, an *unbranching* subfeasible path.

Proof Because of assumption 3, ϕ' will be an equilibrium point at $t = \hat{t}$. By lemma 4.5.8, this means that all strategy combinations $q(\mu) = (q_i(\mu)\phi_{-i})$, $0 \leq \mu \leq 1$, will have the same property. Thus all points of the form $(\hat{t}, q(\mu))$ —that is, all points of J—will belong to graph X. Moreover, in view of assumption 3 and lemma 4.17.5, $L' = L \cup J$ will be unbranching. ∎

LEMMA 4.17.10   Under the assumptions of lemma 4.17.8, suppose that:

4. For all strategy combinations of form $q(\mu)$ with $\mu < \mu^*$, every player $j \neq i$ has only the one best reply ϕ_j to $q_{-j}(\mu)$ but that this assumption fails for the strategy combination $q(\mu^*)$.

If assumption 4 fails because player j has more than one best reply to $q_{-j}(\mu^*)$, then we will say that player j is *destabilized* at the point $(\hat{t}, q(\mu^*))$.
    Then the jump segment J mentioned in lemma 4.17.8 will end at the point $\tilde{x} = (\hat{t}, q(\mu^*))$. On the other hand, the extended path $L' = L \cup J$ will again be an *unbranching* subfeasible path.

Proof of this lemma is similar to that of the preceding lemma.

LEMMA 4.17.11   Suppose that L is an unbranching subfeasible path whose end point is $\hat{x} = (\hat{t}, \phi)$ and whose last segment is a jump segment J, with points of the form $(\hat{t}, (q_i \phi_{-i}))$, where q_i ranges over some or all probability mixtures of ϕ_i and of another pure strategy $\bar{\phi}_i$. Suppose also that at $t = \hat{t}$:

1. Player i has exactly the *two* pure-strategy best replies ϕ_i and $\bar{\phi}_i$ to ϕ_{-i}.

2. Every other player $j \neq i$ has only the *one* best reply ϕ_j to ϕ_{-j}.

3. At some t-value $t = t^* > \hat{t}$, ϕ is a *strong* equilibrium point.

Then L will be joined by a constant segment C with points of the form (t, ϕ) for $\hat{t} \leq t \leq t^{**}$, where $t^{**} = t^* = 1$ if $t^* = 1$, whereas $t^{**} > t^*$ if $t^* < 1$. Moreover the extended path $L' = L \cup C$ will be an *unbranching* subfeasible path.

Proof Existence of C can be established by an argument similar to that used in the proof of lemma 4.17.7. The statement about t^{**} follows from lemma 4.17.4. Finally, the fact that $L' = L \cup C$ will be unbranching follows from lemmas 4.17.5 and 4.17.6. ∎

In computing the two end points of any line segment, but particularly in computing those of a variable segment, the following lemma is useful.

LEMMA 4.17.12 Suppose that $\hat{x} = (\hat{t}, \hat{q})$ is a point of a given line segment S. This point $\hat{x}$ will be an end point of S if and only if an analytic continuation of S beyond $\hat{x}$ would violate any combination of the following:

1. One or more inequalities of form (4.2.3).

2. One or more inequalities of form (4.5.5) as applied to the payoff functions H_i^t.

3. The inequality $0 \leq t \leq 1$.

The lemma follows from the definition of graph $X = X(G, p)$.

4.18 Destabilization Points

By lemma 4.10.1, for almost all games G, almost all prior vectors p will give rise to a separable game $\Gamma^0 = \Gamma^0(G, p)$ having only *one* equilibrium point $q^0 = \phi$, which will be a strong equilibrium point in pure strategies. Moreover, by lemma 4.17.7, if ϕ is also an (isolated) equilibrium point of the original game $\Gamma^1 = G$, then ϕ will be the actual outcome selected by the linear tracing procedure.

On the other hand, if ϕ is *not* an equilibrium point of G, then obviously one or more players will have to *shift* from their original strategies ϕ_i to alternative strategies $q_i \neq \phi_i$ during the tracing procedure. As was indicated in section 4.11, the outcome will crucially depend on which player will be the *first* to shift to another strategy.

Now suppose that player i is the first player to shift, and that this shift occurs at $t = t_i$. This can happen only if, at $t = t_i$, in addition to ϕ_i, he has *another* pure-strategy best reply ϕ_i' to the other players' strategy combination ϕ_{-i} (lemma 4.5.3). If the other assumptions of lemma 4.17.8 are also satisfied (which will always be true in nondegenerate cases), then player i's strategy shift will take the form of a jump segment at this t-value $t = t_i$.

As we know from lemma 4.17.10, in general, this jump segment J may end before player i has moved all the way from strategy ϕ_i to strategy ϕ_i' because another player j may get destabilized before player i can reach ϕ_i'. (An example of this kind will be discussed in section 4.19.) On the other hand, if assumption 3 of lemma 4.17.9 is satisfied, then player i will be able to shift to ϕ_i' without destabilizing any other player.

As we have seen, at the t-value $t = t_i$, the point at which player i shifts to another strategy, he is *indifferent* between his initial best-reply strategy ϕ_i and an alternative best-reply pure strategy $\phi_i' \neq \phi_i$. Thus the t-value $t = t_i$ is defined by the equation

$$tH_i(\phi_i\phi_{-i}) + (1 - t)H_i(\phi_i p_{-i}) = tH_i(\phi_i'\phi_{-i}) + (1 - t)H_i(\phi_i' p_{-i}), \qquad (4.18.1)$$

provided that this t-value satisfies

$$0 \leq t < 1. \qquad (4.18.2)$$

This t-value $t = t_i$ is called player i's *destabilization point*. Strategy ϕ_i is called his *initial strategy*, whereas strategy ϕ_i' is called his *destabilizing strategy*. (Thus, by our definition, this destabilizing strategy ϕ_i' is always a pure strategy, even if player i does not actually shift all the way to ϕ_i'.) To make this destabilizing strategy explicit, we write $t = t_i = t_i(\phi_i')$.

If the t-value defined by (4.18.1) does not satisfy (4.18.2), then we set

$$t_i = +\infty. \qquad (4.18.3)$$

LEMMA 4.18.1   Player i will be the first player to shift to another strategy— with strategy ϕ_i' as his destabilizing strategy—if and only if

$$t_i^* = t_i(\phi_i') = \min_{j \in N} \min_{\hat{\phi}_j \neq \phi_j} t_j(\hat{\phi}_j). \qquad (4.18.4)$$

The lemma follows from our preceding discussion.

As the third example of section 4.11 shows, in degenerate cases it can happen that two (or even more) players $i, j, \ldots$, are destabilized at the same t-value $t_i = t_j = \ldots$. In such a case the linear tracing procedure will not be well defined. (The same is true if one player i has two or more destabilizing strategies ϕ_i', ϕ_i'', ..., at the same t-value $t = t_i$.)

As we have seen, if all assumptions of lemma 4.17.9 are satisfied, then at the t-value $t = t_i$ there will be a jump segment going all the way to the point $\bar{x} = (t_i, \phi') = (t_i, (\phi_i' \phi_{-i}))$. In this case, by lemma 4.17.11, if ϕ' is a strong equilibrium point of game G, we can conclude that ϕ' is the outcome. On the other hand, if ϕ' is not an equilibrium point in game G then, once more, some of the players will have to change their strategies during the remaining part of the tracing procedure. Thus we can again use lemma 4.18.1 to decide which player will change his strategy first in the subinterval $[t_i, 1]$, and so on.

To conclude, the linear tracing procedure takes a particularly simple form when the entire distinguished path consists of *constant segments* and (possibly) of *jump segments* but contains no variable segments. In such cases, by using the lemmas of sections 4.17 and 4.18 (sometimes repeatedly), we can rather easily compute the outcome. In contrast, if the distinguished path contains variable segments, then more computation may be required because we may have to calculate the actual mixed-strategy equilibrium points used on these variable segments numerically as functions of the parameter t. Yet, as we will see in section 4.19, even in such cases there may be possible shortcuts to finding the outcome without computing these mixed-strategy equilibrium points.

4.19   An Example for a Backward-Moving Variable Segment

Suppose that player 3 simultaneously plays two games: One is game G_1, which he plays against player 1.[7] The other is game G_2, which he plays against player 2. Each player has two pure strategies. Those of player 1 will be called a and b, those of player 2 will be called c and d, and those of player 3 will be called e and f. The payoff matrices of games G_1 and G_2 are shown in figures 4.23 and 4.24. (As will be noted, in game G_1 player 2 always obtains a zero payoff. The same is true of player 1 in game G_2.)

We now assume that player 3 is constrained always to use the same strategy in games G_1 and G_2, and that his total payoff is the sum of the payoffs he receives from both games. Under these assumptions games G_1 and G_2 will effectively become one game G, whose payoff matrix is shown in Fig. 4.25.

The strategy space of this game G can be represented by cube $ABCDFIJK$ of figure 4.26. Player 1's strategies will be represented by the up–down

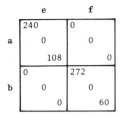

Game G_1

Figure 4.23

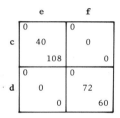

Game G_2

Figure 4.24

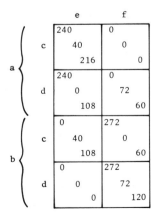

Game G

Figure 4.25

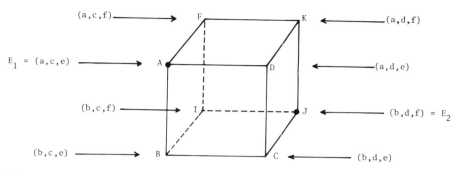

Figure 4.26

coordinate, player 2's by the right–left coordinate, and player 3's by the forward–backward coordinate. The eight corner points of the cube will correspond to various pure-strategy combinations of the game as indicated in figure 4.26.

As is easy to verify, game G has two equilibrium points in pure strategies: $E_1 = (a, c, e) = A$ and $E_2 = (b, d, f) = J$. It has also a third equilibrium point, $E^* = (q_1^*, d, q_3^*)$, where players 1 and 3 use the mixed strategies $q_1^* = (\frac{5}{7}, \frac{2}{7})$ and $q_3^* = (\frac{17}{32}, \frac{15}{32})$, whereas player 2 uses the pure strategy $d = (0, 1)$. In figure 4.26, E^* (not shown) would be located on face $DCJK$, not far from the midpoint of edge DK.

We analyze this game G on the assumption that the players' initial expectations correspond to the prior vector $p = (p_1, p_2, p_3)$, where $p_1 = (\frac{1}{3}, \frac{2}{3})$, $p_2 = (\frac{1}{3}, \frac{2}{3})$, and $p_3 = (\frac{5}{8}, \frac{3}{8})$. Accordingly, the separable auxiliary game Γ^0 has the payoff matrix shown in figure 4.27, whereas a typical auxiliary game Γ^t, $0 \leq t \leq 1$, has the payoff matrix shown in figure 4.28.

Clearly game Γ^0 has only the one equilibrium point $(a, d, f) = K$, which is a strong equilibrium point in pure strategies. But it is not an equilibrium point of the original game $\Gamma^1 = G$. Therefore at least one player must change his strategy during the tracing procedure. The question is which player will be the first to do so.

We can rule out the possibility that it is player 2 because, as long as player 3 keeps on using strategy f, player 2 will always be better off by using strategy d. (Hence $t_2 = +\infty$.) Thus it must be either player 1 or player 3. Using equation (4.18.1), we find that player 1's destabilization point is $t_1 = \frac{3}{20} = 0.15$ because this is the solution of the equation

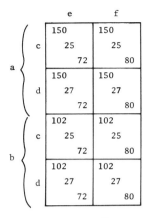

Game Γ^0

Figure 4.27

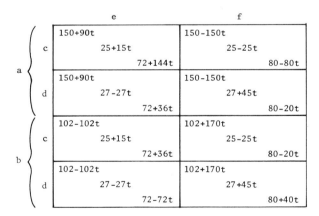

Game Γ^t

Figure 4.28

$$150 - 150t = 102 + 170t. \tag{4.19.1}$$

On the other hand, player 3's destabilization point is $t_3 = \frac{1}{7} = 0.14$ because this is the solution of the equation

$$72 + 36t = 80 - 20t. \tag{4.19.2}$$

Thus $t_3 < t_1$, and so player 3 is the first player to shift his strategy at $t = t_3 = \frac{1}{7}$.

As a result any feasible path L of the linear tracing procedure must start with the *constant segment* $\mathscr{C}$ using the pure-strategy combination $(a, d, f) = K.$[8] But this constant segment $\mathscr{C}$ ends at the t-value $t = \frac{1}{7}$, and the next segment of path L will be a jump segment $\mathscr{J}$ on which players 1 and 2 go on using strategies a and d, respectively, whereas player 3 uses various mixed strategies $q_3 = q_3(\mu) = (\mu, 1 - \mu)$.

The next question we have to ask is whether this jump segment $\mathscr{J}$ will go all the way to the point $(t, \phi') = (\frac{1}{7}, (a, d, e))$ or will end before reaching this point. The answer is that $\mathscr{J}$ will end at the point $\hat{x} = (\frac{1}{7}, (a, d, \hat{q}_3))$ with $\hat{q}_3 = q_3(\frac{3}{4}) = (\frac{3}{4}, \frac{1}{4})$ because at that point player 2 will be *destabilized*.

To verify this, note that

$$H_2^{1/7}(a, d, e) = 27 - 27t = 27 - \frac{27}{7} = \frac{162}{7}, \tag{4.19.3}$$

whereas

$$H_2^{1/7}(a, d, f) = 27 + 45t = 27 + \frac{45}{7} = \frac{234}{7}. \tag{4.19.4}$$

Therefore, if we set $q_3 = (\mu, 1 - \mu)$, then

$$H_2^{1/7}(a, d, q_3) = \frac{162\mu}{7} + \frac{234(1 - \mu)}{7} = \frac{234}{7} - \frac{72\mu}{7}. \tag{4.19.5}$$

On the other hand,

$$H_2^{1/7}(a, c, e) = 25 + 15t = 25 + \frac{15}{7} = \frac{190}{7}, \tag{4.19.6}$$

whereas

$$H_2^{1/7}(a, c, f) = 25 - 25t = 25 - \frac{25}{7} = \frac{150}{7}. \tag{4.19.7}$$

Therefore

$$H_2^{1/7}(a, c, q_3) = \frac{190\mu}{7} + \frac{150(1 - \mu)}{7} = \frac{150}{7} + \frac{40\mu}{7}. \tag{4.19.8}$$

Consequently, as long as $\mu < \frac{3}{4}$,

$$H_2^{1/7}(a, d, q_3) > H_2^{1/7}(a, c, q_3), \tag{4.19.9}$$

and player 2 will keep on using strategy d. But at the point $\mu = \frac{3}{4}$ this inequality will be replaced by an equality, which means that player 2 will be indifferent between strategies d and c. Finally, if player 3 used a strategy q_3 with $\mu > \frac{3}{4}$, player 2 would shift to strategy c; that is, the strategy combination (a, d, q_3) would no longer be an equilibrium point.

This means that the jump segment J will end at the point $(1/7, (a, d, \hat{q}_3))$ with $\hat{q}_3 = (\frac{3}{4}, \frac{1}{4})$. Yet any continuation of path L from this point on *cannot* be in the direction of *increasing* t-values because, in the range $\frac{1}{7} < t < \frac{3}{20}$, the linear tracing graph consists merely of one constant segment $\mathscr{C}'$, which uses the pure-strategy combination $(a, c, e) = A$. (To verify this, note that in this range, strategy a dominates strategy b. On the other hand, if player 1 uses a, then strategy e dominates strategy f. Finally, if player 3 uses strategy e, then strategy c dominates strategy d.) Likewise, L has no continuation in the plane (hyperplane) $t = 1/7$ itself, either, because game $\Gamma^{1/7}$ has no equilibrium points outside $\mathscr{J}$, except for the one equilibrium point $(a, c, e) = A$ belonging to $\mathscr{C}'$.

Thus any continuation of path L must be a path L' going in the direction of *decreasing* t-values and linking $\mathscr{J}$ with $\mathscr{C}'$. Since, by theorem 4.13.2, such a path L' linking $\mathscr{J}$ with $\mathscr{C}'$ must exist, even without knowing the nature of the connecting path L', we can infer that any feasible path must contain the constant segment $\mathscr{C}'$. Moreover it is easy to show that once a feasible path reaches the constant segment $\mathscr{C}'$, which uses the pure-strategy combination $(a, c, e) = A$, it will never deviate from $\mathscr{C}'$ because $(a, c, e) = A = E_1$ is a *strong* equilibrium point of the original game $\Gamma^1 = G$. Consequently we can identify E_1 as the outcome, without actually computing the path L' connecting $\mathscr{J}$ with $\mathscr{C}'$.

Nevertheless, for the reader's convenience, we will describe the connecting path L' in some detail. As has been noted, the jump segment $\mathscr{J}$ ends at the point $\hat{x} = (1/7, (a, d, \hat{q}_3))$ with $\hat{q}_3 = (\frac{3}{4}, \frac{1}{4})$. At this point $\hat{x}$, $\mathscr{J}$ is joined by a *backward-moving* variable segment $\mathscr{V}$ whose points are of the form $(t, \bar{q}(t))$ with $\frac{1}{7} \geq t \geq \frac{1}{21}$, where

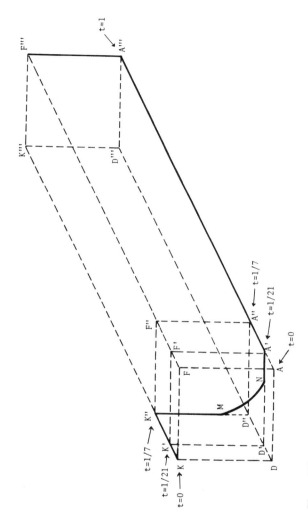

Figure 4.29

$$\bar{q}_1(t) = (1,0) = a = \text{constant}, \tag{4.19.10}$$

$$\bar{q}_2(t) = \left(\frac{1}{21t} - \frac{1}{3}, \frac{4}{3} - \frac{1}{21t} \right), \tag{4.19.11}$$

$$\bar{q}_3(t) = \left(\frac{5}{8} + \frac{1}{56t}, \frac{3}{8} - \frac{1}{56t} \right). \tag{4.19.12}$$

$\mathcal{V}$ ends at the point $\check{x} = (\frac{1}{21}, \bar{q}(\frac{1}{21})) = (\frac{1}{21}, (a, \check{q}_2, e))$, where $\check{q}_2 = \bar{q}_2(\frac{1}{21}) = (\frac{2}{3}, \frac{1}{3})$. At this point $\check{x}$, $\mathcal{V}$ is joined by another *jump segment* $\mathcal{J}'$, whose points are of the form $(\frac{1}{21}, (a, \tilde{q}_2(v), e))$, where $\tilde{q}_2(v) = (v, 1 - v)$ with $\frac{2}{3} \le v \le 1$.

Finally, $\mathcal{J}'$ ends at the point $x^+ = (\frac{1}{21}, (a, c, e))$ and is joined at this point by the *constant segment* $\mathcal{C}'$ which uses the pure-strategy combination $(a, c, e) = A$ over the entire range $\frac{1}{21} \le t \le 1$.

The distinguished path L as a whole, consisting of line segments $\mathcal{C} = KK''$, $\mathcal{J} = K''M$, $\mathcal{V} = MN$, $\mathcal{J}' = NA'$, and $\mathcal{C}' = A'A'''$, is shown in figure 4.29.

The diagram shows a three-dimensional structure, even though in principle the tracing procedure of our example must take place in a four-dimensional space $Y = I \times Q$, where I is the unit interval $I = [0,1]$ representing the set of admissible t-values, while $Q = \text{cube } ABCDFIJK$ of figure 4.26. But it so happens that at all points of the distinguished path L, player 1 always uses strategy a, so that all strategy combinations employed on this path L will actually correspond to points on the upper face $\bar{Q} = ADKF$ of the cube Q. Therefore path L is, in fact, a subset of the three-dimensional space $\bar{Y} = I \times \bar{Q}$. (For convenience, in figure 4.29 this face $ADKF$ has been rotated by $180°$.)

As figure 4.29 shows, the distinguished path starts at point K, that is, at the t-value $t = 0$. Then it proceeds to point K'', that is, to the t-value $t = \frac{1}{7} = 0.14$. Segment $K''M$ throughout stays at this latter t-value. But segment MN *goes back* from $t = \frac{1}{7} = 0.14$ to $t = \frac{1}{21} = 0.05$. Segment NA' stays at the latter lower t-value. Finally, segment $A'A'''$ moves from $t = \frac{1}{21} = 0.05$ to $t = 1$.

Apart from the distinguished path L shown in figure 4.29, the linear tracing graph X of our example has also another branch $\mathcal{B}$ which connects equilibrium points $E_2 = (b, d, f) = J$ and E^* of game G. This latter branch is restricted to t-values with $\frac{3}{20} = 0.15 \le t \le 1$. But to save space, this latter branch will not be described here in detail.[9]

5 The Solution Concept

5.1 Introduction

We have already introduced some of the fundamental ideas pertaining to our solution concept. In this chapter we explain how our theory solves irreducible games. For this purpose we employ a *process of candidate elimination and substitution*. The process starts with a set of natural solution candidates and then generates a finite sequence of sets of equilibrium points, called *candidate sets*. The last candidate set contains only one equilibrium point, the *solution* of the game. As an introduction to this chapter we shall give an informal overview over the new ideas to be introduced. Detailed and precise definitions can be found in sections 5.2, 5.3, and 5.5.

Our theory makes use of special substructures of games, called *formations*. Roughly speaking, a formation is a proper substructure obtained by eliminating some of the agents' choices which are closed with respect to local best replies. Those formations, which are smallest in the sense that they contain no other formation, are called primitive. The primitive formations are of special significance for our theory. In irreducible games with formations we will look at the solutions of all the primitive formations as the natural candidates for a solution of the game. We will try to find the solution among these natural candidates.

Irreducible games without formations are called *basic*. To solve a basic game, the tracing procedure is applied to the centroid of the game—to that strategy combination where each agent uses all his choices with the same probability. The result of doing this is the solution of the game.

In irreducible games with formations we make use of payoff dominance and risk dominance for pairwise comparisons of solution candidates. Our definition of *risk dominance* between two equilibrium points will be based on the tracing procedure applied to a special prior. If this tracing procedure yields one of the equilibrium points, then this equilibrium point risk-dominates the other. The special prior distribution depends on the two equilibrium points and therefore is called the *bicentric prior*.

A risk-dominance comparison is not performed in the original game but in a *restricted game*, a substructure of the smallest formation that contains both equilibrium points. In this formation those players who have the same strategy in both equilibrium points are fixed at these equilibrium strategies. The result is the restricted game.

The bicentric prior is regarded as a preliminary theory to be improved by the tracing procedure. The construction of the bicentric prior starts from a picture of a player's initial beliefs. All other players play their strategies in the same equilibrium point. With subjective probabilities adding up to one, this will be either one of both equilibrium points to be compared: the player plays his central local best reply to the joint mixture corresponding to his beliefs. His *bicentric prior strategy* is the result of averaging over all possible subjective probability distributions over both equilibrium points. The bicentric prior is the mixed-strategy combination for the restricted game that contains the bicentric prior strategies as components.

Risk dominance and payoff dominance are combined to form a *dominance relationship* that gives precedence to payoff dominance. Risk dominance determines dominance, if neither of the two equilibrium points payoff-dominates the other.

Not all dominance relationships are regarded as equally important. It is reasonable to emphasize comparisons between equilibrium points that are similar to each other. For this purpose a measure of *strategic distance* between two equilibrium points is introduced. The definition of strategic distance is closely related to that of the bicentric prior. If the subjective probability of a player for one of both equilibrium points is increased from 0 to 1, this probability will pass a finite number of *critical points* where the central local best reply of the player is changed. The number of critical points for all players in the restricted game is the strategic distance.

The measure of strategic distance is further refined to a measure of *strategic net distance* within a candidate set. For each of both equilibrium points the strategic distance to the next neighbor in the candidate set is subtracted from the strategic distance between the two equilibrium points; the sum of both surpluses plus 1 is the strategic net distance. One is added in order to make sure that the strategic net distance is positive. Strategic net distance is small if both equilibrium points are relatively near to each other compared with the strategic distances to next neighbors in the candidate set.

The stability of an equilibrium point within a candidate set is measured by its *stability index*. The stability index is the greatest strategic net distance assumed in the set, such that within this net distance the candidate is not dominated by another candidate in the set. A candidate is *maximally stable* in a candidate set if its stability index is maximal in the set.

The *process of candidate elimination and substitution* starts with the set of all solutions of primitive formations, the *first candidate set*. Whenever possible an *elimination step* is performed in the transition from one candidate set to the next. An elimination step eliminates all candidates that are not maximally stable.

If a candidate set with more than one element cannot be narrowed down by an elimination step, a *substitution step* has to be performed. For this purpose a *substitute* of the candidate set is determined. The substitute is obtained by tracing the *centroid of the candidate set*. In the centroid of the candidate set each player uses the unweighted average of his strategies in the candidates of the set.

Generally, the substitute is not yet the solution. Among the candidates that have been eliminated before, there may be preferable ones. Therefore in a substitution step a new candidate set is formed that contains the substitute together with all candidates that have been eliminated before but not yet substituted. Once a candidate has been substituted, it is finally removed from consideration, but elimination is canceled if substitution becomes necessary. The flowchart of the process of candidate elimination and substitution is shown in figure 5.3.

Our solution concept is based on a recursive definition. We need to know the solutions of the primitive formations in order to start the process of candidate elimination and substitution. The primitive formations are smaller than the game under consideration; therefore we can assume that their solutions are known.

A primitive formation of an irreducible game may not be irreducible. In this case we have to apply the procedure of decomposition and reduction in order to find the solution (see section 3.13). As we explained at the end of chapter 2, the solution function specified by our theory is meant to be applied to uniformly perturbed games. The limit solution is obtained by letting the perturbance parameter go to zero.

The solution concept combines a number of separate ideas such as cell decomposition, reduction, primitive formations, the tracing procedure, payoff dominance, risk dominance, strategic net distance, candidate elimination, and substitution. The coherence of the composite structure cannot be made clear without a thorough discussion of the building blocks. Therefore we will not follow the shortest path to the completion of mathematical definition of the solution. Auxiliary concepts will be motivated and examined in the light of examples where they are introduced.

5.2   Initial Candidates

Games that arise in the context of economic theory often have many strong
equilibrium points. Obviously in such cases it is more natural to select
a strong equilibrium point rather than a weak one. Of course strong
equilibrium points are not always available, and if they are, they may be
ineligible in view of lack of symmetry invariance.

Even if strongness is not a suitable selection criterion, it is still possible
to look for a principle that helps us to avoid those weak equilibrium points
that are especially unstable. An example of a very unstable equilibrium
point is the completely mixed one in a 2×2 game with two strong ones.
In figure 3.6 this unstable equilibrium point corresponds to the point where
the stability regions of U and V meet. Both U and V are best replies to the
unstable equilibrium point. Mixed equilibrium points at the border of
stability regions of strong ones can be found in more complicated games
as well. It is clearly desirable to restrict the selection of such equilibrium
points to exceptional cases that cannot be avoided for good reasons such
as symmetry considerations.

The way in which we will approach this problem makes use of certain
substructures of games, called formations. With the help of such substructures we will be able to identify a class of equilibrium points without
unnecessary instability properties. Among these we will find natural solution candidates that will be called initial candidates.

Formations

Let $G = (\Phi, H)$, with $\Phi = \bigtimes_{i \in N} \Phi_i$, and $\Phi_i = \bigtimes_{ij \in M_i} \Phi_{ij}$ be a game in
standard form. A subset Ψ of Φ is called *cartesian*, if Ψ is a nonempty proper
subset of Φ of the form $\Psi = \bigtimes_{i \in N} \Psi_i$ with $\Psi_i = \bigtimes_{ij \in M_i} \Psi_{ij}$.

Consider a cartesian set Ψ. Let $G' = (\Psi, H')$ be the game that results from
G by narrowing the choice sets in Φ to Ψ (see section 2.6). Obviously, the
Ψ_{ij} are admissible new choice sets. G' is a substructure of G.

For every agent ij let $B'_{i \setminus ij}$ be the set of all ij-incomplete behavior
strategies in G'. For every player i let $Q'_{.i}$ be the set of all i-incomplete joint
mixtures in G'. The sets $B'_{i \setminus ij}$ and $Q'_{.i}$ are subsets of the corresponding sets
$B_{i \setminus ij}$ and $Q_{.i}$ for G (see section 2.6). $G' = (\Psi, H')$ is a *formation* of $G = (\Phi, H)$
if the following condition is satisfied for every agent ij and for every hybrid
combination $b'_{i \setminus ij} q'_{.i}$ with $b'_{i \setminus ij} \in B'_{i \setminus ij}$ and $q'_{.i} \in Q'_{.i}$:

$$A_{ij}(b'_{i\setminus ij}q'_{.i}) \subseteq \Psi_{ij}. \tag{5.2.1}$$

Here A_{ij} is the local best-reply correspondence of agent ij for G, which was introduced in section 2.7. It is important to notice that on the left-hand side of (5.2.1) we find the set of all pure local best replies to $b'_{i\setminus ij}q'_{.i}$ in G. If G' is a formation, then the local best replies in G' are also local best replies in G. This is a consequence of (5.2.1) and the lemma 2.3.2 on local best replies in section 2.3.

Condition (5.2.1) can be expressed by saying that Ψ is *closed with respect to local best replies* in G. If this is the case, we call $G' = (\Psi, H')$ the formation of G *generated* by Ψ. Let Λ and Ψ both be cartesian subsets of Φ which are closed with respect to local best replies in G, and let Λ be a proper subset of Ψ. Then we say that the formation generated by Λ is a *subformation* of the formation generated by Ψ.

Remarks   A behavior strategy b_i cannot be a best reply to a joint mixture $q_{.i}$ unless it is a local best reply. Therefore (5.2.1) has the following consequence. For every player i and every i-incomplete joint mixture $q'_{.i} \in Q'_{.i}$ we have

$$A_i(q'_{.i}) \subseteq \Psi_i, \tag{5.2.2}$$

where A_i is player i's best-reply correspondence (which was introduced in section 3.5).

It follows by (5.2.2) that an equilibrium point of a formation G' of G is also an equilibrium point of G. Since a formation is a game, it follows by Nash's theorem that every formation has at least one equilibrium point.

A formation is defined by the local condition (5.2.1) rather than the global condition (5.2.2). This has important consequences for the case that G is an interior substructure of a standard form with perfect recall. For such games the notion of a central local best reply $a_i(q_{.i})$ to a joint mixture has been introduced in section 2.7. It follows by (5.2.1) together with the definition of the central local best reply that it does not matter whether $a_i(q'_{.i})$ is computed in G or G' if $q'_{.i}$ is a joint mixture for a formation G' of G.

Interpretation   The stability condition (5.2.2) can be interpreted as follows: Suppose that player i is convinced that the other players will use strategies $\phi_j \in \Psi_j$ in the formation. If player i's expectations are compatible with this assumption, he will never have a pure best reply outside Ψ_i. Whatever his subjective probability distribution over Ψ_{-i} may be, his best replies will be strategies within the formation. A pure strategy outside Ψ_i will always yield less expected payoff than some pure strategy inside Ψ_i. In this respect the stability properties of a formation are similar to those of a strong equilibrium point.

Formations are defined in terms of best replies to joint mixtures rather than to i-incomplete combinations of mixed strategies. As was explained in section 2.3, player i may hold subjective beliefs on his opponents that cannot be expressed by an i-incomplete combination of mixed strategies. In our theory such beliefs occur as preliminary expectations that are gradually revised by the tracing procedure. Of course, after the solution is found, the beliefs of the players become nothing but the i-incomplete mixed-strategy combinations generated by the solution. Preliminary beliefs are disequilibrium beliefs and therefore need not have the same properties as the final solution.

A local best-reply condition rather than a global one is used for the definition of a formation. This seems to be appropriate in the framework of the standard form. A definition in terms of global best replies would not immediately lead to a standard form, but to a normal form. The pure strategy combinations in this normal form do not necessarily form a cartesian set. Any definition that leads to a standard form on the basis of a global best reply condition would have to be more complicated and probably somewhat artificial.

Intersections of Formations

Let $G' = (\Psi, H')$ and $G'' = (\Lambda, H'')$ be two formations of $G = (\Phi, H)$ such that the intersection $\Delta = \Lambda \cap \Psi$ is nonempty. The game $\bar{G} = (\Delta, \bar{H})$ that results from G by narrowing the choice sets in Φ to Δ is called the *intersection* of the formations G' and G''.

LEMMA 5.2.1 (Intersection lemma)   If $\bar{G}$ is the intersection of two formations G' and G'' of G, then $\bar{G}$ is a formation of G.

Proof   Condition (5.2.1) applied to $\bar{G}$ is an immediate consequence of (5.2.1) for G' and G''. ∎

PRIMITIVE FORMATIONS   A formation $G' = (\Psi, H')$ of G is called *primitive*, if G' has no subformation. A *primitive game* is a game without formations.

Remarks It follows by the intersection lemma 5.2.1 that two primitive formations of a game do not intersect. Obviously a game that is not primitive must have at least one primitive formation.

Let ψ be a strong equilibrium point of G. Then $\{\psi\}$ generates a primitive formation of G.

Comment Primitive formations are the smallest substructures with similar stability properties as strong equilibrium points. An equilibrium point in a primitive formation may be weak as far as the strategies in the formation are concerned, but it is strong with respect to outside strategies in the sense that an outside strategy incurs a positive deviation loss. Our solution concept favors the selection of such equilibrium points in order to obtain as much of the desirable stability properties of strong equilibrium points as possible.

Suppose that r is an equilibrium point of a primitive formation G' of G. Then it cannot happen that a strong equilibrium point ψ of G is a best reply for r. The reason for this is that $\{\psi\}$ generates a primitive formation that would have to belong to G'. This is impossible since G' is primitive. The stability property that has been described is certainly a desirable feature of equilibrium points of primitive formations.

It would not be reasonable to prefer strong equilibrium points to weak ones under all circumstances. This can be seen with the help of the game with normal form structure shown in figure 5.1. There $\Psi = \Psi_1 \times \Psi_2$ with

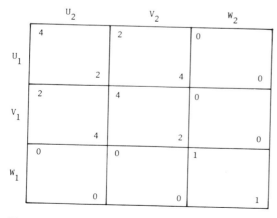

Figure 5.1
A 3×3 game with two primitive formations

$\Psi_1 = \{U_1, V_1\}$ and $\Psi_2 = \{U_2, V_2\}$ generates a primitive formation G' and $\{W\}$ with $W = (W_1, W_2)$ generates another primitive formation G''. The formation G' is equivalent to a matching pennies game and has a unique equilibrium point $r = (r_1, r_2)$ where both players use both strategies with probability $\frac{1}{2}$. The equilibrium payoffs $H(r) = (3, 3)$ are much better for both players than the equilibrium payoffs in $H(W) = (1, 1)$. Because in G' all payoffs are greater than 1, it is of little importance that W is strong and r is weak. Clearly in the case of figure 5.1 it is more reasonable to select r as the solution rather than W. The game has also a third equilibrium point q that is not in a primitive formation $q_i(U_i) = \frac{1}{8}$, $q_i(V_i) = \frac{1}{8}$, and $q_i(W_i) = \frac{3}{4}$. Both r and W are best replies to q.

We will take the view that the solutions of primitive formations are natural candidates for the solution of the whole game. Therefore we must now turn our attention to the question of how to define the solution of primitive games. It may happen that a primitive game has cells, inferior choices, duplicates, or semiduplicates. In such cases one has to apply our procedure of reduction and decomposition in order to find the solution. A direct definition of the solution without reference to substructures is required only for irreducible primitive games.

Solution of Basic Games

A game is called basic if it is primitive and irreducible—in other words, if it has no cells, inferior choices, duplicate classes, semiduplicate classes, or formations. Let $G = (\Phi, H)$ be a basic game. The centroid $c(\Phi)$ of G is that behavior strategy combination where every agent assigns equal probabilities to all his choices. Let $\mathcal{G}_1$ be the set of all basic games in the class $\mathcal{I}(\mathcal{R})$ of interior substructures of standard forms with perfect recall (see section 2.13). We define a solution function L_1 for $\mathcal{G}_1$ as follows: For every $G = (\Phi, H) \in \mathcal{G}_1$ the solution $L_1(G)$ is the result $T[G, c(\Phi)]$ of the logarithmic tracing procedure in behavior strategies applied to G with $c(\Phi)$ as prior distribution. This solution function L_1 is called the *basic solution function*.

Initial Candidates

We say that a game $G = (\Phi, H)$ has size K if K is the number of all choices in G; that is, if K is the sum of all K_{ij} with $ij \in M$, where K_{ij} is the number of agent ij's choices. Let L be a solution function for the class of all games in $\mathscr{I}(\mathscr{R})$ whose size is smaller than K, and let $G = (\Phi, H)$ be an irreducible game of size K. An *initial candidate* for G with respect to L is defined as follows: If G is basic, then the basic solution $L_1(G)$ is the only initial candidate for G. If G is not basic, then the solutions $L(G')$ of the primitive formations G' of G are the initial candidates of G. This definition is a meaningful one since in the case of a nonbasic game the primitive formations must be of smaller size. The set of all initial candidates is denoted by Ω_1. We call Ω_1 the first candidate set. The solutions of primitive formations are also called *primitive equilibria*.

Comment   Since the notion of an initial candidate is a part of the recursive definition of the solution function proposed in this book, it has to be relative to a solution function for games whose primitive formations are all basic. Our proposed solution function agrees with the basic solution function for basic games.

It may happen that the first candidate set of a nonbasic game has only one initial candidate, but generally such games will have many initial candidates. In this case Ω_1 is only the first sequence of candidate sets generated by a process of candidate elimination and substitution that was loosely described in the introduction of the chapter. Our notion of risk dominance is used as an important criterion of candidate elimination. It will be the task of the next section to introduce the formal definition of risk dominance and to discuss the underlying conceptual ideas.

5.3   Risk Dominance

In sections 3.7 to 3.9 the notion of risk dominance was discussed in the framework of 2×2 games. The axiomatization in section 3.9 shows that for this narrow class of games the comparison of Nash-products is a natural criterion of risk dominance. Obviously, a general definition should agree with that of chapter 3 for 2×2 games with two strong equilibrium points. This is of course not the only desirable property that one might want to achieve.

Since we cannot really motivate our general definition by desirable properties, we will emphasize the plausibility of its direct interpretation. In the long run one might want to extend the axiomatic approach to risk dominance beyond the narrow range of 2×2 games, but no attempt in this direction will be made here. In section 5.5 we will discuss some of the desirable properties that distinguish our present notion of risk dominance from other definitions that we considered in earlier stages of the development of our theory.

The Nature of Risk-Dominance Comparisons

Risk dominance is concerned with pairwise comparisons between equilibrium points. Consider two equilibrium points $U = (U_i)_N$ and $V = (V_i)_N$, not necessarily in pure strategies, of a game $G = (\Phi, H)$. Imagine a hypothetical situation where it is common knowledge that all players think that either U or V must be the solution without knowing which of both equilibrium points is the solution. Risk dominance tries to capture the idea that in this state of confusion the players enter a process of expectation formation that may lead to the conclusion that in some sense one of both equilibrium points is less risky than the other.

Bayesian rationality requires that a decision maker must have a subjective probability distribution over the states of the world that determine the consequences of his possible actions. We take the view that in game theory the subjective probabilities of players should not be arbitrary. A rational player should have a rational way of deriving his subjective probabilities from the structure of the game situation.

Imagine a rational outside observer who shares the common knowledge of the players and tries to form expectations on the game. We assume that there is just one rational way in which the outside observer can form his expectations on the behavior of the players. Obviously rational players must form their expectations on other players in the same way as the outside observer as far as the behavior of other players is concerned. This means that we do not have to consider different processes of expectation formation for different players but at just one way of forming expectations, namely that of a rational outside observer.

Our theory looks at the rational formation of expectations as a process that proceeds in two stages. The first stage yields a preliminary theory on the players' behavior. This theory takes the form of a mixed strategy combination, the bicentric prior, which already has been mentioned in the introduction of the chapter. With the help of the tracing procedure the expectations of the preliminary theory are then gradually transformed to final expectations.

Since the preliminary theory will look at the players as Bayesian decision makers, it must involve expectations on the players' expectations. The focus of the preliminary theory is on players rather than agents. The players are the centers of expectation formation, and all agents of the same player must have the same expectations. Consequently expectations on expectations must concern players rather than agents. This is the main reason why our theory had to be developed in terms of the standard form rather than the agent normal form (see section 2.3).

Some of the players may have the same strategy in U and V. Consider a player i with $U_i = V_i$. On the basis of the assumption that either U or V is the solution, it is natural to expect that player i will player his equilibrium strategy $U_i = V_i$; he has no need to know whether U of V is the solution in order to play his solution strategy. Therefore our theory describes a process of forming expectations where expectations on players i with $U_i = V_i$ are always fixed at these equilibrium strategies. Accordingly, risk dominance comparisons will be performed in a restricted game where such players are fixed at their equilibrium strategies.

The restricted game has an additional feature that serves to secure a desirable property called formation consistency. It should not matter whether risk dominance is determined in the game as a whole or in one of its formations which contains both equilibrium points.

Restricted Game Let U and V be two different equilibrium points, not necessarily in pure strategies, of a game $G = (\Phi, H)$ in standard form. Because the intersection of two formations is a formation (intersection lemma 5.2.1), a smallest formation F exists such that U and V belong to F. We call this formation F, the formation *spanned by U and V*. Let D be the set of players i who have the same strategy $U_i = V_i$ in both equilibrium points, and let C be the set of all agents of players in D. The *restricted game* $G' = (\Phi', H')$ *for the comparison between U and V* is the game that results from the formation F spanned by U and V by fixing every agent $ij \in C$ at the local strategy prescribed by the common equilibrium strategy $U_i = V_i$ in both equilibrium points.

Let N' be the set of all $i \in N$ with $U_i \neq V_i$, that is, the player set of the restricted game. Clearly the combinations $U' = (U_i)_{N'}$ and $V' = (V_i)_{N'}$ are equilibrium points of the restricted game G'. We say that U' and V' *correspond* to U and V, respectively, in G'.

Comment In exceptional cases the logarithmic tracing procedure has to be used to determine risk dominance. If this happens, the weights α_i^* of the logarithmic terms (see section 4.15) may have an influence on the result, and it may matter whether the logarithmic tracing procedure is performed in the game as a whole or in one of its formations. The definition of the restricted game as a substructure of the formation spanned by U and V has the consequences that risk dominance in the game as a whole is not different from risk dominance in one of its formations. This is the desirable property of formation consistency that was mentioned earlier.

The restricted game may have cells, inferior strategies, duplicate, or semiduplicate classes. We do not apply our procedure of decomposition and reduction in such cases. We look at the restricted game as a constraint on the process of forming expectations in the original game. Attention is focused on the formation spanned by U and V and expectations on players with $U_i = V_i$ are fixed on these strategies from the beginning to the end of the process. Because of this interpretation of the restricted game we do not attach any significance to structural features not present in the game as a whole.

A Theory of Preliminary Expectations

Let U and V be two equilibrium points of $G = (\Phi, H)$ such that for every player i the strategies U_i and V_i in U and V, respectively, are different. (G may be the original game under consideration or it may be the relevant restricted game.) We continue to look at the hypothetical situation where it is common knowledge that all players believe that either U or V is the solution.

It will be convenient to look at the problem of forming preliminary expectations from the point of view of an outside observer. We approach the problem by asking the following question: What could a player do if he had to make his decision in an initial state of uncertainty, not knowing whether U or V is the solution? Of course he will eventually know; however, the problem at hand is not yet the derivation of final expectations but the derivation of preliminary expectations.

The description of the initial state of uncertainty between U and V must be made more precise. What does player i think about the other players in this state of uncertainty? He must think that in the end they will find out whether U or V is the solution, that they will all follow the same rational reasoning process, and that they will all come to the same final conclusion and therefore act accordingly. Player i being a Bayesian must have subjective probabilities z_i and $1 - z_i$ for both of these possibilities.

A player in the initial state of uncertainty must expect that in the end not only the other players but also he himself will know which of both equilibrium points is the solution. However, if he had to make his decision in his initial state of uncertainty he could do nothing else than to choose a best reply against the i-incomplete mixture with probabilities z_i for U_{-i} and $1 - z_i$ for V_{-i}.

What should the outside observer think about the parameters z_i? As a Bayesian he must form a prior distribution. Obviously the distributions of the z_i should be independent of each other since the players form their expectations independently of each other. Moreover it is natural to form a flat prior on z_i, that is, a uniform distribution over $[0, 1]$. It may happen that among the behavior strategies of player i there is more than one best reply to the joint mixture with probabilities z_i for U_{-i} and $1 - z_i$ for V_{-i}. In this case it is natural for the outside observer to assume that player i will choose his central local best reply to the joint mixture (see section 2.7).

A plausible chain of reasoning has led us to a complete description of a preliminary theory an outside observer should have on the player's behavior in the hypothetical situation. It is convenient to introduce the symbolic expression $z_i U_{-i} + (1 - z_i) V_{-i}$ for the i-incomplete joint mixture with probabilities z_i and $1 - z_i$ for U_{-i} and V_{-i}, respectively. The preliminary theory can be summarized as follows:

1. Each player i believes that either all other players behave according to U_{-i} or all other players behave according to V_{-i}.

2. Each player i has a subjective probability z_i for U_{-i} and subjective probability $1 - z_i$ for V_{-i}.

3. Each player i plays his central local best reply $a_i[z_i U_{-i} + (1 - z_i) V_{-i}]$ to the i-incomplete joint mixture $z_i U_{-i} + (1 - z_i) V_{-i}$.

4. The z_i are independently distributed (subjective) random variables; each of them has an even distribution over the interval $[0, 1]$.

The expectations specified by the preliminary theory take the form of a mixed strategy combination which will be called the *bicentric prior* because it is a special prior distribution concerning a hypothetical comparison between two equilibrium points.

BICENTRIC PRIOR   Let $G = (\Phi, H)$ be an interior substructure of a standard form with perfect recall, that is, a game in $\mathscr{I}(\mathscr{R})$ (see section 2.13). Let U and V be two equilibrium points of G, and let i be a player such that his strategies U_i and V_i in U and V, respectively, are different. For every z with $0 \leq z \leq 1$ define

$$r_i^z = a_i(zU_{-i} + (1 - z)V_{-i}), \tag{5.3.1}$$

where a_i denotes the central local best reply (section 2.7).

The bicentric prior strategy of player i for the comparison of U and V is defined as follows:

$$p_i(\phi_i) = \int_0^1 r_i^z(\phi_i)dz, \quad \text{for every } \phi_i \in \Phi_i. \tag{5.3.2}$$

In the next section we shall prove a lemma that shows that no difficulty arises with respect to the integrability of $r_i^z(\phi_i)$. As we shall see there, the interval $[0, 1]$ can be subdivided into a finite number of subintervals where r_i^z is constant. The bicentric prior for the comparison between U and V is that strategy combination p that contains the bicentric prior strategies as components.

As before let $U = (U_i)_N$ and $V = (V_i)_N$ be two different equilibrium points of a game $G = (\Phi, H)$, but such that we have $U_k = V_k$ for some players k. Let $G' = (\Phi', H')$ be the restricted game for the comparison of U and V, and let $U' = (U_i)_{N'}$ and $V' = (V_i)_{N'}$ be the equilibrium points of G' that correspond to U and V, respectively. Then the bicentric prior strategy of a player i with $U_i \neq V_i$ for the comparison of U and V is the bicentric prior strategy p_i of this player for the comparison of U' and V' in the restricted game G'; the bicentric prior for the comparison between U and V is the bicentric prior p' for the comparison between U' and V' in G'.

RISK DOMINANCE   Let $U = (U_i)_N$ and $V = (V_i)_N$ be two different equilibrium points of a game $G \in \mathcal{I}(\mathcal{R})$, and let p' be the bicentric prior for the comparison between U and V. Let G' be the restricted game for the comparison between U and V. We say that U risk-dominates V if we have

$$T(G', p') = U' = (U_i)_{N'}. \tag{5.3.3}$$

Analogously, V risk-dominates U if we have

$$T(G', p') = V' = (V_i)_{N'}, \tag{5.3.4}$$

where N' is the player set of the restricted game G'.

Interpretation

The definition of risk dominance is based on a hypothetical process of forming expectations starting from a state of uncertainty between U and

V. A preliminary view of the risks involved in the uncertainty between U and V is embodied in the bicentric prior. If the gradual adaptation of expectations with the help of the tracing procedure converges to one of both equilibrium points, then the risks arising from the initial state of uncertainty favor this equilibrium point. The term "risk dominant" can be understood as "dominant in the players' expectation after due consideration of the risks involved in the initial state of uncertainty." This justifies our language use.

As in section 3.9 we permit the possibility that none of both equilibrium points risk dominates the other. $T(G', p')$ may be different both from U' and V'. If this happens, none of both equilibrium points is clearly favored by the risks involved in the uncertainty between U and V.

5.4   Properties of Risk Dominance

It will be the first task of this section to show that the integral in (5.3.2) is always well defined. Since r_i^z is a central local best reply that is obtained as the result of an iterative process, this is not obvious (see section 2.7).

We will prove two lemmas on desirable properties of our notion of risk dominance. The property of *formation consistency* mentioned earlier is expressed by the first lemma. The second concerns another desirable property, *invariance with respect to isomorphisms*. A special class of games, called unanimity games, will be examined in detail. In nondegenerate cases risk dominance in such games can be characterized in a simple way that is reminiscent of Nash's cooperative bargaining theory with fixed threats. Therefore the name Nash-property will be used in this connection.

A lemma on 2×2 games will show that our general concept of risk dominance agrees with the special one axiomatized in section 3.9 for 2×2 games with two strong equilibrium points. We shall also reconsider the payoff monotonicity counterexample from section 3.8, in order to verify that our notion of risk dominance does not have this property. The discussion will show that nevertheless the result is not unreasonable.

Stability Regions with Respect to Central Local Best Replies

Let $G = (\Phi, H)$ be an interior substructure of a standard form with perfect recall or, in other words, a game in the class $\mathscr{I}(\mathscr{R})$. To show that our definition (5.3.2) of the bicentric prior strategy in fact describes a well-defined mixed strategy, we will prove a more general result on central local best replies. Some auxiliary definitions and notations will now be introduced in order to prepare this result.

Let L_i be the set of all behavior strategies r_i of player i, such that for every agent ij of player i the local strategy r_{ij} prescribed by r_i to agent ij is the centroid of some subset of agent ij's choice set Φ_{ij}. Obviously a strategy r_i that is a central local best reply $a_i(q_{.i})$ to some i-incomplete joint mixture must be an element of R_i. Therefore we call L_i the set of *potential central local best replies* of player i. It is clear that R_i is a finite set.

For every $r_i \in L_i$ let $R(r_i)$ be the set of all $q_{.i} \in Q_{.i}$ such that r_i is the central local best reply to $q_{.i}$. We call $R(r_i)$ the *central local best-reply stability region* of r_i (or the *stability region* of r_i where there is no danger of confusion with the stability region $S(\phi_i)$ introduced in chapter 3, section 3.4). One may think of the correspondence R as the inverse of the central local best-reply function a_i.

The following lemma will assert that $R(r_i)$ is *convex*; this means that for $q_{.i} \in R(r_i)$ and $r_{.i} \in R(r_i)$ and $0 < \alpha < 1$ the joint mixture $s_{.i}$ with

$$s_{.i}(\phi_{-i}) = \alpha q_{.i}(\phi_{-i}) + (1 - \alpha)r_{.i}(\phi_{-i}), \tag{5.4.1}$$

for every $\phi_{-i} \in \Phi_{-i}$ is also in $R(r_i)$.

LEMMA 5.4.1 (Convexity lemma) Let $G = (\Phi, H)$ be an interior substructure of a standard form with perfect recall, and let $r_i \in L_i$ be a potential central local best reply of player i in G. Then the central local best-reply stability region $R(r_i)$ of r_i in G is convex.

Proof Let b_i^o, $b_i^1, \ldots$, be a best reply sequence for a joint mixture $q_{.i}$. According to the theorem 2.7.3 on coordination, the sequence b_i^o, $b_i^1, \ldots$, converges after a finite number of steps, and it has been pointed out in the remark after the proof that $|M_i|$ is an upper bound of this number.

In the proof of the theorem 2.7.3 on coordination a partition M_i^1, M_i^2 of M_i has been introduced. The construction was based on a fixed tree K_i of player i (a tree of player i in the game with perfect recall whose substructure G is assumed to be). It is an important property of the construction that for $ij \in M_i^{k+1}$ the forward set $[ij\rangle$ relative to K_i belongs to $M_i^1 \cup \cdots \cup M_i^k$. (For the definition of $[ij\rangle$, see section 2.5.) In a best-reply sequence b_i^o, $b_i^1, \ldots$, for $q_{.i}$ the local strategies of agents in M_i^k do not change any more after b_i^k. The local best replies of agents $ij \in M_i^{k+1}$ to $b_i^k q_{.i}$ maximize his local payoff $H_{ij}(b_{[ij\rangle} q_{.i})$. It is important to note that for fixed $b_{[ij\rangle}$ this local payoff is a linear function of the probabilities $q_{.i}(\phi_{-i})$.

Let c_i be that behavior strategy of player i that for every agent ij assigns equal probabilities to all choices in Φ_{ij}. A best-reply sequence $b_i^o, b_i^1, \ldots$, to a joint mixture $q_{.i}$ will be called *normal*, if it starts from $b_i^o = c_i$. Obviously exactly one normal best-reply structure belongs to every joint mixture $q_{.i}$.

Consider two joint mixtures $r_{.i}$ and $q_{.i}$. Let $b_i^o, b_i^1, \ldots$, and $g_i^o, g_i^1, \ldots$, be the normal best-reply sequences for $r_{.i}$ and $q_{.i}$, respectively. Suppose that we have $b_i^k \neq g_i^k$ for some k. Since the local strategies of agents in M_i^k do not change after b_i^k and g_i^k, respectively, in the two normal best-reply sequences, we must have $a_i(r_{.i}) \neq a_i(q_{.i})$. Therefore the same normal best-reply sequence $b_i^o, b_i^1, \ldots$, belongs to every $r_{.i} \in R(r_i)$.

For every sequence $b_i^o, \ldots, b_i^k$ with $b_i^o = c_i$ and $b_i^m \in L_i$ for $m = 1, \ldots, k$, let $N(b_i^o, \ldots, b_i^k)$ be the set of all joint mixtures $q_{.i}$ such that the first $k + 1$ members of the normal best-reply sequence for $q_{.i}$ are the strategies $b_i^o, \ldots, b_i^k$. We will prove by induction on k that $N(b_i^o, \ldots, b_i^k)$ is convex. Because the same normal best-reply sequence belongs to every $r_i \in R(r_i)$, this is sufficient for the convexity of $R(r_i)$.

Obviously the assertion that $N(b_i^o, \ldots, b_i^k)$ is convex holds for $k = 0$. To see that the assertion holds for $k + 1$ if it holds for k, consider a sequence $b_i^o, \ldots, b_i^{k+1}$ with $b_i^o = c_i$ and $b_i^m \in L_i$ for $m = 1, \ldots, k + 1$. We can assume that $N(b_i^o, \ldots, b_i^{k+1})$ is nonempty since the empty set is convex anyhow. Consider three joint mixtures $q_{.i}, r_{.i},$ and $s_{.i}$ related as in (5.4.1) and with $q_{.i}$ and $r_{.i}$ in $N(b_i^o, \ldots, b_i^{k+1})$. In view of definition of b_i^{k+1} an agent $ij \in M_i^{k+1}$ has the same local best replies to $b_i^k q_{.i}$ and to $b_i^k r_{.i}$. In view of the convexity of $N(b_i^o, \ldots, b_i^k)$ and the linearity of $H_{ij}(b_{[ij\rangle}q_{.i})$ with respect to $q_{.i}$, we can conclude that the local best replies of an agent $ij \in M_i^{k+1}$ to $b_i^k s_{.i}$ are the local best replies of this agent to $b_i^k q_{.i}$ and $b_i^k r_{.i}$. This shows that $N(b_i^o, \ldots, b_i^{k+1})$ is convex. ∎

Consequences for the Bicentric Prior

The convexity of the central local best reply stability regions has the consequence that under the assumptions underlying the definition of the bicentric prior the interval $0 \leq z \leq 1$ is partitioned into finitely many subintervals, where r_i^z is constant. Each of these subintervals corresponds to the intersection of a stability region $R(r_i)$ with the set of all joint mixtures of the form $zU_{-i} + (1 - z)V_{-i}$. The values of z for mixtures in the intersection form the subinterval, which will be denoted by $Z(r_i)$. We call $Z(r_i)$ the *z-line subinterval for* r_i. In many cases $Z(r_i)$ may of course be empty, and in others it may consist of a single point. For every $r_i \in L_i$, let $|Z(r_i)|$ be the length of the subinterval $Z(r_i)$. Obviously, instead of (5.3.2), we can also write

$$p_i(\phi_i) = \sum_{r_i \in L_i} |Z(r_i)| r_i(\phi_i), \quad \text{for every } \phi_i \in \Phi_i. \tag{5.4.2}$$

We say that $Z(r_i)$ is an essential subinterval if $|Z(r_i)|$ is positive. A strategy $r_i \in L_i$ is called essential for p_i if $Z(r_i)$ is an essential subinterval. Obviously, only the essential $r_i \in L_i$ contributes anything to the sum (5.4.2).

It is now clear that no problems arise with respect to the integrability of r_i^z in the definition of the bicentric prior. Moreover (5.4.2) indicates how the bicentric prior can be computed in applications to specific examples. We now turn our attention to the properties of formation consistency and invariance with respect to isomorphisms.

LEMMA 5.4.2 (Formation consistency lemma)   Let G be an interior substructure of a standard form with perfect recall, and let U and V be two different equilibrium points of G, not necessarily in pure strategies. Moreover let $\bar{G}$ be a formation which contains both U and V. Then U risk-dominates V in $\bar{G}$, if and only if U risk-dominates V in G.

Proof   The formation F spanned by U and V in $\bar{G}$ is also the formation spanned by U and V in G. In both cases we receive the same restricted game and the same bicentric prior. ∎

LEMMA 5.4.3 (Lemma on invariance with respect to isomorphisms)   Let f be an isomorphism from a game $G = (\Phi, H) \in \mathcal{I}(\mathcal{R})$ to a game $\bar{G} = (\bar{\Phi}, \bar{H}) \in \mathcal{I}(\mathcal{R})$, and let U and V be two different equilibrium points of G. Then U risk-dominates V in G, if and only if $f(U)$ risk-dominates $f(V)$ in $\bar{G}$.

Proof   Let $G' = (\Phi', H')$ and $\bar{G}' = (\bar{\Phi}', \bar{H}')$ be the restricted games of G and $\bar{G}$, respectively. Obviously the restriction f' of f to Φ' is an isomorphism from G' to $\bar{G}'$.

The linear payoff transformations connected to the isomorphism f' also carry the logarithmic payoffs of the auxiliary games in the logarithmic tracing procedure for G' to the corresponding payoffs for $\bar{G}'$. This can be seen from the definition of the logarithmic tracing procedure. The weights α_i^* of the logarithmic terms are defined as maximal payoff differences and therefore change in the appropriate way (section 4.15).

The isomorphism f' maps the bicentric prior for the comparison between U and V to the bicentric prior for the comparison between $f(U)$ and $f(V)$

since isomorphisms preserve the best-reply structure. It follows that the assertion of the lemma 5.4.3 holds. ∎

Unanimity Games

We will now investigate risk dominance in a special class of games. A *unanimity game* $G = (\Phi, H)$ with $\Phi = \Phi_1 \times \ldots \times \Phi_n$ is a game with normal form structure whose strategy sets and payoffs are as follows: for $i = 1, \ldots, n$, the strategy set Φ_i contains m pure strategies $U_i^1, \ldots, U_i^m$. We use the notation $U^j = (U_i^j, \ldots, U_n^j)$. Payoffs are defined as

$$H_i(\phi) = \begin{cases} u_i^j, & \text{for } \phi = U^j, j = 1, \ldots, m, \\ 0 & \text{otherwise,} \end{cases} \tag{5.4.3}$$

where all u_i^j are positive numbers $(i = 1, \ldots, n; j = 1, \ldots, m)$. We use the notation $u^j = (u_1^j, \ldots, u_n^j)$.

The vectors u^j can be interpreted as payoff vectors attached to possible agreements. A pure strategy consists in voting for one of these agreements. An agreement is reached if and only if the players unanimously vote for it.

The set of all u^j with $j = 1, \ldots, m$ is denoted by X. In view of the interpretation just given, X is called the *agreement set*. Sometimes we shall distinguish the elements of X by different letters $u, v, \ldots$, rather than by upper indexes. In such cases indexed capital letter $U_i, V_i, \ldots$, will be used for the corresponding pure strategies; thereby we avoid double indexes.

The pure strategy combinations U^j are strong equilibrium points of $G = (\Phi, H)$. The game may have additional pure strategy equilibrium points such as (U_1, V_2, W_3) in a three-person unanimity game with $X = \{u, v, w\}$, but these equilibrium points are weak because no player loses anything by deviation.

The *Nash-product* of a strong equilibrium point U is the product $u_1 \cdot u_2 \cdot \ldots \cdot u_n$ of all components of its payoff vector $u = (u_1, \ldots, u_n)$. For the special case of two-person unanimity games this definition coincides with that of section 3.7. Nash's cooperative bargaining theory with fixed threats selects that agreement that has the highest Nash-product. We will show that our concept of risk dominance is in harmony with Nash's theory. To do this, we will compute risk dominance between strong equilibrium points in unanimity games.

The definition of risk dominance has been given for games in the class $\mathscr{S}(\mathscr{R})$, but it can also be applied to other games as long as no difficulties arise. We do not want to discuss the question whether unanimity games belong to $\mathscr{I}(\mathscr{R})$. To compute the limit solution of unanimity games, we would have to look at their ε-perturbations. As we will argue later, the theorem 5.4.1 stated next remains true for ε-perturbations with sufficiently small ε.

THEOREM 5.4.1 (Nash-product theorem)   Let U and V be two strong equilibrium points of a unanimity game $G = (\Phi, H)$. The equilibrium point U risk-dominates V, if the Nash-product of U is greater than of V.

Proof   Since we have $U_i \neq V_i$ for $i = 1, \ldots, n$, no player i is fixed in the restricted game. In the two-person case $\Psi = \Psi_1 \times \Psi_2$ with $\Psi_i = \{U_i, V_i\}$ is the set of pure-strategy combinations of the formation spanned by U and V. For $n > 2$ the whole game is spanned by U and V because every pure strategy is a best reply to an i-incomplete pure-strategy combination where two players j and k use U_j and V_k. Therefore for $n > 2$ the restricted game agrees with the whole game.

To compute the bicentric prior strategies p_i, we look at the following payoffs:

$$H_i(U_i[zU_{-i} + (1 - z)V_{-i}]) = zu_i, \tag{5.4.4}$$

$$H_i(V_i[zU_{-i} + (1 - z)V_{-i}]) = (1 - z)v_i. \tag{5.4.5}$$

The comparison of (5.4.4) and (5.4.5) shows that the following is true for the best reply r_i^z to $zU_{-i} + (1 - z)V_{-i}$:

$$r_i^z = \begin{cases} U_i, & \text{for } 1 > z > \dfrac{v_i}{u_i + v_i}, \\[2ex] V_i & \text{for } 0 < z < \dfrac{v_i}{u_i + v_i}. \end{cases} \tag{5.4.6}$$

Wherever there is only one best reply, this is also the central local best reply. Figure 5.2 graphically represents the result. The joint mixtures $zU_{-i} + (1 - z)V_{-i}$ are shown as points on the line segment $0 \leq z \leq 1$. The essential subintervals $Z(U_i)$ and $Z_1(V_i)$ meet at the *critical point* $v_i/(u_i + v_i)$. The line shown in figure 5.2 will be referred to as *player i's z-line*.

According to (5.4.2) the probabilities assigned to U_i and V_i by player i's bicentric strategy p_i are determined by the length of the subintervals for U_i and V_i:

$$p_i(U_i) = \frac{u_i}{u_i + v_i}, \tag{5.4.7}$$

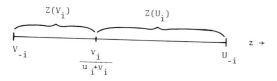

Figure 5.2
Player i's z-line

$$p_i(V_i) = \frac{v_i}{u_i + v_i}, \quad \text{for } i = 1, \ldots, n. \tag{5.4.8}$$

We now look at player i's payoff obtained at p_{-i}. Let N_i be the set of all players except i.

$$H_i(U_i p_{-i}) = u_i \prod_{k \in N_i} \frac{u_k}{u_k + v_k}, \tag{5.4.9}$$

$$H_i(V_i p_{-i}) = v_i \prod_{k \in N_i} \frac{v_k}{u_k + v_k}. \tag{5.4.10}$$

This shows that we have

$$H_i(U_i p_{-i}) > H_i(V_i p_{-i}), \quad \text{for } i = 1, \ldots, n, \tag{5.4.11}$$

if the Nash product of U is greater than that of V. If this is the case, then U is the only best reply to the bicentric prior $p = (p_1, \ldots, p_n)$, and the tracing procedure yields $T(G, p) = U$. Therefore the assertion of theorem 5.4.1 is true. ∎

Comment We will refer to the property of our risk-dominance definition expressed by the Nash-product theorem 5.4.1 as the Nash-property. Our attempts to define risk dominance in a satisfactory way have been guided by the idea that it is desirable to reproduce the result of Nash's cooperative bargaining theory with fixed threats. The Nash-property is not an unintended by-product of our theory.

One might object that other axiomatic bargaining theories such as that of Kalai and Smorodinsky may be equally plausible (Kalai-Smorodinsky 1975). We find that we can reject this point of view because our axiomatic characterization of risk dominance between strong equilibrium points in 2×2 games supports the Nash-product as a selection criterion. A desirable feature of our theory is that the risk-dominating equilibrium point with the higher Nash-product is obtained as the strong best reply to the bicentric prior and not in a more substantial application of the tracing procedure. We think that because unanimity games have a very simple structure, a reasonable equilibrium selection theory should be expected to solve them in a simple way.

For the class $\mathscr{R}$ of 2×2 games with two strong equilibrium points a risk-dominance relation has been characterized by three axioms in chapter 3, section 3.9. The following lemma shows that the definition introduced in this chapter yields the same risk-dominance relation on $\mathscr{R}$.

LEMMA 5.4.4 (Lemma on 2×2 games) Let U and V be two different strong equilibrium points of a 2×2 game, and for $i = 1$, 2 let u_i and v_i be the deviation losses of U and V, respectively (see figure 3.5). Then U risk-dominates v if and only if we have

$$u_1 u_2 > v_1 v_2 \tag{5.4.12}$$

Proof As was shown in section 3.5, the 2×2 game can be transformed into the unanimity game of figure 3.7, without changing the best reply structure. This game is equivalent to the game in figure 3.14 (section 3.9). Figure 3.7 permits the conclusion that the bicentric prior strategy p_i of player i is given by (5.4.7) and (5.4.8) and that U is the only best reply to $p = (p_1, p_2)$ if (5.4.12) holds. Therefore (5.4.10) is sufficient for risk dominance of U over V. Moreover V risk-dominates U for $v_1 v_2 > u_1 u_2$. To see that for $u_1 u_2 = v_1 v_2$ none of both equilibrium points risk-dominates the other, we remember that in this case the game of figure 3.14 has a symmetry f that carries U to V, and vice versa (see section 3.9). In view of the lemma 5.4.3 on invariance with respect to isomorphisms, this excludes risk dominance of one of both equilibrium points over the other. It follows that U risk-dominates V if and only if (5.4.12) holds. ∎

Intransitivities

A unanimity game is called nondegenerate if any two strong equilibrium points have different Nash-products. The Nash-product theorem 5.4.1 shows that in nondegenerate unanimity games risk dominance between strong equilibrium points is a transitive relationship. Unfortunately we cannot expect this kind of transitivity in general.

Consider the game G in figure 3.25. This game has three strong equilibrium points (α, α), (β, β), and (γ, γ). We are going to show that the following are true:

1. (α, α) risk-dominates (β, β),

2. (β, β) risk-dominates (γ, γ),

3. (γ, γ) risk-dominates (α, α).

To see this, we do not need to apply our definition in detail. Any formation consistent risk-dominance relation that agrees with ours on 2×2 games with two strong equilibrium points must satisfy all three conditions. A formation is obtained if γ is removed from the strategy sets of both players. The same is true with respect to the other two pure strategies. These formations are 2×2 games. To determine risk dominance, it is sufficient to compare Nash-products. The Nash-products for the comparison between (α, α) and (β, β) are 21 and 18, those for (β, β) versus (γ, γ) are 18 and 16, and those for (γ, γ) versus (α, α) are 32 and 21.

Comment Our notion of risk dominance is based on the idea of a hypothetical situation where it is generally believed that one of two equilibrium points U and V is the solution. As long as the players follow Bayesian reasoning processes, the uncertainty between U and V cannot move their behavioral inclinations out of the formation spanned by U and V. Therefore the property of formation consistency seems to be unavoidable. This together with our axiomatic characterization of risk dominance for 2×2 games with two strong equilibrium points leads to the conclusion that we should not expect transitivity.

Obviously the intransitivities in the game of figure 3.25 are connected with the impossibility theorem 3.12.1. The cells produced by sequential agent splitting are formations of the game. The cell structure obtained by sequential agent splitting has the consequence that one of the three risk-dominance comparisons becomes irrelevant. This fact is exploited by the proof of the theorem.

The Payoff Monotonicity Counterexample

In section 3.8 we discussed the numerical example of figures 3.12 and 3.13 which throws doubt on payoff monotonicity as a desirable property of a risk-dominance relation. The numbers were chosen in such a way that payoff monotonicity does not hold for the example with the definition introduced in this chapter. We will now show that U risk-dominates V in figure 3.12 and that V risk-dominates U in figure 3.13.

Both games are symmetric with respect to players 1 and 2. Therefore it is sufficient to compute the bicentric prior strategies for players 1 and 3. A player's bicentric prior depends only on his own payoffs. Therefore the bicentric prior strategy p_1 of player 1 is the same in both games. Player 3's bicentric prior strategy in the game of figure 3.12 will be denoted by p_3 and that for figure 3.13 will be denoted by p'_3. We obtain the following results:

$$p_1(U_1) = \frac{7}{11}, \quad p_1(V_1) = \frac{4}{11}, \tag{5.4.13}$$

$$p_3(U_3) = \frac{1}{4}, \quad p_3(V_3) = \frac{3}{4}, \tag{5.4.14}$$

$$p'_3(U_3) = \frac{2}{5}, \quad p'_3(V_3) = \frac{3}{5}. \tag{5.4.15}$$

We can now compute player 1's payoff for U_1 and V_1 if the others use $p_{-1} = p_2 p_3$ or $p'_{-1} = p_2 p'_3$:

$$H_1(U_1 p_{-1}) = \frac{7}{44} \times 7 + \frac{21}{44} \times 3 = \frac{112}{44}, \tag{5.4.16}$$

$$H_1(V_1 p_{-1}) = \frac{4}{44} \times 15 + \frac{12}{44} \times 4 = \frac{108}{44}, \tag{5.4.17}$$

$$H'_1(U_1 p'_{-1}) = \frac{14}{55} \times 7 + \frac{21}{55} \times 3 = \frac{161}{55}, \tag{5.4.18}$$

$$H'_1(V_1 p'_{-1}) = \frac{8}{55} \times 15 + \frac{12}{55} \times 4 = \frac{168}{55}. \tag{5.4.19}$$

The payoff functions for figures 3.12 and 3.13 are denoted by H and H', respectively. Player 3 is faced with $p_{-3} = p_1 p_2$ in both games:

$$H_3(U_3 p_{-3}) = \frac{49}{121} \times 1 = \frac{49}{121}, \tag{5.4.20}$$

$$H_3(V_3 p_{-3}) = \frac{16}{121} \times 3 = \frac{48}{121}, \tag{5.4.21}$$

$$H'_3(U_3 p_{-3}) = \frac{49}{121} \times 2 = \frac{98}{121}, \tag{5.4.22}$$

$$H_3'(V_3 p_{-3}) = \frac{16}{121} \times 3 = \frac{48}{121}. \tag{5.4.23}$$

These computations show that U is the only best reply to the bicentric prior in the game of figure 3.12. Consequently in this game U risk-dominates V.

In the game of figure 3.13 the only best reply to the bicentric prior is (V_1, V_2, U_3). At this strategy combination players 1 and 2 have an incentive to play V_1 and V_2. Therefore in the games G^t that arise in the application of the tracing procedure, their best replies to (V_1, V_2, U_3) will always be V_1 and V_2. At some critical value of t player 3 will switch over to V_3 since his best reply to (V_1, V_2, U_3) is V_3. The final result is V. This shows that in the game of figure 3.13, where player 3 has a higher payoff at U, the equilibrium point V risk-dominates U.

Comment The result obtained for the payoff monotonicity counterexample does not look unreasonable. In figure 3.13 player 3's incentive to use U_3 is stronger than in figure 3.12. Therefore we have $p_3'(U_3) > p_3(U_3)$. Since V_1 and V_2 are very advantageous for players 1 and 2 if player 3 plays U_3, their best replies to the bicentric prior shift from U_1 and U_2 to V_1 and V_2 in the transition from figure 3.12 to figure 3.13.

In many cases the deviation of one player from an equilibrium point decreases the other players' incentive to stick to it. At the equilibrium point V of figures 3.12 and 3.13 the situation is reversed as far as deviations of player 3 are concerned. His deviation to U_3 has a stabilizing effect in the sense that it increases the other players' incentive to stick to V. Therefore it works in favor of V that player 3 is more strongly attracted to U_3 in figure 3.13.

Risk Dominance in ε-Perturbations

In the application of our theory to special classes of games of substantial interest, like bargaining or oligopoly games, risk-dominance comparisons often have to be computed for pairs of strong equilibrium points only. With the exception of degenerate border cases, it rarely makes a difference whether risk dominance between two strong equilibrium points is determined in an ε-perturbation with sufficiently small ε or in the unperturbed game. In the following we will look at the important case where one of both equilibrium points is the only best reply to the bicentric prior. Under a mild regularity condition on the z-line "conspicuous risk dominance" will be used to describe this situation.

Conspicuous Risk Dominance

Let $G = (\Phi, H)$ be a standard form, not necessarily in $\mathcal{I}(\mathcal{R})$, and let U and V be two strong equilibrium points of G. We say that player i has a *regular z-line* if in the interval $0 \leq z \leq 1$, with the exception of finitely many points, there is only one pure strategy ϕ_i for every z such that ϕ_i is a best reply to $zU_{-i} + (1 - z)V_{-i}$. Obviously, ϕ_i is the central local best reply r_i^z if this is the case. Moreover in view of the linearity of $H_i(\phi_i[zU_{-i} + (1 - z)V_{-i}])$ as a function of z, the set $Z(\phi_i)$ of all z such that ϕ_i is a best reply to $zU_{-i} + (1 - z)V_{-i}$ is a subinterval of $0 \leq z \leq 1$. Therefore a bicentric prior strategy p_i can be computed according to (5.3.2) if player i has a regular z-line. We say that U *conspicuously risk-dominates* V in G if every player i in the player set N' of the restricted game G' for the comparison between U and V has a regular z-line and if in G' the equilibrium point U' corresponding to U is the only best reply to the bicentric prior $p' = (P_i)_{N'}$.

LEMMA 5.4.5 (Conspicuous risk dominance lemma)   Let U and V be two strong equilibrium points of a standard form $G = (\Phi, H)$ with perfect recall such that U conspicuously risk-dominates V in G. For every ε-perturbation $G_\varepsilon = (\Phi_\varepsilon, H_\varepsilon)$ of G, let U_ε and V_ε be the strategy combinations whose local strategies $U_{\varepsilon ij}$ and $V_{\varepsilon ij}$ are the ε-extreme local strategies corresponding to the local strategies U_{ij} and V_{ij} in U and V, respectively. Then an $\bar{\varepsilon} > 0$ can be found such that for every $0 < \varepsilon \leq \bar{\varepsilon}$ the strategy combination U_ε and V_ε are strong equilibrium points of G_ε such that U_ε risk-dominates V_ε.

Proof   As can be seen by (2.8.7), the payoff vectors $H(U_\varepsilon)$ and $H(V_\varepsilon)$ are continuous functions of ε. Consequently, for sufficiently small ε, the strategy combinations U_ε and V_ε are strong equilibrium points of G_ε. We shall assume that all players i in G have different equilibrium strategies in U and V. If this is not the case, the argument can be applied to the game that results from G by fixing the players with the same strategy in U and V at their equilibrium strategies in G_ε.

Let $\phi_{\varepsilon i}$ be the ε-*extreme strategy* corresponding to a pure strategy ϕ_i; this means that the local strategies $\phi_{\varepsilon ij}$ prescribed by $\phi_{\varepsilon i}$ are the ε-extreme strategies corresponding to the choices ϕ_{ij} prescribed by ϕ_i. The payoff

$$H_{\varepsilon i}(\phi_{\varepsilon i}[zU_{\varepsilon-i} + (1 - z)V_{\varepsilon-i}])$$

is a continuous function of ε. Consequently, for sufficiently small ε, the ε-extreme strategy $\phi_{\varepsilon i}$ is the only best reply to $zU_{\varepsilon-i} + (1 - z)V_{\varepsilon-i}$ if ϕ_i is the only best reply to $zU_{-i} + (1 - z)V_{-i}$. This shows that for $\varepsilon \to 0$ the bicentric prior p_ε for the comparison between U_ε and V_ε in G_ε converges to the bicentric prior p for the comparison between U and V in G. We can conclude that for sufficiently small ε, the equilibrium point U_ε is the only best reply to p_ε in G_ε. Therefore the assertion of the lemma 5.4.5 holds. ∎

Comment   The conspicuous risk dominance lemma 5.4.5 can be applied to the special case of unanimity games. In this way we receive the following analogy to the Nash-product theorem 5.4.1:

THEOREM 5.4.2 (Nash-product theorem for perturbations)   Let U and V be two strong equilibrium points of a unanimity game $G = (\Phi, H)$, such that the Nash-product of U is greater than the Nash-product of V. For every ε-perturbation G_ε of G, let U_ε and V_ε be defined as in the conspicuous risk-dominance lemma. Then an $\bar{\varepsilon} > 0$ can be found with the property that for $0 < \varepsilon \leq \bar{\varepsilon}$ the strategy combinations U_ε and V_ε are strong equilibrium points of G_ε, such that U_ε risk-dominates V_ε in G_ε.

Proof   The proof of the Nash-product theorem 5.4.1 has shown that U conspicuously risk-dominates V. Unanimity games have normal form structure and therefore are standard forms with perfect recall. The assertion is an immediate consequence of the conspicuous risk-dominance lemma 5.4.5. ∎

5.5   Candidate Elimination and Substitution

The last missing piece in the definition of our solution concept is the process of candidate elimination and substitution that will be described in this section. In the introduction of the chapter we have already mentioned the auxiliary concepts used in the process of candidate elimination and substitution. Here we will define dominance, strategic distance, strategic net distance and maximal stability, and the substitute of a candidate set. The process is described by the flowchart in figure 5.3. In the same way as in earlier chapters we will try to motivate our definitions where they are introduced.

Dominance

Let $U = (U_i)_N$ and $V = (V_i)_N$ be two different equilibrium points, not necessarily in pure strategies, of a game $G = (\Phi, H)$ in the class $\mathscr{I}(R)$. We say that U *dominates* V if one of the following two statements holds:

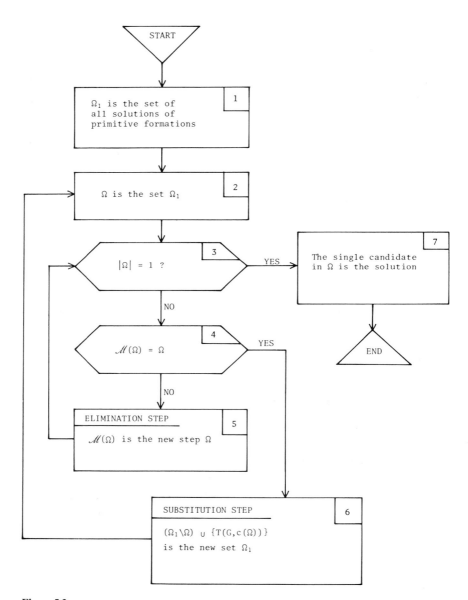

Figure 5.3
Flowchart for the process of candidate elimination and substitution. $\mathcal{M}(\Omega)$ is the set of maximally stable candidates in Ω, and $c(\Omega)$ is the centroid of Ω.

1. $H_i(U) > H_i(V)$, for every $i \in N$ with $U_i \neq V_i$.

2. U risk dominates V and $H_i(U) \geq H_i(V)$, for at least one $i \in N$ with $U_i \neq V_i$.

We write $U \succ V$ if U dominates V and $U|V$ if none of both equilibrium points dominates the other.

Interpretation

Dominance is a combination of payoff dominance and risk dominance. As in the interpretation of risk dominance, we look at a hypothetical situation where it is generally believed that either U or V is the solution. Players with $U_i = V_i$ can be expected to play this strategy. Therefore payoff dominance as well as risk dominance concerns only players with $U_i \neq V_i$, that is, players who belong to the restricted game. Risk dominance of U over V does not matter if V payoff-dominates U in the restricted game. Therefore in statement 2, we require $H_i(U) \geq H_i(V)$ for at least one $i \in N$ with $U_i \neq V_i$.

In the definition of dominance, payoff dominance has priority over risk dominance. We take the point of view that there is no risk involved in a situation where expectations can be coordinated by common payoff interests of the relevant players (see section 3.9).

The Idea of Strategic Distance

Before we formally define the measure of strategic distance, we want to indicate our reasons for doing this. Not all risk-dominance comparisons can be regarded as equally important. We think that it is reasonable to give more weight to comparisons between equilibrium points that are near to each other in a strategically relevant sense. To give a precise meaning to this intuitive idea, one needs a measure of strategic distance.

Consider two equilibrium points U and V of a game G. We think of the strategic distance between U and V as connected to the differences between the strategies used in U and V. Therefore we take the point of view that those players whose strategies in U and V agree do not contribute anything to the strategic distance between U and V.

Consider a player i whose strategies in U and V are different from each other. How can one measure the difference between his equilibrium strategies U_i and V_i? To answer this question, we imagine that player i's beliefs are described by a joint mixture $zU_{-i} + (1 - z)V_{-i}$. This idea has been used already for the definition of the bicentric prior. Suppose that player i first firmly believes in V_{-i} which corresponds to $z = 0$ and then gradually increases his confidence into U_{-i} until $z = 1$ is reached. Each z is connected to a central local best reply r_i^z to $zU_{-i} + (1 - z)V_{-i}$ [see (5.3.1)]. As z is increased from 0 to 1, the strategy r_i^z changes at finitely many critical points and remains constant in the open subinterval between two neighboring critical points of this kind. Our measure of strategic distance will be the number of all critical points summed up over all players with $U_i \neq V_i$.

The greater the number of critical points is the more difficult is the comparison between U and V. One may think of our definition of strategic distance as a measure of the intensity of initial confusion arising in the hypothetical situation where all players believe that either U or V is the solution. The initial confusion is measured before the bicentric prior has been formed in the first stage of the emergence of Bayesian expectations. This seems to be reasonable since the bicentric prior can be considered a preliminary resolution of initial confusion.

Strategic Distance

Let $U = (U_i)_N$ and $V = (V_i)_N$ be two different equilibrium points, not necessarily in pure strategies of a game $G = (\Phi, H)$ in the class $\mathscr{I}(\mathscr{R})$ of interior substructures of standard forms with perfect recall. Let N' be the player set of the restricted game G' for the comparison of U and V. Consider a player $i \in N'$ and the essential subintervals $Z(r_i)$ on his z-line (see consequences for the bicentric prior, section 5.4). There are finitely many points $z_1, \ldots,$ z_s where two adjacent essential subintervals meet. These points $z_1, \ldots, z_s$ are called *critical points* of player i. The number of player i's critical points is denoted by $e_i(U, V)$. The *strategic distance* $e(U, V)$ between U and V is defined as

$$e(U, V) = \sum_{i \in N'} e_i(U, V). \tag{5.5.1}$$

Strategic Distance in Unanimity Games

Consider two strong equilibrium points U and V of a unanimity game G. As we have seen in section 5.4 (see figure 5.2), in this case every player has exactly one critical point, namely $v_i/(u_i + v_i)$. The strategic distance $e(U, V)$ is nothing else than the number of players.

Next Neighbors

Let Ω be a set of equilibrium points for a game $G \in \mathscr{I}(\mathscr{R})$. (We may think of a candidate set, e.g., the first candidate set Ω_1, defined in section 5.2.) We assume that Ω has at least two elements. Consider two different equilibrium points U and V in Ω. We say that V is a *next neighbor of U in Ω* if we have

$$e(U, V) = \min_{W \in \Omega \setminus \{U\}} e(U, W). \tag{5.5.2}$$

We use the notation

$$e(U, \Omega) = \min_{W \in \Omega \setminus \{U\}} e(U, W) \tag{5.5.3}$$

for the distance of U to a next neighbor in Ω.

The Idea of Strategic Net Distance

Our theory gives more weight to dominance comparisons between equilibrium points that are relatively near to each other. The most important dominance comparisons within a candidate set Ω are those between two equilibrium points that are next neighbors in Ω. Note that U is not necessarily a next neighbor of V in Ω if V is a next neighbor of U in Ω. To judge the importance of dominance comparison of U and V relative to a candidate set Ω, our theory looks at the question how close U and V come to being next neighbors in Ω. Closeness to the condition of being next neighbors to each other in Ω can be measured by the sum of the surpluses $e(U, V) - e(U, \Omega)$ and $e(U, V) - e(V, \Omega)$ of the distance between U and V over the distances of U and V to their next neighbors. To avoid distances of zero between two different candidates, we add 1 to this sum of surpluses. In this way we obtain our measure of strategic net distance.

One might ask why we do not take strategic distance rather than strategic net distance as a measure of importance of dominance comparisons within a candidate set. In fact an earlier version of our theory was based on strategic distance rather than strategic net distance. Examples have led us to the conclusion that an equilibrium point should not be judged as extraordinarily stable simply because it is far away from its next neighbors in the candidate set while all other candidates are near to each other. Strategic net distance as a measure of importance of dominance comparisons does not give any advantage to candidates that are far off from other candidates. The stability of each candidate is judged in terms of comparisons with other candidates who are relatively near to it.

Strategic Net Distance

Let Ω be a set of equilibrium points for a game $G \in \mathscr{I}(\mathscr{R})$, and let U and V be two different equilibrium points in Ω. The *strategic net distance $e(U, V, \Omega)$*

of U and V in Ω is defined as

$$e(U, V, \Omega) = 2e(U, V) - e(U, \Omega) - e(V, \Omega) + 1. \tag{5.5.4}$$

It can be seen immediately that $e(U, V, \Omega)$ is equal to $e(V, U, \Omega)$. Moreover it follows by (5.5.3) that $e(U, V, \Omega)$ is always positive.

The use of the symbol e for both strategic distance and strategic net distance should not lead to confusion because distance is a function of two arguments and net distance is a function of three arguments. The *maximal net distance within* Ω is defined as

$$e(\Omega) = \max_{U,V \in \Omega} e(U, V, \Omega). \tag{5.5.5}$$

Stability

As before, let Ω be a set of at least two equilibrium points for a game $G \in \mathscr{I}(\mathscr{R})$. We say that $U \in \Omega$ is *undominated* in Ω if no $V \in \Omega$ with $V \neq U$ dominates U; otherwise, we says that U is *dominated* in Ω. For every $U \in \Omega$ we define a *stability index* $\sigma(U, \Omega)$ of U in Ω:

$$\sigma(U, \Omega) = e(\Omega), \quad \text{if } U \text{ is undominated in } \Omega, \tag{5.5.6}$$

$$\sigma(U, \Omega) = \min\{e(U, V, \Omega) \mid V \in \Omega \text{ and } V \succ U\} - 1,$$
$$\text{if } U \text{ is dominated in } \Omega. \tag{5.5.7}$$

The right-hand side of (5.5.7) is the smallest number k such that no $V \in \Omega$ with $V \neq U$ and $e(U, V, \Omega) \leq k$ dominates U. Equation (5.5.7) has no meaning if U is undominated in Ω. If U is dominated in Ω, then the right-hand side of (5.5.6) is at most $e(\Omega) - 1$. This means that (5.5.6) assigns the highest possible stability index to undominated equilibrium points in Ω if there are any. Define

$$\sigma(\Omega) = \max_{U \in \Omega} \sigma(U, \Omega). \tag{5.5.8}$$

$\sigma(\Omega)$ is the *maximal stability index in* Ω. We say that U is *maximally stable in* Ω if we have

$$\sigma(U, \Omega) = \sigma(\Omega). \tag{5.5.9}$$

The set of all maximally stable elements of Ω is denoted by $\mathscr{M}(\Omega)$.

Remarks If Ω contains equilibrium points that are undominated in Ω, then the set $\mathscr{M}(\Omega)$ of maximally stable elements of Ω is the set of all $U \in \Omega$

that are undominated in Ω. This is an immediate consequence of (5.5.6) and (5.5.7).

The stability index $\sigma(U,\Omega)$ is one of the integers $0,\ldots,e(\Omega)$. It may happen that all the $U \in \Omega$ have the same stability index $\sigma(U,\Omega)$. If this is the case, we have $\mathcal{M}(\Omega) = \Omega$. There are two ways in which $\mathcal{M}(\Omega)$ may fail to be smaller than Ω. It may happen that all elements of Ω are undominated in Ω; then we have $\sigma(U,\Omega) = e(\Omega)$ for all $U \in \Omega$. Since risk dominance may be cyclical, it is also possible that all elements of Ω are dominated by other elements of Ω and that all of them have the same stability index $\sigma(U,\Omega)$.

Comment   On the basis of strategic net distance as a measure for the importance of dominance comparisons, it is reasonable to use the stability index to determine those elements of a candidate set that are considered to be maximally stable relative to this set. Whenever $\mathcal{M}(\Omega)$ is smaller than Ω, our process of candidate elimination and substitution will perform an *elimination step* that eliminates all candidates not in $\mathcal{M}(\Omega)$. Generally, stability indexes with respect to $\Omega' = \mathcal{M}(\Omega)$ are different from stability indexes with respect to Ω, and it may be possible to continue the elimination by the application of the elimination step to the new candidate set. Sometimes the first candidate set Ω can be narrowed down to a single element by repeated application of the elimination step. However, this is not always possible.

If after a number of elimination steps we obtain a candidate set Ω with $\mathcal{M}(\Omega) = \Omega$, all equilibrium points in Ω must be considered equally good, or rather equally bad since no selection can be made among them on the basis of their stability within Ω. In this situation the process of elimination and substitution performs a substitution step. An imprecise description of the substitution step has been given already in the introduction of the chapter.

Before we can proceed to the definition of the substitute of a candidate set, we must first define the centroid of a candidate set. The centroid of a candidate set is a mixed-strategy combination. Like the bicentric prior it has the interpretation of a special prior distribution for the tracing procedure. Each player is expected to use his equilibrium strategy in each of the candidates with the same probability. This means that in the computation of a player's centroid strategy, each equilibrium strategy is counted as many times as it occurs in candidates of the set. The equilibrium strategies are behavior strategies, but the resulting mixture is generally no behavior strategy but a mixed strategy. The substitute of a candidate set is the result of tracing its centroid.

Substitute of a Candidate Set

Let Ω be a set of equilibrium points of a game $G = (\Phi, H)$ in $\mathscr{I}(\mathscr{R})$. Let $b^1, \ldots, b^m$ be the elements of Ω. For every player i in G let b_i^k be player i's behavior strategy in b^k. The *centroid* $c(\Omega)$ of Ω is the mixed-strategy combination c whose elements c_i are defined as

$$c_i(\phi_i) = \frac{1}{m} \sum_{k=1}^{m} b_i^k(\phi_i) \qquad (5.5.10)$$

for every $\phi_i \in \Phi_i$. The *substitute of* Ω is the result $T(G, c(\Omega))$ of tracing the centroid of Ω.

Comment   One might ask why we do not define the substitute in a way that generalizes the bicentric prior to something that could be called the "multilateral prior." One could define i-incomplete joint mixtures of the form

$$q_{.i} = \sum_{k=1}^{m} z_i b_{-i}^k. \qquad (5.5.11)$$

For every vector $z = (z_1, \ldots, z_m)$ with $z_i \geq 0$ and

$$\sum_{i=1}^{m} z_i = 1, \qquad (5.5.12)$$

one could form the central local best reply r_i^z to the corresponding $q_{.i}$. Integration over the simplex of the vectors z would then yield a "multilateral prior strategy," an obvious generalization of the bicentric prior strategy.

We admit that one of the reasons why we did not take this approach is the complexity of the computations that have to be performed if Ω contains many candidates. However, this is not the only reason. We feel that the circumstances that require the computations of a substitute are not exactly analogous to the hypothetical situations where one of two equilibrium points is generally believed to be the solution. If all candidates in a candidate set are maximally stable, then it is quite likely that none of them is the solution. In fact this happens in cases where all the elements of Ω fail to be symmetry invariant and cannot be selected for this reason. In this case the application of the tracing procedure to the centroid of Ω leads to an equilibrium point that is in some sense "between" the equilibrium points of Ω. Of course the same would be true for the tracing procedure when applied to the multilateral prior instead of the centroid. However, there is no strong reason to prefer the "multilateral prior" to the centroid.

We look at the impasse in a situation where all candidates in a candidate set are maximally stable as a "dominance failure" in the sense that considerations of risk dominance and payoff dominance have reached a dead end and therefore must be supplemented by a different principle. This new principle is the coordination of expectations by the application of the tracing procedure to the centroid of the candidate set. Unlike the bicentric prior, the centroid does not even superficially take into account the risk situation that we considered earlier in the determination of dominance. Since dominance considerations have failed, the prior is now formed in the most simple way by taking averages over the candidates.

The Process of Candidate Elimination and Substitution

To distinguish different candidate sets that appear in the process of candidate elimination and substitution, we use lower indexes: $\Omega_1, \Omega_2, \ldots, \Omega_m$ is the sequence of candidate sets in the order in which it is generated by the process. However, in the description of the process by the flowchart of figure 5.3, it is more convenient to use a dynamic notation. Ω stands for the last candidate set generated. At the beginning Ω_1 is the first candidate set, but later it may become the candidate set generated by the last substitution step.

As figure 5.3 shows, the process begins with the determination of the first candidate set in rectangle 1. The process then moves to rectangle 2 where Ω receives the meaning of Ω_1. The process goes on to rhomboid 3. Rhomboids contain questions whose answers determine the next step. Rectangles contain operations including the change of names. In rhomboid 3 the question is asked whether the number $|\Omega|$ of elements in Ω is 1. The process stops after rectangle 1 if the answer is yes. In this case the single element of Ω is the solution.

If Ω has more than one element, the answer to the question in rhomboid 3 is no, and the process moves to rhomboid 4. If the set $\mathscr{M}(\Omega)$ of maximally stable candidates in Ω is smaller than Ω, then an *elimination step* is performed in rectangle 5. The set $\mathscr{M}(\Omega)$ becomes the new set Ω, and the process returns to rhomboid 3.

If all elements of Ω are maximally stable in Ω, the answer to the question in rhomboid 4 is yes, and a *substitution step* has to be performed in rectangle 6. In Ω_1 the elements of Ω are removed and replaced by the substitute $T(G, c(\Omega))$ of Ω. In this way we receive a new set Ω_1. Then the process returns to rectangle 2.

Remark It is clear that the process of candidate elimination and substitution stops after a finite number of candidate sets has been generated. The first candidate set is finite. An elimination step reduces the size of the candidate set. A substitution step temporarily may increase the number of candidates, but each further substitution step results in a number of candidates smaller than after the previous substitution step. Finally, a candidate set with only one element must be reached.

Solution Function

The description of the process of candidate elimination and substitution completes the definition of the solution function L specified by our theory. This solution function L is defined for the class $\mathcal{I}(\mathcal{R})$ of all interior substructures of standard forms with perfect recall.

It is often possible to extend the definition of our solution function L beyond the class $\mathcal{I}(\mathcal{R})$. However, it must be kept in mind that there the six properties mentioned in the extension theorem 3.13, do not necessarily hold. Our solution concept for games in $\mathcal{R}$ is the limit solution function $\underset{\rightarrow}{L}$ for our solution function L (see section 2.10). From now on L will always refer to the solution function specified by our theory and $\underset{\rightarrow}{L}$ to the limit solution function for L.

5.6 Solutions of Special Games

In this section we will apply our solution concept to some special classes of games and to numerical examples that illustrate certain aspects of our definitions. We first show that in nondegenerate unanimity games our solution concept selects the equilibrium point with the highest Nash-product. Then we prove that the proposed solution function for 2×2 games with two strong equilibrium points defined in section 3.9 agrees with our solution function L. Finally, we turn our attention to two numerical examples of special interest.

Nondegenerate Unanimity Games

A unanimity game $G = (\Phi, H)$ is called *nondegenerate* if G has one strong equilibrium point U whose Nash-product is greater than that of every other strong equilibrium point. We do not want to question whether nondegenerate unanimity games belong to the class $\mathscr{I}(\mathscr{R})$, for no difficulties arise in the extension of L to such games.

THEOREM 5.6.1 (Theorem on nondegenerate unanimity games)   Let $G = (\Phi, H)$ be a nondegenerate unanimity game, and let U be that strong equilibrium point of G that has the greatest Nash-product. Then we have

$$L(G) = \underline{L}(G) = U. \tag{5.6.1}$$

Proof   Let $U^1, \ldots, U^m$ be the strong equilibrium points of G. We first show that neither G nor ε-perturbations G_ε of G with sufficiently small ε have cells. To see this, we shall construct an i-incomplete mixed combination q_{-i} of completely mixed strategies with the property that an arbitrarily small deviation of a player k with $k \neq i$ from q_{-i} changes the best replies of player i. This excludes the possibility of a cell that contains i but not k. Since the construction can be based on any pair of players i and k, it can be shown in this way that there is no cell. It will be convenient to use the following notation:

$$\gamma_h = \frac{1}{\sqrt[n-1]{u_i^h}} \tag{5.6.2}$$

and

$$\gamma = \sum_{h=1}^{m} \gamma_h. \tag{5.6.3}$$

Here u_1^h is player 1's payoff in U^h. The components q_j of q_{-i} are

$$q_j(U_j^h) = \frac{\gamma_h}{\gamma}, \tag{5.6.4}$$

for $h = 1, \ldots, m$ and for every q_j in q_{-i}. For this q_{-i} player i's payoffs $H_i(U_i^h q_{-i})$ are the same for every $h = 1, \ldots, m$. Therefore player i's best replies change if a player $k \neq i$ deviates from q_k in the direction of one of the strategies U_k^h. For sufficiently small ε the strategies q_j are completely mixed not only in G but also in G_ε. The same is true for sufficiently small deviations from q_j. We can conclude that neither G nor G_ε for sufficiently small ε have cells.

For $i = 1, \ldots, n$ and $h = 1, \ldots, m$ let $U_{\varepsilon i}^h$ be the extreme strategy corresponding to U_i^h in G_ε. It is clear that for sufficiently small ε the strategy combination $U_\varepsilon^h = (U_{\varepsilon i}^h)_N$ is a strong equilibrium point of G_ε. This shows that in G_ε as well as in G every pure strategy is the only best reply to some i-incomplete strategy combination. Therefore neither G nor G_ε for sufficiently small ε has inferior strategies, duplicates, or semiduplicates. These games are irreducible; it is not necessary to apply the procedure of decomposition and reduction.

In G and G_ε for sufficiently small ε, every pure strategy belongs to a strong equilibrium point. Therefore the primitive formations are exactly those generated by the strong equilibrium points. The first candidate set Ω_1 is the set of all strong equilibrium points.

U cannot be payoff dominated by another strong equilibrium points of G or of G_ε for sufficiently small ε; the Nash-product theorem 5.4.1 permits the conclusion that U dominates all other equilibrium points in the first candidate set Ω_1 of G. Therefore $L(G) = U$ holds. On the basis of the Nash-product theorem for perturbations (theorem 5.4.2), the same argument applied to G_ε with sufficiently small ε yields $L(G_\varepsilon) = U_\varepsilon$, where U_ε is the equilibrium point of G_ε corresponding to U. This shows that we have $\underline{L}(G) = U$. ∎

Global Dominance

Let Ω_1 be the first candidate set for an irreducible game G. We say that an equilibrium point U of G is called *globally dominant in* G if it belongs to the first candidate set Ω_1 of G and in addition dominates every other equilibrium point in Ω_1.

Remarks If U is globally dominant in G, then U is the solution $L(G)$ of G. This follows by $\Omega_2 = \{U\}$. The proof of the theorem 5.6.1 on nondegenerate unanimity games has shown that in such games the equilibrium point U with the highest Nash-product is globally dominant and that for sufficiently small ε the equilibrium point U_ε corresponding to U is globally dominant in the ε-perturbation G_ε.

Comment The Nash-property of our notion of risk dominance leads to a "Nash-property" for our solution concept that is expressed by the theorem 5.6.1 on nondegenerate unanimity games. We feel that it is a desirable feature of our theory that nondegenerate unanimity games are solved in an especially simple way, namely by global dominance. Moreover all dominance comparisons are decided by payoff dominance or conspicuous risk dominance (see section 5.4).

The investigation of 2 × 2 games with two strong equilibrium points will make it necessary to look more closely at the ε-perturbations of such games. Not only in this context, but in general for two-person games with normal form structure, it will be useful to replace an ε-perturbation by an equivalent game with a simpler payoff function. For this purpose we introduce the notion of a modified ε-perturbation.

Modified ε-Perturbations

Let $G = (\Phi, H)$ with $\Phi = \Phi_1 \times \Phi_2$ be a two-person game with normal form structure. Consider an ε-perturbation $G_\varepsilon = (\Phi_\varepsilon, H_\varepsilon)$ of G, For every $\phi_i \in \Phi_i$, let $\phi_{\varepsilon i}$ be the corresponding ε-extreme strategy. The connection between H_ε and H was explored in section 2.8. Analogously to (2.8.4) define

$$\eta_i = 1 - |\Phi_i|\varepsilon, \quad \text{for } i = 1, 2. \tag{5.6.5}$$

Consider a pure-strategy combination $\psi = (\psi_1, \psi_2)$ and the corresponding ε-extreme combination $\psi_\varepsilon = (\psi_{\varepsilon 1}, \psi_{\varepsilon 2})$. From (2.8.7) the payoff vector for ψ_ε can be written

$$H_\varepsilon(\psi_\varepsilon) = \eta_1 \eta_2 H(\psi) + \varepsilon \eta_1 \sum_{\phi_2 \in \Phi_2} H(\psi_1 \phi_2)$$
$$+ \varepsilon \eta_2 \sum_{\phi_1 \in \Phi_1} H(\phi_1 \psi_2) + \varepsilon^2 \sum_{\phi \in \Phi} H(\phi). \tag{5.6.6}$$

The *modified ε-perturbation* $\bar{G}_\varepsilon = (\Phi_\varepsilon, \bar{H}_\varepsilon)$ differs from G_ε only with respect to payoffs. To describe $\bar{H}_\varepsilon$ in a convenient way, we introduce the following notation:

$$\varepsilon_1 = \frac{\varepsilon}{\eta_2} = \frac{\varepsilon}{1 - |\Phi_2|\varepsilon}, \tag{5.6.7}$$

$$\varepsilon_2 = \frac{\varepsilon}{\eta_1} = \frac{\varepsilon}{1 - |\Phi_1|\varepsilon}. \tag{5.6.8}$$

On the right-hand side of (5.6.6) we neglect the last term and divide by $\eta_1 \eta_2$. Obviously this amounts to positive linear payoff transformations. In this way we obtain $\bar{H}_\varepsilon$:

$$\bar{H}_\varepsilon(\psi_\varepsilon) = H(\psi) + \varepsilon_1 \sum_{\phi_2 \in \Phi_2} H(\psi_1 \phi_2)$$

$$+ \varepsilon_2 \sum_{\phi_1 \in \Phi_1} H(\phi_1 \psi_2). \tag{5.6.9}$$

By construction, $\bar{G}_\varepsilon$ and G_ε are equivalent (see section 2.3). Both games have the same solution. For some purposes it will be useful to consider a game $\hat{G}_\varepsilon = (\Phi_\varepsilon, \hat{H}_\varepsilon)$ with an even shorter payoff. We call this game $\hat{G}_\varepsilon$ the *short ε-perturbation* of G. Player i's best replies remain unchanged if the term that does not depend on ψ_i in (5.6.9) is dropped. The payoffs of the short ε-perturbation are

$$\hat{H}_{\varepsilon 1}(\psi_\varepsilon) = H_1(\psi) + \varepsilon_1 \sum_{\phi_2 \in \Phi_2} H_1(\psi_1 \phi_2), \tag{5.6.10}$$

$$\hat{H}_{\varepsilon 2}(\psi_\varepsilon) = H_2(\psi) + \varepsilon_2 \sum_{\phi_1 \in \Phi_1} H_2(\phi_1 \psi_2). \tag{5.6.11}$$

Generally, the short ε-perturbation is not equivalent to the ε-perturbation. Payoff-dominance relationships may differ in both games. However, the best-reply structure is the same, and the weights of the logarithmic terms in the logarithmic tracing procedure are the same in $\hat{G}_\varepsilon$ and $\bar{G}_\varepsilon$ since they are determined by payoff differences where they matter (see section 4.13). This permits us to draw the following conclusion:

LEMMA 5.6.1 (Lemma on ε-perturbations)   Let G_ε be an ε-perturbation of a two-person game G with normal form structure. Let $\bar{G}_\varepsilon$ be the modified ε-perturbation of G, and let $\hat{G}_\varepsilon$ be the short ε-perturbation of G. Payoff-dominance relationships between equilibrium points are the same in G_ε and $\bar{G}_\varepsilon$. Risk-dominance relationships between equilibrium points are the same in G_ε and $\hat{G}_\varepsilon$. The substitute of a candidate set Ω is the same in G_ε and in $\hat{G}_\varepsilon$.

Proof   The proof was given earlier. ∎

THEOREM 5.6.2 (Theorem on 2×2 games)   On the class $\mathcal{K}$ of all 2×2 games with two strong equilibrium points, the solution function L specified by our theory agrees with the proposed solution function defined by (3.9.6).

Moreover on the class $\mathcal{K}$ the limit solution function $\underrightarrow{L}$ of L agrees with L.

Proof   Let U and V be two strong equilibrium points of a game $G \in \mathcal{K}$. Let G_ε be the ε-perturbation, $\bar{G}_\varepsilon$ the modified ε-perturbation, and $\hat{G}_\varepsilon$ the short ε-perturbation of G. Moreover let U_ε and V_ε be the strategy combinations corresponding to U and V in G_ε. For sufficiently small ε, both U_ε and V_ε are strong equilibrium points of G_ε. It is clear that the first candidate set is $\{U, V\}$ in the case of G and $\{U_\varepsilon, V_\varepsilon\}$ in the case of G_ε with sufficiently small ε.

We first show that the payoff-dominance relationship between U_ε and V_ε in G_ε is the same as that between U and V in G. From lemma 5.6.1 on ε-perturbations this question can be examined in $\bar{G}_\varepsilon$. Let $\bar{a}_{ij}$ be player 1's payoff in $\bar{G}_\varepsilon$ which corresponds to a_{ij} in figure 3.5 (chapter 3, section 3.4). Equation (5.6.6) yields:

$$\bar{a}_{11} = a_{11} + \varepsilon_1(a_{11} + a_{12}) + \varepsilon_2(a_{11} + a_{21}), \tag{5.6.12}$$

$$\bar{a}_{22} = a_{22} + \varepsilon_1(a_{22} + a_{21}) + \varepsilon_2(a_{22} + a_{12}). \tag{5.6.13}$$

In view of

$$\varepsilon_1 = \varepsilon_2 = \frac{\varepsilon}{1 - 2\varepsilon} = \bar{\varepsilon}, \tag{5.6.14}$$

we obtain

$$\bar{a}_{11} - \bar{a}_{22} = \frac{1}{1 - 2\varepsilon}(a_{11} - a_{22}). \tag{5.6.15}$$

An analogous equation can be derived for player 2. This shows that payoff dominance does not differ in G and G_ε.

Risk dominance in G_ε can be investigated in the short ε-perturbation $\hat{G}_\varepsilon$. This game is shown in figure 5.4. We shall show that risk dominance in $\hat{G}_\varepsilon$ agrees with risk dominance in G. For this purpose we compute the deviation losses $\hat{u}_{\varepsilon i}$ and $\hat{v}_{\varepsilon i}$ in $\hat{G}_\varepsilon$ and connect them to the deviation losses u_i and v_i in G. We obtain

$$\hat{u}_i = u_i(1 + \bar{\varepsilon}) - \bar{\varepsilon}v_i, \quad \text{for } i = 1, 2, \tag{5.6.16}$$

$$\hat{v}_i = v_i(1 + \bar{\varepsilon}) - \bar{\varepsilon}u_i, \quad \text{for } i = 1, 2. \tag{5.6.17}$$

This yields

$$\hat{u}_1\hat{u}_2 - \hat{v}_1\hat{v}_2 = (u_1u_2 - v_1v_2)(1 + 2\bar{\varepsilon}). \tag{5.6.18}$$

In view of the lemma 5.4.4 on 2×2 games, equation (5.6.18) permits the conclusion that the risk-dominance relationship between U_ε and V_ε in G_ε is the same as between U and V in G. Moreover the lemma has shown that our general notion of risk dominance agrees with the special one of chapter 3.

Our results on payoff dominance and risk dominance show that the dominance relationship between U_ε and V_ε in G_ε is the same as that between U and V, respectively, in G. Suppose that U dominates V. Then the second candidate set contains only U in the case of G and only U_ε in the case of G_ε. Consequently U is selected both by L and $\underrightarrow{L}$. It is also clear that U is selected by the proposed solution function of chapter 3 if U dominates V.

It is now clear that the theorem 5.6.1 holds in all cases where one of both strong equilibrium points dominates the other. Assume that neither U dominates V nor V dominates U in G. Then the same is true with respect to U_ε and V_ε in the case of G_ε. To determine the solution, we have to compute the substitute of $\{U, V\}$ in the case of G and of $\{U_\varepsilon, V_\varepsilon\}$ in the case of G_ε. In both cases Ω_3 contains only this substitute which therefore is the solution. We have to show that the substitute is none of both strong equilibrium points but the mixed equilibrium point which is also selected by the proposed solution function of chapter 3.

The transformations that we applied in chapter 3 to obtain the form of figure 3.14 amount to positive linear transformations of payoff differences and therefore do not influence the path of the logarithmic tracing procedure. In the case of G and $\hat{G}_\varepsilon$ we obtain $u = v$ in the transformed game of figure 3.14. For $\hat{G}_\varepsilon$ this follows by (5.6.18). Obviously the transformed game

	$U_{\varepsilon 2}$	$V_{\varepsilon 2}$
$U_{\varepsilon 1}$	$a_{11}+\bar{\varepsilon}(a_{11}+a_{12})$ $b_{11}+\bar{\varepsilon}(b_{11}+b_{21})$	$a_{12}+\bar{\varepsilon}(a_{11}+a_{12})$ $b_{12}+\bar{\varepsilon}(b_{12}+b_{22})$
$V_{\varepsilon 1}$	$a_{21}+\bar{\varepsilon}(a_{21}+a_{22})$ $b_{21}+\bar{\varepsilon}(b_{11}+b_{21})$	$a_{22}+\bar{\varepsilon}(a_{21}+a_{22})$ $b_{22}+\bar{\varepsilon}(b_{12}+b_{22})$

Figure 5.4
The short ε-perturbation $\hat{G}_\varepsilon$ of the game G of figure 3.5

has only one symmetry-invariant equilibrium point, namely the mixed one, which therefore must be the result of the logarithmic tracing procedure. This follows by the fact that the centroid of the second candidate set and the definition of the logarithmic tracing procedure are invariant with respect to isomorphisms. ∎

Remark The proof of the theorem 5.6.1 has shown that for games $G \in \mathcal{K}$ the dominance relationship between the two strong equilibrium points U and V is the same as the dominance relationship between U_ε and V_ε in an ε-perturbation with sufficiently small ε. Here we have to add the words "for sufficiently small ε" merely because V_ε may not be an equilibrium point of G_ε if ε is not small enough.

Payoff Dominance in G and G_ε

We now look at the numerical example of figure 5.5 to illustrate the point that sometimes $\underrightarrow{L}(G)$ may be different from $L(G)$ since the ε-perturbations G_ε of G show a payoff dominance relationship that is not present in G.

The modified ε-perturbation $\bar{G}_\varepsilon$ of the game G in figure 5.5 is shown in figure 5.6. To determine the solution $L(G_\varepsilon)$ of G_ε, we first apply the procedure of decomposition and reduction to $\bar{G}_\varepsilon$. Since G_ε and $\bar{G}_\varepsilon$ are equivalent, we can solve $\bar{G}_\varepsilon$ instead of G_ε. It can easily be seen that $\bar{G}_\varepsilon$ has no cells. However, the strategies W_1 and W_2 are inferior (both are dominated). After the elimination of W_1 and W_2, we obtain an irreducible game $\bar{G}_\varepsilon^1$ with two

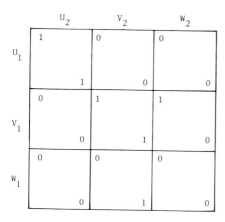

Figure 5.5
A numerical example

	$U_{\varepsilon 2}$	$V_{\varepsilon 2}$	$W_{\varepsilon 2}$
$U_{\varepsilon 1}$	$1+2\bar\varepsilon$ $1+2\bar\varepsilon$	$2\bar\varepsilon$ $3\bar\varepsilon$	$2\bar\varepsilon$ $\bar\varepsilon$
$V_{\varepsilon 1}$	$3\bar\varepsilon$ $2\bar\varepsilon$	$1+3\bar\varepsilon$ $1+3\bar\varepsilon$	$1+3\bar\varepsilon$ $\bar\varepsilon$
$W_{\varepsilon 1}$	$\bar\varepsilon$ $2\bar\varepsilon$	$\bar\varepsilon$ $1+3\bar\varepsilon$	$\bar\varepsilon$ $\bar\varepsilon$

$$\varepsilon_1 = \varepsilon_2 = \frac{\varepsilon}{1-3\varepsilon} = \bar\varepsilon$$

Figure 5.6
Modified ε-perturbation of the game of figure 5.5

strong equilibrium points. Obviously $V_\varepsilon = (V_{\varepsilon 1}, V_{\varepsilon 2})$ payoff-dominates $U_\varepsilon = (U_{\varepsilon 1}, U_{\varepsilon 2})$. The first candidate set is $\{U_\varepsilon, V_\varepsilon\}$, and the second candidate set contains only V_ε. We have $L(\bar{G}_\varepsilon) = V_\varepsilon$. This yields $\underrightarrow{L}(G) = V$.

In the direct application of L to G the procedure of decomposition and reduction also removes W_1 and W_2. According to theorem 5.6.2 on 2×2 games, the mixed equilibrium point is the solution of the game G^1 that results in this way. Consequently $L(G) = (q_1, q_2)$ with $q_i(U_i) = q_i(V_i) = \frac{1}{2}$ for $i = 1, 2$. The solution $L(G)$ is different from the limit solution $\underrightarrow{L}(G)$.

A Degenerate Unanimity Game

To illustrate some aspects of candidate elimination and substitution, we determine the solution $L(G)$ of the degenerate unanimity game shown in figure 5.7. Because no additional insight can be gained in this way, the analysis of the ε-perturbations and the limit solution is omitted here.

The three strong equilibrium points $U = (U_1, U_2)$, $V = (V_1, V_2)$, and $W = (W_1, W_2)$ are the elements of the first candidate set. U and V do not dominate each other (their Nash-products are equal), and both of them payoff dominate W. Therefore U and V are the undominated elements of $\Omega_1 = \{U, V, W\}$. Consequently the second candidate set is $\Omega_2 = \{U, V\}$.

We have to compute the substitute $T(G, c(\Omega_2))$. In $c(\Omega_2)$ player i uses his

	U_2		V_2		W_2	
U_1	6		0		0	
		4		0		0
V_1	0		4		0	
		0		6		0
W_1	0		0		3	
		0		0		3

Figure 5.7
A degenerate unanimity game

strategies U_i and V_i with probabilities $\frac{1}{2}$ and his strategy W_i with probability 0 $(i = 1, 2)$. The linear tracing procedure with the prior $c(\Omega_2)$ fails to be well defined. For $0 \leq t < 0.2$ the games G^t arising in the linear tracing procedure have exactly one equilibrium, namely (U_1, V_2). At $t = 0.2$ the graph of equilibrium points splits into three paths, leading to U, V, and the mixed equilibrium point $q = (q_1, q_2)$ whose components are

$$q_1(U_1) = 0.6, \quad q_1(V_1) = 0.4, \quad q_1(W_1) = 0, \tag{5.6.19}$$

$$q_2(U_2) = 0.4, \quad q_2(V_2) = 0.6, \quad q_2(W_2) = 0. \tag{5.6.20}$$

The symmetry that carries U to V excludes the possibility that either U or V is the result of the logarithmic tracing procedure. Here

$$T(G, c(\Omega_2)) = q. \tag{5.6.21}$$

The substitution step yields the following third candidate set $\Omega_3 = \{W, q\}$. The payoffs attached to q are 2.4 for each of both players. This shows that q is payoff-dominated by W. Therefore $\Omega_4 = \{W\}$ is the fourth candidate set. $L(G) = W$ is the solution.

Comment   At least at first glance it might seem to be natural to look at the substitute as the solution where a substitution step has to be performed. We do not want to define the solution in this way because the substitute may actually be much less stable than one of the candidates eliminated before. This is illustrated by the game of figure 5.7. In the transition from Ω_1 to Ω_2 the payoff-dominated equilibrium point W is eliminated. The substitute of Ω_2 is the mixed strategy equilibrium point q. It would be undesirable to obtain this rather unstable equilibrium point as the solution. The substitution step requires a comparison of q with W and thereby gives the more stable equilibrium point W the chance to emerge as the solution.

The Example of Figure 2.1   This game is a team problem, where both players have the same payoffs. Nevertheless, the players face a coordination problem since both (A, A) and (B, C) yield the same maximal common payoffs. In the ε-perturbations of this game the initial candidates are the equilibrium points $(A_\varepsilon, A_\varepsilon)$ and $(B_\varepsilon, C_\varepsilon)$ corresponding to (A, A) and (B, C). With the help of (5.6.9) it can be seen that at these equilibrium points the payoffs in the ε-perturbations are

$$\bar{H}_{\varepsilon i}(A_\varepsilon, A_\varepsilon) = 2 + 3\varepsilon_1 + 3\varepsilon_2, \tag{5.6.22}$$

$$\bar{H}_{\varepsilon i}(B_\varepsilon, C_\varepsilon) = 2 + 3\varepsilon_1 + 2\varepsilon_2, \quad \text{for } i = 1, 2. \tag{5.6.23}$$

Consequently $(A_\varepsilon, A_\varepsilon)$ payoff-dominates $(B_\varepsilon, C_\varepsilon)$. It follows that (A, A) is the solution.

5.7   Summary of Procedures

In this section we will give an overview of the structure of our theory and outline the steps to be taken in its application to specific examples.

Though our solution concept does not really specify an algorithm, for convenience, we will summarize it somewhat like the description of a computer program. Each step specifies certain tasks that are broken down into subtasks if necessary. Once a task such as finding the solution of an auxiliary game has been completed, one has to go back to the last unfinished task which may involve the solution of further auxiliary games. It is assumed that the game to be solved is given as an unperturbed extensive form with perfect recall or as a game in normal form. The final aim is the determination of its limit solution.

Step 1:
If the game is given in extensive form, construct its standard form (see chapter 2). The standard form is the game to which the theory is applied. A game given in normal form is considered as a standard form with normal-form structure. Continue with step 2.

Step 2:

Select a sufficiently small ε_0 and form the ε-perturbed games with $0 < \varepsilon < \varepsilon_0$ (see section 2.8). Find the solutions for all these games. For each game to be solved, the required procedures begin with step 3. (The procedures must be followed parametrically, but it is convenient to describe them as they apply to single ε-perturbed games.) After finding the solutions of all ε-perturbed games, continue with step 6.

Step 3:

Start with the procedure of decomposition and reduction described by figure 3.29. During this procedure solutions of irreducible games have to be computed (rectangle 10 in figure 3.29). The determination of the solution of each of the irreducible games begins with step 4.

Step 4:

Find out whether the game is basic (it is basic if it has no formation). If the game is basic, find its solution by tracing its centroid. If the game is nonbasic, continue with step 5.

Step 5:

Find the primitive formations. For each primitive formation determine its solution, beginning with step 3. Form the first candidate set (the set of all solutions of primitive formations). Determine the payoff-dominance relationships, strategic distances, strategic net distances, and risk-dominance relationships for all pairs of primitive formation solutions. Follow the process of candidate elimination and substitution described in figure 5.3. In the course of this process substitutes may come in as new candidates. If this happens, payoff-dominance relationships, strategic distances, strategic net distances, and risk-dominance relationships have to be determined between the substitute and the other equilibrium points in the candidate set produced by the substitution step. The end result of the process of candidate elimination and substitution is the solution.

Step 6:

Determine the limit solution (see section 2.10).

6 A Bargaining Problem with Transaction Costs on One Side

6.1 Introduction

Several applications of our theory to specific game models will be presented in this chapter and the remaining chapters of this book. Further applications can be found in the literature (Selten and Güth 1978, 1982a, 1982b; Selten and Leopold 1983; Leopold-Wildburger 1982, 1985; Lutz 1983). In this chapter we will investigate a two-person bargaining situation where one of the participants has transaction costs connected to making a proposal. One may think of an illegal deal where player 1, the seller, faces punishment if he is caught bargaining, whether or not an agreement is reached. The transaction costs express the utility loss involved in this risk.

Bargaining is modeled in the same way as in the unanimity game. Both players make simultaneous decisions. Agreement is reached if both of them make the same proposal. Otherwise, conflict results. Player 1 can choose to make no proposal, in which case he is better off than in a conflict reached by disagreeing proposals. In the bargaining situation considered here, the players can divide a fixed amount of money between themselves. Both players are assumed to have utility functions that are linear in money.

A similar bargaining problem with only two possible agreements, but with transaction costs on both sides, has been explored in the literature (Selten and Leopold 1983). Ulrike Leopold has investigated the much more difficult case of bargaining on the division of a fixed amount of money with transaction costs on both sides (Leopold-Wildburger 1982, 1985). Some remarks on the results obtained there will be made at the end of the chapter. Loosely speaking, one may say that the model examined here is almost a special case of the much more complicated problem treated by Ulrike Leopold. The results presented in this chapter agree with those obtained by Ulrike Leopold for sufficiently small transaction costs of player 2. This is not surprising, though by no means trivial, since the simpler model is not a special case of the more complicated one.

Our theory has been conceived for finite games because this permits us to concentrate efforts on the basic problems of equilibrium selection without running into technical difficulties connected to infinite games. Therefore it will be assumed that money is not infinitely divisible.

6.2   The Model

The model has the form of a two-person game with normal form structure. As we mentioned earlier, the model is similar to a unanimity game. To reach an agreement, each player must make the same proposal on the division of one money unit. However, player 1 has the option not to bargain at all.

The possible agreements can be characterized by the amount x assigned to player 1. The corresponding agreement payoff for player 2 is $1 - x$. It is assumed that there is a smallest piece of money worth $1/M$, where M is a positive even number. This piece of money cannot be further subdivided. Player 1's agreement payoff must be an integer multiple of $1/M$, with $0 < x < 1$. We exclude agreements that do not give positive amounts to both players. The set of all possible agreements is given by

$$X = \left\{ x \mid x = \frac{k}{M}, k = 1, \ldots, M - 1 \right\}. \tag{6.2.1}$$

The symbol W_1 denotes player 1's choice not to bargain. If player 1 selects W_1, he receives a positive payoff α and player 2 receives 0, independently of player 2's strategy. To exclude uninteresting cases that would require special attention, we impose the following conditions on M and the transaction cost parameter α:

$$M > 2, \tag{6.2.2}$$

$$\frac{2}{M - 1} < \alpha < \frac{M - 1}{M}. \tag{6.2.3}$$

Because M is even, (6.2.2) means that M can assume the values $4, 6, \ldots$. We are mainly interested in the behavior of the limit solution for $M \to \infty$. In this respect (6.2.2) and (6.2.3) do not restrict the generality of our analysis. The bargaining situation is described by the following two-person game $G = (\Phi, H)$, with $\Phi = \Phi_1 \times \Phi_2$:

$$\Phi_1 = X \cup \{W_1\}, \tag{6.2.4}$$

$$\Phi_2 = X, \tag{6.2.5}$$

$$H_1(\phi) = \begin{cases} x, & \text{for } \phi_1 = \phi_2 = x, \\ \alpha, & \text{for } \phi_1 = W_1, \\ 0, & \text{for } \phi_1 \neq \phi_2 \text{ and } \phi_1 \neq W_1, \end{cases} \tag{6.2.6}$$

$$H_2(\phi) = \begin{cases} 1 - x, & \text{for } \phi_1 = \phi_2 = x, \\ 0, & \text{for } \phi_1 \neq \phi_2. \end{cases} \qquad (6.2.7)$$

6.3 Properties of ε-Perturbations

To apply our theory to the model, we have to look at the ε-perturbations $G_\varepsilon = (\Phi_\varepsilon, H_\varepsilon)$ of the game G defined by (6.2.4) through (6.2.7). We begin by introducing some notational conventions.

To avoid confusion with algebraic expressions like xy, the notation (x, y) is used for pure-strategy pairs of G; as is usual, the first component is player 1's strategy and the second is player 2's strategy. The ε-extreme strategy corresponding to player i's pure strategy x is denoted by $[x]_{\varepsilon i}$, or $x_{\varepsilon i}$ where the shorter notation does not lead to confusion. $W_{\varepsilon 1}$ is player 1's ε-extreme strategy corresponding to W_1. The symbol $X_{\varepsilon i}$ is used for the set of player i's ε-extreme strategies corresponding to proposals $x \in X$. The pure-strategy sets $\Phi_{\varepsilon 1}$ and $\Phi_{\varepsilon 2}$ in G_ε are

$$\Phi_{\varepsilon 1} = X_{\varepsilon 1} \cup \{W_{\varepsilon 1}\}, \qquad (6.3.1)$$

$$\Phi_{\varepsilon 2} = X_{\varepsilon 2}. \qquad (6.3.2)$$

The payoff function H_ε agrees with H. As much as possible the analysis will be based on the short ε-perturbation $\hat{G}_\varepsilon = (\Phi_\varepsilon, \hat{H}_\varepsilon)$ rather than G_ε or the modified ε-perturbation $\bar{G}_\varepsilon = (\Phi_\varepsilon, \bar{H}_\varepsilon)$ (see section 5.6).

Two Payoff Inequalities

Let m be the smallest integer such that m/M is greater than α:

$$m = \min \left\{ k \,|\, k = 1, \ldots, M - 1 \text{ and } \frac{k}{M} > \alpha \right\}. \qquad (6.3.3)$$

It will be shown that the following two inequalities hold for sufficiently small ε:

$$\hat{H}_{\varepsilon 1}(W_{\varepsilon 1} x_{\varepsilon 2}) > \hat{H}_{\varepsilon 1}(x_{\varepsilon 1} x_{\varepsilon 2}), \quad \text{for } x = \frac{k}{M} \text{ with } k = 1, \ldots, m - 1, \qquad (6.3.4)$$

$$\hat{H}_{\varepsilon 1}(W_{\varepsilon 1} x_{\varepsilon 2}) < \hat{H}_{\varepsilon 1}(x_{\varepsilon 1} x_{\varepsilon 2}), \quad \text{for } x = \frac{k}{M} \text{ with } k = m, \ldots, M - 1. \qquad (6.3.5)$$

To show this, we apply (5.6.10):

$$\hat{H}_{\varepsilon 1}(W_{\varepsilon 1} x_{\varepsilon 2}) = \alpha + \varepsilon_1 (M - 1)\alpha, \tag{6.3.6}$$

$$\hat{H}_{\varepsilon 1}(x_{\varepsilon 1} x_{\varepsilon 2}) = x + \varepsilon_1 x. \tag{6.3.7}$$

Inequality (6.3.4) holds for $\alpha > x$. For $x = (m - 1)/M$ we may have $x = \alpha$. In view of $M > 2$ inequality (6.3.4) holds in this case as well. For sufficiently small ε inequality (6.3.5) is valid in view of $x > \alpha$.

Best Replies to Pure Strategies

$A_{\varepsilon i}$ denotes player i's best-reply correspondence which maps every strategy of the other player to the set of player i's pure best replies in G_ε. Inequalities (6.3.4) and (6.3.5) permit the following conclusion: for sufficiently small ε we have

$$A_{\varepsilon 1}(x_{\varepsilon 2}) = \begin{cases} \{W_{\varepsilon 1}\}, & \text{for } x \le \alpha, \\ \{x_{\varepsilon 1}\}, & \text{for } x > \alpha. \end{cases} \tag{6.3.8}$$

Since $W_{\varepsilon 1}$ assigns the same probability ε to all $x \in X$, player 2's unique best reply to $W_{\varepsilon 1}$ in G_ε is $[1/M]_\varepsilon$. Obviously, for sufficiently small ε, player 2's unique best reply to $x_{\varepsilon 1}$ in G_ε is $x_{\varepsilon 2}$, and we have

$$A_{\varepsilon 2}(x_{\varepsilon 1}) = \{x_{\varepsilon 2}\}, \tag{6.3.9}$$

$$A_{\varepsilon 2}(W_{\varepsilon 1}) = \left\{ \left[\frac{1}{M} \right]_\varepsilon \right\}. \tag{6.3.10}$$

Strong Equilibrium Points

It can be seen immediately that for sufficiently small ε the game G_ε has $M - m$ strong equilibrium points of the form $x_{\varepsilon 1} x_{\varepsilon 2}$ with $x = k/M$ and $k = m, \ldots, M - 1$ and one additional strong equilibrium point $W_{\varepsilon 1}[1/M]_\varepsilon$. There are no further pure-strategy equilibrium points. The symbol x_ε will be used as a short notation for $x_{\varepsilon 1} x_{\varepsilon 2}$.

6.4 Decomposition and Reduction

The procedure of decomposition and reduction has to be applied to G_ε. Here it will always be assumed that ε is sufficiently small in the sense that the results obtained in section 6.3 hold. Neither player 1 nor player 2 forms a cell in G_ε since, otherwise, best replies could not depend on the other player's strategy. Since G_ε is a game with normal form structure, we do not make any distinction between a player and his single agent. Inferior choices may also be called inferior pure strategies.

Inequality (6.3.4) permits the conclusion that player 1's pure strategies $x_{\varepsilon 1}$ with $x = k/M$ and $k = 1, \ldots, m - 1$ are inferior in G_ε. The other pure strategies of player 1 are not inferior because they are unique best replies somewhere. The same is true for all pure strategies of player 2. Let G_ε' be the game that results from G_ε by elimination of inferior choices (pure strategies). We now have to ask whether G_ε' is decomposable (see figure 3.29). The argument used for G_ε also establishes the absence of cells in G_ε'.

It is necessary to examine whether G_ε' has inferior pure strategies. As we shall see, player 2's pure strategies $x_{\varepsilon 2}$ with $x = k/M$ and $k = 2, \ldots, m - 1$ are inferior in G_ε'. Let q_1 be a mixed strategy of player 1 in G_ε'. Equation (5.6.11) yields

$$\hat{H}_{\varepsilon 2}\left(q_1 \left[\frac{k}{M}\right]_{\varepsilon 2}\right) = \varepsilon_2 \frac{M - k}{M}, \quad \text{for } k = 1, \ldots, m - 1. \tag{6.4.1}$$

This is due to the fact that player 1's pure strategies $[k/M]_{\varepsilon 1}$ with $k = 1, \ldots, m - 1$ have already been eliminated. q_1 assigns probability ε to each of the pure strategies $1/M, \ldots, (m - 1)/M$. Obviously, in G_ε', player 2's pure strategy $[1/M]_{\varepsilon 2}$ dominates his pure strategies $[k/M]_{\varepsilon 2}$, with $k = 2, \ldots, m - 1$. No other pure strategies are inferior in G_ε'.

Let $G_\varepsilon'' = (\Phi_\varepsilon'', H_\varepsilon'')$ be the game that results from G_ε' by elimination of inferior choices. Arguments very similar to those just used show that G_ε'' hasn't any cells, inferior strategies, semiduplicates, or duplicates. G_ε'' is irreducible. Define

$$X'' = \left\{ x \,\middle|\, x = \frac{k}{M}, \quad \text{with } k = m, \ldots, M - 1 \right\}. \tag{6.4.2}$$

Let $X_{\varepsilon i}''$ be the set of all ε-extreme strategies of player i corresponding to proposals $x \in X''$. The pure-strategy sets of G_ε'' are

$$\Phi_{\varepsilon 1}'' = X_{\varepsilon 1}'' \cup \{W_{1\varepsilon}\}, \tag{6.4.3}$$

$$\Phi_{\varepsilon 2}'' = X_{\varepsilon 2}'' \cup \left\{ \left[\frac{1}{M}\right]_{\varepsilon 2} \right\}. \tag{6.4.4}$$

Obviously the best replies to pure strategies in G_ε'' are the same as in G_ε', and both games have the same strong equilibrium points.

6.5 Initial Candidates

The process of candidate elimination and substitution has to be followed in G_ε''. To find the first candidate set, we have to determine the primitive formations of G_ε''. Each of the strong equilibrium points generates a primitive formation. Every pure strategy belongs to one of these strong equilibrium points. Consequently the primitive formations of G_ε'' are exactly those generated by the strong equilibrium points. It follows that the first candidate set Ω_1 is nothing else than the set of all strong equilibrium points.

The investigation of dominance relationships between pairs of initial candidates leads to the conclusion that one of the candidates in Ω_1 is globally dominant in G_ε''. As was pointed out in section 5.6, a globally dominant candidate is the solution.

Because the solution is found by global dominance, there is no need to look at strategic distances. The payoff-dominance relationships between pairs of initial candidates are easily obtained. Because $x > \alpha$ for $x \in X''$, each candidate of the form $x_\varepsilon = x_{\varepsilon 1} x_{\varepsilon 2}$ payoff dominates $W_{\varepsilon 1}[1/M]_{\varepsilon 2}$ for sufficiently small ε. It is also clear that for sufficiently small ε there is no payoff dominance between two different candidates of the form $x_\varepsilon = x_{\varepsilon 1} x_{\varepsilon 2}$. The dominance relationship between two such candidates is determined by risk dominance. It can now be seen that for sufficiently small ε, a candidate of the form $x_\varepsilon = x_{\varepsilon 1} x_{\varepsilon 2}$ is globally dominant if it risk-dominates all other strong equilibrium points of this form.

The investigation of risk dominance between pairs of strong equilibrium points of the form $x_\varepsilon = x_{\varepsilon 1} x_{\varepsilon 2}$ leads to the conclusion that one of these strong equilibrium points risk-dominates all others and therefore is the solution of the game.

6.6 Risk Dominance between Pairs of Initial Candidates

The risk-dominance comparisons to be investigated do not require the use of the logarithmic tracing procedure. For a given prior the path of the linear tracing procedure depends only on the best-reply structure. The bicentric prior is also determined by the best-reply structure. Therefore, for the purpose of computing risk-dominance relationships without the logarithmic tracing procedure, a restricted game can be replaced by another game with the same pure-strategy sets, the same best-reply structure, and a simpler payoff function.

In our case ε-perturbation payoffs will be replaced by payoffs of the short ε-perturbation. If in $G_\varepsilon'' = (\Phi_\varepsilon'', H_\varepsilon'')$ the payoff function H_ε'' is replaced by the restriction of the payoff function for the short ε-perturbation to Φ_ε'', we obtain the game $\tilde{G}_\varepsilon = (\phi_\varepsilon'', \tilde{H}_\varepsilon)$. Obviously $\tilde{G}_\varepsilon$ has the same best reply structure as G_ε''.

In our case no agents are fixed in the transition to the restricted game for a risk-dominance comparison between two different strong equilibrium points, $x_\varepsilon = x_{\varepsilon 1} x_{\varepsilon 2}$ and $y_\varepsilon = y_{\varepsilon 1} y_{\varepsilon 2}$. Both players have different strategies at these equilibrium points. Therefore the restricted game for the comparison is the formation spanned by both points. The best-reply structure of the restricted game is fully determined by the best-reply structure of the whole game. (If agents are fixed in the transition to the restricted game, this is not necessarily the case.)

It is now clear that for the purpose of computing risk-dominance relationships without the logarithmic tracing procedure, we can replace G_ε'' by $\tilde{G}_\varepsilon$. As long as the logarithmic tracing procedure is not used, it does not matter whether the computations for the determination of risk-dominance comparisons are based on the restricted game or on some larger formation. The bicentric prior and the result of the application of the linear tracing procedure are the same in both cases. We shall make use of this fact.

A Formation Containing the Restricted Game

Let $x_\varepsilon = x_{\varepsilon 1} x_{\varepsilon 2}$, $y_\varepsilon = y_{\varepsilon 1} y_{\varepsilon 2}$ be two different strong equilibrium points. We want to explore the risk-dominance relationship between these equilibrium points in $\tilde{G}_\varepsilon$. For this purpose we determine a formation F of $\tilde{G}_\varepsilon$ that contains both equilibrium points. In this formation F player 1 has the pure strategies $x_{\varepsilon 1}$, $y_{\varepsilon 1}$ and $W_{\varepsilon 1}$, and player 2 has the pure strategies $x_{\varepsilon 2}$, $y_{\varepsilon 2}$ and $[1/M]_{\varepsilon 2}$. Figure 6.1 shows a bimatrix representation of F.

We have to show that for sufficiently small ε the substructure F is a formation of $\tilde{G}_\varepsilon$. Consider a proposal $s \in X''$ different from x and y, and let $s_{\varepsilon i}$ be the corresponding ε-extreme strategy of player i. Suppose that player 2 uses an arbitrary mixed strategy of F and player 1 plays $s_{\varepsilon 1}$. Then player 1's payoff in $\tilde{G}_\varepsilon$ is $\varepsilon_1 s$. For sufficiently small ε this is smaller than α. Therefore in $\tilde{G}_\varepsilon$ player 1's best reply to a mixed strategy available to player 2 in F cannot be $s_{\varepsilon 1}$.

Now suppose that player 1 uses an arbitrary mixed strategy available in F. Then player 2's payoff for $s_{\varepsilon 2}$ is $\varepsilon_2(1 - s)$ which is smaller than his payoff

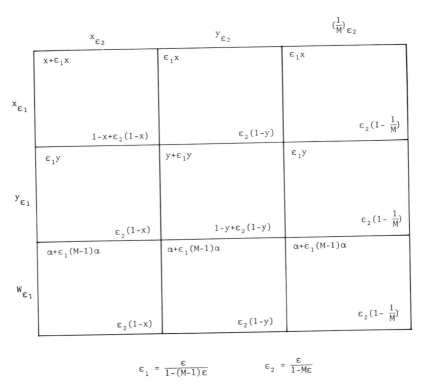

Figure 6.1
The game F which determines the risk-dominance relationship between $x_\varepsilon = x_{\varepsilon 1} x_{\varepsilon 2}$ and $y_\varepsilon = y_{\varepsilon 1} y_{\varepsilon 2}$

for $[1/M]_{\varepsilon 2}$. Therefore in $\tilde{G}_\varepsilon$ player 2's best reply to a mixed strategy of player 1 available in F cannot be $s_{\varepsilon 2}$. It follows that for sufficiently small ε the substructure F is a formation of $\tilde{G}_\varepsilon$. Since this formation contains x_ε and y_ε, it also contains the formation spanned by both equilibrium points—in other words, the restricted game for the comparison of both equilibrium points. To determine risk dominance between x_ε and y_ε, we can concentrate our attention on F.

Player 1's Bicentric Prior

Player 1's bicentric prior p_1 for the comparison between x_ε and y_ε can be determined as indicated in figure 6.2. The vertical axis shows the z-line. Player 1's payoffs for $x_{\varepsilon 1}$, $y_{\varepsilon 1}$ and $W_{\varepsilon 1}$ against strategies of the form $z x_{\varepsilon 2} +$

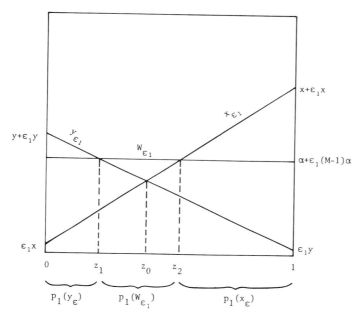

Figure 6.2
Determination of player 1's bicentric prior for the comparison of $x_\varepsilon = x_{\varepsilon 1} x_{\varepsilon 2}$ and $y_\varepsilon = y_{\varepsilon 1} y_{\varepsilon 2}$

$(1 - z) y_{\varepsilon 2}$ are represented by straight lines marked $x_{\varepsilon 1}$, $y_{\varepsilon 1}$ and $W_{\varepsilon 1}$, respectively.

In the case shown in the diagram the intersection of the lines for $x_{\varepsilon 1}$ and $y_{\varepsilon 1}$ is below the line for $W_{\varepsilon 1}$. It may also happen that the intersection is not below this line. We have to distinguish both cases. For this purpose we determine z_0:

$$z_0 = \frac{y}{x + y} + \varepsilon_1 \frac{y - x}{x + y}. \tag{6.6.1}$$

The intersection is below the line for $W_{\varepsilon 1}$ if we have

$$\frac{xy}{x + y}(1 + 2\varepsilon_1) < \alpha(1 + (M - 1)\varepsilon_1). \tag{6.6.2}$$

In view of $M - 1 \geq 3$, inequality (6.6.2) holds for

$$\frac{xy}{x + y} \leq \alpha. \tag{6.6.3}$$

In the opposite case

$$\frac{xy}{x+y} > \alpha \tag{6.6.4}$$

the intersection is above the line for $W_{\varepsilon 1}$ if ε is sufficiently small.

With the help of elementary computations guided by figure 6.2, we can now determine player 1's prior. For sufficiently small ε we obtain the following result:

$$p_1(x_{\varepsilon 1}) = 1 - \frac{\alpha}{x} - \varepsilon_1\left((M-1)\frac{\alpha}{x} - 1\right), \quad \text{for } \frac{xy}{x+y} \le \alpha, \tag{6.6.5}$$

$$p_1(y_{\varepsilon 1}) = 1 - \frac{\alpha}{y} - \varepsilon_1\left((M-1)\frac{\alpha}{y} - 1\right), \quad \text{for } \frac{xy}{x+y} \le \alpha, \tag{6.6.6}$$

$$p_1(W_{\varepsilon 1}) = \alpha\frac{x+y}{xy} - 1 + \varepsilon_1\left((M-1)\alpha\frac{x+y}{xy} - 2\right), \quad \text{for } \frac{xy}{x+y} \le \alpha, \tag{6.6.7}$$

$$p_1(x_{\varepsilon 1}) = \frac{x}{x+y} + \varepsilon_1\frac{x-y}{x+y}, \quad \text{for } \frac{xy}{x+y} > \alpha, \tag{6.6.8}$$

$$p_1(y_{\varepsilon 1}) = \frac{y}{x+y} + \varepsilon_1\frac{y-x}{x+y}, \quad \text{for } \frac{xy}{x+y} > \alpha, \tag{6.6.9}$$

$$p_1(W_{\varepsilon 1}) = 0, \quad \text{for } \frac{xy}{x+y} > \alpha. \tag{6.6.10}$$

Player 2's Bicentric Prior

Player 2's bicentric prior can be computed in essentially the same way as player 1's bicentric prior. One obtains

$$p_2(x_{\varepsilon 2}) = \frac{1-x}{2-x-y} - \varepsilon_2\frac{x-y}{2-x-y}, \tag{6.6.11}$$

$$p_2(y_{\varepsilon 2}) = \frac{1-y}{2-x-y} - \varepsilon_2\frac{y-x}{2-x-y}, \tag{6.6.12}$$

$$p_2\left(\left[\frac{1}{M}\right]_{\varepsilon 2}\right) = 0. \tag{6.6.13}$$

Payoffs Obtained against Bicentric Prior

To determine the risk dominance relationship between x_ε and y_ε, we must apply the tracing procedure to the bicentric prior p. The first step is the determination of the payoffs obtained for the pure strategies in F against the bicentric prior strategy of the other player:

$$\tilde{H}_{\varepsilon 1}(x_{\varepsilon 1} p_2) = \frac{x(1 - x)}{2 - x - y} + \varepsilon_2 \frac{x(y - x)}{2 - x - y} + \varepsilon_1 x, \tag{6.6.14}$$

$$\tilde{H}_{\varepsilon 1}(y_{\varepsilon 1} p_2) = \frac{y(1 - y)}{2 - x - y} + \varepsilon_2 \frac{y(x - y)}{2 - x - y} + \varepsilon_1 y, \tag{6.6.15}$$

$$\tilde{H}_{\varepsilon 1}(W_{\varepsilon 1} p_2) = \alpha + \varepsilon_1 (M - 1)\alpha, \tag{6.6.16}$$

$$\tilde{H}_{\varepsilon 2}(p_1 x_{\varepsilon 2}) = (1 - x)[p_1(x_{\varepsilon 1}) + \varepsilon_2], \tag{6.6.17}$$

$$\tilde{H}_{\varepsilon 2}(p_1 y_{\varepsilon 2}) = (1 - y)[p_1(y_{\varepsilon 1}) + \varepsilon_2], \tag{6.6.18}$$

$$\tilde{H}_{\varepsilon 2}\left(p_1 \left[\frac{1}{M}\right]_{\varepsilon 2}\right) = \varepsilon_2 \frac{M - 1}{M}. \tag{6.6.19}$$

Conditions for $W_{\varepsilon 1}$ Being the Best Reply to p_2

It is necessary to determine the best reply to the bicentric prior. We first ask the question under which circumstances $W_{\varepsilon 1}$ is player 1's unique best reply to player 2's prior strategy p_2. For this purpose we must compare the payoff in (6.6.16) with the payoffs in (6.6.14) and (6.6.15). We will show that for sufficiently small ε, player 1's best reply set $A_{\varepsilon 1}(p_2)$ has the following property:

$$A_{\varepsilon 1}(p_2) = \{W_{\varepsilon 1}\}, \quad \text{if and only if } \alpha \geq \frac{x(1 - x)}{2 - x - y} \text{ and } \alpha \geq \frac{y(1 - y)}{2 - x - y}. \tag{6.6.20}$$

Clearly for sufficiently small ε the strategy $W_{\varepsilon 1}$ is the only best reply to p_2 if the inequalities for α hold with $>$ instead of $\geq$. Moreover for sufficiently small ε the strategy $W_{\varepsilon 1}$ cannot be a best reply to p_2 if one of both inequalities for α does not hold. To show that assertion (6.6.20) holds for border cases as well, we will show that for sufficiently small ε the ε-term in (6.6.16) outweighs the ε-terms in (6.6.14) and (6.6.15):

$$\varepsilon_1(M-1)\alpha > \varepsilon_2 \frac{x(y-x)}{2-x-y} + \varepsilon_1 x, \qquad (6.6.21)$$

$$\varepsilon_1(M-1)\alpha > \varepsilon_2 \frac{y(x-y)}{2-x-y} + \varepsilon_1 y. \qquad (6.6.22)$$

In view of (5.6.7) and (5.6.8) we have

$$\varepsilon_1 = \frac{\varepsilon}{1-(M-1)\varepsilon}, \qquad (6.6.23)$$

$$\varepsilon_2 = \frac{\varepsilon}{1-M\varepsilon}. \qquad (6.6.24)$$

To obtain a relationship between ε_1 and ε_2, we divide ε_1 by ε_2:

$$\frac{\varepsilon_1}{\varepsilon_2} = \frac{1-M\varepsilon}{1-(M-1)\varepsilon} = 1-\varepsilon_1. \qquad (6.6.25)$$

This yields

$$\varepsilon_2 = \frac{\varepsilon_1}{1-\varepsilon_1}. \qquad (6.6.26)$$

Consequently (6.6.21) and (6.6.22) are equivalent to the following inequalities (6.6.27) and (6.6.28), respectively:

$$(M-1)\alpha > \frac{1}{1-\varepsilon_1} \cdot \frac{x(y-x)}{2-x-y} + x, \qquad (6.6.27)$$

$$(M-1)\alpha > \frac{1}{1-\varepsilon_1} \cdot \frac{y(x-y)}{2-x-y} + y. \qquad (6.6.28)$$

We can make use of two simple algebraic identities:

$$\frac{x(y-x)}{2-x-y} + x = \frac{2x(1-x)}{2-x-y}, \qquad (6.6.29)$$

$$\frac{y(x-y)}{2-x-y} + y = \frac{2y(1-y)}{2-x-y}. \qquad (6.6.30)$$

Since $2-x-y$ is the sum of $1-x$ and $1-y$, in both cases the right-hand side is smaller than 2. Therefore for sufficiently small ε the right-hand sides of (6.6.27) and (6.6.28) are smaller than 2. On the other hand, assumption

(6.2.3) has the consequence that the left-hand side is greater than 2. There-fore (6.6.20) holds.

Conditions for $x_{\varepsilon1}$ and $y_{\varepsilon1}$ Being Best Replies to p_2

If one of the conditions on α in (6.6.20) is not satisfied, then $x_{\varepsilon1}$ or $y_{\varepsilon1}$ is a best reply of player 1 to p_2 for sufficiently small ε. To find out where $x_{\varepsilon1}$ or $y_{\varepsilon1}$ is player 1's unique best reply to p_2, we form the difference of his payoffs in (6.6.14) and (6.6.15):

$$\tilde{H}_{\varepsilon1}(x_{\varepsilon1}p_2) - \tilde{H}_{\varepsilon1}(y_{\varepsilon1}p_2) = \frac{(x-y)(1-x-y)}{2-x-y} + \varepsilon_2\frac{y^2-x^2}{2-x-y} + \varepsilon_1(x-y).$$

(6.6.31)

It will be convenient to concentrate our attention on the case $x > y$. After deriving the results for this case, we can simply obtain the results for the opposite case, $y > x$, by exchanging the roles of x and y. With the help of (6.6.31) we will show that for sufficiently small ε player 1's best-reply set $A_{\varepsilon1}(p_2)$ has the following properties:

$$A_{\varepsilon1}(p_2) = \{x_{\varepsilon1}\}, \quad \text{for } x > y \text{ if and only if } x + y < 1 \text{ and } \frac{x(1-x)}{2-x-y} > \alpha,$$

(6.6.32)

$$A_{\varepsilon1}(p_2) = \{y_{\varepsilon1}\}, \quad \text{for } x > y \text{ if and only if } x + y \geq 1 \text{ and } \frac{y(1-y)}{2-x-y} > \alpha.$$

(6.6.33)

Under the condition on α in (6.6.32), strategy $W_{\varepsilon1}$ cannot be a best reply to p_2, and the right-hand side of (6.6.31) is positive for sufficiently small ε. Therefore (6.6.32) holds. Under the condition on α in (6.6.33), strategy $W_{\varepsilon1}$ cannot be a best reply to p_2 either. For $x + y > 1$ the right-hand side of (6.6.31) is negative. Clearly in this case y_ε is player 1's unique best reply to p_2. Now consider the case $x + y = 1$. In this case we have

$$\tilde{H}_{\varepsilon1}(x_{\varepsilon1}p_2) - \tilde{H}_{\varepsilon1}(y_{\varepsilon1}p_2) = (x-y)(\varepsilon_1 - \varepsilon_2).$$

(6.6.34)

Equation (6.6.26) yields

$$\varepsilon_2 > \varepsilon_1.$$

(6.6.35)

This shows that $y_{\varepsilon1}$ is player 1's unique best reply if the conditions of (6.6.33) are satisfied with $x + y = 1$. It is easy to see that the conditions of (6.6.32) and (6.6.33) exhaust the set of all possible pairs with $x > y$, where $W_{\varepsilon 1}$ is not the unique best reply to p_2. Therefore the conditions in (6.6.32) and (6.6.33) are not only sufficient but also necessary for the assertions.

The results show that for sufficiently small ε, player 1's best reply to p_2 is uniquely determined. It will be shown that the analogous statement holds for player 2 as well. The uniqueness of the vector best reply to the prior is important for the applicability of the linear tracing procedure in the determination of the risk-dominance relationship between x_ε and y_ε.

Player 2's Best Replies to the Prior

To determine player 2's best-reply set $A_{\varepsilon 2}(p_1)$, we first notice that for sufficiently small ε player 2's strategy $[1/M]_{\varepsilon 2}$ cannot be a best reply to p_1. This is an immediate consequence of (6.6.17), (6.6.18), and (6.6.19), together with the fact that the main terms of $p_1(x_{\varepsilon 1})$ and $p_1(y_{\varepsilon 1})$ are always positive. To compare the payoffs in (6.6.17) and (6.6.18), it is necessary to distinguish the cases (6.6.3) and (6.6.4). For the sake of notational shortness we introduce the following definition:

$$\Delta = \frac{1}{x - y}[\tilde{H}_{\varepsilon 2}(p_1 x_{\varepsilon 2}) - \tilde{H}_{\varepsilon 2}(p_1 y_{\varepsilon 2})]. \tag{6.6.36}$$

After some computations, (6.6.17) and (6.6.18) combined with (6.6.5) to (6.6.10) yield

$$\Delta = \frac{\alpha}{xy} - 1 + \varepsilon_1\left(\frac{(M-1)\alpha}{xy} - 1\right) - \varepsilon_2, \quad \text{for } \frac{xy}{x+y} \leq \alpha, \tag{6.6.37}$$

$$\Delta = \frac{1 - x - y}{x + y} + \varepsilon_1\frac{2 - x - y}{x + y} - \varepsilon_2, \quad \text{for } \frac{xy}{x+y} > \alpha. \tag{6.6.38}$$

We continue to concentrate our attention on the case $x > y$. With the help of (6.6.37) and (6.6.38) we will show that the following is true:

$$A_{\varepsilon 2}(p_1) = \begin{cases} \{x_{\varepsilon 2}\}, & \text{for } x + y < 1 \text{ or } xy \leq \alpha, \\ \{y_{\varepsilon 2}\}, & \text{for } x + y \geq 1 \text{ and } xy > \alpha. \end{cases} \tag{6.6.39}$$

The condition on α in (6.6.37) can be rewritten as

$$\frac{\alpha}{xy} \geq \frac{1}{x + y}. \tag{6.6.40}$$

In view of $M - 1 \geq 2$, (6.6.40) combined with (6.6.37) yields

$$\Delta \geq \frac{1 - x - y}{x + y} + \varepsilon_1 \frac{2 - x - y}{x + y} - \varepsilon_2. \tag{6.6.41}$$

Inequality (6.6.41) holds regardless of the value of α. It follows that for sufficiently small ε the assertion (6.6.39) holds in the subcase $x + y < 1$.

In the subcase $x + y \geq 1$ and $xy \leq \alpha$ the condition on α in (6.6.37) holds. Consequently Δ is positive for $xy < \alpha$ if ε is sufficiently small. Moreover we have

$$\Delta = \varepsilon_1(M - 2) - \varepsilon_2, \quad \text{for } x + y \geq 1 \text{ and } \alpha = xy. \tag{6.6.42}$$

In view of (6.6.26) and $M \geq 4$ the right-hand side of (6.6.42) is positive for sufficiently small ε. We can conclude that the assertion in the first line of (6.6.39) holds for sufficiently small ε.

Now consider the subcase $x + y \geq 1$ and $xy > \alpha$. If the condition on α in (6.6.37) holds, then Δ is negative for sufficiently small ε. If the condition on α in (6.6.38) holds, then for sufficiently small ε the right-hand side of (6.6.38) is negative for $x + y > 1$. Moreover we have

$$\Delta = \varepsilon_1 - \varepsilon_2, \quad \text{for } x + y = 1 \text{ and } xy > \alpha. \tag{6.6.43}$$

In view of $\varepsilon_1 < \varepsilon_2$ the right-hand side of (6.6.43) is negative for $x > y$. Therefore the assertion of the second line of (6.6.39) holds for sufficiently small ε. Our results show that for sufficiently small ε player 2's best reply to the bicentric prior is always uniquely determined.

Exclusion of $x_{\varepsilon 1} y_{\varepsilon 2}$ and $y_{\varepsilon 1} x_{\varepsilon 2}$ as Best Replies to the Bicentric Prior

For sufficiently small ε neither $x_{\varepsilon 1} y_{\varepsilon 2}$ nor $y_{\varepsilon 1} x_{\varepsilon 2}$ can be vector best replies to the bicentric prior. Without loss of generality we can restrict our attention to the case $x > y$.

Suppose that $x_{\varepsilon 1} y_{\varepsilon 2}$ is the vector best reply to the bicentric prior. Equation (6.6.32) requires $x + y < 1$, and (6.6.39) requires $x + y \geq 1$. Obviously this is impossible. Now assume that $y_{\varepsilon 1} x_{\varepsilon 2}$ is the vector best reply to the bicentric prior. Equation (6.6.33) requires $x + y \geq 1$. This condition permits the following conclusion:

$$xy \geq \frac{y(1 - y)}{2 - x - y}, \quad \text{for } x + y \geq 1. \tag{6.6.44}$$

Therefore (6.6.33) requires $xy > \alpha$. Contrary to the assumption, it follows by (6.6.39) that $y_{\varepsilon 2}$ is player 2's only best reply to the bicentric prior.

Risk-Dominance Relationships

It is clear that x_ε risk-dominates y_ε if x_ε is the vector best reply to the bicentric prior. Analogously y_ε risk-dominates x_ε if y_ε is the vector best reply to the bicentric prior. The only other possibilities for the vector best reply to p are $W_{\varepsilon 1} x_{\varepsilon 2}$ and $W_{\varepsilon 1} y_{\varepsilon 2}$. For these two cases we apply the linear tracing procedure to determine the risk-dominance relationship between x_ε and y_ε. As we shall see, x_ε risk-dominates y_ε if the best reply to p is $W_{\varepsilon 1} x_{\varepsilon 2}$ and y_ε risk-dominates x_ε if the best reply to p is $W_{\varepsilon 1} y_{\varepsilon 2}$.

We will restrict our attention to parameter pairs (x, y) with $x > y$, since for $x < y$ the same arguments can be applied with the roles of x and y interchanged. Let us first consider the case where for sufficiently small ε the best reply to p is $W_{\varepsilon 1} x_{\varepsilon 2}$. It follows by (6.6.20) and (6.6.39) that we must have

$$\alpha \geq \frac{x(1 - x)}{2 - x - y} \tag{6.6.45}$$

and

$$x + y < 1, \quad \text{or } xy \leq \alpha. \tag{6.6.46}$$

Under these conditions the difference (6.6.31) between player 1's payoffs for $x_{\varepsilon 1}$ and $y_{\varepsilon 1}$ against player 2's prior strategy is positive. Therefore we can exclude the possibility that along the path of the tracing procedure applied to p in F, player 1 shifts to $y_{\varepsilon 1}$. Since $\tilde{H}_{\varepsilon 1}(x_\varepsilon)$ is greater than $\tilde{H}_{\varepsilon 1}(W_{\varepsilon 1} x_{\varepsilon 1})$, there will be a reversal point where $x_{\varepsilon 1}$ becomes player 1's best reply. This reversal point can be determined as follows:

$$t_{\varepsilon 1} = \frac{\tilde{H}_{\varepsilon 1}(W_{\varepsilon 1} p_2) - \tilde{H}_{\varepsilon 1}(x_{\varepsilon 1} p_2)}{\tilde{H}_{\varepsilon 1}(W_{\varepsilon 1} p_2) - \tilde{H}_{\varepsilon 1}(x_{\varepsilon 1} p_2) + \tilde{H}_{\varepsilon 1}(x_\varepsilon) - \tilde{H}(W_{\varepsilon 1} x_{\varepsilon 2})}. \tag{6.6.47}$$

With the help of (6.6.14), (6.6.16), and figure 6.1 we can compute the limit t_1 of $t_{\varepsilon 1}$ for $\varepsilon \to 0$:

$$t_1 = \lim_{\varepsilon \to 0} t_{\varepsilon 1} = \frac{\alpha - [x(1 - x)]/[2 - x - y]}{\alpha - [x(1 - x)]/[2 - x - y] + x - \alpha}. \tag{6.6.48}$$

For $x > \alpha$ we have

$$0 \leq t_1 < 1. \tag{6.6.49}$$

Figure 6.1 shows that $\tilde{H}_{\varepsilon 2}(W_{\varepsilon 1}[1/M]_{\varepsilon 2})$ is greater than $\tilde{H}_{\varepsilon 2}(W_{\varepsilon 1} y_{\varepsilon 2})$.

Therefore player 2 cannot be destabilized to $y_{\varepsilon 2}$. However, there will be a reversal point $t_{\varepsilon 2}$, with $0 < t_{\varepsilon 2} < 1$, where player 2 shifts to $(1/M)_{\varepsilon 2}$. This reversal point can be determined as follows:

$$t_{\varepsilon 2} = \frac{\tilde{H}_{\varepsilon 2}(p_1 x_{\varepsilon 2}) - \tilde{H}_{\varepsilon 2}(p_1 [1/M]_{\varepsilon 2})}{\tilde{H}_{\varepsilon 2}(p_1 x_{\varepsilon 2}) - \tilde{H}_{\varepsilon 2}(p_1 [1/M]_{\varepsilon 2}) + \tilde{H}_{\varepsilon 2}(W_{\varepsilon 1} [1/M]_{\varepsilon 2}) - \tilde{H}_{\varepsilon 2}(W_{\varepsilon 1} x_{\varepsilon 2})}.$$

$$(6.6.50)$$

Figure 7.1 together with (6.6.7), (6.6.18), and (6.6.19) shows that for $\varepsilon \to 0$ all payoffs in (6.6.50) with the exception of $\tilde{H}_{\varepsilon 2}(p_1 x_{\varepsilon 2})$ vanish. This yields the conclusion that

$$t_2 = \lim_{\varepsilon \to 0} t_{\varepsilon 2} = 1. \tag{6.6.51}$$

The comparison between (6.6.50) and (6.6.51) shows that for sufficiently small ε we have

$$t_{\varepsilon 1} < t_{\varepsilon 2} \tag{6.6.52}$$

Therefore player 1 is the first to shift. He shifts to $x_{\varepsilon 1}$. Since x_ε is a strong equilibrium point of F, player 2's strategy $x_{\varepsilon 2}$ is his unique best reply on the whole jump segment. x_ε risk-dominates y_ε.

The case where $W_{\varepsilon 1} y_{\varepsilon 1}$ is the best reply to the bicentric prior can be treated in a very similar way. We will not repeat essentially the same arguments in detail. The trace remains at $W_{\varepsilon 1} y_{\varepsilon 2}$ until player 1 shifts to $y_{\varepsilon 1}$ at a point $t'_{\varepsilon 1}$. If in (6.6.48) the roles of x and y are interchanged, one receives the limit t'_1 of $t'_{\varepsilon 1}$ for $\varepsilon \to 0$. The strong equilibrium point y_ε is the result of the tracing procedure which shows that y_ε risk-dominates x_ε.

As we have seen, x_ε risk-dominates y_ε for sufficiently small ε if and only if the best reply to the bicentric prior is either x_ε or $W_{\varepsilon 1} x_{\varepsilon 2}$. In other words, x_ε risk-dominates y_ε for sufficiently small ε if player 2's best reply to p_1 is $x_{\varepsilon 2}$. Analogously, y_ε risk-dominates x_ε if player 2's best reply to p_1 is $y_{\varepsilon 2}$. It is interesting to note that the direction of risk dominance depends only on player 2's best reply to player 1's prior strategy. Our results are summarized by the following theorem:

THEOREM 6.6.1 (Theorem on risk dominance in G''_ε) Let $x_\varepsilon = x_{\varepsilon 1} x_{\varepsilon 2}$ and $y_\varepsilon = y_{\varepsilon 1} y_{\varepsilon 2}$ be two different strong equilibrium points of G''_ε. Then for sufficiently small ε the risk-dominance relationships between x_ε and y_ε in G''_ε are

260 Bargaining Problem with Transaction Costs on One Side

x_ε risk-dominates y_ε, for $x > y$ if $x + y < 1$ or $xy \leq \alpha$, (6.6.53)

y_ε risk-dominates x_ε, for $x > y$ if $x + y \geq 1$ and $xy > \alpha$. (6.6.54)

Remarks The risk-dominance relationships for $x < y$ can be obtained by interchanging the roles of x and y in (6.6.53) and (6.6.54). Since G_ε'' has only finitely many strong equilibrium points, we can find a number ε_0 such that for every ε with $\varepsilon \leq \varepsilon_0$ the risk-dominance relationships between pairs of equilibrium points x_ε and y_ε in G_ε'' are correctly described by (6.6.53) and (6.6.54).

6.7 The Limit Solution

In the following we will assume that ε is sufficiently small in the sense that risk dominance in G_ε'' is correctly described by (6.6.53) and (6.6.54). The theorem (6.6.1) on risk dominance in G_ε'' will be used to determine the limit solution of the bargaining model. For this purpose we will introduce a useful graphical tool, the risk-dominance diagram.

The Risk-Dominance Diagram

Let R be the set of all pairs (x, y) of real numbers with the following properties:

$\alpha < x < 1$, (6.7.1)

$\alpha < y < 1$, (6.7.2)

$x \neq y$. (6.7.3)

Each risk-dominance comparison between two different strong equilibrium points x_ε and y_ε corresponds to a pair (x, y) in R. The risk-dominance diagram is a graphical representation of R that indicates the regions where one equilibrium point risk-dominates the other. x_ε risk-dominates y_ε if we have

$x + y < 1$ or $xy \leq \alpha$, for $x > y$, (6.7.4)

and

$x + y \geq 1$ and $xy > \alpha$, for $x < y$. (6.7.5)

The first condition is taken from (6.6.53) in the risk-dominance theorem

6.6.1. The second condition is obtained by interchanging the roles of x and y. Let R_x be the set of all pairs $(x, y) \in R$ with (6.7.4) or (6.7.5). Analogously, we define R_y as the set of all pairs (x, y) satisfying

$$x + y \geq 1 \quad \text{and} \quad xy > \alpha, \quad \text{for } x > y, \tag{6.7.6}$$

and

$$x + y < 1 \quad \text{or} \quad xy \leq \alpha, \quad \text{for } x < y. \tag{6.7.7}$$

It is clear that y_ε risk-dominates x_ε if (x, y) is in R_y. We call R_x and R_y the *risk-dominance regions* for x and y, respectively. The risk-dominance diagram is a graphical representation of the risk-dominance regions.

Figures 6.3 and 6.4 show the risk-dominance diagrams for $\alpha = 0.2$ and $\alpha = 0.4$. Figure 6.3 is typical for values of α with $\alpha < 0.25$, and figure 6.4 is typical for $\alpha \geq 0.25$. This is due to the fact that the intersection point of $xy = \alpha$ with the 45° line is at $(\sqrt{\alpha}, \sqrt{\alpha})$. For $\alpha < 0.25$ this intersection point is below the line $x + y = 1$. Therefore in these cases the line $x + y = 1$ determines part of the border between both risk-dominance regions. For $\alpha = 0.25$ the line $x + y = 1$ is a tangent of the curve $xy = \alpha$, and for $\alpha > 0.25$ the line is completely below the curve.

The Limit Solution for $\alpha < 0.25$

Consider the case $\alpha < 0.25$. Since M is even, G_ε'' has a strong equilibrium point $\tilde{x}_\varepsilon = [0.5]_{\varepsilon 1}[0.5]_{\varepsilon 2}$. In the risk-dominance diagram all risk-dominance comparisons of this $\tilde{x}_\varepsilon$ with other strong equilibrium points y_ε correspond to pairs (x, y) on the vertical line through $(0.5, 0.5)$. As can be seen in figure 6.3, the intersection of this vertical line with R is completely in R_x. (The 45° line does not belong to R.) Therefore $\tilde{x}_\varepsilon$ risk-dominates all other strong equilibrium points of the form $y_\varepsilon = y_{\varepsilon 1} y_{\varepsilon 2}$. It follows that $\tilde{x}_\varepsilon$ is globally dominant. Therefore $\tilde{x}_\varepsilon$ is the solution of G_ε. Consequently $(0.5, 0.5)$ is the limit solution of G. We have obtained the following result:

Result   For $\alpha < 0.25$ the strong equilibrium point $(0.5, 0.5)$ is the limit solution of G.

The Case $\alpha \geq 0.25$

In the following we will assume $\alpha \geq 0.25$. The intersection point of $xy = \alpha$ and the 45° line in figure 6.4 is at $(\sqrt{\alpha}, \sqrt{\alpha})$. Suppose that $\sqrt{\alpha}$ is an integer

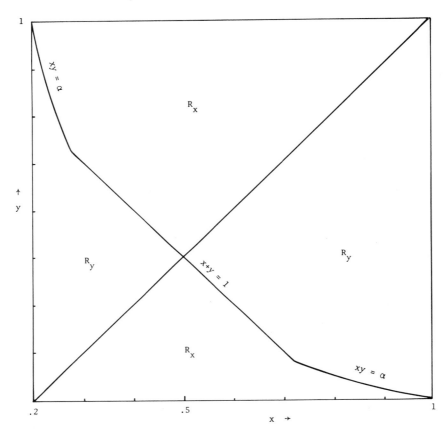

Figure 6.3
Risk-dominance diagram for $\alpha = 0.2$. Border points with $xy = \alpha$ belong to the lower risk-dominance region. Border points with $x + y = 1$ and $xy > \alpha$ belong to the upper risk-dominance region.

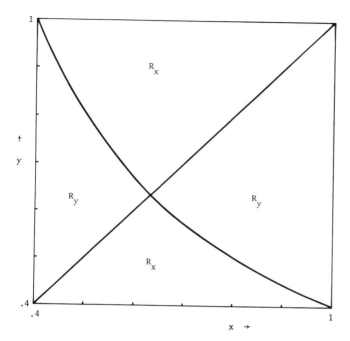

Figure 6.4
Risk-dominance diagram for $\alpha = 0.4$. Border points with $xy = \alpha$ belong to the lower risk-dominance region.

multiple k/M of the smallest money unit. In this exceptional case $[\sqrt{\alpha}]_{\varepsilon 1}$ $[\sqrt{\alpha}]_{\varepsilon 2}$ is the solution of G_ε and $(\sqrt{\alpha}, \sqrt{\alpha})$ is the limit solution of G since all R points on the vertical line through the intersection point belong to R_x.

It is not surprising that the limit solution can be found near $(\sqrt{\alpha}, \sqrt{\alpha})$ if $\sqrt{\alpha}$ is not an integer multiple of the smallest money unit. Let g be that integer which satisfies the following inequality:

$$\frac{g}{M} \leq \sqrt{\alpha} < \frac{g+1}{M}.$$

(6.7.8)

Define

$$\underline{x} = \frac{g}{M}$$

(6.7.9)

and

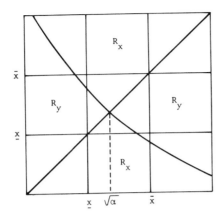

Figure 6.5
Vicinity of $(\sqrt{\alpha}, \sqrt{\alpha})$ in the risk-dominance diagram with $0.25 \le \alpha \le 1$. A case where $\underline{x}_\varepsilon$ is the solution of G_ε.

$$\bar{x} = \frac{g+1}{M}. \tag{6.7.10}$$

We will show that either $\underline{x}_\varepsilon = \underline{x}_{\varepsilon 1}\underline{x}_{\varepsilon 2}$ or $\bar{x}_\varepsilon = \bar{x}_{\varepsilon 1}\bar{x}_{\varepsilon 2}$ is the solution of G_ε.

Not all pairs $(x, y) \in R$ correspond to risk-dominance comparisons, only those that are *grid points* in the sense that both x and y are multiples of $1/M$. To find the solution of G_ε, one has to look at the grid points in the vicinity of $(\sqrt{\alpha}, \sqrt{\alpha})$. Figures 6.5 and 6.6 show two situations that can arise. In figure 6.5 all grid points (x, y) of R belong to R_x. Therefore $\underline{x}_\varepsilon$ is globally dominant. Similarly in figure 6.6 the grid points $(\bar{x}, y)$ belong to R_x, and $\bar{x}_\varepsilon$ is globally dominant.

If the grid points $(\underline{x}, \bar{x})$ and $(\bar{x}, \underline{x})$ are above the curve $xy = \alpha$, then $\underline{x}_\varepsilon$ is the solution of G_ε. This is the case if the following condition is satisfied:

$$\underline{x}\bar{x} > \alpha. \tag{6.7.11}$$

If we have

$$\underline{x}\bar{x} \le \alpha, \tag{6.7.12}$$

then $\bar{x}_\varepsilon$ is the solution of G_ε. The special case $\underline{x}\bar{x} = \alpha$ leads to $\bar{x}_\varepsilon$ as the solution of G_ε since the border points with $xy = \alpha$ belong to the lower risk-dominance region (see figure 6.4). The limit solution of G is $(\underline{x}, \underline{x})$ if $\underline{x}_\varepsilon$ is the solution of G_ε and $(\bar{x}, \bar{x})$ if $\bar{x}_\varepsilon$ is the solution of G_ε. This yields the

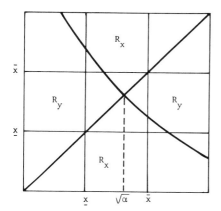

Figure 6.6
Vicinity of $(\sqrt{\alpha}, \sqrt{\alpha})$ in the risk-dominance diagram with $0.25 \leq \alpha \leq 1$. A case where $\bar{x}_\varepsilon$ is the solution of G_ε.

following theorem:

THEOREM 6.7.1 (Theorem on the limit solution)
    Let $\underline{x}$ be the greatest integer multiple of $1/M$ with $\underline{x} \leq \sqrt{\alpha}$, and let $\bar{x}$ be the smallest integer multiple of $1/M$ with $\bar{x} > \sqrt{\alpha}$. The game G described in section 6.2 has the following limit solution:

$$\underrightarrow{L}(G) = \begin{cases} (\frac{1}{2}, \frac{1}{2}), & \text{for } \alpha < 0.25, \\ (\underline{x}, \underline{x}), & \text{for } \alpha \geq 0.25 \text{ and } \bar{x}\underline{x} > \alpha, \\ (\bar{x}, \bar{x}), & \text{for } \alpha \geq 0.25 \text{ and } \bar{x}\underline{x} \leq \alpha. \end{cases} \qquad (6.7.13)$$

6.8   The Asymptotic Solution

A smallest money unit $1/M$ was introduced as a feature of the bargaining model in order to obtain a finite game. It is natural to think of $1/M$ as very small. Therefore we are interested in the behavior of the limit solution for large M. As M goes to infinity, the limit solution approaches $(0.5, 0.5)$ for $\alpha < 0.25$ and $(\sqrt{\alpha}, \sqrt{\alpha})$ for $\alpha \geq 0.25$. Define

$$(\tilde{x}, \tilde{x}) = \begin{cases} (0.5, 0.5), & \text{for } 0 < \alpha < 0.25, \\ (\sqrt{\alpha}, \sqrt{\alpha}), & \text{for } 0.25 \leq \alpha < 1. \end{cases} \qquad (6.8.1)$$

We call $(\tilde{x}, \tilde{x})$ the *asymptotic solution* for large M. A graph of $\tilde{x}$ as a function of α is shown in figure 6.7.

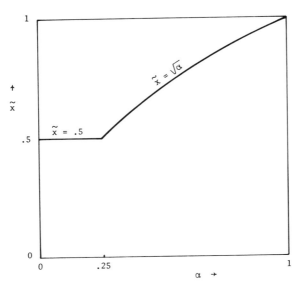

Figure 6.7
Player 1's payoff in the asymptotic solution for large M as a function of the transaction cost parameter α

Interpretation Consider the game that results from our model if W_1 is removed from player 1's pure strategy set. This game is a nondegenerate unanimity game whose limit solution is $(0.5, 0.5)$ (see the theorem 5.6.1 on nondegenerate unanimity games). For $\alpha \leq 0.25$ the availability of W_1 does not change this limit solution. We may say that small transaction costs do not improve the bargaining position of player 1. For $\alpha > 0.25$ player 1 receives more than $\frac{1}{2}$ in the asymptotic solution. Moreover in this range player 1's asymptotic solution payoff $\sqrt{\alpha}$ is an increasing concave function of α; an increase of α strengthens player 1's bargaining position, but the incremental effect becomes weaker for higher α.

It is interesting to compare the asymptotic solution with a naive approach to the same bargaining situation. One might base a naive theory on the levels which the players can guarantee for themselves, namely α for player 1 and 0 for player 2. If the players split the difference above these levels, player 1 receives the following agreement payoff:

$$\hat{x} = \frac{1 + \alpha}{2}. \tag{6.8.2}$$

In the diagram of figure 6.7 equation (6.8.2) could be represented by a straight line connecting the points $(0, 0.5)$ and $(1, 1)$. Obviously $\hat{x}^2$ is greater than α. Therefore we have

$$\tilde{x} < \hat{x}, \quad \text{for } 0 < \alpha < 1. \tag{6.8.3}$$

This shows that the transaction cost parameter α does not improve player 1's bargaining position as much as the naive argument suggests. In fact, this is very reasonable for there is an important difference between both players with respect to the way in which their security levels α and 0 can be guaranteed. Player 1 must risk to get 0 if he tries to get more than α, whereas player 2 receives at least 0 no matter what he does. Inequality (6.8.3) shows that our equilibrium selection theory is sensitive to this difference.

Asymptotic Solutions for Other Models

It is possible to give a more general definition of an asymptotic solution. In the following we will indicate how this can be done without going into formal detail.

Consider a situation that can be modeled as a game in standard form where some of the agents or all agents have choice sets that are convex and compact subsets of some euclidian space. For this purpose of applying our theory, this game is replaced by a sequence of finite games depending on a parameter M such that for sufficiently large M the distance between a choice in the infinite game and the nearest choice of the same agent in the finite game becomes arbitrarily small. The *asymptotic solution* can be defined as the limit approached by the limit solution as M goes to infinity.

An aymptotic solution of course need not exist. The asymptotic solution may also depend on the way in which the infinite game is replaced by a sequence of finite substructures. Difficulties with the convergence to an asymptotic solution do not pose a serious problem for our theory of equilibrium selection. We take the view that infinite games are useful as convenient idealizations of finite games with a large number of pure strategies. Infinite games cannot really be found in a finite world. Therefore difficulties posed by infinite games should be considered as caused by overidealization. In view of Nash's existence theorem for finite games, one should not be worried by the nonexistence of equilibrium points in infinite games. Similarly one may suspect that the infinite game does not represent important features of the underlying finite situation if difficulties with the convergence to an asymptotic solution arise.

6.9   Other Kinds of Transaction Costs

Transaction costs enter the bargaining model in a specific way. They are *offer related* in the sense that player 1 has to bear costs of α whether an agreement is reached or not. Player 1's decision situation is also *simultaneous* rather than sequential. He does not have to commit himself to making a proposal before he selects a specific proposal.

In this section we will look at two variants of the model. In both cases we will sketch the process of finding the limit solution without going into formal detail. The first variant will deal with *agreement-related* transaction costs incurred only if agreement is reached. In the second variant player 1's decision is *sequential* in the sense that he has to commit himself to making a proposal before he selects a specific proposal.

Agreement-Related Transaction Costs

Assume that transaction costs are connected to reaching an agreement. We may think of an illegal trade where bargaining in itself is not punishable but the seller player 1 can be punished if an agreement is reached. This means that the transaction costs can be deducted from player 1's agreement payoff x in order to obtain his payoff for the strategy combination (x, x).

The situation is most naturally modeled by a game G^a where both players have the same pure strategy set X. In G^a the payoff vector for strategy combination (x, x) is $(x - \alpha, 1 - x)$. Strategy combinations (x, y) with $x \neq y$ yield zero for both players. It would make no difference for the analysis if W_1 were included in player 1's pure-strategy set with zero payoffs for both players whenever W_1 is used.

The application of the procedure of decomposition and reduction to G_ε^a first removes player 1's ε-extreme strategies $x_{\varepsilon 1}$ corresponding to $x \in X$ with $x \leq \alpha$. In a second step player 2's ε-extreme strategies $x_{\varepsilon 2}$ with $x \leq \alpha$ are eliminated. For sufficiently small ε and sufficiently large M the resulting game $\hat{G}_\varepsilon^a$ is irreducible.

The game $\hat{G}_\varepsilon^a$ is very similar to the ε-perturbed game of a unanimity game even if the perturbances are different. Suppose that X'' contains exactly one element x_0 where the Nash-product $(x - \alpha)(1 - x)$ assumes its maximum. Similar arguments as in the proof of the theorem 5.6.1 on nondegenerate unanimity games can be used to show that (x_0, x_0) is the limit solution of G^a. Obviously, for almost all values of α and M, the value where $(x - \alpha)(1 - x)$ assumes its maximum is uniquely determined. For large M this value is near to $\hat{x}$ in (6.8.2).

Inequality (6.8.3) shows that agreement-related transaction costs are more favorable for player 1's bargaining position than offer-related transaction costs. This result may be interpreted as due to the fact that under agreement-related transaction costs, player 1 avoids transaction costs in the conflict case where the proposals of both players are different from each other.

Sunk Transaction Costs

Assume that player 1 first has to decide whether he wants to bargain; if he chooses to bargain, he has to make a second decision where he selects his proposal. As before, each player makes his decisions without any information on previous or simultaneous decisions of the other player. Once player 1 has made the decision to bargain, he has to bear the transaction costs α. In this sense the transaction costs are *sunk* when he makes his second decision.

The situation is described by a game $G^s = (\Phi^s, H^s)$ in standard form, where player 1 has two agents 11 and 12. Agent 11 has two choices W_1, and X and the choice set of agent 12 is X. We need not distinguish between player 2 and his single agent. Player 2's choice set is X. If agent 11 chooses W_1, then player 1 receives α and player 2 receives 0, regardless of what agent 12 and player 2 do. If agent 11 chooses X, agent 12 selects x, and player 2 plays y, then the players receive their payoffs for (x, y) in G.

It can be seen easily that the ε-perturbation G^s_ε is decomposable. (G^s is indecomposable.) Agent 12 and player 2 form a cell. This cell is equivalent to the ε-perturbation of a unanimity game. In the solution of the cell both players use their ε-extreme strategies corresponding to the proposal 0.5. The main truncation of G^s_ε is a one-person game where agent 11 chooses between his ε-extreme strategies corresponding to W_1 and X. For sufficiently small ε the solution of this main truncation is X for $0 < \alpha < 0.5$ and W_1 for $0.5 < \alpha < 1$. We do not want to look at the border case $\alpha = 0.5$, for this would force us to investigate ε-terms. We can conclude that for sufficiently small ε the choices of agents 11, 12, and player 2 prescribed by the limit solution of G_ε are ε-extreme strategies corresponding to X, 0.5, 0.5, respectively, for $0 < \alpha < 0.5$ and to W_1, 0.5, 0.5, respectively, for $0.5 < \alpha < 1$.

Player 1's limit solution payoff is the maximum of α and 0.5. For $\alpha > 0.25$ this is below his asymptotic solution payoff $\sqrt{\alpha}$ in G. If player 1 has to sink his transaction costs before he can select a proposal, his bargaining position is not improved. For $0.5 < \alpha < 1$ no agreement is reached. Player 1 knows that his sunk transaction costs do not have any influence on the bargaining outcome and therefore cannot afford to bargain if his transaction costs are greater than 0.5.

The example shows that it is important to find the right way of modeling the internal sequential structure of a player's decision situation. The modeling choice between G and G^s depends on whether player 1 has to commit himself to bargain before he can select a specific proposal or whether the choice to bargain can be delayed until it finally has to be made simultaneously with the selection of a proposal. In the first case G is the adequate model, and in the second case it is G^s.

The game G^s may be described as the game that results from G by splitting off an agent 11 for player 1's choice W_1. The difference between the limit solutions of G and G^s illustrates the lack of invariance with respect to sequential agent splitting discussed in chapter 3, section 3.11. As we have seen there, this lack of invariance is unavoidable if one does not want to sacrifice even more compeling requirements for a theory of equilibrium selection. Our theory takes the point of view that the players face different risk situations in G and G^s. In G the choice W_1 is still available to player 1 when he has the opportunity to select a proposal. In G^s player 1 cannot choose W_1 anymore when he selects a proposal. Therefore player 1's choice W_1 influences risk comparisons between different agreement possibilities in G but not in G^s. Upon reflection, this is not as unreasonable as it may appear to be at first glance.

6.10   Transaction Costs on Both Sides

It is interesting to look at a bargaining situation where not only player 1 but also player 2 has transaction costs. Ulrike Leopold has explored this problem (Leopold-Wildburger 1982). In the bargaining game G^b with transaction costs on both sides, player 2 has an additional pure strategy W_2. The payoffs for (x, W_2) are 0 for player 1 and β for player 2, where β with $0 < \beta < 1$ is player 2's transaction cost parameter. The payoffs for (W_1, W_2) are α for player 1 and β for player 2. Otherwise, the game G^b agrees with the game G.

Ulrike Leopold has shown that an asymptotic solution exists for every parameter combination (α, β). Figure 6.8 summarizes her results. The upper part shows a *parameter diagram* in the (α, β)-plane which indicates the

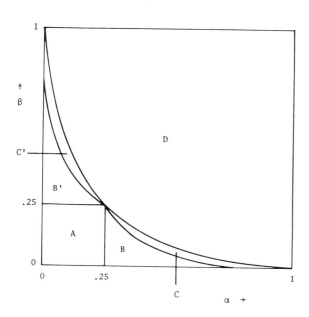

Region	Asymptotic solution	
A	$(.5, .5)$	
B	$(\sqrt{\alpha}, \sqrt{\alpha})$	
B'	$(\sqrt{\beta}, \sqrt{\beta})$	
C	$(\tilde{x}, \tilde{x})$	*)
C'	$(\tilde{x}', \tilde{x}')$	*)
D	(W_1, W_2)	

Figure 6.8
Asymptotic solutions of the bargaining problem with transaction costs on both sides.
(*Explained in the text.)

regions where different types of asymptotic solutions are obtained. The table below the diagram indicates the asymptotic solutions obtained in this regions.

Player 1's payoff $\tilde{x}$ in the asymptotic solution for region C is obtained as a root of the following cubic equation:

$$\tilde{x}^3 - \left(1 + 2\alpha - \frac{\beta}{2}\right)\tilde{x}^2 + (2\alpha + \alpha^2)\tilde{x} - \alpha^2 = 0. \tag{6.10.1}$$

An interchange of the role of both players yields the asymptotic solution for region C'.

The asymptotic solutions for regions A and B are exactly those that were obtained for $\alpha < 0.25$ and $\alpha \geq 0.25$ in the case of transaction costs on one side. This is not surprising but not trivial, since the model with transaction costs on one side is not really a special case of the model with transaction costs on both sides. In the first case both players have a different number of pure strategies, and in the second both have the same number of pure strategies. The difference is small, but it cannot be disregarded in the application of our equilibrium selection theory.

An interesting feature of the model with transaction costs on both sides can be seen in the fact that the asymptotic solution (W_1, W_2) is obtained for parameter combinations with $\alpha + \beta < 1$ where α or β are relatively high. In these cases our theory does not select a payoff-efficient equilibrium point; despite the availability of agreements with payoffs greater than the transaction costs, the asymptotic solution recommends the option not to bargain at all.

The failure to reach a profitable agreement in the presence of relatively high transaction costs is not an unreasonable result. One may say that in such cases the strategic uncertainty underlying the definition of the bicentric prior involves a high risk for making a proposal and therefore points to the selection of the "safe" equilibrium point (W_1, W_2).

7 Trade Involving One Seller and More Than One Potential Buyer

7.1 Introduction

We now analyze a $(k + 1)$-person game G, played by one seller S, and k (potential) buyers i $(i = 1, \ldots, k)$. The set of all $n = k + 1$ players will be called N. The set of the k buyers will be called B. S wants to sell one object, A, to any one of the k buyers. The players' utility payoffs will be called u_s and u_i, respectively. All players have *linear* utility functions for money and derive x units of utility from \$$x$. If S cannot sell A, then $u_S = 0$. If any player i cannot buy A, then $u_i = 0$. S's asking price will be called π_S, whereas i's offer price will be called π_i. Each buyer i would derive 100 units of utility from possessing A so that if he can buy A for \$$\pi$, his net payoff will be $u_i = 100 - \pi$.

The game will be played as follows: All players will simultaneously name a *price*. The price π_S named by player S, and the price π_i named by any player i, will be his *pure strategy* in the game. The set of pure strategies available to each player S or i will be a copy of the interval $I = [0, 100]$. Thus $\Phi_S = \Phi_i = I = [0, 100]$.

Let M be the set of all m buyers i who have named the same price $\pi = \pi_i = \pi_S$ as the seller, player S, has. Each buyer i in M will have the same probability $1/m$ of being able to buy A at this price of \$$\pi$. Buyers not in M will have zero probability of obtaining A. Thus player S's payoff will be

$$u_S = \begin{cases} \pi, & \text{if } m \geq 1, \\ 0, & \text{if } m = 0, \end{cases} \tag{7.1.1}$$

whereas, for any player i in B, his expected payoff will be

$$u_i = \begin{cases} \dfrac{100 - \pi}{m}, & \text{if } i \in M, \\ 0, & \text{if } i \notin M. \end{cases} \tag{7.1.2}$$

7.2 The Discrete Version G^* of G and the Uniformly Perturbed Standard Form G_ε^*

Since formally our theory covers only *finite* games, we have to approximate the *continuous* game G described in the previous section by a *discrete* game G^*. G^* will differ from G in restricting every player's pure-strategy set to a *finite subset* I^* of the closed interval $I = [0, 100]$, the same for all players. (For example, we may assume that the players can propose only a price π_S or π_i that is an integer multiple of \$1 or of 1¢ or of some other small amount of money.) But, to avoid needlessly complicating our computations without any compensating advantage, we will assume that regardless of how the other elements of I^* have been selected, we will always have

$$\pi^* \in I^*, \tag{7.2.1}$$

where

$$\pi^* = \frac{100(2^k - 1)}{k + 2^k - 1} \tag{7.2.2}$$

Here π^* is the price the players will agree on at the equilibrium point that will turn out to be the *solution* of the game. (If π^* were not in I^*, then we would have to worry about whether the solution is associated with a price *slightly larger* or *slightly smaller* than π^*—which of course would depend on the actual numbers included in I^*. In contrast, if π^* is an element of I^*, then, as we shall see, π^* will *always* be the price prescribed by the solution.)

For convenience, we will assume also that both boundary points of $I = [0, 100]$ are likewise always included in I^* so that

$$0 \quad \text{and} \quad 100 \in I^*. \tag{7.2.3}$$

The discrete game G^* just defined is already in *standard form* because each player S or i will have only *one* move π_S or π_i in the game and therefore will have only *one* agent who can be identified with the player himself.

To obtain the uniformly perturbed game G_ε^* corresponding to G^*, we must assume that when any player intends to name a specific price π_S or π_i, he may in fact name *any one* of the other possible prices $\pi_S' \neq \pi_S$ or $\pi_i' \neq \pi_i$ (π_S' and $\pi_i' \in I^*$) instead with a small positive probability ε by mistake. As a result the payoff functions of G_ε^* will no longer be the functions defined by equations (7.1.1) and (7.1.2) but rather will be more complicated functions, involving the mistake-probability parameter ε.

Yet we will assume that ε is small enough that the payoff functions defined by (7.1.1) and (7.1.2) will provide very good approximations and will *neglect* the terms involving ε. Of course we will always point it out when the mathematical properties of the *perturbed* game G_ε^* are significantly different from those of the *unperturbed* game G^*. In particular, we will point it out when some strategies that are best replies in G^* are not best replies in G_ε^*, or when strategy combinations that are equilibria in G^* are not equilibria in G_ε^*.

7.3 Primitive Equilibrium Points

Both in G^* and in G_ε^* every pure-strategy equilibrium $e(\pi)$ will be a $(k + 1)$-vector with $(k + 1)$ identical components, having the form

$$e(\pi) = (\pi, \ldots, \pi), \quad \text{with } \pi \in I^*. \tag{7.3.1}$$

Indeed, in G^* all strategy combinations of this form will be equilibria. In particular, all of them will be *strong* equilibria, except for $e(0)$ and $e(100)$. $e(0)$ will be *weak* for player S because, if all players i in B offer only the price $\pi_i = 0$, player S will be able to obtain his equilibrium payoff $u_S = 0$ not only by naming the same price $\pi_S = 0$ but also by naming any other price $\pi_S \neq 0$. Likewise $e(100)$ will be a weak equilibrium for all players i in B because, if player S asks for the price $\pi_S = 100$, each player i can obtain his equilibrium payoff $u_i = 0$ not only by naming the same price $\pi_i = 100$ but also by naming any other price $\pi_i \neq 100$.

In contrast, in the perturbed game G_ε^*, $e(0)$ and $e(100)$ will not be equilibria at all. First, $e(100)$ will not be an equilibrium because, if any buyer i thinks that the seller's intended strategy is $\pi_S = 100$, he must realize that this seller may in fact use any other strategy $\pi_S \neq 100$ in I^* by mistake with probability ε. Thus, if i uses the strategy $\pi_i = 100$, he will obtain the payoff $u_i = 100 - 100 = 0$, whereas if he uses any other strategy $\pi_i = \pi \neq 100$ in I^*, then he will obtain the expected payoff $u_i = \varepsilon(100 - \pi)m$.[1] Therefore i's expected payoff will be maximized by using the strategy $\pi_i = 0$. Thus i's best reply to $\pi_S = 100$ will not be $\pi_i = 100$ but rather $\pi_i = 0$. Hence $e(100)$ is not an equilibrium in G_ε^* because it would require all players i in B to use non-best-reply strategies.

Likewise, in game G_ε^*, $e(0)$ will not be an equilibrium. For even if all buyers i intend to use the strategies $\pi_i = 0$, each buyer i will actually use any unintended strategy $\pi_i \neq 0$ in I^* with probability ε. Thus the probability of at least one buyer's using a given unintended strategy $\pi_i \neq 0$ will be $1 - (1 - \varepsilon)^k$. Therefore, if player S chooses the strategy $\pi_S = 0$, his payoff will be $u_S = 0$, whereas if he uses any other strategy $\pi_S = \pi \neq 0$, then his expected payoff will be $\pi[1 - (1 - \varepsilon)^k]$.[2] Thus, to maximize his expected payoff, he must use the strategy $\pi_S = 100$. Accordingly S's best reply to all buyers' using the strategies $\pi_i = 0$ will not be $\pi_S = 0$, but rather $\pi_S = 100$. Hence $e(0)$ is not an equilibrium in G_ε^* because it would require player S to use a non-best-reply strategy.

On the other hand, all strategy combinations $e(\pi)$ with $\pi \neq 0$ and $\neq 100$ but $\in I^*$ are equilibria (and, in fact, *strong* equilibria) also in the perturbed game G_ε^*. It is easy to verify that these strong equilibria are also *primitive equilibria*, and the only such equilibria in G_ε^* (see section 5.2).

7.4 Bicentric Priors

Our next task is to investigate risk-dominance and payoff-dominance relations between any two primitive equilibria $e' = e(\pi')$ and $e'' = e(\pi'')$, with $\pi', \pi'' \neq 0, 100$ but $\in I^*$.

It is clear that there cannot be any payoff dominance between e' and e'' because if, say, e' yields a higher payoff $H_S(e') > H_S(e'')$ to player S, then it must yield a *lower* payoff $H_i(e') < H_i(e'')$ to every player i in set B, and conversely. As to risk dominance, we first have to compute the *bicentric priors* induced by e' and e''. The S-incomplete strategy combination that the k players in set B use at e' and at e'' will be denoted as $\pi'_B = (\pi', \dots, \pi')$ and as $\pi''_B = (\pi'', \dots, \pi'')$, respectively.

First, suppose that player S thinks that the players in B will use π'_B, with probability z, and will use π''_B, with probability $(1 - z)$. Thus S's expectations correspond to the jointly randomized mixed strategy

$$\zeta_S(z) = z\pi'_B + (1 - z)\pi''_B. \tag{7.4.1}$$

If S uses the strategy $\pi'_S = \pi'$, his expected payoff will be

$$u'_S = H_S(\pi'_S\zeta_S(z)) = z\pi'. \tag{7.4.2}$$

On the other hand, if he uses the strategy $\pi''_S = \pi''$, his expected payoff will be

$$u''_S = H_S(\pi''_S\zeta_S(z)) = (1 - z)\pi''. \tag{7.4.3}$$

Finally, if he uses any *other* strategy $\pi_S \neq \pi'$ and $\neq \pi''$, his payoff will be zero. Clearly $u'_S \geq u''_S > 0$ if $z \in [z^*, 1]$, where

$$z^* = \frac{\pi''}{\pi' + \pi''} \quad \text{and} \quad 0 < u'_S \leq u''_S, \quad \text{if } z \in [0, z^*]. \tag{7.4.4}$$

The Lebesgue measures associated with the intervals $[z^*, 1]$ and $[0, z^*]$ are $1 - z^* = \pi'/(\pi' + \pi'')$ and $z^* = \pi''/(\pi' + \pi'')$. Since in our model, z is uniformly distributed over the unit interval, the *bicentric prior probabilities* associated with player S's strategies $\pi'_S = \pi'$ and $\pi''_S = \pi''$ are

$$p'_S = p_S(\pi'_S) - \frac{\pi'}{\pi' + \pi''} = r, \tag{7.4.5}$$

and

$$p''_S = p_S(\pi''_S) - \frac{\pi''}{\pi' + \pi''} = 1 - r. \tag{7.4.6}$$

Thus the *bicentric prior probability distribution* associated with player S will be

$$p_S = (p'_S, p''_S). \tag{7.4.7}$$

To compute the bicentric prior probabilities for any player i in B, we introduce the notations π'_{-i} and π''_{-i} which denote the strategy combination used by all k players other than i (including player S) at e' and at e'', respectively. Again, suppose that player i thinks that the other players will use π'_{-i} with probability z and will use π''_{-i} with probability $(1 - z)$. Then i's expectations correspond to the jointly randomized mixed strategy

$$\zeta_i(z) = z\pi'_{-i} + (1 - z)\pi''_{-i}. \tag{7.4.8}$$

If i uses strategy $\pi'_i = \pi'$, his expected payoff will be

$$u'_i = H_i(\pi'_i \zeta_i(z)) = \frac{z(100 - \pi')}{k}. \tag{7.4.9}$$

On the other hand, if he uses strategy $\pi''_i = \pi''$, his expected payoff will be

$$u''_i = H_i(\pi''_i \zeta_i(z)) = \frac{(1 - z)(100 - \pi'')}{k}. \tag{7.4.10}$$

Finally, if he uses any other strategy $\pi_i \neq \pi'$ and $\neq \pi''$, his payoff will be *zero*. Obviously $u'_i \geq u''_i > 0$ if $z \in [z^{**}, 1]$, where

$$z^{**} = \frac{100 - \pi''}{200 - \pi' - \pi''},$$

$$0 < u'_i \leq u''_i \quad \text{if } z \in [0, z^{**}]. \tag{7.4.11}$$

Accordingly the bicentric prior probabilities associated with any player i in set B are

$$p_i' = p_i(\pi_i') = \frac{100 - \pi'}{200 - \pi' - \pi''} = \rho \qquad (7.4.12)$$

and

$$p_i'' = p_i(\pi_i'') = \frac{100 - \pi''}{200 - \pi' - \pi''} = 1 - \rho. \qquad (7.4.13)$$

Hence the bicentric prior probability distribution[3] associated with any player i in set B will be

$$p_i = (p_i', p_i''). \qquad (7.4.14)$$

We will write

$$p_B = p_{-S} = (p_1, \ldots, p_k). \qquad (7.4.15)$$

Thus $p_B = p_{-S}$ is the vector listing the bicentric prior probability distributions p_i associated with all players i in set B (i.e., all players other than player S). We will also write

$$p = (p_S, p_1, \ldots, p_k), \qquad (7.4.16)$$

and

$$p_{-i} = (p_S, p_1, \ldots, p_{i-1}, p_{i+1}, \ldots, p_n). \qquad (7.4.17)$$

Thus p is the vector listing the bicentric prior probability distributions associated with all $(k + 1)$ players. Finally, p_{-i} is a vector listing only the bicentric priors associated with the k players other than player i.

7.5   Risk-Dominance Relations

We now have to compute each player's best reply to the other players' strategies. Starting with player S, if he uses the strategy $\pi_S' = \pi'$ while the other players use the prior-strategy combination p_B, then his payoff will be

$$\bar{u}_S' = H_S(\pi_S' p_B) = \pi'[1 - (1 - \rho)^k]$$

$$= \pi'\left[1 - \left(\frac{100 - \pi''}{200 - \pi' - \pi''}\right)^k\right] = v(\pi', \pi''), \qquad (7.5.1)$$

where $\rho = p_i(\pi_i')$ is the probability defined by (7.4.12). This is so because, if S uses $\pi_S' = \pi'$, he will obtain the payoff π' only if at least one player i in set B uses a similar strategy $\pi_i' = \pi'$. Yet any *given* player i will use this strategy only with probability $\rho = p_i(\pi_i')$. Therefore the probability that at least one of them will do so is $1 - (1 - \rho)^k$. On the other hand, if none of them uses this strategy, then S will obtain a zero payoff. This implies equation (7.5.1).

By similar reasoning, if player S uses the strategy $\pi_S'' = \pi''$ while the other players use the strategy combination p_B, then his payoff will be

$$\bar{u}_S'' = H_S(\pi_S'' p_B) = \pi''(1 - \rho^k)$$

$$= \pi'' \left[1 - \left(\frac{100 - \pi'}{200 - \pi' - \pi''} \right)^k \right] = v(\pi'', \pi'). \tag{7.5.2}$$

Finally, if S uses any other strategy $\pi_S \neq \pi'$ and $\neq \pi''$ while the other players use p_B, then S's payoff will be zero. Consequently $\pi_S' = \pi'$ will be player S's strong best reply to p_B if

$$\bar{u}_S' > \bar{u}_S'' > 0. \tag{7.5.3}$$

In view of (7.5.1) and (7.5.2) this condition can also be written as

$$v(\pi', \pi'') > v(\pi'', \pi') > 0. \tag{7.5.4}$$

On the other hand, if any player i in set B uses the strategy $\pi_i' = \pi'$ while the other players use the strategy combination p_{-i}, then i's payoff $H_i(\pi_i' p_{-1})$ can be evaluated by noting that i will obtain the expected payoff $(100 - \pi')/m$ if and only if:

1. Player S uses the strategy $\pi_S' = \pi'$, which will happen with probability $r = p_S(\pi_S')$, as defined by (7.4.5).

2. Exactly $(m - 1)$ other players j in set B use the strategies $\pi_j' = \pi'$, which will happen with probability

$$\frac{(k - 1)!}{(m - 1)!(k - m)!} \rho^{m-1}(1 - \rho)^{k-m},$$

because every player j will use this strategy $\pi_j' = \pi'$ with probability ρ, as defined by (7.4.12).

Consequently we can write

$$\bar{u}_i' = H_i(\pi_i'p_{-i})$$

$$= (100 - \pi')r \sum_{m=1}^{k} \frac{(k-1)!}{m(m-1)!(k-m)!} \rho^{m-1}(1-\rho)^{k-m}$$

$$= \frac{200 - \pi' - \pi''}{k} r \sum_{m=1}^{k} \frac{k!}{m!(k-m)!} \rho^m (1-\rho)^{k-m} \qquad (7.5.5)$$

$$= \frac{200 - \pi' - \pi''}{k} r[1 - (1-\rho)^k]$$

$$= \frac{200 - \pi' - \pi''}{k(\pi' + \pi'')} \pi' \left[1 - \left(\frac{100 - \pi''}{200 - \pi' - \pi''} \right)^k \right].$$

By similar reasoning, if any player i in set B uses the strategy $\pi_i'' = \pi''$ while the other players use p_{-i}, then his payoff will be

$$\bar{u}_i'' = H_i(\pi_i''p_{-i})$$
$$\qquad\qquad\qquad\qquad\qquad\qquad\qquad\qquad (7.5.6)$$
$$= \frac{200 - \pi' - \pi''}{k(\pi' + \pi'')} \pi'' \left[1 - \left(\frac{100 - \pi'}{200 - \pi' - \pi''} \right)^k \right].$$

Finally, for any other strategy $\pi_i \neq \pi'$ and $\neq \pi''$, we can write $H_i(\pi_i p_{-i}) = 0$. Consequently the strategy $\pi_i' = \pi'$ will be i's strong best reply to p_i if

$$\bar{u}_i' > \bar{u}_i'' > 0. \qquad\qquad\qquad\qquad\qquad\qquad (7.5.7)$$

Now inspection of (7.5.1), (7.5.2), (7.5.5), and (7.5.6) will show that condition (7.5.7) will hold if and only if condition (7.5.4) does. This means that the strategies $\pi_S' = \pi'$ and $\pi_i' = \pi'$ of the $(k+1)$ players will be strong best replies to the bicentric prior vector p if and only if (7.5.4) is satisfied. In other words, we can state:

LEMMA 7.5.1   Let p be the bicentric prior vector generated by the two equilibria $e(\pi')$ and $e(\pi'')$. Then $e(\pi')$ will be a *strong vector best reply* to p if and only if (7.5.4) is satisfied.

LEMMA 7.5.2   If (7.5.4) is satisfied, then the linear tracing procedure applied to game G_ε^* and to the prior vector p will yield the equilibrium point $e(\pi')$ as outcome; that is $T(G_\varepsilon^*, p) = e(\pi')$.

Proof   This follows from the facts that:

1. $e(\pi')$ is a strong vector best reply to p.

2. $e(\pi')$ is a strong equilibrium point in game G_ε^* (see lemmas 4.17.6 and 4.17.7). ∎

LEMMA 7.5.3   If (7.4.4) is satisfied then $e(\pi')$ will have *risk dominance* and, in fact, *conspicuous* risk dominance over $e(\pi'')$.

Proof   This follows from the definitions of risk dominance and conspicuous risk dominance. In particular risk dominance follows from lemma 7.5.2, whereas conspicuous risk dominance follows from propositions (1) and (2) in the proof of that lemma. ∎

7.6   Global Conspicuous Risk Dominance: The Solution

We will say that a given equilibrium point e^* has *global* conspicuous risk dominance over all other equilibrium points $e \neq e^*$ in a given set E of equilibrium points if e has conspicuous risk dominance over all equilibria $e \neq e^*$ in set E. We now want to find out whether there is any primitive equilibrium point $e^* = e(\pi^*)$ with global conspicuous risk dominance over all other primitive equilibria $e(\pi)$ with $\pi \neq \pi^*$. Suppose there is such a globally dominant equilibrium point $e(\pi^*)$. Then $e(\pi^*)$ must satisfy condition (7.5.4) with respect to all other primitive equilibria $e(\pi)$. Writing

$$\pi = \pi^* + u, \tag{7.6.1}$$

$$\Delta(\pi^*, u) = v(\pi^*, \pi^* + u) - v(\pi^* + u, \pi^*), \tag{7.6.2}$$

condition (7.5.4) implies that

$$\Delta(\pi^*, u) > 0, \quad \text{for all } u \neq 0. \tag{7.6.3}$$

On the other hand, by (7.6.2)

$$\Delta(\pi^*, u) = 0, \quad \text{for } u = 0. \tag{7.6.4}$$

Consequently the function $\Delta(\pi^*, u)$ will have a global *minimum* at the point $u = 0$ if π^* is kept constant. Tentatively assuming that this is an *interior* minimum, the function Δ must satisfy the first-order condition

$$\frac{\partial \Delta(\pi^*, u)}{\partial u} = 0 \tag{7.6.5}$$

at the point $u = 0$. Evaluating this partial derivative at $u = 0$, we can conclude that π^* must have the value

$$\pi^* = \frac{100(2^k - 1)}{k + 2^k - 1}.$$ (7.6.6)

It is easy to verify that at $u = 0$ the second-order condition for a minimum is likewise satisfied. Of course this shows only that at $u = 0$ there is at least a local minimum. To verify that this is a global minimum, we have to show that inequality (7.6.3) is satisfied for all $u \neq 0$. Since Δ is a complicated algebraic expression of order k, this can be best shown by numerical computation. It turns out that this is, in fact, a global minimum. Therefore we can state the following theorem:

THEOREM 7.6.1   In the one-seller and k-buyers game, the solution is the equilibrium point $e(\pi^*)$ at which the price asked by the seller and offered by the k buyers is the quantity π^* defined by (7.6.6).

Proof π^* satisfies condition (7.6.3). Therefore the equilibrium point $e(\pi^*)$ will conspicuously risk-dominate all other primitive equilibria of the game. This risk dominance will not be offset by any payoff dominance. Consequently $e(\pi^*)$ will dominate all other primitive equilibria, which will make it the solution of the game. ∎

The principle we have used in this section can be stated in more general terms as follows:

THE MINIMUM PRINCIPLE FOR GLOBAL CONSPICUOUS RISK DOMINANCE   Let $E = \{e(\pi)\}$ a one-parameter family of equilibrium points. Suppose that it can be shown, for any two equilibrium points $e(\pi')$ and $e(\pi'')$ in E, that if $e(\pi')$ has conspicuous risk dominance over $e(\pi'')$, then π' and π'' must satisfy an inequality of the form $v(\pi', \pi'') > v(\pi'', \pi')$. Then a necessary condition for a given equilibrium point $e(\pi^*)$ in E to have global conspicuous risk dominance over all other equilibrium points $e(\pi)$ in E is that the function

$$\Delta(\pi^*, u) = v(\pi^*, \pi^* + u) - v(\pi^* + u, \pi^*)$$ (7.6.7)

should have a global minimum at the point $u = 0$ if π^* is kept constant.

7.7   Analysis of the Game in Terms of Commonsense Subjective-Probability Judgments

This game provides a good illustration of the fact that our concept of risk dominance is merely a mathematical formalization of the informal and qualitative subjective probability judgments that everyone uses in analyzing problems of strategy choice at the commonsense level (*yet* these are barred from classical game theory, as are all subjective-probability arguments). For instance, at the commonsense level one would try to predict the seller's asking price when dealing with several potential buyers on the basis of the following considerations:

1. The higher the price asked by the seller, the more money he will get if a buyer accepts this price

2. But the higher the price, the lower the probability that any given buyer will in fact accept it.

3. The larger the number of potential buyers, the higher the probability that any given price will be accepted at least by one of them. If the probability that any particular buyer will accept this price is ρ, the probability that at least one of k buyers will accept it is $\rho^* = 1 - (1 - \rho)^k$. If k is large enough, ρ^* can be a high probability even if ρ itself is a *low* probability.

All three points are directly used in our theory, and equation (7.5.1) makes use of all three.

In the case of the buyer, at the commonsense level one would try to predict any buyer's offer price on the basis of the following considerations:

1. The lower the price offered by this buyer, the more money he will save if his offer is accepted by the seller.

2. But the lower the price offered, the lower the probability that the seller will accept the offer.

3. The larger the number of potential buyers, the higher the probability that any given price offered by a particular buyer will be matched (or even exceeded) by some other buyers.

All three of these considerations are used in equation (7.5.5).

7.8   Comparision with the Shapley Value

We will now compare the prices predicted by our theory with the Shapley values of the one-seller and k-buyers game. Of course the Shapley value does not directly predict any price, but since in this game the seller's payoff equals the price, the Shapley values of such games to the seller do implicitly

Table 7.1

Number of buyers	Price π^* under our theory	Seller's Shapley value, u_S
1	50.00	50.00
2	60.00	66.67
3	70.00	75.00
4	78.95	80.00
5	86.11	83.33
6	91.30	85.71

provide prices. It is easy to verify that the Shapley value of this game to the seller is

$$u_S = \frac{100k}{k+1}.$$

The prices π^* predicted by our theory and the seller's Shapley values, u_S, are listed in table 7.1 for $k = 1,\ldots, 6$. Both π^* and u_S converge to 100 as k increases, but the convergence of π^* is somewhat faster.

8 Two-Person Bargaining Games with Incomplete Information on One Side

8.1 Introduction

We will now consider a game $G(\alpha)$ in which players I and II have to divide $\$100$. Each player would derive x units of utility from $\$x$. If they cannot agree, then they will obtain the following conflict payoffs:

$$c_I = 0 \quad \text{and} \quad c_{II} = 0 \quad \text{or} \quad \alpha, \tag{8.1.1}$$

where

$$0 < \alpha < 100,$$

with either value of c_{II} having probability $\frac{1}{2}$. This probability is common knowledge to both players as is also the value of c_I, but only player II knows the actual value of c_{II}. Player II will be called subplayer IIA or IIB, according as $c_{II} = 0$ or $c_{II} = \alpha$.

The game is played as follows: Both players will propose a payoff vector $(x, 100 - x)$ by stating the payoff x they want to assign to player I. The x values suggested by players I and II will be called x_I and x_{II}. If $x_I = x_{II} = x$, then the two players will receive the payoffs $u_I = x$ and $u_{II} = 100 - x$, in accordance with their own payoff proposals. In contrast, if $x_I \neq x_{II}$, then the players will receive only their conflict payoffs c_I and c_{II} as defined by (8.1.1). For convenience, we will now reinterpret this game as a *three-person* game by renaming player I as player 1, subplayer IIA as player 2, and subplayer IIB as player 3. We will sometimes refer to players 2 and 3 as "representatives of player II."

The pure-strategy sets $X_1 = \{x_1\}$ and $X_2 = \{x_2\}$ of players 1 and 2 are copies of the closed interval $I = [0, 100]$. In contrast, the pure-strategy set $X_3 = \{x_3\}$ of player 3 is only the smaller closed interval $[0, 100 - \alpha]$ because if he used any pure strategy $x_3 > 100 - \alpha$, he would by this means agree to reduce his own payoff to $u_3 = 100 - x_3 < \alpha$, that is, to less than his conflict payoff, which would always be irrational behavior for him.

8.2 The Discrete Version $G^*(\alpha)$ of Game $G(\alpha)$ and the Uniformly Perturbed Standard Form $G_\varepsilon^*(\alpha)$

To make our solution theory formally applicable, we will again approximate the *continuous* game $G(\alpha)$ under consideration by a *discrete* game $G^*(\alpha)$, in which each player will have only a finite number of pure strategies. We will first select a finite subset I^* of the interval $I = [0, 100]$, subject to some requirements to be stated presently. Then we will define the pure-strategy sets X_1^*, X_2^*, and X_3^* of the three players in $G^*(\alpha)$ as

$$X_1^* = X_2^* = I^*, \tag{8.2.1}$$

$$X_3^* = I^* \cap X_3. \tag{8.2.2}$$

The choice of I^* will be subject to the following requirements:

$$I^* \ni 0, \quad 100 - \alpha, \quad \text{and} \quad 100, \tag{8.2.3}$$

$$I^* \ni 50 \quad \text{and} \quad x^*, \tag{8.2.4}$$

where x^* is the number to be defined later by (8.4.18). Moreover

$$I^* \cap (0, 100 - \alpha) \neq \varnothing, \tag{8.2.5}$$

$$I^* \cap (100 - \alpha, 100) \neq \varnothing. \tag{8.2.6}$$

The purpose of requirement (8.2.3) is to ensure that the extreme strategies corresponding to the boundary points 0, $100 - \alpha$, and 100 of the original strategy sets X_1, X_2, X_3 are available to the players, whereas the purpose of (8.2.5) and (8.2.6) is to ensure that some nonextreme strategies should be likewise available. Finally, (8.2.4) is meant to ensure that two specific strategies that will play important roles in our analysis are available to the players.

The discrete game $G^*(\alpha)$ defined in this way is already in standard form because each player i ($i = 1, 2, 3$) will have only one move x_i in the game and therefore only one agent, who can be identified with the player himself. To obtain the uniformly perturbed game $G_\varepsilon^*(\alpha)$ corresponding to $G^*(\alpha)$, we have to assume that whenever any given player i wants to suggest a specific payoff x_i for player 1, he may in fact come to suggest any alternative payoff $x_i' \neq x_i$ in his strategy set X_i^* with a small positive probability ε by mistake. But again, to simplify our analysis, we will assume that ε is small enough to allow us to omit the terms containing ε from the payoff functions. Yet we will always point out the effects that the actual presence of these ε-terms will have on the best replies and on the equilibrium points in the perturbed game $G_\varepsilon^*(\alpha)$.

8.3 Equilibrium Points

We will first discuss the pure-strategy equilibria of the unperturbed game $G^*(\alpha)$. These equilibria fall into three structurally different classes, A, B, and C.

Class A will consist of strategy triplets of the form $a(x) = (x, x, x)$, representing three-player agreements to assign player 1 the payoff $u_1 = x$ and player 2 or 3 (whichever happens to be present in the game) the payoff $u_2 = u_3 = 100 - x$. Since x must be contained in all three players' strategy sets, we must have

$$0 \leq x \leq 100 - \alpha \quad \text{and} \quad x \in I^*. \tag{8.3.1}$$

Within class A the equilibria $a(0)$ and $a(100 - \alpha)$ will be *weak* equilibria. All others will be *strong*. $a(0)$ will be weak for player 1 because, if the other two players use the strategies $x_2 = x_3 = 0$, he can obtain his equilibrium payoff $u_1 = 0$ by using his equilibrium strategy $x_1 = 0$ as well as any other strategy. For similar reasons, $a(100 - \alpha)$ is weak for player 3.

In contrast, class B will consist of strategy triplets of the form $b(x, y) = (x, x, y)$ which must satisfy

$$100 - \alpha \leq x \leq 100, \quad 0 \leq y \leq 100 - \alpha, \quad \text{and} \quad x, y \in I^*. \tag{8.3.2}$$

Equilibria in this class can be interpreted as agreements between players 1 and 2 that player 3 does not join. (If $x > 100 - \alpha$, then player 3 would lose by joining the agreement because it would yield him a payoff *lower* than his conflict payoff $c_3 = \alpha$, whereas if $x = 100 - \alpha$, then joining the agreement would be a matter of indifference to him because it would yield him a payoff exactly *equal* to his conflict payoff. Indeed, under our definitions, if $x > 100 - \alpha$, joining the agreement would not be even a strategy available to player 3.)

To express his disagreement, player 3 can choose any strategy $y < 100 - \alpha$ in his strategy set X_3^*. As a result, if player 3 is the player representing player II in the game, no agreement will be reached, so players 1 and 3 will receive only their conflict payoffs $u_1 = c_1 = 0$ and $u_3 = c_3 = \alpha$. All in all, an equilibrium point $b(x, y)$ of class B will yield player 1 the expected payoff $\bar{u}_1 = \frac{1}{2}x + \frac{1}{2}0 = x/2$. Hence the payoff vector corresponding to $b(x, y)$ will be $(x/2, 100 - x, \alpha)$. All equilibria $b(x, y)$ in class B will be weak for player 3 since he can choose any strategy $y \in X_3^*$ without affecting his payoff. For the same reason any equilibrium of the form $b(100, y)$ will be weak for player 2. Finally, class C will consist of the one strategy triplet $c^* = (100, 0, 0)$, representing complete disagreement between player 1 and players 2 and 3. It yields the three players only their conflict payoffs $u_1 = u_2 = 0$ and $u_3 = \alpha$.

For the uniformly perturbed game $G_\varepsilon^*(\alpha)$, the pure-strategy equilibria will be a subset of those of the unperturbed game $G^*(\alpha)$. The equilibria will fall again into three classes when $\alpha \geq 50$ but only into two classes when $\alpha < 50$ (because in this case the strategy combination c^* will no longer be an equilibrium).

Class A^o will consist of all strategy triplets that in game $G^*(\alpha)$ belonged to class A, except for the two extreme cases of $a(0)$ and of $a(100 - \alpha)$. $a(0)$ will no longer be an equilibrium because in game G_ε^*, if players 2 and 3 use the strategies $x_2 = x_3 = 0$ as their intended strategies, then player 1's best reply will *not* be $x_1 = 0$. Rather, it will be $x_1 = 100$ if $\alpha > 50$ and $x_1 = 100 - \alpha$ if $\alpha < 50$. Finally, if $\alpha = 50$, both $x_1 = 100$ and $x_1 = 100 - \alpha$ will be best replies.[1] However, by very similar reasoning, in game $G_\varepsilon^*(\alpha)$, $a(100 - \alpha)$ will not be an equilibrium point because player 3's best reply to player 1's strategy $x_1 = 100 - \alpha$ is *not* $x_3 = 100 - \alpha$ but rather the strategy $x_3 = 0$ (which optimally exploits player 1's postulated tendency to use various unintended strategies by mistake).

Class B^o will consist of strategy triplets of the form $b(x) = (x, x, 0)$ with $100 - \alpha \leq x < 100$. Thus class B^o differs from class B by excluding (1) strategy triplets of the form (x, x, y) with $y \neq 0$ and (2) the strategy triplet $b(100) = (100, 100, 0)$. The strategy triplets (x, x, y) with $y \neq 0$ are not equilibrium points in game $G_\varepsilon^*(\alpha)$ because in this game player 3's only best reply to a strategy $x_1 = x$ with $x \geq 100 - \alpha$ is $x_3 = 0$, and $b(100)$ is not an equilibrium because player 2's only best reply to $x_1 = 100$ is $x_2 = 0$. (The reason is again that $x_3 = 0$ and $x_2 = 0$ are the strategies optimally exploiting player 1's postulated inclination to make mistakes.)

Finally, class C^o, like class C, will consist of the one strategy triplet $c^* = (100, 0, 0)$, but only when $\alpha \geq 50$. But if $\alpha < 50$, then c^* will no longer be an equilibrium because then player 1's best reply to the strategies $x_2 = 0$ and $x_3 = 0$ will be strategy $x_3 = 100 - \alpha$, rather then $x_3 = 100$ (see note 1 on page 367). In game $G_\varepsilon^*(\alpha)$ all pure-strategy equilibria—that is, all equilibria in classes A^o, B^o, and C^o—are strong equilibria. They are also primitive equilibria and are, in fact, the only primitive equilibria in the game. Our next task is to investigate risk-dominance and payoff-dominance relations among these equilibria.

8.4   Dominance Relations in Class A^o

An equilibrium point in A^o cannot payoff-dominate another equilibrium point in A^o because one of the two will yield a higher payoff to player 1, whereas the other will yield higher payoffs to players 2 and 3. Therefore we can restrict ourselves to studying risk-dominance relations.

Consider two equilibria $a' = a(x')$ and $a'' = a(x'')$ of class A^o with $x' > x''$. It is easy to verify[2] that the bicentric prior for player 1 will be the probability vector

$$p_1 = (p_1', p_1''), \tag{8.4.1}$$

with

$$p_1' = p_1(x') = \frac{x'}{x' + x''}, \tag{8.4.2}$$

$$p_1'' = p_1(x'') = \frac{x''}{x' + x''}. \tag{8.4.3}$$

The bicentric prior for player 2 will be

$$p_2 = (p_2', p_2''), \tag{8.4.4}$$

with

$$p_2' = \frac{100 - x'}{200 - x' - x''}, \tag{8.4.5}$$

$$p_2'' = \frac{100 - x''}{200 - x' - x''}. \tag{8.4.6}$$

Finally, the bicentric prior for player 3 will be

$$p_3 = (p_3', p_3''), \tag{8.4.7}$$

with

$$p_3' = p_3(x') = \frac{100 - x' - \alpha}{200 - x' - x'' - 2\alpha}, \tag{8.4.8}$$

$$p_3'' = p_3(x'') = \frac{100 - x'' - \alpha}{200 - x' - x'' - 2\alpha}. \tag{8.4.9}$$

What will be player 1's best reply to the bicentric prior vector $p_{-1} = (p_2, p_3)$, consisting of the bicentric priors p_2 and p_3 of the other two players? Clearly his best reply will be the strategy $x_1' = x'$ rather than the strategy $x_1'' = x''$ if

$$H_1(x_1'p_{-1}) > H_1(x_1''p_{-1}),\tag{8.4.10}$$

that is, if

$$x'(\tfrac{1}{2}p_2' + \tfrac{1}{2}p_3') > x''(\tfrac{1}{2}p_2'' + \tfrac{1}{2}p_3'').\tag{8.4.11}$$

(The expressions in parenthesis indicate that (1) player 1 will obtain a positive payoff only if his opponent uses a matching strategy, and (2) his opponent will be either player 2 or player 3, the probability of either possibility being $\tfrac{1}{2}$.) For convenience we will write

$$\bar{x} = \frac{x' + x''}{2}\tag{8.4.12}$$

and

$$x' = \bar{x} + v \quad \text{and} \quad x'' = \bar{x} - v, \quad \text{with} \quad v > 0.\tag{8.4.13}$$

Using (8.4.5), (8.4.6), (8.4.8), (8.4.9), (8.4.12), and (8.4.13), we can write (8.4.11) in the form:

$$
\begin{aligned}
(\bar{x} + v)&\left(\frac{1}{2}\frac{100 - \bar{x} - v}{200 - 2\bar{x}} + \frac{1}{2}\frac{100 - \bar{x} - v - \alpha}{200 - 2\bar{x} - 2\alpha}\right) \\
&> (\bar{x} - v)\left(\frac{1}{2}\frac{100 - \bar{x} + v}{200 - 2\bar{x}} + \frac{1}{2}\frac{100 - \bar{x} + v - \alpha}{200 - 2\bar{x} - 2\alpha}\right).
\end{aligned}\tag{8.4.14}
$$

After simplification this yields the requirement:

$$4\bar{x}^2 - (600 - 3\alpha)\bar{x} + (20{,}000 - 200\alpha) > 0.\tag{8.4.15}$$

This requirement will be satisfied if either

$$\bar{x} = \frac{x' + x''}{2} < x^*,\tag{8.4.16}$$

or

$$\bar{x} = \frac{x' + x''}{2} > x^{**},\tag{8.4.17}$$

where

$$x^* = \frac{600 - 3\alpha - \sqrt{40{,}000 - 400\alpha + 9\alpha^2}}{8},\tag{8.4.18}$$

$$x^{**} = \frac{600 - 3\alpha + \sqrt{40,000 - 400\alpha + 9\alpha^2}}{8}.$$

(8.4.19)

But, in view of (8.3.1), condition (8.4.17) cannot be satisfied because $x^{**} > 100 - \alpha$. Therefore we can conclude:

LEMMA 8.4.1   Player 1's best reply to the bicentric prior vector p_{-1} will be the strategy $x'_1 = x'$ with $x' > x''$ whenever x' and x'' satisfy inequality (8.4.16), and it will be the strategy $x''_1 = x''$ whenever this inequality is reversed.

Table 8.1 lists the values of $x^* = x^*(\alpha)$ for a few selected values of the parameter α:

Table 8.1

α	x^*
0	50.00
10	47.24
20	43.92
30	40.00
40	35.51
50	30.48
60	25.00
70	19.14
80	12.98
90	6.59
100	0

What will be player 2's best reply to player 1's bicentric prior p_1? [Formally, we should ask what will be his best reply to the bicentric prior vector $p_{-2} = (p_1, p_3)$. But since player 2's payoff depends only on his own and on player 1's strategy, and does not depend on player 3's strategy at all, we can consider player 2's best reply to p_1 rather than to (p_1, p_3).] Clearly his best reply to p_1 will be the strategy $x'_2 = x'$ rather than the strategy $x''_2 = x''$ if

$$H_2(x'_2 p_1) > H_2(x''_2 p_1),$$

(8.4.20)

that is, if

$$(100 - x')p'_1 > (100 - x'')p''_1.$$

(8.4.21)

Using (8.4.2), (8.4.3), (8.4.12), and (8.4.13), this becomes

$$(100 - \bar{x} - v)\frac{\bar{x} + v}{2\bar{x}} > (100 - \bar{x} + v)\frac{\bar{x} - v}{2\bar{x}}, \qquad (8.4.22)$$

which reduces to

$$\bar{x} = \frac{x' + x''}{2} < 50. \qquad (8.4.23)$$

Consequently we can state:

LEMMA 8.4.2 Player 2's best reply to the bicentric prior p_1 will be the strategy $x_2' = x'$ with $x' > x''$ whenever x' and x'' satisfy inequality (8.4.23), and it will be the strategy $x_2'' = x''$ whenever this inequality is reversed.

Finally, what will be player 3's best reply to player 1's bicentric prior p_1? It will be the strategy $x_3' = x'$ rather than the strategy $x_3'' = x''$ if

$$H_3(x_3'p_1') > H_3(x_3''p_1''). \qquad (8.4.24)$$

After some computation this reduces to the condition

$$\bar{x} = \frac{x' + x''}{2} < 50 - \frac{\alpha}{2}. \qquad (8.4.25)$$

Equation (8.4.25) implies:

LEMMA 8.4.3 Player 3's best reply to the bicentric prior p_1 will be the strategy $x_3' = x'$ with $x' > x''$ whenever x' and x'' satisfy inequality (8.4.25), and it will be the strategy $x_3'' = x''$ if this inequality is reversed.

It is easy to verify that always

$$50 - \frac{\alpha}{2} < x^* < 50. \qquad (8.4.26)$$

In view of the last three lemmas we can distinguish four possible cases.

Case 1: $\bar{x} < 50 - (\alpha/2)$. In this case the three players' strong vector best reply to the prior vector $p = (p_1, p_2, p_3)$ will be the strategy triplet $(x_1', x_2', x_3') = a(x')$. Since $a(x')$ is a strong equilibrium point of game $G_\varepsilon^*(\alpha)$, by lemmas 4.17.6 and 4.17.7 in this case the equilibrium point $a(x')$ will always conspicuously risk-dominate the equilibrium point $a(x'')$.

Case 2: $50 - (\alpha/2) < \bar{x} < x^*$. In this case the three players' vector best reply to the prior vector p will be (x_1', x_2', x_3'').[3] Consequently, if we apply the tracing procedure to this prior vector p, the players' initial strategy combination at $t = 0$ will be this strategy triplet $\beta^o = (\beta_1^o, \beta_2^o, \beta_3^o) = (x_1', x_2', x_3'')$. Since β^o is not an equilibrium point of game $G_\varepsilon^*(\alpha)$, during the tracing procedure at least one of the three players will have to relinquish his initial strategy. We now have to decide which player will be the *first* to do so.

Clearly it *cannot* be player 2 because, as long as player 1 sticks to his initial strategy $x_1' = x'$, player 2 will have no incentive to move away from his matching strategy $x_2' = x'$. But it *cannot* be player 1 either because, as long as the other two players stick to their initial strategies $x_2' = x'$ and $x_3'' = x''$, for all values of t ($0 \le t \le 1$) we will have

$$H_1^t(x_1' x_2' x_3'') = (1 - t)H_1(x_1' p_{-1}) + tH_1(x_1' x_2' x_3'')$$
$$> H_1^t(x_1'' x_2' x_3'') = (1 - t)H_1(x_1'' p_{-1}) + tH_1(x_1'' x_2' x_3''). \tag{8.4.27}$$

This follows from the fact that, by lemma 8.4.1, we have

$$H_1(x_1' p_{-1}) > H_1(x_1'' p_{-1}) \tag{8.4.28}$$

and from the fact that

$$H_1(x_1' x_2' x_3'') = \frac{x'}{2} = \frac{\bar{x} + v}{2}$$
$$> H_1(x_1'' x_2' x_3'') = \frac{x''}{2} = \frac{\bar{x} - v}{2}. \tag{8.4.29}$$

Consequently the first player to change his strategy during the tracing procedure will be player 3. After he has changed his strategy at the relevant t value, the strategy combination used by the three players will be and will remain $(x_1', x_2', x_3') = a(x')$, which means that, also in this case, equilibrium point $a(x')$ will risk-dominate equilibrium point $a(x'')$.

Case 3: $x^* < \bar{x} < 50$. In this case the players' vector best reply to the prior vector p will be $\bar{\beta}^o = (\bar{\beta}_1^o, \bar{\beta}_2^o, \bar{\beta}_3^o) = (x_1'', x_2', x_3'')$. Again, this strategy combination is *not* an equilibrium point of game $G_\varepsilon^*(\alpha)$, so that during the tracing procedure at least one player must change his strategy. But which player will be the first one to do this? It cannot be player 3, who will have no incentive to move away from strategy $x_3'' = x''$ as long as player 1 uses the matching strategy $x_1'' = x''$. Thus we now have to decide whether it is player 1 or player 2 who will first relinquish his initial strategy.

If the other two players stick to their initial strategies $x_2' = x'$ and $x_3'' = x''$, then player 1 will be destabilized at the t value $t = t_1$, satisfying the equation

$$H_1^t(x_1'x_2'x_3'') = (1 - t)H_1(x_1'p_{-1}) + tH_1(x_1'x_2'x_3'')$$
$$= H_1^t(x_1''x_2'x_3'') = (1 - t)H_1(x_1''p_{-1}) + tH_1(x_1''x_2'x_3''), \tag{8.4.30}$$

where

$$H_1(x_1'p_{-1}) = x'(\tfrac{1}{2}p_2' + \tfrac{1}{2}p_3')$$
$$= x'\left(\frac{1}{2}\frac{100 - x'}{200 - x' - x''} + \frac{1}{2}\frac{100 - x' - \alpha}{200 - x' - x'' - 2\alpha}\right), \tag{8.4.31}$$

$$H_1(x_1'x_2'x_3'') = \frac{x'}{2}, \tag{8.4.32}$$

$$H_1(x_1''p_{-1}) = x''(\tfrac{1}{2}p_2'' + \tfrac{1}{2}p_3'')$$
$$= x''\left(\frac{1}{2}\frac{100 - x''}{200 - x' - x''} + \frac{1}{2}\frac{100 - x'' - \alpha}{200 - x' - x'' - 2\alpha}\right), \tag{8.4.33}$$

and

$$H_1(x_1''x_2'x_3'') = \frac{x''}{2}. \tag{8.4.34}$$

It turns out that the t value $t = t_1$ satisfying equation (8.4.30) will be

$$t_1 = \frac{(600 - 2x' - 2x'' - 3\alpha)(x' + x'') - 400(100 - \alpha)}{(200 - x' - x'' - \alpha)(x' + x'')} \tag{8.4.35}$$

On the other hand, if players 1 and 3 stick to their initial strategies $x_1'' = x''$ and $x_3'' = x''$, then player 2 will be destabilized at the t value $t = t_2$, satisifying the equation

$$H_2^t(x_1''x_2'x_3'') = (1 - t)H_2(x_2'p_1) + tH_2(x_1''x_2'x_3'')$$
$$= H_2^t(x_1''x_2''x_3'') = (1 - t)H_2(x_2''p_1) + tH_2(x_1''x_2''x_3''), \tag{8.4.36}$$

where

$$H_2(x_2'p_1) = (100 - x')p_1' = (100 - x')\frac{x'}{x' + x''}, \tag{8.4.37}$$

$$H_2(x_1''x_2'x_3'') = 0, \tag{8.4.38}$$

$$H_2(x_2''p_1) = (100 - x'')p_1'' = (100 - x'')\frac{x''}{x' + x''}, \tag{8.4.39}$$

$$H_2(x_1''x_2''x_3'') = 100 - x''. \tag{8.4.40}$$

The t value $t = t_2$ satisfying equation (8.4.36) is

$$t_2 = \frac{(x' - x'')(100 - x' - x'')}{x'(200 - x' - x'')}. \tag{8.4.41}$$

Numerical computation shows that both $t_1 > t_2$ and $t_1 < t_2$ are possible cases. Accordingly we will distinguish:

Subcase 3A: $t_1 > t_2$. If this subcase obtains, then in the tracing procedure at the t value $t = t_2$ player 2 will shift to strategy $x_2'' = x''$, and from that point on the players will stick to the strategy combination $a(x'') = (x_1'', x_2'', x_3'')$, so that equilibrium point $a(x'')$ will risk-dominate equilibrium point $a(x')$.

Subcase 3B: $t_1 < t_2$. If this subcase obtains, then risk dominance will always go the opposite way so that it will be equilibrium point $a(x')$ that risk-dominates equilibrium point $a(x'')$. Yet subcase 3B must be itself subdivided into two sub-subcases.

In sub-subcase 3B*, at the t value $t = t_1$, player 1 will shift to strategy x_1' so that the strategy combination used by the players will become (x_1', x_2', x_3''). Then, later at some t value $t = t_3 > t_1$, player 3 will likewise shift to strategy x_3', and from that point on the players will stick to the resulting strategy combination $a(x') = (x_1', x_2', x_3')$.

In contrast, in sub-subcase 3B**, at the t value $t = t_1$, both players 1 and 3 will move over to *mixed* strategies whereas player 2 will stick to his strategy $x_2' = x'$. Then the path defined by the tracing procedure will turn *backward* toward smaller t values $t < t_1$ and will reach the pure-strategy combination $a(x') = (x_1'x_2'x_3')$ at some t value $t^* < t_1$. After that point the path of the tracing procedure will again move toward *increasing* t values while the players will stick to this strategy combination $a(x')$.

Case 4: $\bar{x} > 50$. In this case the players' strong vector best reply to the bicentric prior vector p will be the strategy combination $a(x'') = (x_1'', x_2'', x_3'')$, which is of course an equilibrium point of game $G_\varepsilon^*(\alpha)$. As a result equilibrium point $a(x'')$ will always conspicuously risk-dominate equilibrium point $a(x')$.

Using the quantity $x^* = x^*(\alpha)$ defined by (8.4.18), we can summarize our analytical results for cases 1, 2, and 4, as well as our computational results for case 3, as follows:

THEOREM 8.4.1   Suppose that $a(x)$ and $a(x^o)$ are two equilibrium points of class A^o of a given game $G_\varepsilon^*(\alpha)$. Then we can define a function $\xi(\alpha, x)$ with the following properties:

1. If $x < x^*(\alpha)$, then $a(x)$ will risk-dominate $a(x^o)$ in case $x^o < x$ or $x^o > \xi(\alpha, x)$, and risk dominance will go the opposite way if the last two inequalities are both reversed.

2. If $x = x^*(\alpha)$, then $a(x)$ will risk-dominate $a(x^o)$ for *all* $x^o \neq x$.

3. If $x > x^*(\alpha)$, then $a(x)$ will risk-dominate $a(x^o)$ in case $x^o < \xi(\alpha, x)$ or $x^o > x$, and risk-dominance will go the opposite way if the last two inequalities are both reversed.

COROLLARY   The equilibrium point $a^* = a(x^*)$ risk-dominates, and indeed dominates, all other equilibrium points of class A^o. (That it risk-dominates them follows from part 2 of the theorem. That it dominates them follows from the fact that there is no payoff dominance between equilibrium points of class A^o.)

As to the numerical values of the function $\xi = \xi(\alpha, x)$, our results in cases 2 and 4 imply that

$$2x^*(\alpha) < \xi(\alpha, x) < 100 - x. \tag{8.4.42}$$

The actual numerical values of ξ we obtain are as follows: For any given α and x, let $x^o = \vartheta(\alpha, x)$ be that particular x^o value for which $t_1 = t_2$ if we set

$$x' = \max(x, x^o) \quad \text{and} \quad x'' = \min(x, x^o), \tag{8.4.43}$$

where t_1 and t_2 are the quantities defined by equations (8.4.35) and (8.4.41). Theorem 8.4.1 would be a fortiori true if we defined $\xi(\alpha, x) = \vartheta(\alpha, x)$. But since both x and x^o must be smaller than $100 - \alpha$ (because they must represent possible strategies for player 3), we will actually define

$$\xi(\alpha, x) = \min[\vartheta(\alpha, x), 100 - \alpha]. \tag{8.4.44}$$

Table 8.2 below lists the values of ξ for a few selected values of α and x:

Table 8.2

α \ x	10	20	30	40	50	60	70	80	90
10	86.07	75.87	65.57	55.08	44.73	35.34	25.71	15.96	6.13
20	80.00	70.56	59.85	48.61	38.81	29.86	20.53	10.99	
30	70.00	63.79	52.49	40.00	32.11	23.42	14.30		
40	60.00	55.31	43.15	32.37	24.50	15.90			
50	50.00	44.98	31.26	23.90	15.86				
60	40.00	32.67	21.86	14.42					
70	30.00	18.67	11.86						
80	17.86	8.46							
90	4.46								

Intuitive Interpretation   In game $G_\varepsilon^*(\alpha)$ player 1 has probability $\frac{1}{2}$ of facing player 2 and has probability $\frac{1}{2}$ of facing player 3. Thus $G_\varepsilon^*(\alpha)$ is halfway between a game G_{12}, where player 1 would always have player 2 as his opponent, and a game G_{13}, where he would always have player 3 as his opponent. Now in game G_{12}, both by the Nash solution and by our own solution theory, the two players would obtain the payoffs $u_1^o = u_2^o = 50$, whereas in game G_{13} player 1 would obtain the payoff $u_1^* = 50 - (\alpha/2)$ and player 3 would obtain the payoff $u_3^* = 50 + (\alpha/2)$.

Since game $G_\varepsilon^*(\alpha)$ is halfway between these two games, it would be natural to expect that it should yield the payoffs

$$\bar{u}_1 = \frac{1}{2}u_1^o + \frac{1}{2}u_1^* = 50 - \left(\frac{\alpha}{4}\right),$$

$$\bar{u}_2 = \bar{u}_3 = 100 - \bar{u}_1 = 50 + \left(\frac{\alpha}{4}\right)$$

(8.4.45)

to the three players. In fact, as we shall see, for small and for middling α values, our theory chooses $a^* = a(x^*)$—that is, the dominant equilibrium point of class A^o—as the solution of $G_\varepsilon^*(\alpha)$, giving the players the payoffs

$$u_1 = x^* \quad \text{and} \quad u_2 = u_3 = 100 - x^*. \tag{8.4.46}$$

(For large values of α, an equilibrium point of class B^o is chosen as the solution.) When α is small, these payoffs u_1, u_2, and u_3 are very close to the payoffs $\bar{u}_1$, $\bar{u}_2$, and $\bar{u}_3$ defined by (8.4.45). But for somewhat larger α values, u_1 is smaller than $\bar{u}_1$, while u_2 and u_3 are larger than $\bar{u}_2$ and $\bar{u}_3$. This has to be the case because player 3's payoff u_3 must exceed his conflict payoff $c_3 = \alpha$ for all values of α. Yet, if his payoff were only $u_3 = \bar{u}_3 = 50 + (\alpha/4)$, then this requirement would not be met for $\alpha > 66.67$.

8.5   Dominance Relations in Class B^o

Again, one equilibrium point in B^o cannot payoff-dominate another equilibrium point in B^o because if one of them yields a higher payoff to player 1, then the other will yield a higher payoff to player 2. Hence we can restrict our attention to risk-dominance relations.

Consider two equilibria $b' = b(x')$ and $b'' = b(x'')$ with $x' > x''$. By the definition of class B^o equilibria, both at b' and at b'' player 3 will use the same equilibrium strategy $x_3 = 0$. As was stated in section 5.3, in such cases we will always perform risk-dominance comparisons within a restricted game G', which differs from the original game by restricting player 3 to this specific strategy $x_3 = 0$, while imposing no restrictions on the strategies used by players 1 and 2. Consequently we have to define bicentric priors only for players 1 and 2.

Reflection will show that these priors will again be defined by equations (8.4.1) through (8.4.6). But since player 3 is now restricted to using strategy $x_3 = 0$, the prior vector p will take the form

$$p = (p_1, p_2, 0). \tag{8.5.1}$$

Player 1's best reply to p will be strategy $x_1' = x'$ if

$$
\begin{aligned}
H_1(x_1' p_2 0) &= x' \left(\frac{1}{2} \frac{100 - x'}{200 - x' - x''} \right) \\
&> H_1(x_1'' p_2 0) = x'' \left(\frac{1}{2} \frac{100 - x''}{200 - x' - x''} \right)
\end{aligned}
\tag{8.5.2}
$$

Using the notations defined in (8.4.12) and (8.4.13), this reduces to

$$\bar{x} = \frac{x' + x''}{2} < 50. \tag{8.5.3}$$

But player 1's best reply to p will be $x_1'' = x''$ if this inequality is reversed. Similarly player 2's best reply to p will be strategy $x_2' = x'$ if

$$H_2(p_1 x_2' 0) = (100 - x')\frac{x'}{x' + x''}$$

$$> H_2(p_1 x_2'' 0) = (100 - x'')\frac{x''}{x' + x''}. \tag{8.5.4}$$

Using the notations of (8.4.12) and (8.4.13), this likewise reduces to (8.5.3). If inequality (8.5.3) is reversed, Player 2's best reply to p will be $x_2'' = x''$.

Condition (8.5.3) has been obtained on the assumption that $x' > x''$. An equivalent condition, independent of the relative magnitude of x' and of x'', is

$$|50 - x'| < |50 - x''|. \tag{8.5.5}$$

Thus we can conclude that regardless of whether $x' > x''$ or $x' < x''$, in the restricted game G' the best replies of players 1 and 2 to p will be $x_1' = x'$ and $x_2' = x'$ if inequality (8.5.5) is satisfied. Moreover, since in game G' player 3 is restricted to strategy $x_3 = 0$, we can say also that in G' the three players' strong vector best reply to p will be the strategy combination $(x', x', 0) = b(x') = b'$. Since b' is a strong equilibrium point in G' [just as in $G_\varepsilon^*(\alpha)$ itself], b' will have conspicuous risk dominance over b'' if (8.5.5) is satisfied, and the opposite will be true if (8.5.5) is reversed.

THEOREM 8.5.1   Suppose that $b' = b(x')$ and $b'' = b(x'')$ are equilibria of class B^o in a given game $G_\varepsilon^*(\alpha)$. Then b' will risk-dominate and, indeed, dominate b'' if inequality (8.5.5) holds, and the opposite will be true if this inequality is reversed.

COROLLARY   If $\alpha \geq 50$, then equilibrium $b^* = b(50)$ will dominate all other equilibria of class B^o. On the other hand, if $\alpha < 50$, then equilibrium $b^{**} = b(100 - \alpha)$ will be the dominant equilibrium in class B^o. [If $\alpha < 50$, then $b(50)$ will not be an equilibrium because all equilibria $b(x)$ of class B^o must satisfy $100 - \alpha \leq x < 100$.]

Intuitive Interpretation   A choice between two equilibria of class B^o is essentially a two-person bargaining game with complete information between players 1 and 2. The equilibrium point b^* (or b^{**}) will correspond to the Nash solution of that game.

8.6 Risk-Dominance and Payoff-Dominance Relations between Two Equilibria Belonging to Different Classes

THEOREM 8.6.1 Equilibrium point c^*, which alone belongs to class C^o (when it is an equilibrium point at all because $\alpha \geq 50$), is risk dominated by every equilibrium $a(x)$ in class A^o and by every equilibrium $b(x)$ in class B^o. It is also payoff dominated by every equilibrium in class A^o. But it has no payoff-dominance relations with equilibria in class B^o in either direction.

As is easy to verify, the first two statements are consequences of the fact that c^* yields all three players' payoffs only slightly above their conflict payoffs (the difference being of order of ε). The third statement is due to the fact that both c^* and equilibria $b(x)$ in class B^o yield player 3 exactly the same payoff $u_3 = \alpha + (100 - \alpha)\varepsilon$ (plus the same term of order ε^2).

Now consider an equilibrium point $a' = a(x')$ of class A^o and an equilibrium point $b'' = b(x'')$ of class B^o. These two equilibria will generate the following bicentric priors. Since $H_1(a') = x'$ whereas $H_1(b'') = x''/2$, the bicentric prior for player 1 will be

$$p_1 = (p_1', p_1''), \tag{8.6.1}$$

with

$$p_1' = \frac{x'}{x' + (x''/2)} = \frac{2x'}{2x' + x''}, \tag{8.6.2}$$

$$p_1'' = \frac{x''/2}{x' + (x''/2)} = \frac{x''}{2x' + x''}. \tag{8.6.3}$$

But, since $H_2(a') = 100 - x'$ and $H_2(b'') = 100 - x''$, the bicentric prior for player 2 is again defined by equations (8.4.4) to (8.4.6). Finally, since $H_3(a') = 100 - x'$ and $H_3(b'') = \alpha + (100 - \alpha)\varepsilon$, the bicentric prior for player 3 is

$$p_3 = (p_3', p_3''), \tag{8.6.4}$$

with

$$p_3' = \frac{100 - x' - \alpha}{(100 - x' - \alpha) + (100 - \alpha)\varepsilon},$$ (8.6.5)

$$p_3'' = \frac{(100 - \alpha)\varepsilon}{(100 - x' - \alpha) + (100 - \alpha)\varepsilon}.$$ (8.6.6)

However, for our purposes p_3' and p_3'' are sufficiently closely approximated by setting

$$p_3' = 1 \quad \text{and} \quad p_3'' = 0.$$ (8.6.7)

What will be player 1's best reply to the bicentric prior vector p? It will be strategy $x_1' = x'$ if

$$H_1(x_1' p_2 p_3) = x' \left(\frac{1}{2} \frac{100 - x'}{200 - x' - x''} + \frac{1}{2} \cdot 1 \right)$$

$$> H_1(x_1'' p_2 p_3) = x'' \left(\frac{1}{2} \frac{100 - x''}{200 - x' - x''} + \frac{1}{2} \cdot 0 \right),$$ (8.6.8)

and it will be $x_1'' = x''$ if this inequality is reversed. After simplification, (8.6.8) can be written as

$$-2(x')^2 + (300 - x'')x' + [(x'')^2 - 100x''] > 0.$$ (8.6.9)

This in turn is equivalent to the requirement that

$$y^* < x' < y^{**},$$ (8.6.10)

where

$$y^* = \frac{300 - x'' - \sqrt{90,000 - 1,400x'' + 9(x'')^2}}{4}$$ (8.6.11)

and

$$y^{**} = \frac{300 - x'' + \sqrt{90,000 - 1,400x'' + 9(x'')^2}}{4}.$$ (8.6.12)

Yet $y^{**} > 100$. Therefore (8.6.11) reduces to

$$x' > y^*.$$ (8.6.13)

Thus we can state:

LEMMA 8.6.1   Player 1's best reply to the bicentric prior vector p will be $x_1' = x'$ if $x' > y^*$, and will be $x_1'' = x''$ if $x' < y^*$.

What will be player 2's best reply to p? It will be $x_2' = x'$ if

$$H_2(p_1 x_2') = (100 - x') \frac{2x'}{2x' + x''}$$

$$> H_2(p_1 x_2'') = (100 - x'') \frac{x''}{2x' + x''},$$

(8.6.14)

and it will be $x_2'' = x''$ if this inequality is reversed. After simplification, (8.6.14) can be written as

$$-2(x')^2 + 200x + [(x'')^2 - 100x''] > 0.$$ (8.6.15)

This is equivalent to the requirement

$$\check{y} < x' < \hat{y},$$ (8.6.16)

where

$$\check{y} = \frac{100 - \sqrt{10{,}000 - 200x'' + 2(x'')^2}}{2},$$ (8.6.17)

$$\hat{y} = \frac{100 + \sqrt{10{,}000 - 200x'' + 2(x'')^2}}{2}.$$ (8.6.18)

Hence we can state:

LEMMA 8.6.2   Player 2's best reply to the bicentric prior vector p will be $x_2' = x'$ if $\check{y} < x' < \hat{y}$, and it will be $x_2'' = x''$ if either $x' < \check{y}$ or $x' > \hat{y}$.

Finally, player 3's best reply to p will always be the strategy $x_3' = x'$ he uses at equilibrium point $a' = (x', x', x')$, rather than the strategy $x_3'' = 0$ he uses at equilibrium point $b'' = (x'', x'', 0)$ because, for sufficiently small ε, we will always have

$$H_3(p_1 x_3') = 100 - x' > H_3(p_1 x_3'') = \alpha + (100 - \alpha)\varepsilon.$$ (8.6.19)

LEMMA 8.6.3   Player 3's best reply to the bicentric prior vector p will always be $x_3' = x'$.

Numerical computation shows that the following inequality is always satisfied:

$$y^* < \check{y} < \hat{y}. \tag{8.6.20}$$

Consequently we can distinguish four cases.

Case 1: $x' < y^*$.   In this case the three players' vector best reply to p will be (x_1'', x_2'', x_3'). It is easy to verify that neither player 1 nor player 2 will have any incentive to change his strategy, so at some t value $t = t_3$ it will be player 3 who will shift from strategy $x_3' = x'$ to strategy $x_3'' = 0$. From this point on the three players will stick to the strategy combination $(x_1'', x_2'', 0) = b(x'')$. Therefore in this case $b(x'')$ will risk-dominate $a(x')$.

Case 2: $y^* < x' < \check{y}$.   In this case the three players' vector best reply to p will be $\beta^o = (x_1', x_2'', x_3')$. Since this is not an equilibrium point of the game $G_\varepsilon^*(\alpha)$, at least one player must switch to another strategy during the tracing procedure. For each player i ($i = 1, 2, 3$), this will occur at the t value $t = t_i$ at which player i will obtain the same payoff by using strategy x_i' as he will by using strategy x_i'' on the assumption that the other two players will stick to their initial strategies used in β^o. Simple computation shows that these t values are

$$t_1 = \frac{(300 - 2x')x' - (100 + x' - x'')x''}{(100 - x')(x' + x'')} \tag{8.6.21}$$

in the case of player 1,

$$t_2 = \frac{(100 - x'')x'' - (200 - 2x')x'}{(200 - x' - x'')x''} \tag{8.6.22}$$

in the case of player 2, and

$$t_3 = 1^- \tag{8.6.23}$$

in the case of player 3, where 1^- denotes a number smaller than 1 by a quantity of order ε.

Thus, we have to distinguish two subcases: In subcase 2A, $t_1 < t_2$. In this subcase at all t values with $t > t_1$, players 1 and 2 will always use strategies x_1'' and x_2'', and at a t-value close to $t = 1$, player 3 will likewise shift to strategy x_3''. Hence in this subcase, as in case 1, $b(x'')$ will risk-dominate $a(x')$.

In subcase 2B, $t_1 > t_2$. In this subcase, at all t values with $t > t_2$, the three players will use the strategies x'_1, x'_2, and x'_3. Therefore $a(x')$ will risk-dominate $b(x'')$.

Case 3: $\breve{y} < x < \hat{y}$. In this case the three players' vector best reply to p will be $(x'_1, x'_2, x'_3) = a(x')$. Consequently $a(x')$ will conspicuously risk-dominate $b(x'')$.

Case 4: $x > \hat{y}$. In this case the players' vector best reply to p will be (x'_1, x''_2, x'_3), just as in case 2. Consequently the situation is the same as in case 2. That is to say, we must again distinguish two subcases according as $t_1 < t_2$ or $t_1 > t_2$. But in each subcase we obtain the same results as we did in the corresponding subcase of case 2.

For any x'' value, let $x' = \sigma(x'')$ be that particular x' value for which $t_1 = t_2$. We can now state:

THEOREM 8.6.2   Suppose that $a(x')$ is an equilibrium of class A^o, whereas $b(x'')$ is an equilibrium of class B^o. Then $a(x')$ will risk-dominate $b(x'')$ if $x' > \sigma(x'')$, and the opposite will be true if $x' < \sigma(x'')$.

The theorem is true because

1. In case 1, always $x' < \sigma(x'')$.

2. In case 3, always $x' > \sigma(x'')$.

3. In cases 2 and 4, $x < \sigma(x'')$ if $t_1 > t_2$ but $x > \sigma(x'')$ if $t_1 < t_2$.

Table 8.3 lists the value of the function $\sigma = \sigma(x'')$ for a few selected values

Table 8.3

x''	σ
0	0
10	3.67
20	6.88
30	9.49
40	11.36
50	12.30
60	12.15
70	10.80
80	8.25
90	4.59
100	0

of x''. The maximum value of this function $\sigma(x'')$ is

$$\sigma_{max} = 12.38, \tag{8.6.24}$$

which is reached when

$$x'' = 53.51. \tag{8.6.25}$$

THEOREM 8.6.3   Theorem 8.6.2 remains true even if we replace the term "risk-dominate" by the term "dominate."

Proof   We have to show that no risk-dominance relation established by theorem 8.6.2 can ever be overridden by an opposite payoff-dominance relation. First, take the case where $a' = a(x')$ risk-dominates $b'' = b(x'')$. It cannot happen that b'' should payoff-dominate a' because, for sufficiently small ε, $H_3(b'') = \alpha + (100 - \alpha)\varepsilon < H_3(a') = 100 - x'$. Next take the case where b'' risk-dominates a'. In that case we must have $x' < \sigma(x'')$. Yet inspection of table 8.3 will show that for all values of x'', $\sigma(x'') < x''/2$, which means that $x' < x''/2$. But for a' to have payoff dominance over b'' we would have to have $H_1(a') = x' > H_1(b'') = x''/2$. Thus in neither case can the risk-dominance relation be overridden by an opposite payoff-dominance relation. ∎

COROLLARY 8.6.1   The dominant equilibrium point $a^* = a(x^*)$ of class A^o will dominate *all* other primitive equilibria of the game if $x^* = x^*(\alpha) > \sigma_{max} = 12.38$. Numerical computation shows that this will be the case whenever $\alpha < 80.76$.

COROLLARY 8.6.2   As table 8.3 shows, the dominant equilibrium point $b^* = b(50)$ of class B^o will dominate all other primitive equilibria of the game if all equilibria $a(x)$ of class A^o satisfy the inequality $x < 12.30$. By requirement (8.3.1), this will be the case whenever $\alpha \geq 100 - 12.30 = 87.70$.

In view of these two corollaries we can state:

THEOREM 8.6.4   When $\alpha < 80.76$, then the solution of game $G_\varepsilon^*(\alpha)$ will be $a^* = a(x^*)$, and when $\alpha \geq 80.76$, then its solution will be $b^* = b(50)$.

To find the solution in cases where $80.76 \leq \alpha < 87.70$, we now have to study dominance relations between the two "class leaders," the equilibrium points $a^* = a(x^*)$ and $b^* = b(50)$.

8.7 Dominance Relations between the Two Class Leaders

We can immediately state:

LEMMA 8.7.1   Equilibrium point a^* will dominate equilibrium point b^* if

$$x^* > 12.30, \tag{8.7.1}$$

and the opposite will be true if this inequality is reversed.

The lemma follows from theorems 8.6.2 and 8.6.3 and from the fact that, as table 8.3 shows, $\sigma(50) = 12.30$.

LEMMA 8.7.2   Equilibrium point a^* will dominate equilibrium point b^* if

$$\alpha < 81.08, \tag{8.7.2}$$

and the opposite is true if this inequality is reversed.

The lemma follows from the previous lemma and from the fact that, by equation (8.4.18), $x^*(81.08) = 12.30$ and that the quantity $x^*(\alpha)$ is a strictly decreasing function of the parameter α. The only further information we need are the strategic net distances between primitive equilibrium points of various kinds.

8.8 Strategic Net Distances

First, we have to compute the strategic (gross) distances between various equilibria (see section 5.5). Reflection will show that in this game the strategic distance between two pure-strategy equilibria will always equal the number of players using different strategies at the two equilibria. Thus, for two equilibria $a = a(x) = (x, x, x)$ and $a' = a(x') = (x', x', x')$ of class A^o, their strategic distance will be 3. In contrast, for two equilibria $b = b(x) = (x, x, 0)$ and $b' = b(x') = (x', x', 0)$ of class B^o, their strategic distance will be 2, because player 3's strategy will be the same strategy $x_3 = 0$ at both equilibria. In particular,

$$e(a, a') = 3, \quad \text{for } a, a' \in A^o. \tag{8.8.1}$$

$$e(b, b') = 2, \quad \text{for } b, b' \in B^o, \tag{8.8.2}$$

$$e(a, b) = 3, \quad \text{for } a \in A^o \text{ and } b \in B^o, \tag{8.8.3}$$

$$e(a, c^*) = 3, \quad \text{for } a \in A^o \text{ and } c^* \in C^o, \tag{8.8.4}$$

$$e(b, c^*) = 2, \quad \text{for } b \in B^o \text{ and } c^* \in C^o. \tag{8.8.5}$$

Let Ω be the set of *all* primitive equilibria, corresponding to the union of classes A^o, B^o, and C^o. In view of (8.8.1) through (8.8.5), the strategic distances of various primitive equilibria from their closest neighbors within Ω will be

$$e(a, \Omega) = 3, \quad \text{for any } a \in A^o, \tag{8.8.6}$$

$$e(b, \Omega) = 2, \quad \text{for any } b \in B^o, \tag{8.8.7}$$

$$e(c^*, \Omega) = 2, \quad \text{for } c^* \in C^o. \tag{8.8.8}$$

Accordingly the strategic *net* distances are

$$e(a, a', \Omega) = 2 \times 3 - 3 - 3 + 1 = 1, \quad \text{for } a, a' \in A^o, \tag{8.8.9}$$

$$e(b, b', \Omega) = 2 \times 2 - 2 - 2 + 1 = 1, \quad \text{for } b, b' \in B^o, \tag{8.8.10}$$

$$e(a, b, \Omega) = 2 \times 3 - 3 - 2 + 1 = 2, \quad \text{for } a \in A^o \text{ and } b \in B^o, \tag{8.8.11}$$

$$e(a, c^*, \Omega) = 2 \times 3 - 3 - 2 + 1 = 2, \quad \text{for } a \in A^o \text{ and } c^* \in C^o, \tag{8.8.12}$$

$$e(b, c^*, \Omega) = 2 \times 2 - 2 - 2 + 1 = 1, \quad \text{for } b \in B^o \text{ and } c^* \in C^o. \tag{8.8.13}$$

8.9   The Solution

We are now in a position to define the solution for games $G_\varepsilon^*(\alpha)$ with $80.76 \leq \alpha < 87.70$. According to the solution-constructing procedure explained in section 5.5, we start off with defining our first candidate set as $\Omega_1 = \Omega$. Within this candidate set all other equilibria $a \neq a^*$ of class A^o will be dominated by their class leader a^*; all equilibria $b \neq b^*$ of class B^o and the one equilibrium c^* of class C^o will be dominated by b^*, the class leader of B^o. Thus, except for the two class leaders, a^* and b^*, all equilibria in Ω will be dominated by some equilibria at a strategic net distance of 1. In contrast, a^* will be dominated only by some equilibria in class B^o, whose strategic net distance from a^* is 2; and b^* will be dominated only by some equilibria in class A^o, whose strategic net distance from b^* is likewise 2.

Consequently a^* and b^* have a stability index of $2 - 1 = 1$ unit, whereas any other equilibrium in Ω_1 will have only a stability index of $1 - 1 = 0$ units. Therefore we must define our second candidate set as

$$\Omega_2 = \{a^*, b^*\}. \tag{8.9.1}$$

Within Ω_2, a^* and b^* will be trivially each other's closest neighbors so that

$$e(a^*, b^*, \Omega_2) = 1. \tag{8.9.2}$$

Consequently our third candidate set will be

$$\Omega_3 = \begin{cases} \{a^*\} & \text{if } a^* \text{ dominates } b^*, \\ \{b^*\}, & \text{if } b^* \text{ dominates } a^*. \end{cases} \tag{8.9.3}$$

By lemma 8.7.2, the former outcome will arise if $\alpha < 81.08$, and the latter outcome will arise if $\alpha > 81.08$. Hence in the former case a^* will be the solution, while in the latter case b^* will be the solution.

Finally, if $\alpha = 81.08$, the solution will have to be selected by our substitution procedure, which will in fact select b^* as the solution. In view of these results, and our earlier results summarized by the two corollaries to theorem 8.6.3, we can now state:

THEOREM 8.9.1   The solution of game $G_\varepsilon^*(\alpha)$ is the equilibrium point $a^* = a(x^*)$ when $0 < \alpha < 81.08$ and is the equilibrium point $b^* = b(50)$ when $81.08 \leq \alpha < 100$.

Intuitive Interpretation   For all values of α, equilibrium point a^* yields higher payoffs than b^* to players 2 and 3. When $\alpha < 60$, the same is true for player 1. But when $\alpha > 60$, player 1 would obtain a higher payoff from b^* than from a^*. But as α increases beyond $\alpha = 60$, at first the difference is not very great. Yet, when $\alpha = 81.08$, $H_1(a^*) = 12.30$, whereas $H_1(b^*) = 50/2 = 25$. According to our theory at this point player 1 will put that much pressure on player 2 that the latter will agree to accept equilibrium point b^* as the outcome. (Player 3's consent is not needed because b^* is a two-player agreement involving only players 1 and 2.)

Note on Computing the Solution   In this chapter we have tried to give the reader a reasonably full picture of the dominance relations among the various primitive equilibrium points, which of course required a lot of computation. But if all one wants to do is to find the solution, then very much less computation is required. All one has to establish is that:

1. a^* dominates all other equilibria of class A^o.

2. b^*, when it is an equilibrium point (which is the case when $\alpha \geq 50$) or

b^{**} (when b^* is not an equilibrium point) dominates all other equilibria of class B^o as well as the one equilibrium c^* of class C^o.

3. a^* dominates b^* (and b^{**}) when $\alpha < 81.08$, and b^* dominates a^* when $\alpha > 81.08$.

4. The strategic net distances are as stated in section 8.8.

These four pieces of information can be established by a very modest amount of computation.

9 Two-Person Bargaining Games with Incomplete Information on Both Sides

9.1 Introduction

We will now consider another family of games $G(\alpha)$ in which players I and II have to divide $100. But now *both* players will be assumed to be uncertain about each other's conflict payoffs in that both players' conflict payoffs will now be defined as

$$c_i = 0 \text{ or } \alpha, \quad \text{for } i = \text{I, II}, \quad \text{with } 0 < \alpha < 50, \qquad (9.1.1)$$

and with all four possible conflict-payoff combinations $(0, 0)$, $(0, \alpha)$, $(\alpha, 0)$, and (α, α) having the same probability $\frac{1}{4}$. These probabilities will be a matter of common knowledge to both players, but the actual value of each conflict payoff c_i will be known only to player i. Each player will be assumed to have a linear utility function for money and to derive x units of utility from $\$x$.

Since having a higher conflict payoff is an advantage in a bargaining game, each player will be said to be *strong* if $c_i = \alpha > 0$ and will be said to be *weak* if $c_i = 0$. When player I (or II) is weak, he will be called subplayer IA (or IIA), and when he is strong, he will be called subplayer IB (or IIB). The game will be played (at most) in two stages so as to permit each player potentially to make inferences about his opponent's strength by observing the latter's behavior at stage 1 and to use this information at stage 2.

At stage 1 each player i ($i = \text{I, II}$) may make a payoff demand x_i^1, or may say "PASS" to indicate that he will not make a payoff demand at that stage as yet. In this case we will say that the player has made a P-move. At stage 2 (if the game did not end at stage 1) each player i will have to make a payoff demand x_i^2. But neither player will be permitted to increase his payoff demand so that, if he made a payoff demand x_i^1 at stage 1, then his payoff demand x_i^2 at stage 2 will have to satisfy

$$x_i^2 \leq x_i^1. \qquad (9.1.2)$$

To discourage the players from needlessly prolonging the game, we will assume that each player i will have to pay a small *penalty* δ if:

1. He uses a P-move at stage 1.

2. Or his payoff demand x_i^1 at stage 1 turns out not to be equal to his final payoff demand (i.e., if $x_i^1 \neq x_i^2$).

Thus his final payoff u_i^* will become

$$u_i^* = u_i - \delta;$$ (9.1.3)

if otherwise, it would be u_i, where δ is a small positive number.[1] We will call u_i the *gross* payoff and u_i^* the *net* payoff of the player in question. (But where no confusion can arise, we will omit the * sign.)

Of course, if player I makes a payoff demand $x_I^k = x (k = 1, 2)$, this can be interpreted as a proposal to make the payoff vector $(u_1, u_{II}) = (x, 100 - x)$ the outcome of the game. By the same token, if player II makes a payoff demand $x_{II}^k = y$, this can be interpreted as a proposal to make the payoff vector $(u_1, u_{II}) = (100 - y, y)$ the outcome. We will assume that the game will end at stage 1 if both players make proposals at that stage and that it will end at stage 2 if at least one of the players uses a P-move at stage 1. Specifically, at either stage the game will end with an *agreement* if both players propose the *same* payoff vector, that is, if

$$x_I^k + x_{II}^k = 100,$$ (9.1.4)

yielding the payoffs

$$u_i = x_i^k, \quad \text{for } i = \text{I, II,}$$ (9.1.5)

subject to (9.1.3). In contrast, the game will end with a *conflict* if the two players propose *different* payoff vectors, that is, if

$$x_I^k + x_{II}^k \neq 100.$$ (9.1.6)

In this case the payoffs will be

$$u_i = c_i, \quad \text{for } i = \text{I, II,}$$ (9.1.7)

again subject to (9.1.3).

It will now be convenient to reinterpret the game as a four-person game by renaming subplayer IA as player 1, subplayer IB as player 2, subplayer IIA as player 3, and subplayer IIB as player 4. We will say that players 1 and 2 represent side I and players 3 and 4 represent side II. The Arabic numeral subscripts 1, 2, 3, and 4 will always refer to these new players. But for convenience we will go on using roman numeral subscripts I and II: they will refer to those players who happen to represent sides I and II, respectively, on any given occasion when the game is played.

As our game has potentially two stages, each player's pure strategies will be more complicated than were the players' pure strategies in the game we analyzed in earlier chapters. Any pure strategy of any player will now contain two parts. One will be the move he plans to use at stage 1. The other will be a mathematical function defining the payoff demand he will use at stage 2, depending on his own move and his opponent's move at stage 1.

Each player will have only *one* agent at stage 1. But he will have a *separate* agent for each information set he can be in at stage 2. This means that he will have one agent who will become active if the move combination (P, P) was used at stage 1 and a separate agent for all possible move combinations of the forms (P, x_2^1) and (x_1^1, P). There will be no stage 2 agents corresponding to move combinations of the form (x_1^1, x_2^1) because, if any such move combination is used at stage 1, the game will immediately end and will not proceed to stage 2.

We will require that any payoff demand x_i^k made by the *weak* players 1 and 3 should satisfy

$$x_i^k \in I = [0, 100], \quad \text{for } i = 1, 3 \quad \text{and } k = 1, 2. \tag{9.1.8}$$

However, any payoff demand x_i^k made by the *strong* players 2 and 4 should satisfy

$$x_i^k \in \bar{I} = [\alpha, 100], \quad \text{for } i = 2, 4 \quad \text{and } k = 1, 2, \tag{9.1.9}$$

because a strong player i cannot rationally demand less than his conflict payoff $c_i = \alpha$.

9.2   The Discrete Version $G^*(\alpha)$ of Game $G(\alpha)$ and the Uniformly Perturbed Games $G_\varepsilon^*(\alpha)$

Once more, to make our solution theory formally applicable, we will approximate any *continuous* game $G(\alpha)$ by a *discrete* game $G^*(\alpha)$, in which each player i, and each agent ij of any player i, will have only a finite number of pure strategies. We will first select a finite subset I^* of $I = [0, 100]$, subject to some requirements to be stated shortly. Then we will define the local-pure-strategy set of the stage 1 agent $i1$ of either *weak* player as

$$X_{i1}^1 = I^* \cup \{P\}, \quad \text{for } i = 1, 3. \tag{9.2.1}$$

We will define that of the stage 1 agent $i1$ of either *strong* player as

$$X_{i1}^1 = (I^* \cap \bar{I}) \cup \{P\}, \quad \text{for } i = 2, 4. \tag{9.2.2}$$

For a stage 2 agent ij who becomes active only when player i made *no* payoff demand at stage 1, his local-pure-strategy set will be defined as

$$X^2_{ij} = \text{I}^*, \quad \text{for } i = 1, 3, \tag{9.2.3}$$

or as

$$X^2_{ij} = \text{I}^* \cap \bar{\text{I}}, \quad \text{for } i = 2, 4. \tag{9.2.4}$$

Finally, for a stage 2 agent ij who becomes active only when player i *did* make a payoff demand x^1_i at stage 1, his local-pure-strategy set will be defined as

$$X^2_{ij} = \text{I}^* \cap [0, x^1_i], \quad \text{for } i = 1, 3, \tag{9.2.5}$$

or as

$$X^2_{ij} = \text{I}^* \cap [\alpha, x^1_i], \quad \text{for } i = 2, 4. \tag{9.2.6}$$

The choice of set I^* itself will be subject to the following requirements:

$$\text{I}^* \ni 0, \quad \alpha, \quad \text{and} \quad 100, \tag{9.2.7}$$

$$\text{I}^* \ni 50, \quad (50 + \tfrac{1}{2}\alpha), \quad \text{and} \quad (75 - \tfrac{1}{2}\alpha + \zeta), \tag{9.2.8}$$

where ζ is a small positive number. For any x with $x \in \text{I}^*$,

$$(100 - x) \in \text{I}^*. \tag{9.2.9}$$

The purpose of requirement (9.2.7) is to make available to the players those extreme payoff demands that are the boundary points of the intervals $\text{I} = [0, 100]$ and $\bar{\text{I}} = [\alpha, 100]$. Requirement (9.2.8) ensures that two specific strategies that will play important roles in our analysis are available. Finally, (9.2.9) ensures that, for any payoff demand $x^k_i = x$ available to one side, a complementary payoff demand $x^k_j = 100 - x$ is available to the other side (subject of course to the individual-rationality requirement $x^k_j \geq c_j$).

In accordance with our solution theory, we will now shift our analysis from the discrete game $G^*(\alpha)$ just defined to the corresponding *uniformly perturbed* games $G^*_\varepsilon(\alpha)$. The latter will be based on the assumption that whenever any agent ij of any given player i *intends* to use a specific local pure strategy ϕ_{ij}, he may end up using any one of his *unintended* local pure strategies $\phi'_{ij} \neq \phi_{ij}$ by mistake, the probability of his using any particular unintended strategy ϕ'_{ij} being equal to a small positive number ε, the same for all unintended local strategies ϕ'_{ij} of all agents ij of all players i. We will assume that this number ε is very small in relation to the penalty δ mentioned in (9.1.3), even though δ is already a very small positive number. For example, we may assume that

$$\varepsilon < \delta^2. \tag{9.2.10}$$

In view of this postulated mistake probability ε, the players' payoffs will often contain terms involving various powers of ε. In view of (9.1.3) they will often contain also terms involving δ. We will assume, however, that ε and δ are small enough to be neglected in most of our numerical computations and will usually omit all terms containing them. Of course we will always point out when these ε and/or δ terms make a qualitative difference by influencing best-reply relations and the nature of the equilibrium points existing in the game.

9.3 Maximin Payoff Demands and Maximin Payoffs

Suppose the game ends at stage k $(k = 1, 2)$, with player i's payoff demand being x_i^k. If he sets $x_i^k = c_i$, he will ensure that his payoff will be exactly $u_i = c_i$. But he can actually ensure slightly higher expected payoff than that. In particular:

LEMMA 9.3.1   By choosing a payoff demand

$$c_i < x_i^k \le 100 - \alpha, \tag{9.3.1}$$

he can ensure that his expected payoff will be at least

$$u'_i = (1 - \varepsilon)c_i + \varepsilon x_i^k, \tag{9.3.2}$$

whereas by choosing a payoff demand

$$100 - \alpha < x_i^k \le 100, \tag{9.3.3}$$

he can ensure that his expected payoff will be at least

$$u''_i = (1 - \tfrac{1}{2}\varepsilon)c_i + \tfrac{1}{2}\varepsilon x_i^k. \tag{9.3.4}$$

Proof If i's payoff demand is $x_i^k \le 100 - \alpha$, then he will have at least probability ε that x_i^k will be matched inadvertently by a complementary payoff demand $100 - x_i^k$ of his opponent (whether the latter is a weak player or a strong player), leading to an agreement, and will have at most probability $(1 - \varepsilon)$ that a noncomplementary payoff demand will be made by his opponent, leading to a *conflict*. In contrast, if i's payoff demand $x_i^k > 100 - \alpha$, then these probabilities will be $\frac{1}{2}\varepsilon$ and $(1 - \frac{1}{2}\varepsilon)$ because in this case only a *weak* opponent could make a complementary payoff demand. [For if $x_i^k > 100 - \alpha$, then $100 - x_i^k < \alpha$, which by (9.1.4) will prevent a strong opponent from making a complementary payoff demand $100 - x_i^k$.]

In view of (9.3.1) and (9.3.2), the quantity u_i' will reach its maximum value

$$\hat{u}_i' = c_i(1 - \varepsilon) + (100 - \alpha)\varepsilon = c_i + (100 - \alpha - c_i)\varepsilon \qquad (9.3.5)$$

when

$$x_i^k = 100 - \alpha. \qquad (9.3.6)$$

But, in view of (9.3.3) and (9.3.4), the quantity u_i'' will take its maximum value

$$\hat{u}_i'' = c_i(1 - \tfrac{1}{2}\varepsilon) + 50\varepsilon = c_i + (50 - \tfrac{1}{2}c_i)\varepsilon \qquad (9.3.7)$$

when

$$x_i^k = 100. \qquad (9.3.8)$$

We will write

$$\bar{u}_i = \max(\hat{u}_i', \hat{u}_i''). \qquad (9.3.9)$$

We will write also $x_i^k = \bar{x}_i$ to denote the payoff demand(s) by which player i can ensure to obtain at least $\bar{u}_i$ as his (expected) payoff.

Now if i is a *weak* player, then $c_i = 0$, and we always have

$$\bar{u}_i = \hat{u}_i' > \hat{u}_i''. \qquad (9.3.10)$$

But, if i is a *strong* player, then $c_i = \alpha$ so that

$$\bar{u}_i = \hat{u}_i' > \hat{u}_i'', \quad \text{if } \alpha < 33\tfrac{1}{3}, \qquad (9.3.11)$$

whereas

$$\bar{u}_i = \hat{u}_i'' = \hat{u}_i', \quad \text{if } \alpha > 33\tfrac{1}{3}, \qquad (9.3.12)$$

$$\bar{u}_i = \hat{u}_i' = \hat{u}_i'' = 33\tfrac{1}{3} + 33\tfrac{1}{3}\varepsilon, \quad \text{if } \alpha = 33\tfrac{1}{3}. \ \blacksquare \qquad (9.3.13)$$

We can now state:

LEMMA 9.3.2   If player i is a *weak* player, then he can always secure at least the payoff $\bar{u}_i = 100\varepsilon > c_i = 0$ by making the payoff demand $\bar{x}_i = 100 - \alpha$. But if i is a *strong* player, then $\bar{u}_i$ and $\bar{x}_i$ will depend on the parameter α. If $\alpha < 33\frac{1}{3}$, then $\bar{u}_i = \alpha + (100 - 2\alpha)\varepsilon > c_i = \alpha$, and i can ensure to obtain at least this payoff $\bar{u}_i$ by making the payoff demand $\bar{x}_i = 100 - \alpha$. If $\alpha > 33\frac{1}{3}$, then $\bar{u}_i = \alpha + (50 - \frac{1}{2}\alpha)\varepsilon > c_i = \alpha$, and i can ensure to obtain at least this payoff $\bar{u}_i$ by making the payoff demand $\bar{x}_i = 100$. Finally, if $\alpha = 33\frac{1}{3}$, then $\bar{u}_i = 33\frac{1}{3} + 33\frac{1}{3}\varepsilon > c_i = \alpha = 33\frac{1}{3}$, and i can ensure to obtain at least this payoff $\bar{u}_i$ by making either the payoff demand $\bar{x}_i = 100 - \alpha$ or the payoff demand $\bar{x}_i = 100$.

We will call $\bar{u}_i$ player i's *maximin payoff* and the payoff demand(s) $\bar{x}_i$, his *maximin demand(s)*. As we shall see, at some equilibrium points the equilibrium strategy of a particular player will involve making a maximin demand. Under our theory, in those cases where any player i has two alternative maximin demands $\bar{x}_i = 100 - \alpha$ and $\bar{x}_i = 100$, he will use either of them will probability $\frac{1}{2}$.

9.4   Equilibrium Points

To save space, we will restrict our discussion to the equilibria—in fact, to the primitive equilibria—of a perturbed game $G_\varepsilon(\alpha)$. These equilibria fall into four classes, A_o, A_2, A_4, and B.

Class A_o

This class consists of equilibrium points $a(x)$, characterized by one parameter x. Each $a(x)$ can be interpreted as an agreement by all four players to make the payoff vector $(u_1, u_{11}) = (x, 100 - x)$ the outcome of the game. (Of course only the two players actually present in the game can make the actual moves bringing about this desired outcome. But the other two players *would* do the same if they were present, as shown by their equilibrium strategies.) In particular, any equilibrium point $a(x)$ requires the players—that is, those two players who happen to be present in the game—to make payoff demands already at stage 1. These prescribed payoff demands are $x_1^1 = x_2^1 = x$ and $x_3^1 = x_4^1 = 100 - x$. We can write

$$y_1 = y_2 = x \quad \text{and} \quad y_3 = y_4 = 100 - x, \tag{9.4.1}$$

and we will call these quantities y_1 to y_4 the players *equilibrium demands*.

In view of (9.2.2) x must satisfy the inequality $\alpha \leq x \leq 100 - \alpha$. In fact by lemma 9.3.2, x must satisfy also the stronger inequality

$$\alpha < x < 100 - \alpha. \tag{9.4.2}$$

If neither side makes a mistake at stage 1, then the game will end already at that stage with an agreement, yielding the net payoffs

$$u_1 = u_2 = x \quad \text{and} \quad u_3 = u_4 = 100 - x. \tag{9.4.3}$$

We now have to consider the payoff demands the players have to make a stage 2 if the game did not end at stage 1 because one or both sides made a mistaken move at that stage. We will call these the players' *postmistake* payoff demands. To decide what these demands ought to be, we will make use of three principles:

Principle 1 No player can increase his payoff demand at stage 2. [This follows from assumption (9.1.2)]

Principle 2 Suppose that player i finds that at stage 1 his opponent, player j, made a move that can only be a mistaken move. Then at stage 2 player i cannot make a payoff demand smaller than his equilibrium demand. Otherwise, he would reward player i for having made a mistake.[2]

Principle 3 At stage 2 each player must act on the expectation that his opponent's payoff demand will conform to principle 2.
We must distinguish two cases:

Case 1 Both sides used P-moves at stage 1 by mistake. In this case, by principles 2 and 3, both sides must use their equilibrium payoff demands $x_i^2 = y_i$ and $x_j^2 = y_j$ at stage 2.

Case 2 Player i used a P-move by mistake while his opponent, player j, made a payoff demand x_j^1 at stage 1. (We need not distinguish between the two subcases where x_j^1 was equal or was not equal to the equilibrium demand y_j that player j was supposed to make.) In this case our three principles imply that player j at stage 2 must make the payoff demand

$$x_j^2 = \min(y_j, x_j^1), \tag{9.4.4}$$

whereas player i must make a complementary payoff demand $x_i^2 = 100 - x_j^2$, provided that the latter $> c_i$. (This qualification is necessary in view of lemma 9.3.2.) Thus

$$x_i^2 = 100 - \min(y_j, x_j^1) = z_j, \quad \text{if } z_j > c_i, \tag{9.4.5}$$

and

$$x_i^2 = \bar{x}_i, \quad \text{if } z_i \leq c_i, \tag{9.4.6}$$

where $\bar{x}_i$ is the quantity defined in lemma 9.3.2. (If $\alpha = 33\frac{1}{3}$, then *both* $\bar{x}_i = 100 - \alpha$ and $\bar{x}_i = 100$ will qualify as acceptable $\bar{x}_i$ values. As we have already indicated, in this case under our theory player i will use both of these payoff demands with the same probability $\frac{1}{2}$.)[3]

Classes A_2 and A_4

The next two classes of equilibria, A_2 and A_4, will consist of strategy combinations $a(x)$ similar to those belonging to class A_o, except that the parameter x characterizing any given $a(x)$ will now *fail* to satisfy condition (9.4.2). In particular, class A_2 will consist of equilibria $a(x)$, satisfying

$$0 < x \leq \alpha. \tag{9.4.7}$$

Any such equilibrium point $a(x)$ can be interpreted as an agreement among players 1, 3, and 4 to achieve the payoff vector $(u_1, u_{11}) = (x, 100 - x)$, with player 2 refusing to join this agreement because it would yield him a payoff $u_2 = u_1 = x$ lower than, or at best equal to, his conflict payoff $c_2 = \alpha$.

At such an equilibrium point $a(x)$, player 1 will make the payoff demand $x_1^1 = x$, whereas player 3 or 4 will make the payoff demand $x_3^1 = x_4^1 = 100 - x$ at stage 1. In contrast, player 2 will make the payoff demand $x_2^1 = \bar{x}_2$ defined by lemma 9.3.2. (Again, in the special case where $\alpha = 33\frac{1}{3}$, he will make both the payoff demands $\bar{x}_2 = 100 - \alpha$ and $\bar{x}_2 = 100$ with probability $\frac{1}{2}$.) Accordingly we now define the players' equilibrium demands as

$$\hat{y}_1 = x, \quad \hat{y}_2 = \bar{x}_2, \quad \hat{y}_3 = \hat{y}_4 = 100 - x. \tag{9.4.8}$$

If the players make no mistake at stage 1, then the game will end already at that stage. It will yield the expected payoffs:

$$u_1 = x,$$

$$u_2 = \bar{x}_2,$$

$$u_3 = \tfrac{1}{2}(100 - x), \tag{9.4.9}$$

$$u_4 = \tfrac{1}{2}(100 - x) + \tfrac{1}{2}\alpha.$$

The payoffs of players 1 and 2 are self-explanatory. Those of players 3 and 4 reflect the fact that with probability $\frac{1}{2}$ their opponent will be player 1, in which case they will obtain the payoff $(100 - x)$, but that with probability $\frac{1}{2}$ their opponent will be player 2, in which case they will obtain only their conflict payoffs $c_3 = 0$ or $c_4 = \alpha$. In case one or both sides made mistakes at stage 1, the game might proceed to stage 2. To determine the players' *postmistake payoff demands*, we will use the three principles we used before. We will again distinguish two cases.

Case 1:
Both sides used P-moves at stage 1 by mistake. In this case at stage 2 each player i ($i = 1, 2, 3, 4$) must simply use his equilibrium demand $x_i^2 = \hat{y}_i$, as defined by (9.4.8).

Case 2:
Player i used a P-move at stage 1 by mistake while his opponent, player j, made a payoff demand x_j^1 at stage 1. In this case at stage 2 player j must make the payoff demand

$$x_j^2 = \min(\hat{y}_j, x_j^1), \tag{9.4.10}$$

while player i must make the payoff demand

$$x_i^2 = \hat{y}_2 = \bar{x}_2, \quad \text{if } i = 2, \tag{9.4.11}$$

whereas, if $i \neq 2$, then he must make the payoff demand

$$x_i^2 = \begin{cases} 100 - \min(100 - x, x_j^1) = \hat{z}_1, & \text{if } i = 1, \\ 100 - \min(x, x_j^1) = \hat{z}_3 = \hat{z}_4, & \text{if } i = 3, 4, \end{cases} \tag{9.4.12}$$

as long as $\hat{z}_i > c_i$, and must make the payoff demand

$$x_i^2 = \bar{x}_i, \quad \text{if } \hat{z}_i \leq c_i, \tag{9.4.13}$$

where $\bar{x}_i$ is the quantity defined by lemma 9.3.2.

  Whereas equilibria $a(x)$ in class A_2 must satisfy (9.4.6), those in class A_4 must satisfy

$$100 - \alpha \leq x < 100. \tag{9.4.14}$$

Any equilibrium point $a(x)$ in class A_4 can be interpreted as an agreement among players 1, 2, and 3 to achieve the payoff vector $(u_1, u_{11}) = (x, 100 - x)$, with player 4 refusing to join this agreement because it would yield him a payoff $u_4 = u_{II} = 100 - x$ lower than, or at best equal to, his conflict payoff $c_4 = \alpha$. We will not discuss the equilibria in class A_4 in any detail because their properties are the same as those in class A_2, except that the roles of players 2 and 4, and those of the quantities x and $(100 - x)$, are interchanged.

For convenience, the union of classes A_o, A_2, and A_4 will be called class A. Within class A, the equilibria of class A_o will be called *pooling* equilibria because they prescribe the same equilibrium demands for the weak and the strong player on any given side. (Thus players 1 and 2 are assigned the same equilibrium demands, and the same is true for players 3 and 4.) In contrast, the equilibria in classes A_2 and A_4 will be called *semipooling* because equilibria in class A_2 prescribe the same equilibrium demands for players 3 and 4 but prescribe different ones for players 1 and 2, whereas equilibria in class A_4 do the converse.

We will now discuss equilibria in class B, which are *separating* equilibria that make the weak and strong players on any given side follow quite different strategies. In particular, any equilibrium point $b(y, v, w)$ in class B will depend on the three parameters y, v, and w, where y is the payoff demand of the strong player on side I (i.e., of player 2), v is the payoff demand of the weak player on side I against a weak opponent (i.e., the payoff demand of player 1 against player 3), and w is the payoff demand of the weak player on side I against a strong opponent (i.e., the payoff demand of player 1 against player 4).

At such an equilibrium point $b(y, v, w)$, the four players' strategies will be as follows: A weak player (i.e., 1 or 3) will make a P-move at stage 1. This will enable him to observe his opponent's move at that stage and to decide whether the latter is a weak or a strong player, before committing himself to a specific payoff demand at stage 2. In contrast, each strong player (i.e., player 2 or 4) will announce his final payoff demand already at stage 1 and will repeat the same payoff demand at stage 2 (unless the game ended at stage 1). In particular, player 2's payoff demand will be $x_2^1 = x_2^2 = y$, whereas player 4's payoff demand will be $x_4^1 = x_4^2 = 100 - w$. (Thus it will be complementary to the payoff demand w of his opponent if the latter is a weak player, i.e., player 1.) We will assume that

$$x_2^1 + x_4^1 = y + (100 - w) > 100, \tag{9.4.15}$$

so that if both sides are represented by strong players (players 2 and 4), then the game will end with a conflict already at stage 1, yielding the payoffs

$u_2 = u_4 = \alpha$ to these two players. Note that after simplification, inequality (9.4.15) reduces to

$$y > w. \tag{9.4.16}$$

However, if the game did not end at stage 1, then by stage 2 both players will *know* whether the other side is represented by a weak or by a strong player. In particular, if at stage 1 both sides made P-moves, then they can infer that both of them are weak players (players 1 and 3). In this case at stage 2 player 1 will make the payoff demand $x_1^2 = v$, whereas player 3 will make the complementary payoff demand $x_3^2 = 100 - v$, and the game will end with an agreement, yielding the gross payoffs $u_1 = w$ and $u_3 = 100 - w$ (which will correspond to the net payoffs $u_1 = w - \delta$ and $u_3 = 100 - w - \delta$).

In contrast, if side I made the payoff demand $x_I^1 = y$ at stage 1 while side II made a P-move, then the former must be the strong player on side I (player 2), whereas the latter must be the weak player on side II (player 3). In this case player 3 will expect player 2 to make the same payoff demand $x_2^2 = x_2^1 = y$ also at stage 2 and will himself make the complementary payoff demand $x_3^2 = 100 - y$. The result will be an agreement, with the gross payoffs $u_2 = y$ and $u_3 = 100 - y$ (corresponding to the net payoffs $u_2 = y$ and $u_3 = 100 - y - \delta$).

Finally, if side II made the payoff demand $x_{II}^1 = 100 - w$ at stage 1 while side I made a P-move, then the latter must be the weak player on side I (player 1), whereas the former must be the strong player on side II (player 4). In this case player 1 will expect player 4 to make the same payoff demand $x_4^2 = x_4^1 = 100 - w$ also at stage 2 and will himself make the complementary payoff demand $x_1^2 = w$. The result will be an agreement, with the gross payoffs $u_1 = w$ and $u_4 = 100 - w$ (corresponding to the net payoffs $u_1 = w - \delta$ and $u_4 = 100 - w$).

Altogether, equilibrium point $b(y, v, w)$ will yield the four players the expected net payoffs

$$\bar{u}_1 = \tfrac{1}{2}(v + w) - \delta,$$

$$\bar{u}_2 = \tfrac{1}{2}(y + \alpha),$$

$$\bar{u}_3 = 100 - \tfrac{1}{2}(y + v) - \delta, \tag{9.4.17}$$

$$\bar{u}_4 = \tfrac{1}{2}(100 - w + \alpha).$$

Next we have to discuss the payoff demands the players must make at stage

2 if at stage 1 one of them made a move that must have resulted from a mistake. Such a move would be a payoff demand x_I^1 by side I with $x_I^1 \neq y$, or a payoff demand x_{II}^1 by side II with $x_{II}^1 \neq 100 - w$. (If both players make such mistaken moves, then the game will end at stage 1 so that no payoff demand will be made at stage 2.)

Case 1: $x_I^1 \neq y$, with a P-Move by Side II
By principle 3, side I cannot ask for a payoff higher than v—the payoff it would ask for if it were the weak player on side I (if it were player 1). In view of principle 2, side I's actual payoff demand at stage 2 will have to be

$$x_I^2 = \min(v, x_I^1), \tag{9.4.18}$$

whereas side II's payoff demand will have to be

$$x_{II}^2 = 100 - \min(y, x_I^1) = \bar{z}_{II}, \quad \text{if } \bar{z}_{II} > c_{II}, \tag{9.4.19}$$

and

$$x_{II}^2 = \bar{x}_{II}, \quad \text{if } \bar{z}_{II} \leq c_{II}. \tag{9.4.20}$$

Here c_{II} and $\bar{x}_{II}$ stand for c_3 and $\bar{x}_3$, or for c_4 and $\bar{x}_4$, according as side II is represented by player 3 or player 4.

Case 2: $x_{II}^1 \neq 100 - v$, with a P-Move by Side I.
By the same reasoning as in case 1, we must now have

$$x_{II}^2 = \min(100 - v, x_{II}^1), \tag{9.4.21}$$

$$x_I^2 = 100 - \min(100 - v, x_{II}^1) = z_I, \quad \text{if } \bar{z}_I > c_I, \tag{9.4.22}$$

but

$$x_I^2 = \bar{x}_I, \quad \text{if } \bar{z}_I \leq c_I. \tag{9.4.23}$$

But there are a few additional requirements that the parameters y, v, and w must satisfy for $b = b(y, v, w)$ to be an equilibrium point. One requirement is that the payoff demand x_i^1 or x_i^2 that b prescribes for any player i must be at least as large as his conflict payoff c_i. In view of lemma 9.3.2 this payoff demand must be strictly larger than c_i. We must have $y > \alpha$ as well as $(100 - y) > 0$, which can be written as

$$\alpha < y < 100. \tag{9.4.24}$$

Likewise, we must have $(100 - w) > \alpha$ as well as $w > 0$, which can be written as

$$0 < w < 100 - \alpha. \tag{9.4.25}$$

Finally, we must have $v > 0$ as well as $(100 - v) > 0$, which can be written as

$$0 < v < 100. \tag{9.4.26}$$

Furthermore, for b to be an equilibrium point, it is necessary that the players on neither side should have any incentive to shift from their own equilibrium strategies to the *other* player's equilibrium strategy on their own side. Thus player 1 should have no incentive to shift to player 2's equilibrium strategy, and conversely. Neither should players 3 and 4 have incentives to "steal" each other's equilibrium strategies. This yields a number of inequalities that the parameters y, v, and w must satisfy. If b is to be a strong equilibrium point, then these inequalities must be satisfied with a strong inequality sign.

Now, if player 1 uses his equilibrium strategy, he will obtain the expected payoff $\bar{u}_1 = \frac{1}{2}(v + w) - \delta$, whereas if he uses player 2's strategy, he will obtain the expected payoff $\bar{u}'_1 = \frac{1}{2}(y + c_1) = \frac{1}{2}y$. We must have $\bar{u}_1 > \bar{u}'_1$, which implies that we must have

$$y - w < v. \tag{9.4.27}$$

By the same token, if player 3 uses his equilibrium strategy, he will obtain $\bar{u}_3 = 100 - \frac{1}{2}(y + v) - \delta$, whereas if he uses player 4's strategy, he will obtain $\bar{u}'_3 = \frac{1}{2}[(100 - w) + c_3] = \frac{1}{2}(100 - w)$. We must have $\bar{u}_3 > \bar{u}'_3$, which implies that

$$y - w < 100 - v. \tag{9.4.28}$$

On the other hand, if player 2 uses his equilibrium strategy, he will obtain $\bar{u}_2 = \frac{1}{2}(y + \alpha)$, whereas if he uses player 1's strategy, he will obtain $\bar{u}'_2 = \frac{1}{2}(v + w) - \delta$. We must have $\bar{u}_2 > \bar{u}'_2$. If δ is small enough, then this will imply that

$$v - \alpha < y - w. \tag{9.4.29}$$

Likewise, if player 4 uses his equilibrium strategy, he will obtain $\bar{u}_4 = \frac{1}{2}(100 - w + \alpha)$, whereas if he uses player 3's strategy, he will obtain $\bar{u}'_4 = 100 - \frac{1}{2}(y + v) - \delta$. We must have $\bar{u}_4 > \bar{u}'_4$. If δ is small enough then this will imply

$$100 - v - \alpha < y - w. \tag{9.4.30}$$

Requirements (9.3.22) through (9.3.25) are jointly equivalent to the one requirement that

$$\max(v, 100 - v) - \alpha < y - w < \min(v, 100 - v). \tag{9.4.31}$$

To sum up our discussion, if a strategy combination $b(y, v, w)$ is to be an equilibrium point, the parameters y, v, and w must satisfy (9.4.16), (9.4.24) through (9.4.26), and (9.4.31).

As is easy to verify, for all α values with $\alpha \neq 33\frac{1}{3}$, all equilibrium points in classes A and B will be strong and therefore will be primitive equilibria. In the special case where $\alpha = 33\frac{1}{3}$, some of these equilibria will lose this strongness property because, by lemma 9.3.2, players 2 and 4 will have a choice between two alternative maximin payoff demands: $\bar{x}_i = 100 - \alpha$ and $\bar{x}_i = 100 (i = 3, 4)$. But even in this case in equilibria in classes A and B will be primitive equilibria. Moreover, for all values of α, the equilibria in these two classes will be the only primitive equilibria of any perturbed game $G_\varepsilon^*(\alpha)$.

9.5   Dominance Relations in Class A

To save space, we will state the following lemma without proof:

LEMMA 9.5.1   Equilibrium point $a_2 = a(\alpha)$ risk-dominates all other equilibria in class A_2, equilibrium point $a_4 = a(100 - \alpha)$ risk-dominates all other equilibria in class A_4, whereas equilibrium point $a^* = a(50)$ risk-dominates all other equilibria in the entire class $A = A_o \cup A_2 \cup A_4$.

LEMMA 9.5.2   The last lemma remains true even if we replace the term "risk-dominates" by the term "dominates."

Proof   This lemma follows from the fact that one equilibrium point $a' = a(x')$ cannot payoff-dominate another equilibrium point $a'' = a(x'')$ of class A. For denote player i's equilibrium payoffs as $u_i' = H_i(a')$ and as $u_i'' = H_i(a'')$, respectively. Then $u_1' + u_3' = u_1'' + u_3'' = 100$, which means that if $u_1' > u_1''$, then $u_3' < u_3''$, and conversely. Hence it is impossible that $u_i' > u_i''$ (or $u_i'' > u_i'$) for all four players i. ∎

9.6   Dominance Relations in Class B

We will pay special attention to two equilibrium points in class B. One is $b^* = b(y^*, v^*, w^*)$, with $y^* = 50 + \frac{1}{2}\alpha$, $v^* = 50$, and $w^* = 50 - \frac{1}{2}\alpha$. The other is $b^{**} = b(y^{**}, v^{**}, w^{**})$, with $y^{**} = 75 - \frac{1}{2}\alpha + \xi$, $v^{**} = v^* = 50$, and $w^{**} = 25 + \frac{1}{2}\alpha - \xi$, where ξ is the small positive number occurring in (9.2.8). We will assume that $y^{**} = 75 - \frac{1}{2}\alpha + \xi$ is the smallest number larger than $(75 - \frac{1}{2}\alpha)$ within set I* (see section 9.2).

In view of (9.4.17), b^* will yield the expected payoffs

$$u_1^* = u_3^* = 50 - \frac{1}{4}\alpha - \delta \quad \text{and} \quad u_2^* = u_4^* = 25 + \frac{3}{4}\alpha, \tag{9.6.1}$$

whereas b^{**} will yield the expected payoffs

$$\begin{aligned} u_1^{**} &= u_3^{**} = 37\frac{1}{2} + \frac{1}{4}\alpha - \frac{1}{2}\xi - \delta, \\ u_2^{**} &= u_4^{**} = 37\frac{1}{2} + \frac{1}{4}\alpha + \frac{1}{2}\xi. \end{aligned} \tag{9.6.2}$$

LEMMA 9.6.1   In all games $G_\varepsilon^*(\alpha)$ with $\alpha > 25$, b^* is an equilibrium point. But in games $G_\varepsilon^*(\alpha)$ with $\alpha \leq 25$ this is not the case.

Proof When $\alpha > 25$, then b^* satisfies (9.4.31) and the other requirements defining class B. But if $\alpha \leq 25$, then b^* fails to satisfy (9.4.31).
By similar reasoning we can establish the following lemma:

LEMMA 9.6.2   For all admissible values of α, b^{**} is an equilibrium point.

We now introduce the notation

$$b^o = b(y^o, v^o, w^o) = \begin{cases} b^*, & \text{if } \alpha > 25, \\ b^{**}, & \text{if } \alpha \leq 25. \end{cases} \tag{9.6.3}$$

LEMMA 9.6.3   For $\alpha > 25$, within class B equilibrium point b^* risk-dominates all other equilibrium points $b = b(y, v, w)$ differing from b^* in *one* parameter only, and b^* is the *only* equilibrium point with this property.

Preliminary Discussion   We must consider three cases.

Case 1: $y \neq y^*$ but $v = v^*$ and $w = w^*$
In this case a choice between b^* and b will amount to a two-person bargaining game, Γ_{23}, between players 2 and 3 at stage 2, played in order to decide whether the two of them should receive the payoff vector $u_{23}^* = (u_2^*, u_3^*) = (y^*, 100 - y^*) = (50 + \frac{1}{2}\alpha, 50 - \frac{1}{2}\alpha)$ or the payoff vector $u_{23} = (u_2, u_3) = (y, 100 - y) \neq u_{23}^*$. Even though Γ_{23} is part of the four-person game $G_\varepsilon^*(\alpha)$, which is a game with incomplete information, Γ_{23} itself is a game with complete information because by stage 2 players 2 and 3 will know each other's conflict payoffs, $u_2 = \alpha$ and $u_3 = 0$.

If Γ_{23} were a self-contained game, then both the Nash solution and our own solution theory would define the predicted outcome of Γ_{23} as the payoff vector u_{23}^*. The Nash solution would do so because the Nash-product

$$\pi = (u_2 - c_2)(u_3 - c_3) = (u_2 - \alpha)u_3 \qquad (9.6.4)$$

is maximized, subject to the conditions

$$u_2 + u_3 = 100 \qquad (9.6.5)$$

as well as

$$u_2 \geq c_2 = \alpha \quad \text{and} \quad u_3 \geq c_3 = 0, \qquad (9.6.6)$$

if we set

$$u_2 = u_2^* = 50 + \tfrac{1}{2}\alpha \quad \text{and} \quad u_3 = u_3^* = 50 - \tfrac{1}{2}\alpha. \qquad (9.6.7)$$

Our own solution theory would likewise select u_{23}^* as the outcome because the equilibrium point yielding u_{23}^* would risk-dominate this and any other equilibrium point (see our discussion of unanimity games in section 5.6). (Γ_{23} is actually not a self-contained game, but our theory still defines u_{23}^* as the outcome of Γ_{23}.)

Case 2: $w \neq w^*$ but $y = y^*$ and $v = v^*$
In this case a choice between b^* and b will amount to a two-person bargaining game, Γ_{14}, between players 1 and 4 at stage 2, played in order to decide whether the two of them should receive the payoff vector $u_{14}^* = (u_1^*, u_4^*) = (w^*, 100 - w^*) = (50 - \tfrac{1}{2}\alpha, 50 + \tfrac{1}{2}\alpha)$ or the payoff vector $u_{14} = (u_1, u_4) = (w, 100 - w) \neq u_{14}^*$. Again, even though Γ_{14} is part of the four-person incomplete-information game $G_\varepsilon^*(\alpha)$, Γ_{14} itself is a game with complete information because by stage 2 players 1 and 4 will know each other's conflict payoffs, $c_1 = c_4 = 0$.

For similar reasons to those adduced in discussing case 1, both the Nash solution and our own theory will define the predicted outcome of Γ_{14} as the payoff vector u_{14}^*.

Case 3: $v \neq v^*$ but $y = y^*$ and $w = w^*$
In this case a choice between b^* and b will amount to a two-person bargaining game, Γ_{13}, between players 1 and 3 at stage 2, played in order to decide whether the two of them should receive the payoff vector $u_{13}^* =$

$(u_1, u_3) = (v^*, 100 - v^*) = (50, 50)$ or the payoff vector $u_{13} = (u_1, u_3) = (v, 100 - v) \neq u_{13}^*$. Once more, Γ_{13} in itself will be a game with complete information because by stage 2 players 1 and 3 will know each other's conflict payoffs, $c_1 = c_3 = 0$.

For similar reasons to those adduced in the other two cases, both the Nash solution and our own theory define the predicted outcome of Γ_{13} as the payoff vector u_{13}^*.

Proof of Lemma 9.6.3 To convert the preceding heuristic argument into a rigorous proof, all we have to show is that the risk-dominance relations in the relevant game Γ_{ij} (with $ij = 23$ or 14 or 13) will be the same when Γ_{ij} is part of the larger game $G_\varepsilon^*(\alpha)$, as they would be if Γ_{ij} were a self-contained independent game.

Under our theory, the risk-dominance relation (if any) between the two equilibrium points b^* and b will not be defined within the game under consideration—that is, within the game $G_\varepsilon^*(\alpha)$—but rather within a *restricted game*, in which the only active players and active agents are those players i and those agents ij of players i who use *different strategies* at b^* and at b (see section 5.3). As a result, even though $G_\varepsilon^*(\alpha)$ is a four-person game, the restricted game derived from $G_\varepsilon^*(\alpha)$ will always be a two-person game— between players 2 and 3 in case 1, between players 1 and 4 in case 2, and between players 1 and 3 in case 3. Moreover, as is easy to verify, this restricted game will have exactly the same *mathematical structure*, and therefore also exactly the same *risk-dominance* relations, as the relevant game Γ_{ij} would have if it were a self-contained two-person game. ∎

LEMMA 9.6.4 For $\alpha \le 25$, within class B the equilibrium point b^{**} risk-dominates all other equilibrium points $b = b(y, v, w)$ differing from b^{**} in one parameter only, and b^{**} will be the only equilibrium point with this property.

Proof By lemma 9.6.1, when $\alpha \le 25$, b^* is not an equilibrium point [because it would violate requirement (9.4.31)]. Our task is to show that in this case the role of b^* will be taken over by b^{**}. We again must distinguish three cases:

Case 1: $y \neq y^{**}$, but $v = v^{**}$ and $w = w^{**}$.

Case 2: $w \neq w^{**}$, but $y = y^{**}$ and $v = v^{**}$.

Case 3: $v \neq v^{**}$, but $y = y^{**}$ and $w = w^{**}$.

Again, case 1 will give rise to a two-person bargaining game, Γ_{23}, between players 2 and 3 at stage 2, when they already know each other's conflict payoffs, $c_2 = \alpha$ and $c_3 = 0$. Likewise case 2 will give rise to game Γ_{14} between players 1 and 4, with $c_1 = 0$ and $c_4 = \alpha$. Finally, case 3 will give rise to game Γ_{13} between players 1 and 3, with $c_1 = c_3 = 0$.

We have to show that in each of these games Γ_{ij}, equilibrium point b^{**} risk-dominates any equilibrium point b of the required form. To show this, we can use much the same approach as we used in the proof of the last lemma. Actually, in case 3 and in the corresponding game Γ_{13} we can use exactly the same approach because the v-parameter for b^{**} and for b^* is the same, that is, $v^{**} = v^* = 50$.

In contrast, $y^{**} = 75 - \frac{1}{2}\alpha + \xi > y^* = 50 + \frac{1}{2}\alpha$, whereas $w^{**} = 25 + \frac{1}{2}\alpha - \xi < 50 - \frac{1}{2}\alpha$. Hence in cases 1 and 2 we must use a modified version of the approach used in the proof of the last lemma. For instance, in game Γ_{23}, associated with case 1, the payoff vector $u_{23}^{**} = (u_2^*, u_3^*) = (y^*, 100 - y^*) = (50 + \frac{1}{2}\alpha, 50 - \frac{1}{2}\alpha)$ is no longer available to the players because if $\alpha \leq 25$, this payoff vector u_{23}^* would violate requirement (9.4.31). But, among the payoff vectors satisfying this requirement, both the Nash solution and our own theory predict the payoff vector $u_{23}^{**} = (u_2^{**}, u_3^{**}) = (y^{**}, 100 - y^{**}) = (75 - \frac{1}{2}\alpha + \xi, 25 + \frac{1}{2}\alpha - \xi)$ as the outcome of game Γ_{23}. [Note that among the payoff vectors satisfying (9.4.31), u_{23}^{**} is numerically closest to the unavailable payoff vector u_{23}^*.] Accordingly, our theory assigns risk dominance to equilibrium point b^{**}, associated with this payoff vector u_{23}^{**}, over any equilibrium point b differing from b^{**} only in its y-parameter.

Likewise, in game Γ_{14} associated with case 2, the payoff vector $u_{14}^* = (w^*, 100 - w^*) = (50 - \frac{1}{2}\alpha, 50 + \frac{1}{2}\alpha)$ is no longer available because it would violate (9.4.31). As a result both the Nash solution and our own theory now predict the payoff vector $u_{14}^{**} = (w^{**}, 100 - w^{**}) = (25 + \frac{1}{2}\alpha - \xi, 75 - \frac{1}{2}\alpha + \xi)$ as the outcome of game Γ_{14}. Accordingly, our theory assigns risk dominance to equilibrium point b^{**}, associated with this payoff vector u_{14}^{**}, over any equilibrium point b differing from b^{**} only in its w-parameter.

To sum up, in all three cases, b^{**} will have risk dominance over any equilibrium point b differing from b^{**} in one parameter only. ∎

LEMMA 9.6.5   Suppose that $b' = b(y', v', w')$ and $b'' = b(y'', v'', w'')$ are two equilibria of class B. Then neither can payoff-dominate the other.

Proof   Suppose that b' payoff-dominates b''. We will denote player i's payoff $(i = 1, 2, 3, 4)$ from b' and from b'' as u_i' and as u_i'', respectively. By payoff dominance we must have $u_i' > u_i''$ for all i. By (9.4.17) this implies that

$$v' + w' > v'' + w'' \quad \text{and} \quad y' > y'', \tag{9.6.8}$$

but also that

$$y' + v' < y'' + v'' \quad \text{and} \quad w' < w''. \tag{9.6.9}$$

Yet (9.6.8) implies that $y' + v' + w' > y'' + v'' + w''$, whereas (9.6.9) implies that $y' + v' + w' < y'' + v'' + w''$, which is a contradiction. ∎

In what follows, we will call $a^* = a(50)$ and $b^o = b^*$ or b^{**} (according as $\alpha > 25$ or ≤ 25) the *class leaders* of classes A and B, respectively. We will also call $a_2 = a(\alpha)$ and $a_4 = a(100 - \alpha)$ *subclass leaders* because they are class leaders of classes A_2 and A_4, respectively, which are subclasses of class A. We can now state:

LEMMA 9.6.6   Regardless of the value of the parameter α, within class B equilibrium point b^o risk-dominates any equilibrium point differing from b^o in one parameter only, and b^o is the only equilibrium point with this property.

The lemma follows from lemmas 9.6.3 and 9.6.4.

LEMMA 9.6.7   Lemma 9.6.6 remains true even if we replace the term "risk-dominates" by the term "dominates."

This lemma follows from lemma 9.6.5.

9.7   Dominance Relations between the Two Class Leaders a^* and b^o

LEMMA 9.7.1   Equilibrium point $b^o = b^*$ has *conspicuous* risk dominance over equilibrium point a^* when $\alpha > 29.71$.

Proof   To prove the lemma, we first have to compute the *bicentric priors* p_1, p_2, p_3, and p_4 for the four players. In the present case we cannot rely on the formula in note 3 to chapter 7 (as we often did before) but rather must go back to the basic definitions stated in section 5.3.

We will use the following notations: player i's strategy at equilibrium point $a*$ will be called a_i^*, and his strategy at equilibrium point $b*$ will be called b_i^*. Moreover we will write

$$N = \{1, 2, 3, 4\}, \quad W = \{1, 3\}, \quad \text{and} \quad S = \{2, 4\}. \tag{9.7.1}$$

Thus N will be the set of all four players, W the set of the two weak players (players 1 and 3), whereas S will be the set of the two strong players (players 2 and 4). For each player i, the probability that his prior p_i assigns to his $a*$-strategy a_i^* will be called p_i', and the probability that p_i assigns to his $b*$-strategy b_i^* will be called p_i''.

We will compute p_i first for a weak player i with $i \in W$. Player i's opponent will be called player j. Under our assumptions i will expect j to use strategy a_j^* with probability z and strategy b_j^* with probability $1 - z$. Moreover i will expect that $j \in W$ with probability $\frac{1}{2}$ and that $j \in S$ also with probability $\frac{1}{2}$. But $a*$ prescribes the same strategy a_j^* for a weak and for a strong player, whereas $b*$ prescribes different strategies b_j^* for them. Consequently we have to consider only three cases:

Case 1:
j uses strategy a_j^*. This case will occur with probability z.

Case 2:
j uses strategy b_j^* and $j \in W$. This case will occur with probability $\frac{1}{2}(1 - z)$.

Case 3:
j uses strategy b_j^* and $j \in S$. This case will occur also with probability $\frac{1}{2}(1 - z)$.

If a weak player i uses strategy a_i^*, he will obtain the payoff

$$H_i(a_i^* a_j^* | i \in W, j \in N) = 50, \quad \text{with probability } z, \tag{9.7.2}$$

while obtaining the payoff

$$H_i(a_i^* b_j^* | i \in W, j \in W) = 50, \quad \text{with probability } \tfrac{1}{2}(1 - z), \tag{9.7.3}$$

and the payoff

$$H_i(a_i^* b_j^* | i \in W, j \in S) = 0, \quad \text{also with probability } \tfrac{1}{2}(1 - z). \tag{9.7.4}$$

Consequently his expected payoff will be

$$\bar{H}_i(a_i^* | i \in W) = 50z + 50 \cdot \tfrac{1}{2}(1 - z) + 0 = 25 + 25z. \tag{9.7.5}$$

In contrast, if a weak player i uses strategy b_i^*, he will obtain the payoff

$$H_i(b_i^* a_j^* | i \in W, j \in N) = 50, \quad \text{with probability } z, \tag{9.7.6}$$

while obtaining the payoff

$$H_i(b_i^* b_j^* | i, j \in W) = 50, \quad \text{with probability } \tfrac{1}{2}(1-z), \tag{9.7.7}$$

and the payoff

$$H_i(b_i^* b_j^* | i \in W, j \in S) = 50 - \tfrac{1}{2}\alpha, \quad \text{also with probability } \tfrac{1}{2}(1-z). \tag{9.7.8}$$

Consequently his expected payoff will be

$$\begin{aligned}
\bar{H}_i(b_i^* | i \in W) &= 50z + 25(1-z) + (25 - \tfrac{1}{4}\alpha)(1-z) \\
&= 50 - \tfrac{1}{4}\alpha + \tfrac{1}{4}\alpha z.
\end{aligned} \tag{9.7.9}$$

Clearly

$$\bar{H}_i(b_i^* | i \in W) \geq \bar{H}_i(a_i^* | i \in W), \quad \text{for all } z \in [0, 1], \tag{9.7.10}$$

and the $\geq$ sign can be replaced by the $=$ sign only at the one point $z = 1$. Hence, for a weak player i, we must associate the Lebesgue measure $\mu = 1$ with strategy b_i^* and the Lebesgue measure $\mu = 0$ with strategy a_i^*. Thus, for a weak player i, we obtain the bicentric prior

$$p_i = (p_i', p_i''), \tag{9.7.11}$$

with

$$p_i' = 0 \quad \text{and} \quad p_i'' = 1, \quad \text{for } i \in W. \tag{9.7.12}$$

Our next task is to compute the bicentric prior p_i for a strong player i. If a strong player i uses strategy a_i^*, he will obtain the payoff

$$H_i(a_i^* a_j^* | i \in S, j \in N) = 50, \quad \text{with probability } z, \tag{9.7.13}$$

while obtaining the payoff

$$H_i(a_i^* b_j^* | i \in S, j \in W) = 50, \quad \text{with probability } \tfrac{1}{2}(1-z), \tag{9.7.14}$$

and the payoff

$$H_i(a_i^* b_j^* | i, j \in S) = \alpha, \quad \text{also with probability } \tfrac{1}{2}(1-z). \tag{9.7.15}$$

Consequently, if a strong player i uses strategy a_i^*, his expected payoff will be

$$\bar{H}_i(a_i^*|i \in S) = 50z + 25(1 - z) + \tfrac{1}{2}\alpha(1 - z)$$
$$= 25 + \tfrac{1}{2}\alpha + 25z - \tfrac{1}{2}\alpha z. \tag{9.7.16}$$

In contrast, if a strong player i uses strategy b_i^*, he will obtain the payoff

$$H_i(b_i^* a_j^*|i \in S, j \in N) = \alpha, \quad \text{with probability } z, \tag{9.7.17}$$

while obtaining the payoff

$$H_i(b_i^* b_j^*|i \in S, j \in W) = 50 + \tfrac{1}{2}\alpha, \quad \text{with probability } \tfrac{1}{2}(1 - z), \tag{9.7.18}$$

and the payoff

$$H_i(b_i^* b_j^*|i, j \in S) = \alpha, \quad \text{also with probability } \tfrac{1}{2}(1 - z). \tag{9.7.19}$$

Consequently his expected payoff will be

$$\bar{H}_i(b_i^*|i \in S) = \alpha z + (25 + \tfrac{1}{4}\alpha)(1 - z) + \tfrac{1}{2}\alpha(1 - z)$$
$$= 25 + \tfrac{3}{4}\alpha - 25z + \tfrac{1}{4}\alpha z. \tag{9.7.20}$$

Now simple computation shows that

$$\bar{H}_i(a_i^*|i \in S) \geq \bar{H}_i(b_i^*|i \in S), \quad \text{if } z \in [z^*, 1], \tag{9.7.21}$$

but

$$\bar{H}_i(b_i^*|i \in S) \geq \bar{H}_i(a_i^*|i \in S) \quad \text{if } z \in [0, z^*], \tag{9.7.22}$$

where

$$z^* = \frac{\alpha}{200 - 3\alpha}. \tag{9.7.23}$$

For a strong player i we must associate the Lebesgue measure $\mu = 1 - z^* = (200 - 4\alpha)/(200 - 3\alpha)$ with strategy a_i^*, and the Lebesgue measure $\mu = z^* - 0 = \alpha/(200 - 3\alpha)$ with strategy b_i^*. Thus, for a strong player i, we obtain the bicentric prior

$$p_i = (p_i', p_i''), \tag{9.7.24}$$

with

$$p_i' = \frac{200 - 4\alpha}{200 - 3\alpha} \quad \text{and} \quad p_i'' = \frac{\alpha}{200 - 3\alpha}, \quad \text{for } i \in S. \tag{9.7.25}$$

In accordance with our usual notation, we will write $p = (p_1, p_2, p_3, p_4)$

and use the symbol p_{-i} to denote the vector we obtain from p if we omit its ith component p_i. Thus p will denote the *complete* bicentric prior combination, whereas p_{-i} will denote the *i-incomplete* bicentric prior combination. Our next task now is to compute each player i's best reply to the i-incomplete bicentric prior combination p_{-i}.

When player i expects his opponent, player j, to act in accordance with p_{-i}, he must consider four possible cases:

Case 1:
$j \in W$ and j uses strategy a_j^*. By (9.7.12) this case will occur with probability $\frac{1}{2} \cdot 0 = 0$.

Case 2:
$j \in W$ and j uses strategy b_j^*. By (9.7.12) this case will occur with probability $\frac{1}{2} \cdot 1 = \frac{1}{2}$.

Case 3:
$j \in S$ and j uses strategy a_j^*. By (9.7.25) this case will occur with probability $\frac{1}{2}(200 - 4\alpha)/(200 - 3\alpha) = (200 - 4\alpha)/(400 - 6\alpha)$.

Case 4:
$j \in S$ and j uses strategy b_j^*. By (9.7.25) this case will occur with probability $\frac{1}{2}\alpha/(200 - 3\alpha) = \alpha/(400 - 6\alpha)$.

Accordingly, if a weak player i uses strategy a_i^*, while his opponent, player j, acts in accordance with p_{-i}, then i's expected payoff will be

$$H_i(a_i^* p_{-i}|i \in W) = \frac{1}{2} \cdot 50 + \frac{200 - 4\alpha}{400 - 6\alpha} \cdot 50 + \frac{\alpha}{400 - 6\alpha} \cdot 0. \qquad (9.7.26)$$

In contrast, if he uses strategy b_i^*, then his expected payoff will be

$$H_i(b_i^* p_{-i}|i \in W) = \frac{1}{2} \cdot 50 + \frac{200 - 4\alpha}{400 - 6\alpha} \cdot 50$$

$$+ \frac{\alpha}{400 - 6\alpha} \cdot \left(50 - \frac{1}{2}\alpha\right). \qquad (9.7.27)$$

Clearly, for all permissible values of α, we have

$$H_i(b_i^* p_{-i}|i \in W) > H_i(a_i^* p_{-i}|i \in W). \qquad (9.7.28)$$

This means that, for a weak player i, his best reply to the other players' priors is always his b^*-strategy b_i^*.

On the other hand, if a strong player i uses strategy a_i^* while his opponent, player j, acts in accordance with p_{-i}, then i's expected payoff will be

$$H_i(a_i^* p_{-i} | i \in S) = \frac{1}{2} \cdot 50 + \frac{200 - 4\alpha}{400 - 6\alpha} \cdot 50 + \frac{\alpha}{400 - 6\alpha} \alpha. \tag{9.7.29}$$

In contrast, if he uses strategy b_i^*, then his expected payoff will be

$$H_i(b_i^* p_{-i} | i \in S) = \frac{1}{2}\left(50 + \frac{1}{2}\alpha\right) + \frac{200 - 4\alpha}{400 - 6\alpha}\alpha + \frac{\alpha}{400 - 6\alpha}\alpha. \tag{9.7.30}$$

Simple computation shows that

$$H_i(b_i^* p_{-i} | i \in S) > H_i(a_i^* p_{-i} | i \in S), \tag{9.7.31}$$

if and only if

$$11\alpha^2 - 1{,}000\alpha + 20{,}000 < 0. \tag{9.7.32}$$

The roots of this inequality are $\alpha' = 29.71$ and $\alpha'' = 61.20$. Since α is always in the range $0 < \alpha < 50$, (9.7.32) is equivalent to the requirement that

$$\alpha > \alpha' = 29.71. \tag{9.7.33}$$

In view of (9.7.28) we can conclude that if (9.7.33) is satisfied, then both the two weak players i and the two strong players i will find that their best reply to p_{-i} is their b^*-strategy b_i^*. Hence, if (9.7.28) is satisfied, then b^* will have conspicuous risk dominance over a^*, as desired. ∎

LEMMA 9.7.2 a^* payoff-dominates b^* if $\alpha < 33\frac{1}{3}$.

Proof   By (9.6.1), for any weak player i

$$H_i(a^*) = 50 > H_i(b^*) = 50 - \tfrac{1}{4}\alpha - \delta. \tag{9.7.34}$$

But for a strong player j

$$H_j(a^*) = 50 > H_j(b^*) = 25 - \tfrac{3}{4}\alpha \tag{9.7.35}$$

if and only if $\alpha < 33\frac{1}{3}$. ∎

LEMMA 9.7.3   For any permissible α-value, a^* payoff-dominates b^{**}.

Proof   By (9.6.2), for any weak player i

$$H_i(a^*) = 50 > H_i(b^{**}) = \frac{75}{2} + \frac{1}{4}\alpha - \frac{1}{2}\xi - \delta. \tag{9.7.36}$$

Likewise, for any strong player j

$$H_j(a^*) = 50 > H_j(b^{**}) = \frac{75}{2} + \frac{1}{4}\alpha + \frac{1}{2}\xi \qquad (9.7.37)$$

if ξ is small enough. ∎

The last three lemmas imply:

LEMMA 9.7.4   If $\alpha \geq 33\frac{1}{3}$, then $b^o = b^*$ dominates a^*. But if $\alpha < 33\frac{1}{3}$, then a^* dominates b^o. (This is equally true when $25 < \alpha < 33\frac{1}{3}$ so that $b^o = b^*$, and when $0 < \alpha < 25$ so that $b^o = b^{**}$.)

9.8   Essential Strategic Distances

Since game $G_\varepsilon^*(\alpha)$ is played (potentially) in two stages, each player i will have a large number of agents, of whom only one will be a stage 1 agent but very many will be stage 2 agents. Yet at any specific equilibrium point, most stage 2 agents will be completely inactive except if one or both sides made a mistaken move at stage 1. Because of there being so many stage 2 agents, finding the strategic distances between equilibrium points will involve rather cumbersome computations if we use the strategic-distance concept defined in chapter 5, section 5.5.

For this reason in this chapter we will use a computationally much more convenient distance concept, to be called *essential* strategic distance, or simply *essential distance*. Although essential distances are much easier to compute than strategic distances are, they rank risk-dominance relations between equilibrium points in the same way as strategic distances would do and therefore will select the same solution for $G_\varepsilon^*(\alpha)$ as strategic distances would select.

To introduce the concept of essential distance, we will start with distinguishing between *essential* and *inessential* agents with respect to a given equilibrium point U. An essential agent is an agent who will become active with a positive probability, even if all n players exactly follow their equilibrium strategies prescribed by U, without making any mistaken move. On the other hand, an inessential agent is one who will remain inactive with probability one if all players follow their equilibrium strategies without any mistake.

The essential distance $d_i(U, V)$ for a given player i between two equilibrium points U and V will be the number of critical points for this player

i (as defined in section 5.5), except that we will now disregard all critical points associated with those agents ij who are inessential agents with respect to both equilibrium points U and V. Then we define the essential distance $d(U, V)$ between U and V as the sum of the distance $d_i(U, V)$ for the individual players, that is,

$$d(U, V) = \sum_{i \in N} d_i(U, V). \tag{9.8.1}$$

Suppose that $U \in \Omega$, and that Ω contains at least one other equilibrium point W. Then we define the essential distance of U from its *nearest neighbor* in Ω as

$$d(U, \Omega) = \min_{W \in \Omega \setminus U} d(U, W). \tag{9.8.2}$$

Next suppose that both U and $V \in \Omega$. Then we define the *essential net distance* between U and V in Ω as

$$d(U, V, \Omega) = 2d(U, V) - d(U, \Omega) - d(V, \Omega) + 1. \tag{9.8.3}$$

Sometimes for convenience we will use the symbol d^* to denote essential *net* distances.

The concepts of *maximal* net distance and of *stability index* will be defined in the same way as in section 5.5, except that the function e used in 5.5 will have to be replaced by the function d just defined. In terms of these definitions, we obtain the following essential distances:

$d = 4$ if both equilibrium points belong to class A_o, or if they belong to two different subclasses of class A.

$d = 3$ if both of them belong to class A_2, or if both of them belong to A_4.

$d = 2, 4,$ or 6 if both belong to class B and differ in one parameter or in two or all three parameters.

$d = 20$ if one equilibrium point belongs to class A, whereas the other belongs to B, with no common parameters being associated with both of these two equilibrium points.

$d = 8$ if one equilibrium point is a^*, whereas the other is b^* or b^{**} (because they share the common parameter $x = v = 50$).

The corresponding essential net distances are as follows:

$d^* = (4 - 4) + (4 - 4) + 1 = 1$ if both equilibrium points belong to class A_o.

$d* = (3 - 3) + (3 - 3) + 1 = 1$ if both belong to class A_2, or if both belong to A_4.

$d* = (4 - 4) + (4 - 3) + 1 = 2$ if one belongs to class A_o, whereas the other belongs to A_2 or to A_4.

$d* = (2 - 2) + (2 - 2) + 1 = 1$ if both belong to class B, and they differ only in one parameter.

$d* = (4 - 2) + (4 - 2) + 1 = 5$ if both belong to class B, and they differ in two parameters.

$d* = (6 - 2) + (6 - 2) + 1 = 9$ if both belong to class B, and they differ in all three parameters.

$d* = (20 - 4) + (20 - 2) + 1 = 35$ if one belongs to class A_o, whereas the other belongs to class B with no common parameter.

$d* = (8 - 4) + (8 - 2) + 1 = 11$ if one is $a*$, whereas the other is $b*$ or $b**$.

$d* = (20 - 3) + (20 - 2) + 1 = 36$ if one belongs to class A_2 or A_4, whereas the other belongs to class B, with no common parameter.

9.9   The Solution

Under our definitions in section 5.5, the first candidate set will be

$$\Omega_1 = A \cup B. \tag{9.9.1}$$

Within set Ω_1 the class leaders $a*$ and b^o, together with the subclass leaders a_2 and a_4, will be the only equilibrium point not dominated by any equilibrium points at an essential net distance of $d* = 1$. But both a_2 and a_4 will be dominated by $a*$ at an essential net distance of $d* = 2$, whereas $a*$ and b^o will not be dominated at the distance $d* = 2$ by any equilibrium point. Now we must distinguish two cases.

Case 1: $\alpha < 33\frac{1}{3}$
In this case $a*$ will dominate b^o at an essential net distance of $d* = 11$, whereas $a*$ will not be dominated by any equilibrium point at this distance. Hence $a*$ will be the only equilibrium point with a stability index σ of at least 11. Hence the second candidate set will be the one-point set

$$\Omega_2 = \{a*\}, \tag{9.9.2}$$

making $a*$ the *solution* of the game.

Case 2: $\alpha \geq 33\frac{1}{3}$

In this case $b^o = b^*$ will dominate a^* at an essential net distance of $d^* = 11$, whereas b^* will not be dominated by any equilibrium point at this distance. Hence now b^* will be the only equilibrium point with a stability index σ of at least 11, and the second candidate set will be the one-point set

$$\Omega_2 = \{b^*\}, \tag{9.9.3}$$

making b^* the *solution*. This implies the following theorem:

THEOREM 9.9.1   If $\alpha < 33\frac{1}{3}$, then a^* will be the solution of the game, whereas if $\alpha \geq 33\frac{1}{3}$, then the solution will be b^*.

The intuitive interpretation is that, even though for $\alpha > 29.71$ risk-dominance considerations would favor b^*, it is the common interest of all four players to choose a^* as long as $\alpha < 33\frac{1}{3}$. But when $\alpha \geq 33\frac{1}{3}$, then the strong players will prefer b^* over a^*, and since b^* risk-dominates a^*, they will be able to get their way—even though a^* would be preferred by the two weak players.

10 Postscript

10.1   Introduction

In this postscript[1] we will start by making some general remarks about our one-point solution theory. Then we will discuss various stability criteria for equilibrium points and will state our reasons for choosing the perfect equilibria of a game, and more specifically its *uniformly* perfect equilibria, as the basis of our theory. Next we will discuss various aspects of the game-theoretic rationality concept underlying our work. Finally, we will briefly outline some possible further refinements to our theory that we intend to explore in future research.

10.2   The Basic Aim of Our Theory

As we have already stated, our basic objective has been to offer rational criteria for selecting *one* equilibrium point as the solution of any non-cooperative game, as well as any cooperative game remodeled as a non-cooperative bargaining game. In the last twenty years we have seen the fruitfulness of modeling a wide variety of economic situations as non-cooperative games, with or without some form of incomplete information. In most of this work, however, the great multiplicity and diversity of equilibrium points (even if one restricts one's attention to perfect equilibria or to those with other special properties) has become a serious problem. In many cases, if all we can say is that the outcome will be an equilibrium point—even if one possessing special properties—we will be saying little more than that almost anything can happen in the game, which is not a very informative conclusion. Even if our interest is primarily qualitative rather then quantitative, we usually want to know at least the general direction of the way increases or decreases in some basic parameters will affect the outcome (comparative statics). Yet, even to make such qualitative predictions, we need a theory associating a specific outcome, or at least a rather narrow range of possible outcomes, with any specific profile of parameter values.

To be sure, it is often possible to select one equilibrium point by some reasonable *ad hoc* criteria as the predicted outcome. But it is preferable to attack the equilibrium-selection problem head on by a systematic general theory, and this is what we have tried to do in this book.

No doubt the problem we have tried to solve is one of considerable difficulty. We certainly do not claim that the theory we are proposing here is the best final solution to it. Indeed, as we have just stated, we plan to outline some possible refinements to our theory. But we think that we have made substantial progress in solving the problem, and we think that even researchers who do not like our theory will often find some of the game-theoretic concepts and methods we have developed to be useful in their research.

Our theory proposes to define a one-point solution concept for any noncooperative game. When we discussed this project with other game theorists we were often told that we were trying to do the impossible. But we always felt it was not really useful to discuss the feasibility or infeasibility of such a solution concept a priori in general philosophical terms. Rather, the only way one can decide its feasibility is to make a serious attempt to produce one. All we can ask the reader is to approach our work with an open mind and to decide for himself how far our attempt has been successful.

10.3   Endogenous Expectations

The basic task of game theory is to tell us what strategies rational players will follow and what expectations they can rationally entertain about other rational players' strategies. The problems of rational strategies and rational expectations are strongly interdependent and require simultaneous solutions, since for any player's strategy to be a rational strategy, it must be a best reply to his rational expectations about the other players' strategies.

Yet there is an inherent ambiguity in the notion of rational expectations. To the question of what expectations are rational we may get one answer if we assume that these expectations are strictly endogenous, in the sense of being based solely on factors internal to the game such as this game's mathematical structure (as specified by its extensive or normal form) and the assumption that all players will act rationally in the game. We may get a very different answer if we assume that the players' expectations will depend also on factors external to the game.

For example, suppose that two players have to divide $100 in a perfectly symmetric bargaining game. In this case all game-theoretic solution concepts yielding a definite outcome will specify a 50:50 split as the solution. But this 50:50 split will represent a reasonable prediction only on the assumption of endogenous expectations. For suppose the two players live in a society where it is a general custom to give 60 percent of the money to the older one of the two bargaining parties. Then it may be perfectly rational for both sides to agree on a 60:40 split. The older party will obviously benefit by insisting on a \$60 payoff if he thinks he can get away with it, whereas the younger party may very well come to the conclusion that it would be hopeless for him to insist on a payoff larger than \$40. In other words, although rational behavior and endogenous expectations will lead to a 50:50 split, rational behavior with exogenous expectations may lead to quite different outcomes (see Schelling 1960; Roth 1985). Needless to say, like most other game-theoretic solution theories, our theory is fully dependent on the assumption of endogenous expectations.

STABILITY CRITERIA FOR EQUILIBRIUM POINTS

10.4 Uniform Perfectness versus Perfectness

Our one-point solution theory is based on the uniformly perfect equilibria of any given game G–on those equilibria that can be obtained as the limits of the Nash equilibria of the uniformly perturbed standard form G_ε of game G when ε goes to zero. We have chosen to work with the set of uniformly perfect equilibria rather than with the set of *all* perfect equilibria because the former is often a much smaller set, which makes it easier to analyze. Moreover uniformly perfect equilibria are easier to compute than perfect equilibria are because they are simply the limits of the Nash equilibria of game G_ε. Finally, by requiring uniform perfectness, we often get rid of many unwanted equilibria that are needless "duplicates" of a given equilibrium point.

To illustrate our last remark, in the family of games discussed in chapter 8, player I has only one type, whereas his opponent, player II, has two possible types. This one type of player I is called player 1, whereas the two types of player II are called players 2 and 3. Either of these two latter types will participate with probability $\frac{1}{2}$ in the game.

In this family of games each equilibrium $b(x, y)$ of class B has the following interpretation: The rules of the game require each player i to name the payoff x_i he wants to assign to player 1. Player 1 himself will name the payoff $x_1 = x$. Player 2 (if *he* is representing player II in the game) will name the *same* payoff $x_2 = x$ and therefore will reach an *agreement* with player 1, yielding the payoffs $u_1 = x$ and $u_2 = 100 - x$. In contrast, player 3 (if *he* is the one representing player II) will name a different payoff $x_3 = y < x$ because if he named the payoff $x_3 = x$, he would reduce his own payoff below his conflict payoff $c_3 = \alpha$. The result will be a *conflict* between players 1 and 3, yielding the conflict payoffs $u_1 = c_1 = 0$ and $u_3 = c_3 = \alpha$.

Any equilibrium $b(x, y)$ is formally characterized by both parameters x and y, but two equilibria with the same x value will yield the same payoffs to the players, even if they involve different y values (as long as $y \neq x$). In this sense all equilibria $b(x, y)$ involving the same x value can be regarded as variants of the same equilibrium. (The value of y is a rather unimportant detail because it indicates merely the specific payoff proposal player 3 would use in rejecting player 1's payoff proposal.)

This problem automatically disappears if the game is analyzed in terms of its uniformly perfect equilibria, because the uniform perfectness requirement reduces the set of admissible y values to $y = 0$. Thus for any admissible x value there is only one admissible class B equilibrium: $b(x, 0)$ In contrast, the set of all perfect equilibria contains many different equilibria $b(x, y)$ with a given x value but with different y values.

10.5   Perfectness versus Sequentiality

Kreps and Wilson (1982) have suggested that it is often preferable to work with sequential equilibria rather than with perfect equilibria because the former are easier to compute. But the computation difficulties posed by perfect equilibria largely disappear is we work with uniformly perfect equilibria. Moreover, as Kohlberg and Mertens (1982, pp. 4–5) have pointed out, unlike perfect equilibria, sequential equilibria often have the undersirable property of using dominated strategies.

10.6   Normal-Form Dependence: An Example

As one of us has shown (Selten 1975), imperfect equilibria cannot always be recognized in the normal form of the game. Hence perfect equilibria must be defined either in the extensive form or, more conveniently, in the agent normal form or the standard form. (In this respect sequential equilibria have similar properties.)

In contrast, Myerson's (1978) *proper* equilibria, Kalai and Samet's (1984) *persistent* equilibria, as well as Kohlberg and Mertens's (1986) various types of *stable* equilibria, do admit definition in the normal form of a game. This property we will call *normal-form dependence*. It is no doubt prima facie a very desirable mathematical property. We have not chosen a stability concept displaying this property as a basis of our theory because our solution theory simply cannot be made normal-form dependent without seriously distorting what Kohlberg and Mertens call backward-induction rationality (1986, p. 1004), which we regard an essential aspect of game-theoretic rationality in dealing with sequential games.

We will illustrate the problem by means of three examples. Each example will show in a different way how the requirement of normal-form dependence would violate the principles of subgame consistency and truncation consistency (see section 3.11), which we regard as essential aspects of backward-induction rationality.[2] (These two consistency requirements can be considered also as consequences of the principle of endogenous expectations as applied to subgames and to truncation games.)

Subgame consistency means that in any subgame Γ^* of an extensive game Γ the players should use the same local strategies as the solution $L(\Gamma^*)$ of Γ^* would require them to use if Γ^* were an independent game. Now suppose that if the players did use these strategies, they would obtain the payoff vector u. Then we define the truncation game Γ^{**} associated with this subgame Γ^* as the game we obtain from game Γ if we replace this subgame Γ^* with the payoff vector u. Truncation consistency means that in that part of game Γ that does not belong to subgame Γ^*, the players should use the same local strategies as the solution of the truncation game Γ^{**} would require them to use if Γ^{**} were an independent game.

Our first example involves the normal-form game in figure 10.1 and the two extensive-form games in figures 10.2 and 10.3. (Apart from omitting

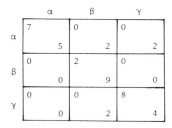

	α	β	γ
α	7 5	0 2	0 2
β	0 0	2 9	0 0
γ	0 0	0 2	8 4

Figure 10.1

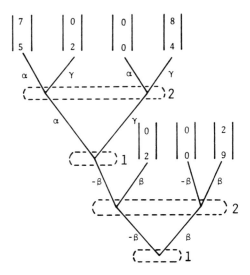

Figure 10.2

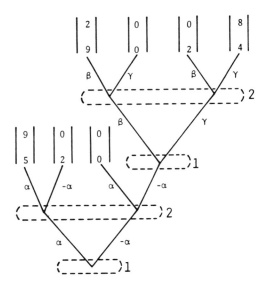

Figure 10.3

any reference to agent splitting, these are the same as figures 3.25, 3.27, and 3.28.) The game in figure 10.1 has three equilibria in pure strategies, called α, β, and γ. The risk-dominance relations among them are circular because $\alpha \succ \beta \succ \gamma \succ \alpha$. There are no payoff-dominance relations. As a result the outcome of the game will depend on the specific *order*, if any, in which the extensive form of the game will make the players choose among the three equilibrium points. Both games in figures 10.2 and 10.3 have the game in figure 10.1 as their normal form. But they have different solutions because they make the players choose in a different order among the three equilibrium points.

In particular, the game in figure 10.2 asks the two players first to choose between accepting and rejecting β. (Acceptance of β is denoted as β, whereas rejection of β is denoted as $-\beta$.) If both choose $-\beta$, then at the second stage of the game they can choose between α and γ. Since $\gamma \succ \alpha$, they would choose γ rather than α at this second stage, and both of them know this. Therefore, when at the first stage they have to choose between β and $-\beta$, their choice will be really between β and γ. Since $\beta \succ \gamma$, they will actually choose β so that the game will end already at the first stage with β as the solution. To verify that this game has the game of figure 10.1 as its normal form, all we have to do is to identify each player's strategies in the two games as follows: $\beta\alpha = \beta\gamma = \beta$, $-\beta\alpha = \alpha$, and $-\beta\gamma = \gamma$.

In contrast, the game in figure 10.3 asks the two players at first to choose between α and $-\alpha$. If both of them choose $-\alpha$, then at the second stage they can choose between β and γ. Since $\beta \succ \gamma$, both of them would choose β at this second stage, and both know this. Therefore, when at the first stage they have to choose between α and $-\alpha$, their choice will be really between α and β. Since $\alpha \succ \beta$, they will actually choose α so that the game will already end at the first stage with α as the solution. To verify that this game also has the game in figure 10.1 as its normal form, we can identify each player's strategies in the two games as follows: $\alpha\beta = \alpha\gamma = \alpha$, $-\alpha\beta = \beta$, and $-\alpha\gamma = \gamma$.

Using the concepts of subgame and of truncation game, we can restate this argument as follows: Each of the two games in figures 10.2 and 10.3 contains a subgame, consisting of the last two information sets. The subgame in figure 10.2 has equilibrium (γ, γ) as its solution because (γ, γ) risk-dominates (α, α). (γ, γ) would yield the payoff vector $u = (8, 4)$. If we now replace the entire subgame with this payoff vector, we obtain the truncated game shown in figure 10.4. This game has equilibrium (β, β) as its solution

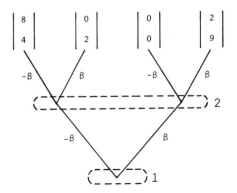

Figure 10.4

because (β, β) risk-dominates $(-\beta, -\beta)$. Consequently the solution of the entire game in figure 10.2 is $(\beta\gamma, \beta\gamma)$. But since in the normal form we can identify either player's strategies $\beta\gamma$ and $\beta\alpha$, we can write $\beta\gamma = \beta\alpha = \beta$ and can describe the solution also as (β, β).

By the same token, the subgame in figure 10.3 has equilibrium (β, β) as its solution because (β, β) risk-dominates (γ, γ). (β, β) would yield the payoff vector $u = (2, 9)$. If we now replace the entire subgame with this payoff vector then we obtain the truncation game shown in figure 10.5. This game has the equilibrium (α, α) as its solution because (α, α) risk-dominates $(-\alpha, -\alpha)$. Consequently the solution of the entire game in figure 10.3 is $(\alpha\beta, \alpha\beta)$. But since in the normal form we can identify either player's strategies $\alpha\beta$ and $\alpha\gamma$, we can write $\alpha\beta = \alpha\gamma = \alpha$ and describe the solution also as (α, α).

This example clearly shows that in general the solution of a game with a sequential structure simply *has* to depend on this sequential structure and cannot be made dependent on the normal form only without seriously distorting our intuitive standards of sequential (or of backward-induction) rationality. It also shows that if we insisted on normal-form dependence, then we would have to give up the intuitively very compelling requirements of subgame and truncation consistency.

10.7   Another Example

To illustrate the problem from a different angle, we will now consider a game with a subgame whose solution is based on payoff dominance (Pareto superiority) rather than on risk dominance; see figure 10.6. (This game is a

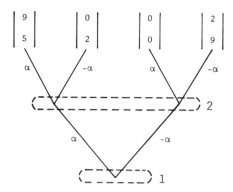

Figure 10.5

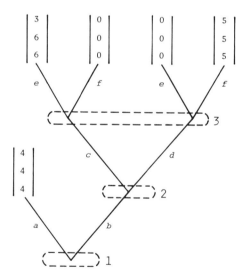

Figure 10.6

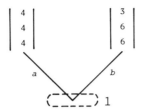

Figure 10.7

simplified version of the game in figure 3.21.) The game in figure 10.6 will be called Γ. The information sets of players 2 and 3 form a subgame, to be called Γ*. In the latter player 1 has no move, so only 2 and 3 are active players. In Γ*, from these two players' points of view, equilibrium (c, e) payoff-dominates equilibrium (d, f), making (c, e) the solution of Γ*. (c, e) would yield the payoff vector $u = (3, 6, 6)$. If we now replace the entire subgame Γ* with this payoff vector then we obtain the truncation game Γ** shown in figure 10.7.

Obviously Γ** has player 1 as its only active player, who will choose strategy a, which is the solution of Γ**. In other words, player 1 must realize that if he makes move b, the other two players will choose the payoff vector $(3, 6, 6)$. In view of this he will make move a rather than move b. Thus, if all players act rationally, the outcome of the game will be equilibrium (a, c, e), yielding the payoffs $(4, 4, 4)$—even though equilibrium (b, d, f) would yield the payoffs $(5, 5, 5)$, making all three players better off.

Although the strategic considerations favoring (a, c, e) are absolutely cogent in the extensive form of the game, they remain completely obscured in its normal form, shown in figure 10.8. This normal form shows only that (b, d, f) would yield higher payoffs than (a, c, e) would yield to all three players. But it does not indicate the strategic reasons making the latter equilibrium the only rational outcome.

10.8   A Third Example

We will now discuss a third undesirable implication of the requirement of normal-form dependence. Consider the game shown in figure 10.9, to be called game Γ. In this game player 1's second information set and the one information set belonging to player 2 form a subgame Γ*, whose solution is equilibrium (c, e), which risk-dominates the other pure-strategy

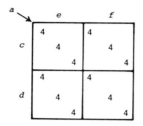
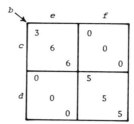

Figure 10.8

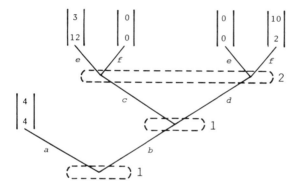

Figure 10.9

equilibrium (d, f). (There is no payoff dominance either way.) If the players use the strategies c and e required by this solution, they will obtain the payoff vector $u = (3, 12)$.

On the other hand, if we replace the entire subgame Γ^* with this payoff vector u, we obtain the truncation game Γ^{**} shown in figure 10.10. In this game player 1 is the only active player, and the only equilibrium is strategy a, which is of course the solution of this game. Consequently subgame and truncation consistency imply that in game Γ of figure 10.9 the two players must use equilibrium (ac, e) as the solution of the entire game.

Yet, if we look only at the normal form of this game, we do not notice that it contains a subgame. Therefore it would be natural to argue as Kohlberg and Mertens do (1986, p. 1015) that if we delete any dominated strategy, this should not change the solution. Now, in the game as a whole, player 1's strategy bc is dominated by ac and ad, so that player 2's strategy

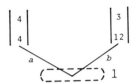

Figure 10.10

e is dominated by f. Yet if we delete bc and f, then (bd, f) becomes the only equilibrium of the remaining game, making the latter the solution.

Informally, the same argument can be restated as follows: Since player 1 prefers outcome (bd, f) to outcome (ac, e), he will make move b at the beginning of the game if he can rationally expect player 2 to respond by move f. Yet it is rational for 2 to entertain this expectation. For if 2 sees 1 making move b, then he must infer that 1 is doing this to obtain a payoff higher than 4 (which he would obtain by move a). Accordingly, 2 must infer that 1 plans to make move d later in the game. This in turn will induce 2 to make move f. Thus it will be rational for 1 to use strategy bd and for 2 to use strategy f.

We can state this informal argument also as follows. By making move b, player 1 can convincingly *signal* to player 2 that he intends to make move d later in the game, and thereby he will induce 2 to respond with move f. Nevertheless, we feel that both the formal and informal arguments favoring equilibrium (bd, f) are inconsistent with backward-induction rationality. Backward-induction rationality requires that the players should first decide how to act in subgame Γ^*. Once this has been decided, it will be obvious for player 1 whether to choose move a or move b before subgame Γ^* is reached. This means that we cannot delete move c in subgame Γ^* because it is an undominated move within this subgame. The fact that in the entire game Γ, strategy bc is a dominated strategy is irrelevant because backward-induction rationality requires us to decompose analysis of game Γ into two separate steps, the first involving analysis of subgame Γ^* and the second involving analysis of the truncation game Γ^{**}. Thus, if the internal mathematical structure of subgame Γ^* makes (c, e) the solution of Γ^*, we cannot refuse accepting (ac, e) as the solution of the entire game Γ even though bc is a dominated strategy in the entire game Γ—as long as no similar dominance relations appear in subgame Γ^* and in truncation game Γ^{**} themselves.

The informal argument favoring (bd, f) is likewise inconsistent with backward-induction rationality. Before deciding whether player 1 can effectively signal his strategic intentions, we must first decide what strategies are the rational strategies for the two players in subgame Γ^*, and accordingly what strategy is the rational strategy for player 1 in the truncation game Γ^{**}. Suppose we find as we did that in Γ^* the only rational strategies are c and e and that because of this in Γ^{**} the only rational strategy is a. Then we are no longer logically free to argue that if player 1 nevertheless makes move b, this should be interpreted by player 2 as a *signal* of player 1's intention to make move d later on. Rather, we must say that player 2 must interpret move b by player 1 as a *mistake*—such that rational players in player 1's position will make with a very small, yet positive, probability. Unless we are making some very special assumptions about the mathematical structure of the game,[3] when a given player i makes such a "mistake," this will not justify any inference by another player j to the effect that player i will make similar mistakes also in the future. Even if i made an obvious mistake at one of his information sets, player j must expect him to make rational moves at his future information sets with near-unity probabilities and to make "mistaken" moves only with very small probabilities.

Thus, even if at the first stage of the game player 1 made the "mistaken" move b, player 2 cannot rationally infer that at the second stage player 1 will again make the "mistaken" move d. Rather, 2 must expect 1 to make the "rational" move c with near-unity probability, and to make the mistaken move d only with a very small probability. By the same token, player 1 must expect player 2 to make the rational move e with near-unity probability and to make the mistaken move f only with very small probability. As a result of these expectations, even if player 1 makes the mistaken move b, in the resulting subgame Γ^*, both players will have a strong incentive to use strategies c and e as required by the solution of Γ^*.

10.9 The Assumption of Specific Mistake Probabilities

One important source of these differences between our solution theory and the Kohlberg-Mertens stability theory is one, more fundamental, difference. Under our theory analysis of any given game G must start with specific assumptions about the probability distribution Π_ε governing the probabilities of mistaken moves by the players at any of their information sets. This probability distribution Π_ε then becomes part of the mathematical definition of the game. In our solution theory we deal only with equilibria stable against this specific mistake-probability distribution Π_ε, but we do not in general require that they should be stable also against other possible mistake-probability distributions.

In contrast, Kohlberg and Mertens are looking for equilibria (and sets of equilibria) stable against all possible small strategy perturbations (i.e., against all possible mistake-probability distributions with small mistake probabilities) and even against small payoff perturbations unconnected with strategy perturbations. Obviously this is a mathematical problem of great intrinsic interest whether equilibria with such very strong stability properties exist at all, and what their properties are if they do exist. We are all indebted to Kohlberg and Mertens for clarifying many important aspects of this problem for us.

Yet it is a different question whether we should insist that the solution of a noncooperative game should always satisfy these very strong stability requirements. As we have seen, if we did insist on this, we would have to give up some fundamentally important principles of game-theoretic rationality. We feel this would be much too high a price to pay.

10.10   Preference for Equilibria with Stability Properties Additional to Uniform Perfectness

Although our theory does not positively require that the solution of a game should have stronger stability properties than uniform perfectness, it does give strong preference to equilibria with stronger stability properties. (We will see presently why our theory cannot actually require the solution to possess these stronger stability properties.)

First, our theory always tries to choose as the solution a uniformly perfect equilibrium belonging to a primitive formation (see section 5.2). Second, if a primitive formation contains two or more uniformly perfect equilibria, our theory will generically choose as the "solution" of this primitive formation an equilibrium whose source set (see section 4.14) is a full-dimensional subset of the strategy space of the game. (This is so because the solution of a primitive formation is chosen by the tracing procedure, which will obviously "almost always" select an equilibrium with a full-dimensional source set and will select one with a less-than-full-dimensional source set only in "exceptional" cases.)

For a uniformly stable equilibrium point to belong to a primitive forma-

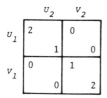

Figure 10.11

tion, or to have a full dimensional source set, are clearly stability properties
going beyond uniform perfectness. In fact both properties are neighborhood-
stability properties related to Kalai and Samet's concept of persistent
equilibria. (Possession of a full-dimensional source set is particularly closely
related to persistence. Every persistent equilibrium has a full-dimensional
source set. But at this point it is not known whether the converse is true,
too.)

To verify the fact that we cannot insist on a solution belonging to a
primitive formation or on one having a full-dimensional source set, consider the 2×2 game shown in figure 10.11. This game has two strong
equilibria in pure strategies: $U = (U_1, U_2)$ and $V = (V_1, V_2)$. It also has a
mixed-strategy equilibrium point, $M = (\frac{2}{3}U_1 + \frac{1}{3}V_1, \frac{1}{3}U_2 + \frac{2}{3}V_2)$. Both U
and V belong to primitive formations. (In fact, either of them is a one-point
primitive formation.) Moreover, both U and V have full-dimensional (two-
dimensional) source sets. Finally, both of them are persistent equilibria.
In contrast, M does not belong to any primitive formation, has a one-
dimensional source set, and is not persistent. Yet, since M is the only
equilibrium displaying the symmetries of the game, our theory has to
choose M as the solution. In other words, given the symmetric structure of
the game, there cannot be any mathematical criterion that could justify
choosing U in preference to V or that could justify choosing V in preference
to U as the solution. Therefore, we have no other option but to choose M
as the solution.

GAME-THEORETIC RATIONALITY

10.11 Payoff Dominance and Risk Dominance

In choosing between two equilibria as solution candidates, our theory uses
two different choice criteria: payoff dominance and risk dominance. We say

that one equilibrium E_1 payoff-dominates another equilibrium E_2 when E_1 yields every player a strictly higher payoff than E_2 does. On the other hand, the notion that E_1 risk-dominates E_2 is meant to capture the intuitive idea that when the players do not know whether the other players will lean toward E_1 or toward E_2, it will be less risky for them to opt for E_1 and to use their E_1-strategies than it would be to opt for E_2 and to use their E_2-strategies.

In cases where payoff dominance and risk dominance go in opposite directions, our theory in general gives precedence to payoff dominance. This is so because risk dominance is important only in those cases where the players would be initially uncertain whether the other players would choose one equilibrium or the other. Yet, if one equilibrium would give all players higher payoffs than the other would—and if the former meets the requirement of uniform perfectness and other relevant requirements— then, under our theory, every player can be quite certain that the other players will opt for this equilibrium, which will make risk-dominance considerations irrelevant.

This means that our theory uses two independent, and ostensibly very different, criteria of rationality. One of them, risk dominance, is based on *individual* rationality: it is an extension of Bayesian rationality from one-person decisions to n-person games involving strategic interaction among n players, each of them guided by Bayesian rationality. If equilibrium point E_1 risk-dominates equilibrium point E_2, this means that in a situation where the players are uncertain whether E_1 or E_2 will be the actual outcome, any player who tries to maximize his expected payoff in terms of rationally chosen subjective probabilities over the other players' strategies (see section 10.13) will opt for E_1.

In contrast, payoff dominance is based on *collective* rationality: it is based on the assumption that in the absence of special reasons to the contrary, rational players will choose an equilibrium point yielding all of them higher payoffs, rather than one yielding them lower payoffs. That is to say, it is based on the assumption that rational individuals will co-operate in pursuing their common interests if the conditions permit them to do so.

No doubt, we would obtain a simpler and a more elegant solution theory if we used only one choice criterion instead of two different choice criteria. But we have felt that one cannot do justice to our intuitive notion of game-theoretic rationality without making use of both of our choice criteria because both are essential aspects of rational behavior in game situations.

To be sure, some readers will disagree. They will feel that payoff dominance —which requires the players to cooperate in promoting their common interests—is a principle of morality rather than one of game-theoretic rationality, and that it is out of place in a game-theoretic solution theory. We strongly disagree with this point of view. Other things being equal, if, of two equally admissible equilibrium points, one yields higher payoffs to all players, it will be surely rational for the players to choose this equilibrium point, and it will be surely irrational for them to choose the other. By choosing the former, they will obtain higher payoffs, regardless of any moral consideration pushing in the same direction.

The point is that in cases where cooperation is in all participants' personal interest, both game-theoretic rationality and morality will favor cooperation. Of course morality goes further then that: it will sometimes require us to help other people and to cooperate with them even in cases where we cannot derive any personal benefit from doing so, whereas game-theoretic rationality will require cooperation only when this will increase all participants' payoffs. Our concept of payoff dominance requires cooperation only in the latter case. Accordingly, by making payoff dominance one of our rationality criteria, we are certainly not obscuring the distinction between rationality and morality.

Nevertheless, under our theory both payoff dominance and risk dominance are choice criteria only in choosing between two otherwise equally admissible equilibrium points. For instance, a nonequilibrium strategy combination may very well yield all players higher payoffs than any equilibrium point of the game does (as it is the case in a Prisoner's Dilemma game). But this cannot justify choosing this nonequilibrium strategy combination as the solution.

10.12   Would a Solution Theory Based Solely on Risk Dominance be Preferable?

We want to add that some time ago we seriously considered proposing a solution theory based solely on risk dominance. Even then we took the view that, whenever possible, rational players would prefer payoff-dominant equilibrium points over payoff-dominated ones. But we thought that this fact need not be made explicitly part of our solution theory but rather would automatically emerge from any sufficiently flexible bargaining process among the players: if this bargaining process permitted the players a clear choice between any payoff-dominated equilibrium point and the equilibrium point(s) payoff-dominating the latter, then, barring special reasons to the contrary (e.g., symmetry consideration; see figure 10.6), they would always choose (one of) the payoff-dominating equilibrium point(s).

Later, however, we decided to include payoff dominance explicitly into our solution theory. One reason was that by doing so we would make it clearer that we did regard payoff dominance as an essential aspect of game-theoretic rationality. Another reason was that if we wanted to use bargaining models always permitting a direct choice between payoff-dominated equilibria and payoff-dominating equilibria, we would often had been forced to use needlessly complicated and unwieldy bargaining models.

Yet an important example recently proposed by Aumann (1985, pp. 24–25) has now provided a much more fundamental reason why negotiations between the players cannot be relied upon to implement the payoff-dominance criterion. His example is the two-person game shown in figure 10.12.

This has two pure-strategy equilibria: $C = (c, c)$ and $D = (d, d)$. (There is also a mixed-strategy equilibrium.) In our terminology, C payoff-dominates D. At the same time, D very strongly risk-dominates C—that is, for either player to choose strategy c associated with C is a much riskier choice than to choose strategy d associated with D. For if he chooses c, he is risking to obtain a zero payoff; while if he chooses d, then he cannot obtain less than 7.

To put it differently, choosing C is a much riskier choice because C is a much less stable equilibrium than D is. For C will be destabilized if either player thinks that the other player may shift to D with a probability larger than $\frac{1}{8}$, whereas D will be destabilized only if either player thinks that the other player may shift to C with a probability larger than $\frac{7}{8}$.

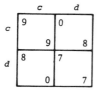

Figure 10.12

Now suppose that both players expect each other to follow a rationality concept that includes a respect for payoff dominance as an essential ingredient, and that this is a matter of common knowledge for them (in the sense of Aumann 1976). Then they will obviously use their c-strategies, making C the outcome of the game.

In contrast, suppose it is common knowledge that the two players follow a strictly individualistic rationality concept based solely on risk dominance. In this case they will follow their d-strategies, making D the outcome. Moreover in this case *no amount of preplay negotiations between the players can make any difference.* This is so because, regardless of whether a given player uses strategy c or d, he will be better off if the other player uses c than if he uses d. Therefore, regardless of which strategy he actually intends to use, he will have an interest to *say* that he intends to use strategy c (in order to give the other player an incentive to use strategy c too). This of course means that when either player says he will use c, he cannot be believed because he will say this regardless of whether this is his true intention or not.

Consequently, if the players are permitted to negotiate before playing the game, they will no doubt verbally "agree" to use their c-strategies. But this agreement will be completely useless because it will not be kept by either player. In other words, the only way we can obtain the payoff-dominant equilibrium point C as the outcome is to assume that payoff dominance is part of both players' *concept of rationality* and that it is their common knowledge that this is so. Otherwise, C will not be the outcome of the game, regardless of whether the players can talk to each other or not and regardless of what rules may govern the negotiations between them.

This shows that in general we cannot expect the players to implement payoff dominance unless, from the very beginning, payoff dominance is *part of the rationality concept* they are using. Free communication among the players in itself may not help. Thus, if one feels that payoff dominance is an essential aspect of game-theoretic rationality, then one must *explicitly* incorporate it into one's concept of rationality.

10.13   Bicentric Priors and the Tracing Procedure

Our concept of risk dominance is defined in terms of two other concepts, the bicentric priors generated by the two equilibrium points and the tracing procedure applied to these bicentric priors. Both concepts try to answer the following question. Suppose the players are *uncertain*; which one of two equilibria E_1 and E_2 the other players will choose as the outcome of the game. In this situation of uncertainty, what subjective probability distribution will a rational player assign to another rational player's pure strategies as expressing his expectation about the latter's future behavior in the game?

Our theory answers this question by a construction procedure involving two steps. The first step consists in specifying a probability distribution p_i for each player i, interpreted as the other players' initial expectations about player i's behavior. This distribution p_i is called the *bicentric prior* for player i. Informally speaking, p_i is based on the principle that the probability of player i's using any given pure strategy of his will be initially judged to be proportional to the range of the relevant situations in which this strategy would be i's best reply to the other players' strategies. (A more precise formal definition of the bicentric priors is found in section 5.3.)

Thus under our theory the n priors $p_1, \ldots, p_n$ will represent the players' initial expectations about one another's strategy choices. But, in general, they will not represent their final expectations about these strategy choices because these priors do not—and, short of inadmissible self-reference, cannot—take account of the players' strategic reactions to these initial expectations corresponding to these very priors.

The second step of our construction procedure is the *tracing procedure*, applied to these bicentric priors $p_1, \ldots, p_n$. Its purpose is to model how the players will gradually reassess their expectations about the other players' behavior in the light of what they know must be these players' strategic *reactions* to their own expectations.

The tracing procedure assumes that initially the expectations of every player i will be based completely on the priors $p_1, \ldots, p_{i-1}, p_{i+1}, \ldots, p_n$ that this player will associate with the other $(n-1)$ players. On the other hand, his tentative strategy plan will be to use a strategy s_i that is his best reply to these priors. But later he will gradually reassess his expectations by giving increasing weight to the strategies $s_1, \ldots, s_{i-1}, s_{i+1}, \ldots, s_n$ that represent what he knows must express the other players tentative strategy plans, and by giving decreasing weight to the priors $p_1, \ldots, p_{i-1}, p_{i+1}, \ldots, p_n$ that represent his initial assessment of the other players' likely behavior. At the same time, he will change this own tentative strategy plan to using a strategy s_i that is his best reply to his current reassessed expectations. In other words, as his expectations change so will his planned strategy. Of course he will know that the other players will change their own tentative strategy plans in a similar way, which will necessitate further changes in his expectations about their behavior, and so on. (A more exact formal definition and discussion of the tracing procedure can be found in chapter 4.)

In the end both the players' expectations about the other players' behavior and their own strategy plans will converge to a specific uniformly perfect equilibrium of the game, called the outcome of the tracing procedure. If this outcome is E_1 (or E_2), then this is interpreted as an indication that the initial uncertainty about whether E_1 or E_2 will be the outcome of the game will be resolved in favor of E_1 (or E_2). This is expressed by saying that E_1 risk-dominates E_2 (or that E_2 risk-dominates E_1). (If the tracing procedure leads to a third equilibrium different from both E_1 and E_2, then we say that neither of these two equilibria risk-dominates the other.)

By studying numerical examples, the reader will find that our concept of risk dominance is in excellent agreement with our intuitive judgment about which one of two equilibria is the "less risky" choice for the players.

10.14 The Role of Strategic Net Distance

Obviously payoff dominance is a transitive relation (simply because "larger than" is a transitive relation). But, in general, risk dominance is not a transitive relation (see the game of figure 10.1 analyzed in section 10.6). As a result, our dominance relation, defined in terms of both payoff dominance and risk dominance, likewise lacks transitivity. Therefore it is a common occurrence that within a given set of equilibria (e.g., within the various "candidate sets" discussed in section 5.5), there is no equilibrium dominating all the others. This fact makes it natural to establish a ranking among the existing dominance relations according to their importance. The ranking we use is based on the strategic net distance between the dominating and the dominated equilibria.

This strategic net distance (just as the strategic distance itself used in defining the "net" distance concept) is a measure of dissimilarity between the strategies used at one equilibrium and those used at another. Our theory gives greater weight to dominance relations between equilibria at small strategic net distance from each other, that is between equilibria involving fairly similar equilibrium strategies.

In games whose equilibria fall into two or more natural similarity classes, the strategic net distance between equilibria belonging to the same class is usually smaller than that between equilibria belonging to two different classes. This is the case, for example, for the family of games discussed in chapter 8. The result is that our theory first identifies the "strongest" equilibrium in each of the two similarity classes and then selects as solution one of these two "class leaders" according to which one of the two dominates the other. We feel this is an intuitively vary desirable feature of our theory.

The solution for the family of games discussed in chapter 9 is also selected by matching the two "class leaders" against each other. But the situation is more complicated than in chapter 8 because every equilibrium $b(y, v, w)$ of class B is characterized by three independent parameters y, v, and w. In this case the ranking of dominance relations according to strategic net distance has two further desirable implications:

1. It enables us to find the parameter values y^*, v^*, and w^* characterizing the "class leader" of class B, the equilibrium $b^* = b(y^*, v^*, w^*)$, separately for each of the three parameters. This greatly simplifies the computations and makes it much easier to interpret the results intuitively.

2. It also ensures that b^* will make the players agree on the same payoffs as they would agree in an otherwise comparable bargaining game with complete information. This is a desirable property because if the players follow the strategies prescribed by b^*, they will agree on their payoffs only at stage 2 of the game, when they will already know each other's types.

10.15   Possible Refinements to Our Theory

We have recently considered several possible changes in our theory. But we have decided to refrain from incorporating them in this book, partly because we have not fully evaluated them as yet and partly because we do not want to delay its publication any further. (Even so, it has been in the works for more than fifteen years.)

One possible change we have in mind is to replace our present concept of *payoff dominance* by a somewhat stronger concept. At present, to establish payoff dominance, we require that all players should prefer one equilibrium to another. But it may be desirable to extend payoff dominance to the case where all "important" players prefer the first equilibrium to the second, even if some very weak players may have preferences going the other way, or maybe indifferent between the two. Of course we would have to find convincing criteria for deciding who the "important" and who the "un-important" players would be in any given case.

Another possible change may be to replace our present concept of *risk dominance* by a much stronger concept. Under our present concept it happens quite often that *neither* of two equilibria risk-dominates the other. Such cases cannot be completely avoided under any possible definition of risk dominance. For example, in the game of figure 10.11 (discussed in section 10.10), given the complete symmetry of the game, no conceivable concept of risk dominance can make U risk-dominate V or can make V risk-dominate U (as long as risk dominance remains an antisymmetric relation). But it may be possible to find a risk-dominance concept under which such cases would become "exceptional." That is to say, even though a given game G may contain two equilibria displaying no risk dominance in either direction, it might always be possible to find a suitably chosen arbitrarily small perturbation of G that would establish a risk-dominance relation between these two equilibria in one direction or the other.

We want to add that the new payoff-dominance and risk-dominance relations we are considering would represent "conservative" changes: they would not destroy the payoff-dominance and the risk-dominance relations existing under our present theory but would merely add new relations of these two types in some cases where none would exist under our present theory.

There are also some other possible refinements we are considering but their discussion must be left for other occasions.

Notes

Chapter 1

1. A given strategy q_i of player i is a *best reply* to the other players' strategies $q_1, \ldots, q_{i-1}$, $q_{i+1}, \ldots, q_n$ if this strategy q_i maximizes player i's payoff $H_i(q_1, \ldots, q_{i-1}, q_i, q_{i+1}, \ldots, q_n)$ when all other players' strategies are kept constant.

2. A *finite game* is a game with a finite number of players and with a finite number of pure strategies for every player.

3. The great strategic importance of an ability or an inability to make firm commitments in playing a game was first pointed out by Schelling (1960).

4. Our theory assumes that the random fluctuations in the payoffs are governed by an *absolutely continuous* joint probability distribution.

5. $E_2 = (B, Y)$ is an "undesirable" equilibrium point, not only because it is *imperfect* but also because it uses a weakly *dominated* strategy (since strategy Y weakly dominates strategy X). It can be shown that in any game containing only two information sets, an imperfect equilibrium point will always involve at least one weakly dominated strategy. But this theorem is not true for games containing three or more information sets. Therefore the problem posed by imperfect equilibria cannot be reduced to the problem posed by dominated equilibria.

6. For every game with *perfect recall*, its agent normal form will have exactly the same equilibrium points as the original game does in its extensive form (or, equivalently, in its normal form). (See Selten 1975.) But, in general, this is not true for games with *imperfect recall*. In view of this fact we will always assume that any game we are dealing with has been modeled as a game with perfect recall. This is not a restrictive assumption because every game with imperfect recall can be easily transformed into one with perfect recall. This is so because any game with imperfect recall is always based on considering some team(s)—some set(s) of players with identical interests—as single player(s), and it can always be transformed into a game with perfect recall by treating every member of any such team as a separate player. For instance, bridge is sometimes modeled as a two-person game with imperfect recall. But it can be just as readily modeled as a four-person game with perfect recall.

7. We will follow the principle that in the absence of specific reasons to the contrary, our analysis of a given game will always be based on the *uniformity assumption*, and therefore on the uniformly perturbed game. The uniformity assumption is a very useful part of our theory: it is a rather natural assumption to make, and it greatly simplifies computation of the solution in many cases. Despite this, it is *not* an indispensable assumption of our theory.

Should anybody feel that he has good reasons to think that in a given game G the players' mistakes would follow a *nonuniform* probability distribution, then all he has to do is to select a specific family of nonuniform mistake-probability distributions Π_ε that he feels to be appropriate, and to use these distributions Π_ε for constructing the corresponding non-uniformly perturbed agent normal forms $\bar{G}_\varepsilon$ of game G. Then he can apply our solution theory to these perturbed games $\bar{G}_\varepsilon$.

On the other hand, if the analysis of any given game G were to be based on such a family of mistake-probability distributions Π_ε, then the latter would have to be included in the *definition* of this game G, along with other defining characteristics, such as the players' strategy sets and payoff functions.

Thus, if two games had identical agent normal forms but were assumed to have different mistake-probability distributions Π_ε, then they would have to be regarded as being two different games with perhaps different solutions.

8. In contrast to Nash's bargaining model where the players make simultaneous offers to each other, Rubinstein's (1982) retains the real-life sequential structure of the bargaining process with a sequence of consecutive offers and counteroffers. But to ensure an agreement after a finite number of bargaining rounds, the players are given incentives to try for an early

agreement. These incentives may take the form of *discounting* payoffs accruing in the future because of time preference or because of uncertainty about when the bargaining process might break down. They may take also the form of *extra costs* for any additional round of bargaining. Even though Rubinstein's bargaining models typically have many different Nash equilibria, only *one* of these will be perfect (subgame perfect) and will be chosen as the solution of the game. Binmore (1982) has shown that Rubinstein's model with discounted payoffs will yield a solution closely related to Nash's bargaining solution. Rubinstein's approach can be extended also to bargaining games with incomplete information. See Rubinstein (1985) and the references quoted there.

Rubinstein's approach provides an interesting alternative in many cases to our own theory for selecting a unique solution to sequential games. But in its present form it seems that it cannot be extended to games involving simultaneous moves by the players.

Chapter 4

1. Of course any probability distribution $[q_{-i}]$ generated by an i-incomplete mixed-strategy combination q_{-i} is a joint mixture of a rather special kind: it is a joint mixture *without* any statistical correlation between the pure strategies ϕ_j used by the different players j $(j = 1, \ldots, i - 1, i + 1, \ldots, n)$.

2. Since the strategy part of each point $x = (t, q)$ of this graph X must be an equilibrium point of game Γ^t, it must satisfy a finite number of equations and inequalities of forms (4.5.4) and (4.5.5). Any given arc X' of X will be an *algebraic* curve if at every point x of X' the same set S of equations and inequalities is binding. On the other hand, any arc X'' of X will be merely a *piecewise* algebraic curve if different subarcs of X'' are subject to *different* sets S of binding equations and inequalities. It is easy to verify that the set S of binding equations and inequalities can change only at such points $x = (t, q)$ whose strategy part q lies on the *boundary* δQ of the strategy space Q.

3. We may of course imagine that all n players go through the solution process at the same speed, so that at any given moment all players will have the same position point $x^t = (t, q)$. But this assumption is not required by our model, which envisages the solution process as consisting of n independent computation processes performed by the n players and requiring no interaction or communication between different players. The different players' computation processes are coordinated by the fact that all of them are based on the *same* distinguished path $L = L(G, p)$, so that all of them will lead to the *same* solution $q^* = T(G, p)$. But it is completely immaterial whether the different players move along this path L at the same speed or not.

4. By the very definition of a distinguished path L, the value of the t-coordinate will always *increase* from $t = 0$ to $t = 1$ as we move from the starting point of L to its end point. But it is quite possible for L to "bend backward" temporarily, that is, to contain segments along which t temporarily *decreases*.

5. As will be explained in chapter 5, before applying the tracing procedure, we will always subject any game to a *reduction procedure*. In the reduced game, case 1 can occur but case 2 cannot. (In fact our reduction procedure transforms any game coming under case 2 into a game coming under case 1.)

6. As has been pointed out in note 2, the merely piecewise algebraic nature of graph X is due to the fact that at border points $x = (t, q)$, that is, at points x with $q \in \delta Q$, the set of binding equations and inequalities may *change*. In contrast, graph $\bar{X}$ is everywhere governed by the same $\bar{K}$ equations of forms (4.13.5) and (4.13.7). Moreover, by lemma 4.13.1, graph $\bar{X}$ does not contain any border points at all (except possibly in the region $t = 1$).

7. The material in section 4.19 is based partly on Drees's (1979) unpublished *Diplomarbeit* for the Faculty of Mathematics, University of Bielefeld.

8. Line segments will now be denoted by script capitals to distinguish them from the corner points of the cube $ABCDFIJK$ of figure 4.26.

9. For the convenience of any reader who may wish to compute branch $\mathscr{B}$, we note that at all points of $\mathscr{B}$, player 2 always uses strategy d.

Chapter 7

1. We have neglected the fact that player i himself will also deviate from his intended strategy π_i with a positive probability. But it can be shown that in computing the local best reply of a given agent ij to the other agents' strategies, or in computing the best reply of a given one-agent player i to the other players' strategies, we will obtain the correct result even if we disregard the fact that this agent or this player will also deviate from his own intended strategy with a positive probability.

In the game G_e^* we are discussing, suppose that I^* contains μ elements. Then, if a given player i intends to use strategy $\pi_i = \pi$, there will be $(\mu - 1)$ unintended strategies $\pi_i' = \pi' \neq \pi$ he might use by mistake, and each of these will be used with probability ε. Therefore he will use his intended strategy $\pi_i = \pi$ only with probability $1 - \varepsilon(\mu - 1)$. If he does so, his expected payoff will be $\varepsilon(100 - \pi)$, as indicated in the text. On the other hand, if he uses one of his unintended strategies $\pi_i' = \pi'$, his expected payoff will be $\varepsilon(100 - \pi')$. If we multiply all these payoffs with the relevant probabilities and simplify, we will find that his total expected payoff will be $u_i = \varepsilon(100 - \pi) + \varepsilon^2(\mu\pi - \mu\bar{\pi})$, where $\bar{\pi}$ is the arithmetic mean of all elements of set I^*. This quantity will be maximized by choosing the strategy $\pi_i = 0$. That is to say, even though in the text we disregarded the mistake probability $\varepsilon(\mu - 1)$ for i's own strategy choice, we have obtained the correct best reply strategy for player i.

2. Again, we are neglecting the fact that player S himself will also deviate from his intended strategy π_S with probability $\varepsilon(\mu - 1)$. See note 1.

3. The reader may have noticed that in this game, for any pair of pure-strategy equilibria e' and e'', the bicentric prior probability distribution $p_j = (p_j', p_j'')$ for any player j ($j = S$ or $= 1, \ldots, k$) can be computed by the formulas

$$p_j' = \frac{u_j' - c_j}{(u_j' - c_j) + (u_j'' - c_j)} \quad \text{and} \quad p_j'' = \frac{u_j'' - c_j}{(u_j' - c_j) + (u_j'' - c_j)},$$

where u_j' and u_j'' are player j's equilibrium payoffs at e' and at e'', respectively, and c_j is his conflict payoff. In many other bargaining games the players' bicentric priors can be computed by the same formulas, including the bargaining games we will discuss in chapters 8 and 9.

Chapter 8

1. This can be verified as follows. Player 2's strategies, like player 1's, range over the interval $[0, 100]$, whereas those of player 3 range only over the shorter interval $[0, 100 - \alpha]$. As a result, if the intended strategies of players 2 and 3 are $x_2 = x_3 = 0$, and if player 1 uses a strategy $x_1 = x$ with $0 < x \leq 100 - \alpha$, he will have probability ε of encountering a matching strategy $x_2 = x$ or $x_3 = x$ as a result of his opponent's mistake (whether his opponent is player 2 or 3). Therefore his expected payoff will be $u_1^* = x\varepsilon$, which will take its maximum value $u_1^* = (100 - \alpha)\varepsilon$ when player 1's strategy is $x_1 = 100 - \alpha$.

However, if player 1 uses a strategy $x_1 = x'$ with $100 - \alpha < x' \leq 100$, then he will have only probability $\varepsilon/2$ of encountering a matching strategy $x_2 = x'$ by his opponent (because this can occur only if his opponent is player 2, which will be the case with probability $\frac{1}{2}$). Therefore his expected payoff will be only $u_1^{**} = x'\varepsilon/2$, which will take its maximum value $u_1^{**} = 50\varepsilon$ when player 1's strategy is $x_1 = 100$.

Now $u_1^*(\max) = (100 - \alpha)\varepsilon > u_1^{**}(\max) = 50\varepsilon$ if $\alpha < 50$, so in this case player 1's best reply will be $x_1 = 100 - \alpha$. By similar reasoning, his best reply will be $x_1 = 100$ if $\alpha > 50$, and both strategies will be best replies if $\alpha = 50$.

2. See the equation of note 3 in chapter 7.

3. According to the notations used in section 4.15, this strategy combination should be called b^o rather than β^o. Actually we call it β^o because in this chapter we want to use the letter b to denote equilibrium points of class B^o (or B).

Chapter 9

1. Both assumptions (9.1.2) and (9.1.3) will significantly simplify our analysis.

2. If player i could obtain a higher payoff by making a mistake, or by pretending to make a mistake, this would give him an incentive to deviate from his equilibrium strategy so that the latter would cease to be an equilibrium strategy.

3. Note that player i can compute the quantity y_j, even though he will not know whether player j is the weak player or the strong player on the opposite side because, by (9.3.1), the quantity y_j will be the same in both cases.

Chapter 10

1. In writing this Postscript we have benefited from very helpful comments by four anonymous editorial readers. One of us (Harsanyi) is indebted also to Robert J. Aumann of the Hebrew University, Jerusalem, for very stimulating personal discussions. We are grateful also to Eric van Damme for helpful comments on the material discussed in section 10.8.

2. Our solution concept is directly defined for a game G_ε in *perturbed* standard form, characterized by a specific mistake-probability distribution Π_ε (see note 9 to chapter 1). Therefore our two consistency requirements apply primarily to such perturbed games. In fact, our solution concept does generically satisfy these two requirements also with respect to games G in unperturbed standard form. But, in some degenerate cases, truncation consistency will be lost (whereas subgame consistency will always persist) with respect to the unperturbed game. This anomaly is due to the fact the unperturbed game conceals an important piece of information—that concerning the mistake-probability distribution Π_ε—which is an essential part of the mathematical definition of the game (see our discussion of figures 3.22 and 3.23 in chapter 3).

3. For instance, we could assume that player i has two or more different types, each of them making mistakes with different probabilities. If we are making this assumption, then any mistake by player i will make it more likely in the eyes of the other players that he is one of the "mistake-prone" types. But without such an assumption we cannot argue that a "mistake" by a given player will make it more likely that he will make similar "mistakes" also in the future.

Bibliography

Aumann, R. J. 1959. "Acceptable Points in General Cooperative *n*-Person Games." In *Contributions to the Theory of Games*. Vol. 4. Edited by A. W. Tucker and R. D. Luce. Princeton: Princeton University Press, pp. 287–324.

Aumann, R. J. 1976. "Agreeing to Disagree." *Annals of Statistics* **4**, 1236–1239.

Aumann, R. J. 1985. "Correlated Equilibria as an Expression of Bayesian Rationality." Working Paper, mimeo.

Aumann, R. J., and M. Maschler 1964. "The Bargaining Set for Cooperative Games." In *Advances in Game Theory* (*Annals of Mathematics Studies* 52). Edited by M. A. Dresher, L. S. Shapley, and A. W. Tucker. Princeton: Princeton University Press, pp. 443–475.

Aumann, R. J., and M. Maschler 1966. "Game Theoretic Aspects of Gradual Disarmament: Development of Utility Theory for Arms Control and Disarmament." In *Mathematica Report* (a). Princeton, NJ, chapter 5.

Aumann, R. J., and M. Maschler 1967. "Repeated Games with Incomplete Information." In *Mathematica Report* (b). Princeton, NJ, chapter 3.

Aumann, R. J., and M. Maschler 1968. "Repeated Games with Incomplete Information: The Zero-Sum Extensive Case." In *Mathematica Report* (c). Princeton, NJ, chapter 2.

Binmore, K. G. 1982. "Perfect Equilibria in Bargaining Models." International Centre for Economics and Related Disciplines. London School of Economics, Discussion Paper 82/58,

Drees, M. 1979. "Auswahl von Gleichgewichtspunkten in einer Klasse von 2 × 4-Spielen mit Hilfe des allgemeinen Lösungskonzepts Harsanyi/Selten." Unpublished master thesis (*Diplomarbeit*). University of Bielefeld, Bielefeld.

Gillies, D. B. 1959. "Solutions to General Non-Zero-Sum Games." In *Contributions to the Theory of Games*. Vol. 4. Edited by A. W. Tucker and R. D. Luce. Princeton: Princeton University Press, pp. 47–85.

Harsanyi, J. C. 1967–68. "Games with Incomplete Information Played by 'Bayesian' Players." Parts I–III. *Management Science* **14**, 159–182, 320–334, and 486–502.

Harsanyi, J. C. 1973a. "Games with Randomly Disturbed Payoffs: A New Rationale for Mixed-Strategy Equilibrium Points." *International Journal of Game Theory* **2**, 1–23.

Harsanyi, J. C. 1973b. "Oddness of the Number of Equilibrium Points: A New Proof." *International Journal of Game Theory* **2**, 235–250.

Harsanyi, J. C. 1975. "The Tracing Procedure." *International Journal of Game Theory* **4**, 61–94.

Harsanyi, J. C. 1977a. "Time and the Flow of Information in Noncooperative Games." In *Quantitative Wirtschaftsforschung*. Edited by H. Albach et al. Tübingen: J. C. B. Mohr, pp. 255–267.

Harsanyi, J. C. 1977b. *Rational Behavior and Bargaining Equilibrium in Games and Social Situations*. Cambridge: Cambridge University Press.

Harsanyi, J. C. 1982. "Solutions for Some Bargaining Games under the Harsanyi-Selten Solution Theory, I: Theoretical Preliminaries; II: Analysis of Specific Bargaining Games." *Mathematical Social Sciences* **3**, 179–191 and 259–279.

Harsanyi, J. C. 1982a. "Noncooperative Bargaining Models." In *Games, Economic Dynamics, and Time Series Analysis*. Edited by M. Deistler et al. Vienna: Physica-Verlag.

Harsanyi, J. C., and R. Selten 1972. "A Generalized Nash Solution for Two-Person Bargaining Games with Incomplete Information." *Management Science* **18**, no. 5, part II, 80–106.

Harsanyi, J. C., and R. Selten 1977. "Simple and Iterated Limits of Algebraic Functions." Working Paper CP-370. Center for Research in Management, University of California, Berkeley.

Kalai, E., and D. Samet 1984. "Persistent Equilibria in Strategic Games." *International Journal of Game Theory* **13**, 129–144.

Kalai, E., and M. Smorodinsky 1975. "Other Solutions to Nash's Bargaining Problem." *Econometrica* **43**, 513–518.

Kohlberg, E., and J. F. Mertens 1982. "On the Strategic Stability of Equilibria." *CORE Discussion* Paper No. 8248.

Kohlberg, E., and J. F. Mertens 1986. "On the Strategic Stability of Equilibria." *Econometrica* **54**, 1003–1037.

Kreps, D., and R. Wilson 1982. "Sequential Equilibria." *Econometrica* **50**, 863–894.

Kuhn, H. W. 1953. "Extensive Games and the Problem of Information." In *Contributions to the Theory of Games*. Vol. 2. Edited by H. W. Kuhn and A. W. Tucker. Princeton: Princeton University Press, pp. 193–216.

Leopold-Wildburger, U. 1982. *Gleichgewichtsauswahl in einem Verhandlungsspiel mit Opportunitätskosten*. Bielefeld: Pfeffersche Buchhandlung.

Leopold-Wildburger, U. 1985. "Equilibrium Selection in a Bargaining Problem with Transaction Costs." *International Journal of Game Theory* **14**, 151–172.

Luce, R. D., and H. Raiffa 1957. *Games and Decisions*. New York: Wiley.

Lutz, B. 1983. "Spieltheoretische Elemente bei der Entscheidungsfindung in der Energiepolitik." Dissertation. Institut für Kernenergetik und Energiesysteme, University of Stuttgart, Stuttgart.

Mathematica, *Reports to the U.S. Arms Control and Disarmament Agency:*
   (a) Final Report on Contract ACDA/ST-80, Princeton, NJ, June 1966.
   (b) Final Report on Contract ACDA/ST-116, Princeton, NJ, September 1967.
   (c) Final Report on Contract ACDA/ST-143, Princeton, NJ, November 1968.

Myerson, R. B. 1978. "Refinements of the Nash Equilibrium Concept." *International Journal of Game Theory* **7**, 73–80.

Nash, J. F. 1950a. "Equilibrium Points in *n*-Person Games." *Proceedings of the National Academy of Sciences* (US) **36**, 48–49.

Nash, J. F. 1950b. "The Bargaining Problem." *Econometrica* **18**, 155–162.

Nash, J. F. 1951. "Non-Cooperative Games." *Annals of Mathematics* **54**, 286–295.

Nash, J. F. 1953. "Two-Person Cooperative Games." *Econometrica* **21**, 128–140.

Roth, A. E. 1985. "Toward a Focal-Point Theory of Bargaining." In *Game-Theoretic Models of Bargaining*. Edited by A. E. Roth. Cambridge: Cambridge University Press, pp. 259–268.

Rubinstein, A. 1982. "Perfect Equilibrium in a Bargaining Model." *Econometrica* **50**, 97–109.

Rubinstein, A. 1985. "A Bargaining Model with Incomplete Information about Time Preference." *Econometrica* **53**, 1151–1172.

Sard, A. 1942. "A Measure of Critical Values of Differentiable Maps." *Bulletin of Mathematical Society* **48**, 883–890.

Schelling, T. C. 1960. *The Strategy of Conflict*. Cambridge, MA: Harvard University Press.

Selten, R. 1965. "Spieltheoretische Behandlung eines Oligopolmodells mit Nachfrageträgheit." Parts I–II. *Zeitschrift für die Gesamte Staatswissenschaft* **121**, 301–324 and 667–689.

Selten, R. 1975. "Reexamination of the Perfectness Concept for Equilibrium Points in Extensive Games." *International Journal of Game Theory* **4**, 25–55.

Selten, R., and W. Güth 1978. "Macht Einigkeit stark?—Spieltheoretische Analyse einer Verhandlungssituation." *Schriften des Vereins für Socialpolitik, Gesellschaft für Wirtschafts und*

Sozialwissenschaften. Vol. 98. Berlin: Neuere Entwicklungen in den Wirtschaftswissenschaften, pp. 197–217.

Selten, R., and W. Güth 1982a. "Original oder Fälschung—Gleichgewichtsauswahl in einem Verhandlungsspiel mit unvollständiger Information." IMW Working Paper 113, University of Bielefeld, Bielefeld.

Selten, R., and W. Güth 1982b. "Equilibrium Point Selection in a Class of Market Entry Games." In *Games, Economic Dynamics and Time Series Analysis.* Edited by M. Deistler et al. Würzburg and Vienna: Physica-Verlag, pp. 101–116.

Selten, R., and U. Leopold 1982. "Equilibrium Point Selection in a Bargaining Situation with Opportunity Costs." *Economie Appliquée,* 611–648.

Shapley, L. S. 1953. "A Value for *n*-Person Games." In *Contributions to the Theory of Games.* Vol. 2. Edited by H. W. Kuhn and A. W. Tucker (*Annals of Mathematics Studies* 28). Princeton: Princeton University Press, pp. 307–317.

Stearns, R. E. 1967. "A Formal Information Concept for Games with Incomplete Information." In *Mathematica Report* (b). Princeton, NJ, chapter IV.

von Neumann, J., and O. Morgenstern 1944. *Theory of Games and Economic Behavior.* Princeton: Princeton University Press.

Index